D1572102

TAOIST RITUAL IN CHINESE SOCIETY AND HISTORY

TAOIST RITUAL IN CHINESE SOCIETY AND HISTORY

JOHN LAGERWEY

MACMILLAN PUBLISHING COMPANY
NEW YORK

COLLIER MACMILLAN PUBLISHERS
LONDON

WITHDRAWN
UTSA Libraries

Copyright © 1987 by Macmillan Publishing Company
A Division of Macmillan, Inc.

All rights reserved. No part of this book may be reproduced or
transmitted in any form or by any means, electronic or mechanical,
including photocopying, recording, or by any information storage
and retrieval system, without permission in writing from the
Publisher.

Macmillan Publishing Company
866 Third Avenue, New York, N. Y. 10022

Collier Macmillan Canada, Inc.

Library of Congress Catalog Card Number: 86-17963

Printed in the United States of America

printing number
1   2   3   4   5   6   7   8   9   10

Library of Congress Cataloging-in-Publication Data
Lagerwey, John.
  Taoist ritual in Chinese society and history.

  1. Taoism—Rituals.   2. Taoism—Influence.
3. China—Civilization.   I. Title.
BL1923.L34   1987   299′.51438   86-17963
ISBN 0-02-896480-2

LIBRARY
The University of Texas
at San Antonio

PLYMOUTH
PUBLIC LIBRARY

For my family

CONTENTS

INTRODUCTION: What is Taoism?   ix

Acknowledgments   xvii

PART I The Context of Taoist Ritual

Chapter 1   Liturgy and Cosmology: Chinese Numerology   3

Chapter 2   Liturgy in Time: The Chinese Festival Calendar   18

Chapter 3   Liturgy in Space: The Taoist Altar   25

PART II Basic Taoist Rituals

Liturgy for the Living: The Offering

Chapter 4   The Basic Program   51

Chapter 5   Preparations   60

Chapter 6   The Announcement   68

Chapter 7   Sealing the Altar and Nocturnal Invocation   90

Chapter 8   The Land of the Way   106

Chapter 9   The Presentation of the Memorial   149

Liturgy for the Dead: The Ritual of Merit

Chapter 10   The Basic Program   169

Chapter 11   Opening a Road in the Darkness   195

Chapter 12   Dispatching the Writ of Pardon   202

Chapter 13   The Attack on Hell   216

PART III Liturgical Taoism and Chinese Society

Chapter 14   Taoism and Popular Religion   241

Chapter 15   Taoism and Political Legitimacy   253

CONCLUSION: What is Taoism?   265

Appendix A: A Note on Vestments   291

Appendix B: Tables   293

Appendix C: Illustrations   295

Appendix D: Glossary   322

Bibliographies   345

Index   353

INTRODUCTION: WHAT IS TAOISM?

What is Taoism? The religion of nature, comes the instant reply, the religion of the cosmos. And so indeed it is. But what is that? The question has been at the root of any number of debates, ancient and modern. To the Buddhists, Taoism was a carbon copy of Buddhism, having pilfered from Buddhism its vocabulary, its ritual, its organization—everything, in fact, but Buddhism's profound analysis of life as suffering and its lofty ethical vision of redemption. Taoists, in spite of all they learned from Buddhism, continued to consider long life—immortality—as the supreme good, and they were even prepared to engage in ritual sex to obtain it. To the Confucians, with some notable exceptions, religious Taoism was a degenerate form of Taoist philosophy: the great Taoist philosophers, Lao-tzu and Chuang-tzu, had already entered the realm of the acceptable, if not the orthodox, in the Former Han dynasty (206–9 B.C.), and this place was secured for them permanently by the practitioners of Hsüan-hsüeh, Mystery Learning, in the third and fourth centuries of our era. Taoist religion, on the other hand, first enters the "standard (Confucian) histories" as the "deception of the people by the fabrication of symbols and documents" (*History of the Latter Han, chüan* 75; on my translation of *fu* as "symbol," see p. 155). The Confucian press, before lapsing into a virtu-ally complete "conspiracy of silence" in the last four centuries, rarely did more than elaborate on this point: Taoism is rank superstition. Worse, it is politically dangerous, because it misleads the people and, occasionally, the emperor.

Modern Sinologists and missionaries have generally confirmed this picture, the Sinologists (Sun K'o-k'uan, Chin Chung-shu; see Bibliography) by their historical studies which drew together the widely scattered references to specific political episodes—most of which ended tragically— in which Taoists played major roles, and the missionaries by filling in the details of Chinese daily life, the very tissue of which proved to be cut of the same cloth as Taoism.

One thinks in the first place of the work whose very title reveals this judgment: *Researchers into Chinese Superstitions*, by Henri Doré, S.J. But the greatest work of this kind is, without any doubt, that of a non-missionary, of an ethnologist, who, although he began his career as a convinced proponent of European liberalism, ended it an ardent champion of the missionary cause: J.J.M. De Groot. In the general preface to his magnum opus, *The Religious System of China*, De Groot affirms:

The reader will soon become aware that, as with semi-civilized peoples in general, so in China religious ideas and usages pervade social life to its inmost recesses, that these are, so to say, the backbone of the manners and customs, of the domestic and political institutions of the nation, and to a large extent of its legislation. Whoever is acquainted with its religion, knows the people. (1892; 1:x)

De Groot devoted nearly two hundred pages of the sixth volume of this work to the "Priesthood of Animism." Nearly a century later, his description of Taoist priests (*sai kong*), "who in the eyes of the people themselves are the most important representatives of the Wu-ist priesthood" (p. 1244), remains the standard reference on the subject. His descriptions of their "initiation vigil," their confraternity (the "Lao-chün association"), their vestments, and their work, both exorcistic and sacrificial, may all be consulted with profit, and they leave one fairly confident that, had he in fact written his promised volume on Taoism, in which he was to treat "the most important part of the function of the *sai kong*," to wit, their "sacrificial work" (p. 1255), it would not have been necessary to rediscover Taoism in the 1960s.

But De Groot abandoned his monumental undertaking, and for nearly half a century liturgical Taoism fell back into the oblivion from which De Groot had nearly succeeded in rescuing it. Important work continued to be done on Taoism, particularly in Paris, but it did not include field work. It was not until 1968, when Kristofer Schipper, after a prolonged stay in Taiwan, presented a paper entitled "Taoism: the Liturgical Tradition" to the First International Conference on Taoism, that field studies of Taoist ritual were placed once again on the Sinological agenda. Since that time, Schipper has published a number of important articles (see Bibliography) and, most recently, a full-length book, *Le corps taoïste* (*The Taoist Body*). In ten tightly packed chapters he describes the "Masters of the Gods," their relationship to the religion of the people, the mythology that underlies their rituals, and the relationship of that mythology to Taoist philosophy. The great chasm between Taoist philosophy and religion—with the one seen as a degenerate form of the other—is thus definitively bridged. We have now as well a clearer view of the relationship between the private aspects of eremetic Taoism detailed by Henri Maspero—alchemy, breath circulation, hygiene, diet—and the public, liturgical forms first brought to the attention of the West by De Groot.

If Schipper's synthetic overview of Taoism focuses more on philosophy and mythology than on those liturgical forms which are the "living heart" of the "Taoist body," Ofuchi Ninji's volume, *Chūgokujin no shūkyō girei*, by contrast, is all ritual and virtually no explanation. Neither attempts to answer the following fundamental questions: first, what is the relationship of Taoist ritual and mythology to Chinese cosmology and numerology? The magisterial work of Marcel Granet on this subject, *La pensée chinoise* (*The Chinese Way of Thinking*) provides background information which must be taken into account if we are to make sense of Taoist ritual. Second, what is the relationship of religious Taoism to political history and theory? Unless the issue of the Taoist role at court is assessed dispassionately, in the light of our new knowledge concerning the inner workings of Taoism itself, we will never bridge the second chasm opened up by traditional historiography, that between the "superstitious" masses, deceived and duped by their priests, and the "enlightened" aristocracy, who labored patiently, against overwhelming odds, for the common weal.

This self-congratulatory Confucian view of its own social and political role in Chinese history, of which they were the literary guardians, was transmitted to the West by the first Christian missionaries, the Jesuits. Throughout the famous "Rites controversy" of the seventeenth century, the Jesuits tried to convince Rome that Confucianism was a rational philosophy, a rational preparation for the supernatural truths of Christianity, as Plato had been in the West. They lost the battle within the Catholic Church to their sectarian rivals the Franciscans, but they won the war in Western society at large, for their light on Chinese civilization, refracted through the prism of the Enlightenment, still shines in virtually every text on Chinese history and thought, where China is the land of Plato's Republic come true, China is the land ruled by philosopher-kings.

This sanguine picture of Chinese history has fallen on hard times recently: it is less easy to credit it in the wake of the Cultural Revolution that began in the 1960s, less easy after one has been treated to the spectacle of millions of human beings, all dressed alike, massed into the world's largest open square, brandishing the Little Red Book of the Thoughts of Chairman Mao. Having witnessed this scene of contemporary religio-political fervor, is it still possible to affirm of China that it is the great humanistic model, held up against the theocentric model of the West? It is still affirmed.

And yet, the Chinese themselves have had doubts in this century. In one of the most brilliant of his vignettes of Chinese society, the great writer Lu Hsün penetrates behind the idyllic smoke screen of the literati landscape. After listening in on the romantic imaginings of a group of literati in a boat, idly conversing about the bucolic peasant scenes visible to them in the distance, he zooms in on shore upon the reality of that scene, and finds the peasants squabbling and cursing the world and each other. The reality of Chinese society, says Lu Hsün in his most famous story, "Ah Q," is dog-eat-dog. Chinese society is a vicious, stratified order, in which even the lowest beggar, like those above him, can think of nothing better to do with his frustrations than to take them out on the next creature down in the chain of being, which is, for the hapless Ah Q, a stray dog.

The picture of Chinese society painted by modern ethnography is not much more complimentary. Maurice Freedman writes:

[In an earlier work] I discussed what evidence I had managed to find on hostile relations between lineages in Fukien and Kwangtung. It seemed to me then, and now seems even more certain, that fighting between lineages, governed by rules, was an important characteristic of social life in southeastern China. (1966, 104)

No one who has read Margery Wolf's *The House of Lim* (1968) would spend any more of his spare time dreaming of belonging to an extended Chinese family. Intrafamily violence and cruelty would seem to be as much a part of Chinese life as fighting between lineages.

Nor have questions been asked of Chinese society exclusively by anthropological observers. The historians too have tried to explain why China, far ahead of the West in the time of Marco Polo, in the end developed neither modern science nor modern democracy. Instead, the stream of creativity slowed to a trickle, and the Chinese state became ever more autocratic and arbitrary. Various answers to these questions have been adduced—the hydraulic society theories of Wittfogel, the "high-level equilibrium trap" of Elvin—and each has its merits. Strangely, no one has suggested that there might be religious factors at work as well, as in the case of the rise of capitalism. Strangely, I say, because thanks to Joseph Needham, it has come to be fairly widely accepted that Chinese science is the product of a Taoist, not a Confucian mentality. Strangely also in that Taoist messianism carried in it, all through Chinese history, the seeds of a profoundly democratic society (Schipper 1982, 22; Seidel 1969, 245).

Thus great puzzles remain for our understanding of Chinese history. Great puzzles?—great contradictions! What is the truth of Chinese history? What is its real shape? And what is Taoism, as revealed by that history? Is it simply the innocent victim of a conspiracy of silence? Or is it a tangled web of superstitions used to deceive people? If it is all too true that China is, at the end of its imperial history, irrevocably split between a class of lettered bureaucrats and the "real country" of its religious masses, whose religion was Taoism (Schipper 1982, 27-31), we must still ask *why* this chasm gradually developed until it became unbridgeable. Why did the national religion of the T'ang (618-907) and of the Sung (960-1279), even of the Ming (1368-1644), fall into such discredit by the end of the Ch'ing (1644-1911)?

No one book can answer all questions, and the questions answered in any case inevitably engender new questions. I shall try, in the pages that follow, to answer three questions: what is Taoist ritual? what has it to do with Chinese cosmology? what have the two of them to do with the shape of Chinese history? We will take them up in the order, cosmology*, ritual, history. The section on cosmology will be introductory; that on history will draw some preliminary conclusions. But the heart of the book will be the

---

* The reader who finds the cosmology rough going should skim that part rapidly and then refer back to it when it is needed to understand a given rite.

description and explanation of the ritual practice of a single Taoist priest in present-day Taiwan.

It is crucial to the comprehension of what follows that this point be clearly understood: this book will ask, at the end as at the beginning, what is Taoism? But it will respond to this very general question from the very specific standpoint of the liturgical specialist, no, even more explicitly, from the stance of the married Taoist priest (*huo-chü tao-shih*, "hearth-dwelling Taoist"), whose position is normally hereditary. This is the Taoism of China's plains and people.

There is another Taoism, that of (often) mountain-dwelling mystics, of wanderers and visionaries, of alchemists, poets, and philosophers. Most of the early Taoists of whom we know, from *Lieh-hsien chuan* ("The Biographies of the Immortals"; trans. Kaltenmark 1953) for example, are of this sort. This kind of Taoism has been ably described, by Isabelle Robinet in particular, and she has shown as well that it is not without influence on liturgical Taoism (Robinet 1984, 1:232 ff.). But "whereas meditation aims at the obtaining of the supreme Tao, ritual aims at universal salvation: universality versus the Absolute" (1:240). The subject of the present book is the Taoists whose rituals are designed to save.

That individual Taoist mystics have played an important part in both Chinese society and history is undeniable. If nothing else, they were proof that the Chinese, often pictured as utterly pragmatic and down-to-earth, are also capable of aspiring after transcendance and eternal life. By comparison, the type of Taoist priest we shall be describing is down-to-earth indeed: for him, as for his clients, the goal of Taoist ritual is health, wealth, and longevity. At an Offering I attended in 1985 in Fukien province, for example, I was constantly reminded not to bump into the *tou-teng* (lamps of destiny). Each of the forty community leaders whose lamps were inside the temple had paid at the very least a thousand (Chinese) dollars (about ten months of an average salary!) for the privilege of placing his lamp inside the temple for the duration of the Offering, and should it go out, not only would his money be down the drain, he would no doubt be in for further bad luck as well.

This anecdote gives some idea of the importance of the Taoist Offering in the eyes of the people who pay for it, and then watch it, as we shall see, without really understanding what it is they are watching. The following quotation, from a missionary observer of the last century, will give some idea of the importance of the Taoist priest generally in traditional Chinese society:

> Judging from the number of Tauist priests and the number of temples which are exclusively devoted to the worship of gods of the Tauist sect in this place (Foochow, Fukien), this religion is much less popular than the Buddhist. There are only four or five temples belonging to the Rationalists or Tauists, and connected with them are not more than twelve or fourteen priests. . . .

The above remarks relate to the class of priests called in this dialect Tö-ing, and believed to be, strictly speaking, *Tauist priests*. There is another class of priests called Tö-tai, who also belong to the Tauist sect. These have been frequently referred to as a "certain kind" of Tauist priest. They are, however, very different in several respects from the former, as well as from the Buddhist priests.

They, except when officiating, usually wear the dress of the common citizen.

They do not live in temples, but in common dwelling-houses, and among the common people.

They marry and raise families. . . . As a general thing, fathers train up their children to follow the same calling. . . . It would appear that this class of priests become or continue priests in order to obtain a livelihood, just as other persons become doctors, fortune-tellers, musicians, etc.

They derive their living principally from the regular pay they receive for the performance of the ceremonies of their sect. . . .

This class of priests is quite numerous, probably much more numerous than the Buddhist priests. They are also much oftener employed than are the Buddhist priests. Their services are very frequently in requisition, on mourning or funeral occasions, for the performance of so-called meritorious ceremonies in cases of sickness of adults or children, male or female, etc. On a multitude of occasions, in all seasons of the year, and relating to almost all subjects, they are invited to perform their singular, superstitious, or idolatrous ceremonies. Their great harvest is in the seventh Chinese month. . . . On the birthdays of gods and goddesses, and on established festival days, they are also very busy. . . .

The mandarins, if they have occasion for the services of these priests in *saving the sun or the moon when eclipsed*, or in *praying for rain in a time of drought* (italics in original), etc. have only to apply to their head man. (Doolittle, 1:246-9)

How far back was what Doolittle observed true?—and for what portion of China? These are questions future research will hopefully be able to answer more precisely. I myself believe that each new archaeological discovery will push the prehistory of the rituals described in this work farther back in time—the Step of Yü, for example (see plate 10), is now known from a third century B.C. manuscript (Harper, 98–101)—and reveal them ever more clearly to be—like the major rituals of every great religion—the synthesis of the very essence of the Chinese experience of and reflection upon man-in-the-universe. In analyzing and describing Taoist ritual, then, we are analyzing and describing the quintessence of the Chinese experience. Put another way, Taoist ritual is the deposit of Chinese society and mentality: its study gives us a privileged glimpse of both.

My methodology, therefore, will be that of a literary critic. Wherever possible, I will give the priest's own understanding of his rituals, but I will also supplement that with references to Chinese cosmology and mythology, as well as to earlier versions of the rituals. My purpose in so proceeding is to give some idea both of the antiquity of Taoist ritual and of its perfect compatibility, not to say its homogeneity, with Chinese mind and society in general. It is this homogeneity which explains its social and historical importance.

But Taoist ritual is not just a vestige of the past, of interest only for our understanding of traditional Chinese society and history. It also has much to teach us about what it is to be, or rather, become human. That is why, using certain categories taken from psychoanalysis, and others from theology, I shall make bold, in the conclusion, to hold up the Taoist mirror to our own religious tradition and vice versa. Taoism, I will suggest, is what existed in Rome before Christianity: paganism. This word, of course, will be used, not in its degenerate, pejorative sense but in its etymological and descriptive sense: from the Latin *paganus*, "peasant, villager," whence "religion of the people of the land."

After fifteen hundred years and more of monotheism in the West, we no longer understand paganism. We understand neither what was so attractive in it to a Marcus Aurelius, to a Julian the Apostate, nor what was so repulsive about it to the Old Testament prophets and to the Church Fathers. Accustomed as we are to the secular rationalism which, in fact, grew out of monotheism, we cannot even imagine what all the fuss was about. How could a multi-racial, multi-linguistic empire like that of Rome rest so securely on the foundations of such an incoherent congery of local cults and superstitions. And yet it did, in Rome and also in China. When, in Rome, those cults gave way before the onslaught of Christianity, so did the empire, as Gibbon saw. But in China both the cults and the empire survived, thanks, at least in part, to the "new testament of the Tao" (Seidel 1978).

We have, then, in Taoism, a rare opportunity to get a glimpse of both what we have gained and what we have lost. May the religious movements of the future be the wiser for it!

ACKNOWLEDGMENTS

This book began as a series of lectures given during the January, 1983, interim at Calvin College in Grand Rapids, Michigan. The translations and descriptions of basic rituals underwent a first revision in preparation for a week-long seminar in June, 1983, with a group of young Taoist scholars working with Professor Hans Steininger at the University of Würzburg. The lectures given to these two groups were based, essentially, on field notes, slides, and audio recordings, as well as on notes from two seminars given in the spring of 1977 at the Ecole Pratique des Hautes Etudes in Paris by the Taoist master Ch'en Jung-sheng of Tainan, Taiwan.

Two events occurred in the summer of 1983 that led to a second complete revision of the manuscript. The first was the return of my friend Patrice Fava from Taiwan with video recordings of virtually all of Master Ch'en's ritual repertoire. The visual descriptions were revised on the basis of these tapes. The second event was the publication of a massive tome, most of it concerning Taoist ritual in Taiwan and Hong Kong, by Ofuchi Ninji. The complete scenario and a systematic description of Ch'en's ritual which occupy some five hundred pages of this remarkable work, *Chūgokujin no shūkyō girei*, spared me many an error.

But so complex is Taoist ritual, so intricate and so precise, that even Ofuchi's exhaustive study is not altogether free of errors. To clarify points on which my tapes and notes disagreed with Ofuchi's description, I had recourse to the only possible arbiter, Master Ch'en himself: he graciously took the time, during my autumn, 1983, visit to Taiwan, to settle each point in dispute. He also allowed me to tape some forty hours of ritual, which meant accepting the inconvenience of spotlights for the video and of a clip microphone for the audio recording. This material was of considerable help in making further adjustments in the manuscript.

My last tangible debt is to Sandy Koffler, who not only read through each successive version of the text, but also listened to most of the oral musings and self-interrogations that preceded them.

My intangible debts are to all those who have educated me. A full accounting would constitute an autobiography. I shall restrict myself, therefore, to what cannot be left unnoticed.

Before I came to France at the end of 1975 to study with Professor Kristofer Schipper at the Ecole Pratique des Hautes Etudes, I had no idea that Chinese history and society had secreted its own "higher religion." I thought, as most Sinologists still do, that Chinese history belonged to an "agnostic" Confucian elite, and Chinese society to the "superstitious" masses. I loved Taoist philosophy; I believed the scornful judgment of others concerning Taoist religion. Professor Schipper's courses hit me, therefore, with the full force of revelation: "It is not so. What you believed is false. The truth is . . ." something like what I have tried to describe in this book.

My greatest debt of all—one learns from the Chinese it is unpayable—is to my parents. Deeply rooted themselves in the Hebraic half of our own Western tradition, they transmitted to their children both their knowledge of and their love for that tradition. From them I learned that the Eternal One of Israel is not subject to our images: we are His. Our language and existence have meaning insofar as they are grounded in His reality and strive for His approval.

I do not believe that Taoism, in the end, in spite of far-reaching differences to be explored in the conclusion, says anything incompatible. Like Biblical religion, it is profoundly humanistic: both open paths to man's becoming, rather than trapping him in immutable Platonic being. The characteristic form of the language of the two Testaments is history (not myth!); the characteristic form of the language of the Covenant of Orthodox Unity is ritual. To pretend that two such different forms did not utterly transform their respective contents would be absurd. But not to assume the identity of the deep structures from which all informed content springs is folly.

John Lagerwey
Paris, March 30, 1984

In the nearly two years since the above was written I have benefited from the advice of numerous friends and colleagues. I would like to thank in particular Ms. Anna Seidel and Ms. Isabelle Robinet, who both read through the entire manuscript and offered many valuable suggestions.

Paris, January 6, 1986

PART

I

The
Context of
Taoist Ritual

CHAPTER

1

Liturgy and Cosmology: Chinese Numerology

One rainy day in Taipei I came home to the Chinese family where I was staying. After taking off my coat and rubbers, I began to close my umbrella. My hostess, Mrs. Wang, who had come to greet me, said, "Just leave it open so the rain can drip off." I looked at her surprised, and replied, "But the floor will get all wet!" "It doesn't matter," she said with a laugh.

I reopened my umbrella, put on my slippers and came to sit at the dining room table, where hot water had already been poured and a snack set out. We talked a bit about the weather, my day, theirs, and then, still uneasy, I said, "Do you really think I should leave the umbrella open like that?" Seeing they didn't understand my concern, I added: "In France they say that to leave an umbrella open in the house brings bad luck." At that, they all broke out in laughter. When they had recovered, one of the daughters said, "We also have a saying about umbrellas open in the house: it brings friends!"

It is a fact: the Chinese love company. They like to be in company. They also know how to make good company. I recall an occasion at an international conference on Chinese studies when a film was to be shown at 9 P.M. People began to gather in the lobby at 8:45, and by 9 o'clock there was already quite a crowd. As the minutes passed and the doors remained shut, the crowd began to grow restive. Around 9:15, we were informed that the projector bulb had burned out; a replacement was being sought, it would be a matter of minutes now. Nine-twenty went by, then 9:25, 9:30. The doors remained closed. Behind it people could be heard talking, rushing about, calling across the room. But the doors remained shut, and no further explanation was forthcoming.

Meanwhile, something remarkable had happened. Spontaneously, the milling crowd had separated into its component parts. On one side of the room were all the Chinese: they had long since ceased to look at the door to see whether an explanation, at least, would emerge, and had set themselves to doing imitations. Forming a single group, they were laughing hilariously as an elderly man danced about with a lady's hat on, singing in falsetto at the top of his lungs and looking for all the world like a transvestite from Pigalle. When he had finished, everyone applauded, and it was the turn of the next person. On the other side of the room quite a different spectacle met one's eye. The Westerners had broken up into groups of four or five—in-groups and out-groups—and one overheard here wisecracks about the conference's organizers, there serious talk about the day's proceedings, and everywhere conversations were punctuated by constant glances at the door to see whether we were ever going to be delivered from the prison of enforced sociability.

Not that the Westerners had nothing to say to each other, but they had come to see a film; talking had already been done at the dinner table. As for the idea of playing a game, no one would have thought of it in a million years. That was why it was such a surprise that the idea had occurred to others.

One could go on endlessly with such stories, but it is time to come to the point: what has such a story to do with Chinese religion? The answer is: everything. For religion is people coming together, assembling: we might say, the Chinese love to form a crowd, therefore they are religious. More precisely, in the waiting scene just described, we saw how the Westerners (1) continued to wait, (2) got impatient, (3) broke up into small groups, (4) made up for the time being lost by engaging in "serious" talk, though interrupted by glances at the door, and/or (5) made ironic remarks about the "organizers," to voice their irritation at being made to wait. The Chinese, by the time the doors opened at 10 o'clock, had completely forgotten why they had come. Indeed, several of them left at that point, as if to say, "I've gotten what I came for." (In fact, it turned out they were going to a party.) And while they had waited and improvised, they had formed *one body*.

The One Body: no people on earth is better at forming one body. However hierarchical the structures of the Chinese state may have been throughout history, Chinese people of all ages and conditions, when thrown together, naturally coalesce. They are, in that very concrete sense, one of the most democratic people on the face of the earth.

There are, of course, counter-examples: one has heard of Chinese factionalism (the "tong wars" of Hollywood fame); one has heard of footbinding and other forms of Chinese misogyny; one has heard of Chinese nepotism and Chinese authoritarianism. And all this hearsay has its foundation in reality, and its implications for Chinese society, history, religion. But by and large, at bottom, in the end—however one wants to put it—the first and fundamental fact about China and the Chinese is the One Body: the Tao is One Body, so big as to contain all, so small as to penetrate everthing.

This One Body is ever-present, not only in Chinese society, but also in the Chinese language: Chinese has none of the distinctions so familiar to us of gender and time, not to mention those of social hierarchy which characterize Japanese. Parts of speech do, of course, exist in Chinese: there are subjects and objects, verbs and adverbs. But even there, Chinese is characterized by an extraordinary degree of suppleness, far greater even than English, for a word does not change form in passing from the state of adjective to adverb, or even from verb to noun or noun to verb: its change in function is signaled not by a change in external form but by a change in relative position. As such, Chinese language mirrors Chinese society, and vice versa. One is refreshed, through these basic facts of language, at the inexhaustible spring of democratic social relations: One Body.

But there is one fact of the Chinese language which is more revelatory than all the rest: its vast reservoir of reduplicatives. The reality hidden behind that dreadfully serious word is a childish one: pa-pa, ma-ma, da-da, do-do virtually exhaust the supply in a Western language. But Chinese is full of these reduplicatives which in Western languages exist only as baby talk—as anyone who has ever tried to translate Chinese poetry knows. And one finds the greatest concentration of such words in the most refined use of language: in lyrical poetry. Their most characteristic use is descriptive, of human emotions, of natural phenomena: the vast expanse of the sky, or of a lake; sorrow; joy; the bluish tint of the mountains in the distance. They are often mood words, words from an impressionist's brush, words which give a feeling, paint a scene, blur a distinction. These words make the world one vast resonant body: "Where there is solicitation (*kan*), there is response (*ying*)" is the Chinese equivalent of "Knock, and it will be opened." But in Chinese, this is not the wise saying of one man, this is the endlessly repeated faith of all. *Kan*: evoke, provoke, stir up, set in motion. The same word is used in stories of the divine origin of great men: a woman walks in the foot print of a Big Man, or is "covered by a red cloud," or swallows a grain of rice, and she is suddenly "stirred within" (*kan*). She later gives birth to a founding hero, the answer to her prayers. The Chinese universe is a giant womb: all is eternally present, both good and evil. It is up to man to "stir up," to elicit the answers he ardently desires. This is the function of Chinese ritual: to keep things right if they have not yet gone wrong; to set things back on the right track when they have. The universe is in man's image, it responds to him: "Of all beings in the universe," say the Chinese religious texts, "man is the most potent" (*ling*);° "man's fate depends on himself," they add, "not on Heaven." *The Book of Solicitations and their Responses (Kan-ying p'ien,* see Legge), is the name of the most popular religious tract of modern times.

"Man is potent," and the simplest way to define Taoism is as the "religion which teaches how to nurture and perfect potency." The Real Man (*chen-jen*) is the man of pure potency: he "accomplishes without having to act" (*Lao-tzu* 47). His very presence in an area will produce perfect weather—rain and shine in their seasons—and, hence, abundant harvests. A Real Man, a man of sheer potency, will increase the fertility of the fields, or rather, elicit from the fields what is best in them, as opposed to what is worst or simply mediocre, and he will do so by harmonizing the energies in his body and so causing the rain to fall and the sun to shine in due time and in proper amounts in the body of Nature. Fertility and harmony are the natural responses to human perfection.

Every man coming into the world has the seed of this perfection: his *yüan-ch'i*, his primordial energy, and it is situated in the depths of his bowels, between his two kidneys, in what is called the Sea of Energy (*ch'i-hai*). On the conservation and refinement (*lien*) of one's stock of

---

° The word *ling* refers in general to that which is of celestial origin (Kaltenmark 1960), whence "spirits, gods," or "spirit, soul." The Chinese conceive of such entities as numinous, efficacious, penetrating, powerful. The aim of the present discussion is to show that the ascription of these attributes to *ling* is grounded in cosmological theory—whence the translation "potent."

primordial energy depends one's destiny (*ming*), a word which also means one's life. "The newborn babe," says Lao-tzu, is "virility at its height" (*Lao-tzu 45*), by which he means that the newborn, especially the male newborn, has still his entire endowment of primordial energy. As a result, his "male member will stir" without solicitation.

The association of potency with erection is a natural one. It is also, in the context of Taoism, a fundamental one, for the primordial energy is identified with the spermatic essence and, in early texts, the "receptacle" from which emerges the sperm in the sex act was thought of as comparable to the receptacle from which emerged the blood of the menstrual flow. It was thus called the Cinnabar Field, "field" for the receptacle, "cinnabar" for the redness of whatever, like the sun, is sheer energy, pure potency. Every individual has, so to speak, a sperm bank at birth: one can either expend one's energy in making children and, in general, running after the things of this world, or one can "return the semen to repair the brain" and thus, gradually, develop—refine—one's original potency into perfect potency. The perfectly potent man is one who has come full cycle: he no longer has a sexual organ which erects spontaneously, like the male infant's; on the contrary, he has an atrophied organ. In the place of the erect penis of his beginning he now has a bulging forehead, the head of an immortal. His entire life endowment has been recycled from the Sea of Energy between his kidneys to the mountainous paradise atop his head, and he can now direct his thoughts at will, wander on the clouds to eternity and back, and, above all, summon the gods to do his bidding.

That is why the man of perfected potency is like a local treasure, capable of making the rain fall and the sun shine. He has *realized* man's *potential* to be, of all beings, the most potent and so naturally all the less potent beings of the body of the universe—the Count of the Wind, the Master of the Rain (plate 19)—are at his beck and call. Whenever he solicits, Nature responds. This Real Man, described already in the third century B.C. text of the *Chuang-tzu*, is the prototype of the modern Taoist priest.

We have much yet to learn about Chinese cosmology before we can understand its priests. We have seen that the universe is a giant body, or rather, a womb, a receptacle pregnant with beings and events. We have seen within that womb, within that vast sea of the primordial chaos of Genesis, a spark of light, the primordial energy. And we have seen emerge, by virtue of the presence of that spark of light, a new possibility, the possibility of expending its energy or, shall we say, capitalizing on it. To expend is bad because it means the extinction of the flame and hence a return to darkness; to refine and recycle is good because it means a long and happy life, not to mention paradise itself.

We are confronted here by a rather puzzling paradox: without the original body of the Tao, there would be nothing at all; but once we distinguish within the body of the Tao a spark of light, it suddenly becomes clear that that without which there is nothing is itself negative, dark, chaotic, and abysmal, in contrast with the light of life. The appearance of light, in other words, produces an awareness of the pre-existence of darkness, and while it is true that where there is both light and darkness, it is the light—*yang*, male—which is good and the darkness—*yin*, female—which is bad, it is also true that the good-light-male could not exist were it not for the bad-dark-female. Indeed, it is within the womb of the bad, dark female that the good, light male gestates and while gestating learns the "embryonic breathing" (*t'ai-hsi*) by means of which he will later save himself.

But if, in one sense, gestation goes on forever in the spacious womb of the universe, parturition occurs in sequential time: the light breath floats up to form the heavens, the dark settles down to form the earth. Henceforth, the universe has become di-verse: a composite of heaven (*t'ien*) and earth (*ti*)—giving *t'ien-ti*, the Chinese word for "universe"—of good and bad. Henceforth, man, who dwells between heaven and earth, will have to learn how to put the pieces back together, how to symbolize, if he wishes to realize his potential as the "most potent being in the universe" (cf. Robinet 1979, 43). True, man alone can redeem the universe; but he can also, if he follows his natural bent, if he gives in to his desire for pleasure and power, cause the waters of Chaos to well up and plunge the whole earth into the Ninefold Obscurity, as the Chinese call hell. On man's behavior now depends the fate of the universe.

But let us not be too eager to rush to judgment; let us go back to the Beginning: before the Beginning was the Tao. Let us call the Tao zero, neither negative nor positive: pure potential (*ling*). Then the primordial energy will be one; it will be a kind of treasure (*pao*), and that is exactly what the Chinese call it, comparing it to a single pearl in the midst of a boundless ocean (we will see later what they did with the combined term, *ling-pao*). But the emergence of one thing in the ocean of nothing provoked the conversion of nothing into something, and that something which is also nothing is at once positive, insofar as it makes everything possible, and negative, insofar as it is no-thing, as opposed to one thing. It is, in short, two, and two is female, that is, cracked in two, like the female sex organ, as opposed to the One Thing of the male.

The really crucial point in this cosmologic is the fact that, as in the sexual act itself, what thus breaks open the virgin womb of the world is the male organ. Chuang-tzu says:

> Heaven and earth were born at the same time I was, and the ten thousand
> things are one with me.

> We have already become one, so how can I say anything? But I have
> just *said* that we are one, so how can I not be saying something? The
> one and what I said about it make two. (Chap. 2; trans. Watson, 43)

In Chuang-tzu, then, it is not the penis which splits open the primal
unity of the universe. It is the tongue, the male organ of the microcosm
of the head, which, like its counterpart in the microcosm of the body,
that is, of the trunk of the body, is the source of *ming*, which means
"life" but also means "orders, commands." The tongue is an agent of
creation, just like the penis, but the life it gives is that given by *naming*
a thing. A thing exists only after it has been, as by Adam, properly
named. To give a name (*ming*, a different word, in second tone) is to
give an order (*ming*, as above, fourth tone; cf. Robinet 1979, 41; also,
137, on the relationship between the saliva and the spermatic essence).
It is to give an order to the universe of things, to bring a thing to life,
that is, to light it up, to elicit from the darkness of the chaos of things
the spark of life.

This, we shall see, is how the Taoist priest converts hell into heaven,
brings the dead back to life, and in general controls the forces of
Nature. The capacity to give orders is also what distinguishes an
emperor from his ministers (on the religious roots of this capacity, see
Vandermeersch 1980, 483). For the moment, however, we simply insist
on the parallel function in Chinese cosmologic of the penis and the
tongue. This is given explicit expression in successive commentaries to
the oldest extant Taoist text on how to refine the primordial energy, the
Huang-t'ing wai-ching (Outer Scripture of the Yellow Court), where the
term *ling-ken*, "root of potency," is glossed both as the tongue and the
"sperm chamber" (Schipper 1975a, 332). In the *Lao-tzu*, on the other
hand, we read:

> The nameless was the beginning of heaven and earth;
> The named was the mother of the myriad creatures.
>> Hence always rid yourself of desires in order to observe its secrets;
>> But always allow yourself to have desires in order to observe its
> manifestations. (chap. 1; trans. Lau, 57)

There is no naming without desiring; there is no desiring without
naming: naming and desiring enter the world simultaneously, breaking
it in two.

Lao-tzu suggests, therefore, an alternation between ridding oneself
of and allowing oneself to have desires so as to understand both the
secrets and the manifestations. "One *yin*, one *yang*: that is the Tao,"
says the *Hsi-tz'u* commentary on *The Book of Changes* (p. 40; cf. Granet
1968, 104). But Chuang-tzu is worried by the implications of such logic;
he concludes the passage quoted above, "The one and what I have said
about it make two," with "and two and the original one make three."
That poses a dilemma:

If we go on this way, then even the cleverest mathematician can't tell where we'll end, much less an ordinary man. If by moving from nonbeing to being we get to three, how far will we get if we move from being to being? Better not to move, but to let things be! (Watson, 43)

Wise advice indeed! But we, in counting to three above, found just how hard it is to interrupt the spontaneous generation of the numbers: heaven (1) + earth (2), we found, engendered (=, the mathematical copula) both man (3) and the "waters of Chaos" (3). That is, the number three, which is the first odd (male) number after one, and which stands in relation to one as a newborn son to his hoary grandfather—representing a new generation, a renewed creation—the number three, like its ancestor, splits the world into two, but now two sets of three exist: heaven, earth, and man; heaven, earth, and water. We may call these the natural and the cultural triads.

$1 + 2 = 3 + 3 = 6$. The hexagrams of *The Book of Changes* are in fact composed of two trigrams. But here again we must not proceed too quickly: 6, yes, but also 4 (heaven, earth, man, and water). And, more significantly, 5: heaven and earth twice each because they are different by virtue of the differing center, plus the center which, though different in *substance*, is identical in *function*.

Thus, when we reach the number five in Chinese cosmologic, we reach a kind of plateau of stability, created by the doubling of the center, which thereby becomes a pivot (cf. Granet 1968, 264). The doubling of the center, as top (heaven) and bottom (earth) are put into relationship by that which joins them together, the = sign, the copula, man and water. Linguists and psychoanalysts will appreciate that this is a rather different understanding of the relationship between words and things, the signifier and the signified, than that current in the West. "The symbol," says Lacan, echoing Mallarmé and, ultimately, the story of the Fall, "manifests itself first of all as the murder of the thing" (tr. Wilden, p. 84). Lacan follows modern linguistics in symbolizing that understanding $\frac{S}{s}$, in which the big S, the signifier, crushes the little s, the signified. In China, by contrast, where the model body is that of the female rather than that of the male, it is not the male act of procreation which is seen as primary, even if it is primordial; it is the female non-act of gestation. Behind the named, the manifest, therefore, is the nameless, the secret. Names plus things together make up the universe, but things exist even when they have not been named. Naming may bring things alive for man, for his use; it does not create out of nothing.

The infinite sense of mystery, eternal, impenetrable, virgin, undisturbed by human presence that one experiences when looking at Chinese landscape paintings comes from this fact of the Chinese psyche: Mother Nature before Father Verb. The Verb of the Father *orders* the primeval Chaos of Mother Nature, but it would have nothing to order were the Chaos not there to begin with, and He could not maintain that order with His law if Chaos did not continue to exist underneath the order. So Chuang-tzu says:

> Words exist because of meaning; once you've gotten the meaning, you can forget the words. Where can I find a man who has forgotten words so I can have a word with him? (Chap. 26; Watson, 302)

If Chaos is eternal, the order introduced into the chaos of the universe has an end, as it had a beginning. This is because slowly names given cease to fit; political systems invented in simpler times cease to function; old irrigation ditches get choked up with new vegetation; the waters of chaos begin to mount. The mythic villain Kun tries to dam the waters with swelling mold, but it is far too late to stop the rising flood. Kun is executed for "disobedience," literally, "neglect of orders" (*fang-ming;* Karlgren, 3), and his son, the Great Yü, is appointed in his stead. Yü rushes tirelessly about the empire ("all under heaven"), getting to know—what?—the names of the gods of the rivers and mountains, in other words, the "veins of the earth" (*mai-li:* see below, p. 160). His intimate knowledge of the deep structure of the earth—his capacity to summon the gods of every hillock and every water course—enables him at last to "draw the waters off," out the Door of Earth in the southeast. There they flow out to sea and thence into the abyss, from whence they are recycled in the vast bosom of the universe, eventually to reenter the system via the Gate of Heaven in the northwest as "showers of blessing."

What Yü did in this myth for all China, the modern Taoist priest still does for the local community: he recycles the "old energy" (*ku-ch'i*), and so gives the community a new lease on life. We shall see later how literally true this is. We shall also see that it is his intimate knowledge of deep structures, of secret names, that enables him to do this, together with a dance called the Step of Yü.

But once again we have let the wild horses of Chinese cosmologic lead us to anticipate ourselves, and we must retrace our steps, back to the beginning:

> The Way gives birth to one; one gives birth to two; two gives birth to three; three gives birth to the ten thousand things. (*Lao-tzu* 42)

We now see why, or rather how, the three gives birth to the myriad things. The Tao here is clearly zero. One is the primordial energy. Two is *yin-yang*, usually referred to as the "two aspects" (*liang-yi*). Three is often called the "three virtualities" (*san-ts'ai*), which refers to the cultural triad of heaven, earth, and man. (When the natural triad of heaven, earth, and the waters is referred to, the texts use the term "three

office(r)s" [*san-kuan*]. We will see why later.) Four, in Chinese, is invariably associated with the seasons (*ssu-shih*). Four is thus essentially temporal, a *succession*, as two is an *alternation*. Five, third in the series of odd numbers, is associated with a *spatial* disposition. One is a thing; three is a linear disposition, either horizontal or vertical; five results from the combination of these two triadic linear dispositions, giving
• • • , the five directions, our four directions plus the center, from which China derives its name, Land of the Center (*chung-kuo*). The stability of five is thus underscored (more of this later). But five is also in motion insofar as it presupposes the alternation and succession of two and four: the five phases (*wu-hsing*), literally, "five goings" (wood, fire, earth, metal, and water).

These first five numbers are called "raw numbers" or "numbers of generation" (*sheng-shu*). It is not hard to see why. They are completed by a second series of five (the logic is becoming familiar; a new unit is formed by each odd, male number, and this unit then instantaneously engenders its "double"), 6 through 10, called "cooked numbers," or "numbers of maturation" (*ch'eng-shu*). With these two sets of five, we can now manufacture one of the components of Chinese time, the so-called Heavenly Trunks (*t'ien-kan*), two—a male and a female—for each direction:

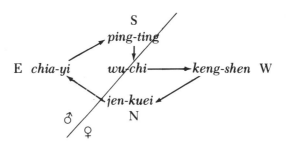

As the letters indicate, on their maps the Chinese invert, from our point of view, both the horizontal (east-west) and the vertical (north-south) axes. (The Pole Star remains north.) Each direction, plus the center, is associated with one of the five phases. The series starts in the east, with the element (phase) wood, corresponding to spring; wood "gives birth to" fire (south, summer), fire to earth (center, late summer), earth to metal (west, autumn), and metal to water (north, winter). This cycle, the first one, is called the cycle of "mutual generation" (*hsiang-sheng*). All but the last two generations are obvious enough: new vegetation burns in the heat of the summer, producing the "ashes" of which the earth is composed; the last two are explained by the fact that in the bosom of the earth grow—everything in China grows—metals and, as illustrated by much Chinese mirror lore, water gathers—drops of water grow—on mirrors, which in ancient China were made of metal.

The cycle of mutual generation is doubled by one of mutual conquest (*hsiang-k'o*): metal conquers wood (with an axe), fire conquers metal (in the foundry), water conquers fire, earth conquers water (Kun's dam), and wood conquers earth (by growth). As is clear from the conclusion of this cycle, it brings us back to the beginning of the cycle of generation: everything, in China, grows; life is always more abundant than death. This greatly facilitates the work of the priest, whose job it is to overcome the forces of evil and death. Confronted by a sick person, for example, he need simply readjust that person's cyclical situation, which has been thrown out of order, either by misguided or immoral behavior on his part, or by the mechanical conflict of the individual's cycles with those of nature, or, as is very often the case, by eruption into his psychic life of ghosts, who nurse a grudge against the living and so refuse to do what is natural, that is, move on. The Taoist priest, therefore, must have an intimate acquaintance with the structure of the universe and its cycles if he is to fulfill his task. It is by conformity with the laws of nature that he evokes from Nature a positive response to his prayers on behalf of his client. By "laws of nature," of course, he means the elaborate system of cosmologic of which we have just examined a rather small portion. Inasmuch as the same laws of situation, relation, and movement apply to every body, including the human body, it is not hard to see why the work of the Chinese doctor and that of the priest overlapped, why indeed, they were often, in the past, the same person.

But to return to cosmology. As the Heavenly Trunks are composed by a doubling of the five phases and then the coupling of the result (*chia* is the husband of *yi*, etc.), so the Earthly Branches (*ti-chih*)—which, combined with the Trunks, serve the Chinese as a system by which to measure time—are formed by the doubling of the female number six from which five, by a movement of return, had been produced. The twelve Earthly Branches, however, are not then coupled, nor do they have a center. They are arranged in cyclical fashion:

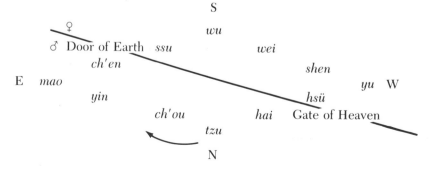

The earthly cycle, like the heavenly, moves clockwise. It starts, however, not in the land of the rising sun but in the deep north, at midnight, in the dead of winter, at the time when the sun begins to come back to life, the winter solstice. *Tzu* means newborn child (especially male, of course). The winter solstice is the time of the Newborn Son. This is symbolized most pregnantly in Chinese by the trigram *k'an*

☵ , two fractured female lines carrying in their bosom one solid male line.

Tzu is thus symbolized in one of two arrangements of the trigrams, and it is with these arrangements that we will finish our survey of Chinese cosmology and numerology. The trigrams summarize perfectly the cosmology we have discussed thus far: "One *yin* – –, one *yang* ——: that is the Way." Indeed, the trigrams are thus composed of two and only two types of lines, but the lines are arranged in threes, because one —— + two – – = three. Two to the third power gives eight, and there are, therefore, in both arrangements, eight trigrams. In Chinese numerology the number eight automatically brings to mind the trigrams, in one or the the other of the following arrangements:

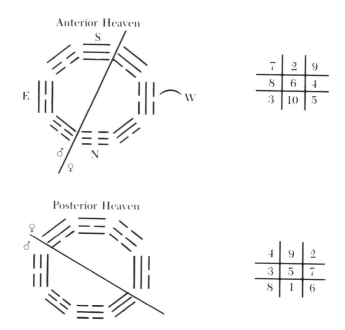

Anterior Heaven (*hsien-t'ien*) represents heaven before things start to turn, heaven before time, and Posterior Heaven (*hou-t'ien*) represents heaven after change has begun. The arrangement of Anterior Heaven is identified with Fu-hsi, a kind of Chinese Adam. It is spatial in character, and is determined by binary oppositions. The "father" (☰) is placed across from the "mother" (☷), the "first son" (☳) from the "first daughter" (☴), the second (☵) from the second (☲), and the third (☶) from the third (☱). In addition, one might say that the "family" is arranged according to "natural" order, with the father on top (the sun at its zenith) and the mother on the bottom (midnight). There is but one exception to this orderly and static universe of Anterior Heaven: the second daughter has been transferred to the male, the second son to the female side. This inversion introduces, into the very structure of the universe, the *potential* for change which will be mirrored in the arrangement identified with King Wen, Posterior Heaven.

The logic of this latter arrangement is far more subtle than the logic of the universe before time began. It is, in the first place, cyclical, as the Earthly Branches are cyclical. Both cycles start in the north and turn as the sun's shadow turns around a gnomon in the northern hemisphere. They have therefore an invisible, "empty" center which serves as an axis, and have as male directions the north and the east and as female the south and the west (by contrast, the Heavenly Trunks and Anterior Heaven have south and east as male, west and north as female, and have a "full" center). This arrangement starts in the northwest, at the Gate of Heaven, with the plenipotentiary father. Inasmuch as male lines represent energy and life force, that is, concentration (*chü*), as opposed to dispersal (*san*) and death, the three male lines of the father ☰ engender the newborn son *k'an* ☵ .

The next principle to be taken into consideration for the understanding of this temporal arrangement is that all that is male is on the male side and all that is female is on the female side. There is no inversion such as gave potential motion to Anterior Heaven. Given this principle, there now remain but two males, the youngest and the eldest son. Their positions are determined by the fact that *chen* ☳ , the eldest son, represents thunder, to which Chinese mythology assigns a major role in the awakening of earth in springtime: it is thus appropriate for the eldest son to be in the position of the rising sun. That leaves for the youngest son, *ken* ☶ , representing mountain, the northeast corner, the Gate of Demons.

On the female side of the line, positions are determined in the first place by the fact that *li* ☲ , the second daughter, must remain opposite *k'an*, as in Anterior Heaven. *Li* and *k'an* being thus the only pair in binary opposition carried over from Anterior to Posterior

Heaven, their axis—east-west in Anterior, north-south in Posterior Heaven—is called the axle of the universe in the famous text of symbolic alchemy, the *Ts'an-t'ung ch'i*. *Li* having thus taken the place of the father ☰ in Anterior Heaven (as *k'an* that of the mother ☷), it is only natural that its concentrated yin disperses to form ☷ , which is therefore in the southwest corner. This corner is generally called the Door of Man, probably because *k'un* (mother) is there, and man issues from the Mother. Note that the Door of Man is thus opposite the Gate of Demons, as the Gate of Heaven in the northwest is opposite the Door of Earth in the southeast. The latter, the last of the crucial corners, is assigned to the eldest daughter, leaving the land of the setting sun, the west, to the youngest daughter. A weak, secondary axis is formed by this pairing of the youngest daughter with the eldest son.

It is Posterior Heaven, the temporal arrangement of the trigrams which is most immediately important in Taoist ritual. When, for example, the southern Taiwan altar (*t'an*) today is described as composed of "eight trigrams, nine palaces, and ten directions" (see below, p. 36f), Posterior Heaven is referred to. The eight trigrams are those of King Wen, the nine palaces result when the center is added, and the ten directions result when the center is doubled into top and bottom. The nine palaces are represented by the two magic squares shown next to the arrangements of the trigrams. They are magic because, no matter which way one adds the numbers, horizontally, vertically, or diagonally, one obtains, in the square related to Anterior Heaven, 18, and in that related to Posterior Heaven, 15.

It will be noted that whereas the Anterior Heaven square starts from the top with the *yin* number 2 and goes down to the *yin* number 10, the Posterior Heaven square starts at the bottom with the *yang* number 1 and goes up to the *yang* number 9 at the top. Thus, as far as vertical motion is concerned, these squares are consistent with the celestial and terrestrial character of Anterior and Posterior Heaven respectively. They are inconsistent, however, in that the celestial square starts with a *yin* and the terrestrial with a *yang* number. We have here, once again, the familiar feature of a tension-producing inversion, which injects a kind of potential energy into the whole scheme. For Granet, "this exchange is the result of a hierogamy" (1968, 166). However that may be, it certainly produces a hierogamy, for these two squares are literally drawn to each other. If the one is placed on top of the other, the result of the additions of all nine pairs of superimposed slots is 11, or 1(0) + 1, from which are engendered all numbers beyond the first ten, right up to the 1(0,000) things which constitute, symbolically, a "full universe" (on the number ten, see Granet, 127, 141).

We now know the bare minimum of what a Taoist priest must

know, or rather, assumes when he does his job. One final remark: one learns, from the secret manuals handed down from high priest to high priest, that the high priest has this "whole world in his hands"—in his left hand, to be precise (cf. Granet, 496):

(based on *Hsüan-ko miao-chüeh*, p. 30)

CHAPTER

2

Liturgy in Time: the Chinese Festival Calendar

The reader can find, in any one of a number of books, complete surveys of Chinese festivals, both in antiquity (Bodde 1975) and in modern times (De Groot 1886). He will surely be impressed, when he has finished perusing these volumes, by the multiplicity of the festivals and, of course, of the gods in whose honor they are held. He is likely to wonder, however, whether there is not, after all, some system, some principle of order, behind the apparent heterogeneity of Chinese religious activity. There is.

We may start by giving, in its barest outline, the calendar year as described by De Groot for Amoy at the end of the last century. Some elements of the liturgical year will be discussed in their Taoist aspects in Parts 2 and 3. Here we start at the end of the year rather than at the beginning. On the 16th day of the 12th month, the local god of the soil receives his last offering of the year and, in principle, all debts are settled (De Groot 1886, 577). On the 24th the domestic gods are banqueted before they leave for the grand year-end celestial assembly. Particular attention is paid at this time to the god of the fireplace (*tsao-chün*), who is in charge of the family's destiny (*ssu-ming*). This means that he is to the family what the god of the soil is to the neighborhood, a detached member of the celestial bureaucracy entrusted with the task of observing the humans in his charge and making regular reports on their behavior to his superiors. Clarence Day (1940, 89) cites a popular religious book to this effect:

> Let there be no careless deportment before the kitchen range, for here resides the arbiter of destiny. It is from hence that good and evil are reported to high Heaven, that blessing and calamity may be apportioned among men.

The god of the hearth makes his report at year's end, during the assembly of the gods presided over by their chief, Yü-huang, the Jade Emperor. Yü-huang is also called T'ien-kung, Duke of Heaven. This year-end event explains why the Chinese begin their preparations for the new year by settling accounts. In China, as in the West, sins and debts are the same thing; a sin puts one in the debt of the gods, as a good deed puts them in your debt. One of the most characteristic of popular religious books in China is, therefore, *The Register of Merits and Demerits* (*Kung-kuo ko*). Its ratings enable one to know precisely the worth of one's deeds, good and bad, and so to keep check, not only on oneself, but also on one's divine censors, and so ensure that justice is done. In the same vein, one of the most characteristic acts of popular Chinese religion for at least the last millennium is the burning of paper money and thus to pay debts, to buy services, and to accumulate merits. Capitalization has a long history in China; it was simply never adequately secularized.

New Year's day, the first day of spring in the Chinese calendar, is a time for spring cleaning and a complete bath, the only such bath in the entire year, according to De Groot (p. 5). The family, having stayed up all night, sets out an offering just before dawn to T'ien-kung. This ceremony is officiated by the family head and is followed by a similar offering for the Three Officers, that is, the lords in charge of the three offices of heaven, earth, and the waters under the earth. This early morning double offering is repeated on each of the first three days of the new year. Offerings are also presented on these three days to the domestic gods and to the ancestors. Thereafter, the domestic gods will be honored by an offering on the 1st and 15th of every month, that is, on the days of the new and the full moon.

By contrast, the "solitary souls" (*ku-hun*), those who have no descendants to tend to their needs, will be offered to on the 2nd and the 16th of every month. The implication of this contrast is clear: 1 and 15 are odd, male numbers, 2 and 16 are even and female (because they split into two equal halves). Thus is signified the celestial, divine character of the gods and the terrestrial, demonic character of the solitary souls.

On the 4th of the month, the domestic gods return from heaven and are given refreshments upon their arrival. On the 5th the New Year period as such comes to an end; people go back to their usual occupations. On the 9th a major domestic offering is made to T'ien-kung (De Groot, 47) and on the 10th to his terrestrial counterpart, Ti-kung (p. 84). It will be recalled that 9 is the highest *yang* number, located in the highest position in the magic square of Posterior Heaven, while 10 is the highest *yin* number, but in the lowest position in the magic square of Anterior Heaven. Significantly, a Taoist will often be asked to come at midnight between the 8th and the 9th to invite T'ien-kung, and Taoist "masses," as De Groot translates (p. 55) *chiao* ("offering"), will be held in temples of Taoist affiliation. The 8th to the 10th may also be a time for three-day Offerings. Taoists do *not* come to invite the Duke of Earth (Ti-kung).

On the 15th occurs the famous Lantern Festival held in honor of the Officer of Heaven. The other two of the three "days of origin" (*san-yüan jih*) are the 15th of the seventh month, when a festival is held in honor of the Officer of Earth, and the 15th of the tenth month, when one is held for the Officer of Water. De Groot has little to say about the latter two festivals, presumably because little was made in Amoy of the Water Festival, and the Earth Festival had long since been appropriated by the Buddhists. The three "days of origin" are nonetheless among the oldest of Taoist festivals, because they represent the three nodes of the Chinese year, the three poles around which the year is constructed. As De Groot points out, the 7th month is the beginning of autumn, and on the 1st day of that month, the gates of hell swing open wide. The 7th month is, therefore, the most crucial time for feeding all the solitary, untended, and hence famished souls of hell. This feeding—the festival of Universal Salvation (*p'u-tu*)—goes on throughout the seventh month, but its high point, even where performed by Buddhist priests, remains the 15th of the month. To understand this practice it is crucial to realize that hell (or hells, for there are many) are called "earth prisons" (*ti-yü*). If heaven is *yang* and divine, earth must be *yin* and demonic. But the demonic, by the inexorable logic of the system of correspondences, is simply that to which one owes a debt: the hungry souls, therefore, also go by the name "resentful souls" (*yüan-hun*). For one reason or another, they resent the living, and the living have, therefore, no choice but to try and relieve this resentment, this hunger for revenge, by appeasing it. Thus the *P'u-tu,* offered not only during the 7th month but also towards the end of every major temple festival and every requiem service, is a kind of insurance system, in which ones buys protection against the claims made on the living by the resentful dead.

The dead make these claims on the living—in the end, all the dead, even the ancestors, do—because they cannot do otherwise: it is natural for the dead to resent and envy the living. The natural, inevitable character of this resentment is brought out in yet another term used to describe them, "obstructed souls" (*chih-hun*). They are trapped, in earth-prison. The earth, to which the dead belong, which they in fact resemble, is composed of thick, sluggish, turbid energy, which is another way of saying it is utterly devoid of light. The term "obstructed souls" also recalls the story of the flood, for obstructed souls are like obstructed water. A portion, the terrestrial portion, the so-called seven p'o-souls, of every individual belongs to the earth; but the three *hun*-souls should naturally, like water, return to their celestial source. If they do not, it is because they are obstructed, as the result of their own unenlightened, sinful behavior no doubt, but dammed up and raging to get out they are, if necessary by going on a rampage. (Thus *hun* is the word used when referring to the "obstructed, resentful, or solitary" souls). It is up to the living to see to it they get out of prison, or else.

All of this, it will be noticed, is simply a matter of definition, of cosmologic: the Chinese are, *by definition,* all members one of another, all members of One Body. As the term "earth-prison" suggests, moreover, the imprisoned dead are comparable to the imprisoned living. The dregs of society have claims on that society, and few Chinese in traditional society were so bold as to turn the beggars or the local hoods (*liu-mang*) away empty-handed.

The day of the Aquatic Officer, the third of the three Days of Origin, does not appear, in De Groot's account, to be the occasion for a public festival. But that is rather misleading, for the aquatic quarter of the year, the winter months—especially the first of the winter months, the tenth month, the month of the third Day of Origin—is the time the most Taoist Offerings are celebrated. It was, moreover, a fundamental part of traditional Taoist practice to observe all three Days of Origin (Schipper 1982, 91). As a devotee and/or priest of the religion of the cosmos, the Taoist was in the first place accountable to its Three Officers. They were to him what the gods of the fire and soil were to the uninitiated, his censors, his "big brothers." It was during the celestial assemblies held on the three Days of Origin that he could, by fasting and prayer, improve his balance sheet and progress toward immortality.

One final thing, the most important of all, remains to be said about the three Days of Origin. Although all are "heavenly" days, in that they occur on odd-numbered days of the month, two—earth and water—are terrestrial and only one celestial. Moreover, their distribution has the effect of dividing the year into two equal parts: six months of *yang*—spring and summer, months one through six—followed by six months of *yin*. (Note that this division of the seasons corresponds to that of Anterior Heaven.) But the *yang* is thus one solid bloc of time, while the *yin* is further subdivided into two equal parts, one belonging to earth (autumn) and one to water (winter). The Chinese liturgical year is thus divided into three parts: $1 + 2 = 3$.

The complicity of earth and water in Chinese cosmologic is confirmed by the fact that hell, before it came, under Buddhist influence, to be called "earth-prison," was called "yellow springs" (*huang-ch'üan*), that is, the springs in the yellow earth. These were springs that could be obstructed, no doubt, but also springs from which sprang new life, the ancestors (Granet 1922). New life, in the Chinese imagination, was only indirectly the result of "showers of blessing": the showers, having fallen, had to soak into the earth and form subterranean rivers. It was knowledge of the deep structure formed by this subterranean network that enabled Yü to succeed in drawing off the waters: everything, in China, ultimately works together for good—for life—to them that love Nature.

Virtually all other days on the festival calendar of a Chinese community are incidental to the basic structure we have outlined above. They are chiefly saints days, the birth days of the gods. Two of these deserve, however, a special mention: the birthday of the god of the soil (plate 24) on the 2nd day of the second month, and of Lao-tzu (plate 2) on the 15th day of that month. The day of the first offering of the new year to the all-important god of the soil, 2/2, is like the day of his last offering, 12/16, a day doubly *yin*. The terrestrial character of this appropriately named god is thus clearly marked. How then can he be considered a member of the celestial bureaucracy, albeit detached? The answer is that he, like the waters, *falls* from heaven to earth—he is literally detached!—and there, in the depths of the eternal night (*ch'ang-yeh*), he brings life and light. He gathers in underground cisterns, forms subterranean rivulets, and springs unexpectedly, mysteriously, to the surface. Underground, he circulates, a hidden treasure of untapped—potential—energy; above ground, the community, by rendering him a cult, taps this limitless source of heaven-sent, but earth-derived life. He is therefore also called the Correct God of Wealth and Virtue (Fu-te cheng-shen), "correct" because he is a duly certified member in good standing of the celestial bureaucracy, "of wealth and virtue," because good fortune is the result of good behavior. The word translated "virtue" (*te*) also means "virtuality," power. The earth god is thus god of the earth because he is the spirit—water—which gives it life, which redeems the sluggish, turbid energy of earth by making it fertile. He can do so precisely because he comes from heaven.

We see, thus, in the earth god, the mediating, redeeming function of water in the context of the natural triad. It is what circulates between the two fixed—inert, *yin*—poles of heaven and earth. It will hardly come as a surprise, then, to learn that he who "led the waters off," the Great Yü, was god of the soil during the Han period (206 B.C.-220 A.D. (Kaltenmark 1967, 17), when Taoism in its religious form first began to take shape. Nor will it be a surprise to learn that the mediating function, in the context of the cultural triad, of the man who performs the Step of Yü is conceived to be analogous to that of water in the natural triad. Nor, finally, will we be surprised to see the Taoist priest, at the crucial moment of the Lighting of the (Incense) Burner in the Land of the Way, addressing himself to the god of the soil as to his alter ego.

As for Lao-tzu, whose birthday is also singled out among the other gods, he is the divine founder of Taoism and the third member of its triad: Yüan-shih t'ien-tsun, Ling-pao t'ien-tsun, Tao-te t'ien-tsun, the Heavenly Worthies of the Primordial Beginning (heaven), of the Numinous* Treasure (earth), and of the Way and its Virtue, or Power (water/man). Lao-tzu, by his very name, embraces—redeems—opposites: his name means "old infant." It summarizes the alchemical search for immortality: by refinement, or sublimation (*lien*), newborn potency becomes the potency, perfect and inexhaustible, of the Tao itself. Lao-tzu is, finally, the one who comes down from heaven to earth regularly, like rain, at first to serve as "counsellor to the Emperor" (*ti-shih*) and later, after he has transferred this power to the first of the Heavenly Masters (*t'ien-shih*) in the 2nd century A.D. (Seidel 1970, 228), to serve as divine "lord of the religion." Taoist histories in the Taoist canon are written as so many miraculous—redemptive—interventions by Lord Lao in the political history familiar to all from the orthodox (Confucian) histories. Taoist history may therefore be described as the history, not of the Messiah himself, not of the Annointed One who comes to establish a kingdom, but of his Spirit. Taoist history is Pentecostal history, as we shall see.

But why is the Taoist Spirit honored on the 15th day of the second month? First, because it is the central day of spring, the day when the Gate of Heaven opens wide. Second, this second month is the first month of the earth and its god: a savior who stayed eternally up in heaven with the Jade Emperor would be of no use to men here on earth. Third, the date of Lao-tzu's birthday coincides, on the Chinese calendar, with the day of the Buddha's extinction, and thus takes its

---

*On the translation of the term *ling*, see above, p. 8.

place as the conclusive word in the great religious debate of Chinese history: which is superior, Buddhism or Taoism? The answer given by the Taoists as early as the fifth century text *San-t'ien nei-chieh ching* (TT 1205) was: the religion of life, Taoism, was superior to Buddhism, the religion of extinction.

A final historical note on the three Days of Origin is needed here. While in modern times these days occur on the 15th day—the day of the full moon—of the first, seventh, and tenth months, there is considerable evidence that they were originally on the 7th (or 5th) days of those months (Stein 1979, 70). An early text of the Heavenly Masters describes the development of the new Taoist church as an imitation of Lao-chün's (Lao-tzu) establishment in heaven of the Upper Eight dioceses on 7/7 of the first year of the Shang-huang era, of the Middle Eight on 10/5 of the same year, and of the Lower Eight on 1/7 of the second year of that era (Lagerwey, 103-4). The importance of the seventh day of the month, and especially of 1/7 and 7/7, has been recently highlighted by Yü Ying-shih:

> There can be little doubt that in the minds of the ancient Chinese the midnight of the seventh day marked the beginning of the *chi-sheng-pa* ("after the birth of the crescent") quarter of the month . . . . The primitive Chinese conception of the soul was derived analogously from the birth of the crescent. (1981, 84)

CHAPTER

3

Liturgy in Space: the Taoist Altar

Wherever the contemporary Taoist performs—in a private home, to improve the owner's fortunes; outdoors, for a requiem service; inside a temple, for any number of reasons—he sets up his own altar (*t'an*). (The altar is the whole arena upon which the ceremony is performed, not just a table.) The great hermitages of the past often had permanent three-stage altars of beaten earth, but even then the altar had to be "constructed" prior to the ritual by means, essentially, of symbolic banners. The altars constructed in northern Taiwan today differ from those in southern Taiwan, and the Taoist canon contains a large variety of altar designs. There is, nonetheless, an underlying unity, as we shall try to show in examining, first, three altars described in a text of the sixth century and, second, the altar used in southern Taiwan today.

ALTARS IN *WU-SHANG PI-YAO*

(*Wu-shang pi-yao*, TT 1138) ("The Essence of the Supreme Secrets") was compiled circa 580 at imperial behest. It contains instructions for three different types of altar. The first is for the Fast of the Three Sovereigns (*san-huang chai;* Lagerwey, 152). The Three Sovereigns are the cosmic lords of heaven, earth, and man, and the texts devoted to them, although re-edited in later times, belong to the most archaic strata of Taoist literature. The altar is called either an "altar of the spirits" (*ling-t'an*), meaning the Three Sovereigns in this case, or an "open-air altar" (*lu-t'an*), open, that is, to receive the visitation of the spirits. Its plan is given here, based on descriptions in *Wu-shang pi-yao:*

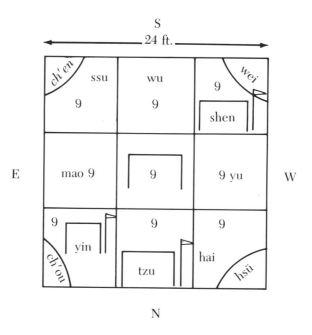

One table and banner are assigned to each of the Three Sovereigns on this square altar area. The 24-foot long sides (about six meters) are subdivided into three equal parts. Twenty-four is the number of the "segmental energies" (*chieh-ch'i*) in a year (each of the twelve months is divided into a male and a female "energy"). It is also the number of "dioceses" (*chih*, literally, "governances") into which in 142 A.D. Lao-chün (Lao-tzu "divinized"; see Seidel 1969) instructed Chang Tao-ling, the founder of Taoism as a religion, to divide his new church. These instructions formed the basis of the new Covenant of Orthodox Unity with the Powers (*Cheng-yi meng-wei*) (on the significance of the term "unity," cf. Robinet 1979, 184 ff). These twenty-four dioceses were in turn divided into three groups of eight, the Upper, Middle, and Lower Eight, in imitation of Lao-tzu's organization of Heaven. Inasmuch as the upper, middle, and lower regions of the universe—the realms of the Three Sovereigns—are also to be found in man himself—in the head (heaven), the thorax (man), and the abdomen (earth; cf. Seidel 1978, 161)—it is likely that the tables or thrones (*wei*) of the Three Sovereigns have correspondences in the human body. Each of these three portions of the body has its center, its "palace" (*kung*); these palaces are equivalent to the thrones of the Three Sovereigns in the diagram above: the *ni-huan* (between the eyes), the heart, and the Cinnabar Field (*tan-t'ien*) between the kidneys (cf. Robinet 1979, 192; 1984, 129).

The division of the altar into sides of $3 \times 8 = 24$ feet must not lead us to neglect the altar viewed as a unity, for just as the human body is sometimes viewed in Taoist texts as divided vertically into three segments, it is viewed in others as a unity. As a unity, abstraction is made of the head (the head is also a separate, self-sufficient microcosm) and only the trunk counts, especially the belly, the womb. Thus on the altar above, the Celestial Sovereign's table and flag are at *tzu*, the Human Sovereign's at *yin*, and the Terrestrial's at *shen*. According to *The Scripture of the Three Sovereigns*, these sovereigns control the three vital forces which lodge in these centers, to wit, energy (*ch'i*), life (*ming*), and spirit (*shen*) (Lagerwey, 82).

Energy and life are probably to be identified with the two kidneys. The spirit is normally located in the heart (south-north, heart-kidneys is the axis of the body's trunk); it may be that it is here displaced to *shen* in the southwest because the Terrestrial Sovereign must be in the corner of the Mother ☷ . (The cosmologic of the altar follows that of Posterior Heaven.) Whatever bodily correspondences we find for the three table-palaces on the altar, it is clear that the Human and Celestial Sovereigns are placed together in the north, in opposition to the Terrestrial Sovereign in the south. The Celestial Sovereign occupies the north, which is always the honorable direction to occupy in China, because whoever occupies it faces south, faces the sun, *yang*. At the same time, he is in the position which is at the center of the heavens, corresponding to *tzu*, the infant of the winter solstice, and *k'an* ☵ .

Thus, in a Chinese temple, the chief deity is always seated in the recess

in the middle of the north wall, and the Taoist priest creates his altar
in modern times by hanging up in front of this recess the scrolls of the
Triad.

But if the location of the sovereigns of earth and heaven is not
surprising, that of the Human Sovereign is. He is positioned in the
northeast, that is, at the Gate of Demons. Is man demonic? Not while
alive, certainly; but after death is another matter, as we have seen in
discussing the solitary souls. Placing the Human Sovereign in the Gate
of Demons is designed to control those former humans who have
become demons. The celebrant, moreover, is identified with the Human
Sovereign, for he enters the altar by the Gate of Demons and not, as is
customary, by the Gate of Heaven (Lagerwey, 182).

We must note here that the first Heavenly Master Chang Tao-ling's
Covenant of Orthodox Unity with the Powers is a contract with the
four (directional) generals of the supreme heavenly body T'ai-sui
(Lagerwey, 43). They are sworn to assist him in overcoming the
demonic forces of the Six Heavens so as to inaugurate the reign of the
Three (pure) Heavens (TT 1205 *San-t'ien nei-chieh ching* 1.5b). Chang
Tao-ling is thus in the first place an exorcist. This is symbolized in
modern iconography by setting him astride a tiger (plate 1), emblem of
demonic forces, and, in modern ritual, by a combat between the high
priest and a tiger-skin-clad demon which ends with the "fixing" of the
demon, significantly, in the northeast (plate 11). The high priest is thus
clearly re-enacting the foundational struggle of Chang Tao-ling with the
forces of evil.

Given these parallels, it is tempting to think that one of the things
Chang Tao-ling learned from Lao-chün was the fast for which the altar
we are examining was constructed. After all, the Three Sovereigns *are*
the Three Energies (that is, Heavens), as the hymns sung later in the
ritual show (Lagerwey, 153, 155). This equivalence means that the
Human Sovereign is none other than the Lao-chün who revealed the
"Way of the Three Heavens" to Chang. As the modern high priest
repeats the combat of Chang Tao-ling, so did Chang imitate that of the
Human Sovereign. The Human Sovereign (Lao-chün, also called Lao-
kuei, Old Demon; cf. Stein 1979, 64), having won his battle with the
demons of the Six Heavens (such battles are a common theme of later
Chinese popular fiction), takes up his post in the crucial northeast corner
of the altar, and so enables those to whom he transmits his way to carry
on the struggle by bringing the tiger demons directly to him.

Conjectural as this interpretation may be from the historical point
of view, it is clearly justified from a ritual point of view: the high priest
fights the battle of the gods, on behalf of the gods. The traditional
phrase used to describe this, found in virtually every liturgical manual,
is "to carry out transformations in the place of heaven" (*tai-t'ien hsing-*

hua). The transformational work of the Taoist priest is one of recycling. Like Yü, he "draws off the waters," he gets the "obstructed souls"—the demons—to move on and leave the living alone.

To return to our altar: in each of the nine component squares is placed a mat and, on each of the mats, nine lamps and an incense burner. Nine is the highest *yang* number; $9^2 = 81$, the number of years spent by Lao-tzu (Lao-chün) in his mother's womb before birth. The long gestation is one explanation of a meaning of "Lao-tzu," Old Infant, for he is a newborn king who is already ancient in days, one whose potency is at once pure, fresh, new, and perfect, refined, fully sublimated. The central square is distinguished by the placement of its burner—associated with the "basic destiny" (*pen-ming*) of the householder for whom the fast is being performed—on a table.

On each of the sovereign's tables are placed a plate and a cup (for the banquet, *chiao*). In front of the table is a mat with an incense burner and behind the table, hanging from a twelve-foot long green bamboo pole, is a five-foot long green flag, on which is written in red the "esoteric writ" (*nei-wen*) of the sovereign. Esoteric writs are described in *chüan* 25 of the *Wu-shang pi-yao* (Lagerwey, 106–7). The writ of the Celestial Sovereign enables one to "enter the mountains." This is probably to be understood both literally and figuratively, for the word "body" is a synonym for the word "mountain" (TT 614 *Sheng-hsüan pu-hsü chang* 4b), and a body is, as we have seen, in the first place a womb, whether it be the body of the Tao (that is, the universe), the human body, or the altar itself. Put another way, a mountain is a cave, a treasure-filled receptacle. For example, the Taoist canon itself is divided into Three Caverns (*san-tung*), one for each of the Three Sovereigns (Lagerwey, 82), or for each of the "venerable gods of the Three Energies" (*san-ch'i tsun-shen*; Lagerwey, 104).

The writ, red on a green background, combines the colors of the two *yang* directions of Anterior Heaven, east and south. The writ itself is the red, pure *yang*. In modern Taiwan, the placard (*pang*) posted outside a temple during an Offering, although written in ordinary black ink, uses a sheet of red paper bordered by strips of green paper. "Red writ" (*ch'ih-wen*) is the standard name for a revealed writing and, more particularly, for the symbols (*fu*) used in virtually every Taoist rite. Today they are often still written in red ink, though usually on yellow paper.

The final instruction for the establishment of the altar concerns the four corners: at *ch'en, hsü, ch'ou*, and *wei*, four of the Earthly Branches, "open doors" are created by means of silk curtains. As Chinese swinging doors are intended, we may imagine them to look very much like those still in use in Taiwan today: curtain doors are created by hanging two rectangular embroidered cloths from a horizontal bar supported by two uprights attached to the back of a table and then drawing back and tying these cloths to the uprights much as one would tie curtains. These curtain doors nowadays open out on the hanging scroll of a divinity (plate 14), but this would seem to be a relatively recent development. However, it is certainly worth noting that the Taoists of northern Taiwan, who consider themselves to be Orthodox Unity (*cheng-yi*), as opposed to the Numinous Treasure (*ling-pao*) Taoists of southern Taiwan, still construct an altar which has such curtain doors at the four corners. Even though the southern Taiwanese Taoist altar has no such curtain doors in the corners, the corners remain important not only in the construction of their altar but also in their rite of entry onto the altar, as discussed later.

The second altar described in the *Wu-shang pi-yao* (Lagerwey, 159) is for the fast of the three Days of Origin. Its plan, reproduced from *Wu-shang pi-yao* (*chüan* 52), is given below:

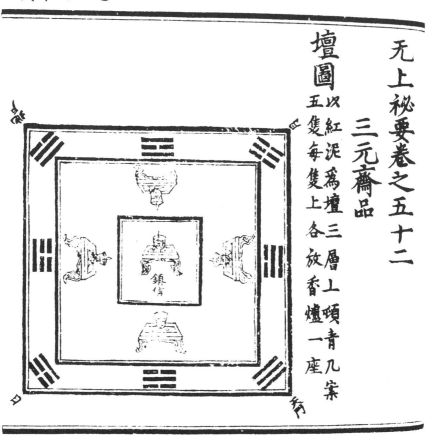

This altar is explicitly described as being composed of three superimposed (square) stages (*ts'eng*). These stages seem to be not actually built up of pounded earth, but simply traced using "red mud." The three stages represent heaven, earth, and water. The four gates created at the corners of the altar are the Gates of Heaven (NW), Earth (SE), the Sun (NE), and the Moon (SW).

On the outer, lower stage of this "ziggurat" (cf. Schipper 1982, 126), we find the eight trigrams in the King Wen disposition. Why? According to a story in *T'ai-p'ing kuang-chi* (*chüan* 291) which quotes from the *Shih-yi lu*, we learn that "when Yü was drilling through the Dragon Pass (in the NW), also called Gate, he came within this gate to a hollow cave." He penetrated deeper and deeper into this cave ("entering the mountain") until at last, having passed through dense darkness, "he felt it growing gradually lighter." Then he met Fu-hsi, who

> showed Yü the diagram of the eight trigrams, arranged on a sheet of gold. There were also eight gods standing in waiting by the side of the diagram. . . . Then he pulled out a jade tablet, which he gave to Yü. The tablet was twelve inches long, in accord with the number of the Earthly Branches, and it was to be used to measure the heavens and the earth. Holding this tablet, Yü then levelled the land and tamed the waters.

Although the text does not say so explicitly, it is clear that the "diagram" (*t'u*), with the eight gods attached to it, is what enables Yü to "tame the waters," not the twelve-inch tablet, which is for measuring the universe (or more accurately, the di-verse). We have already mentioned the role played in Taoist ritual by the Step of Yü (cf. plate 10), which is a way of treading on these trigrams. We now see why: by stepping on these points, the priest activates the principles of the trigrams and so summons their gods, who then do his bidding by leading off the waters (which stand for evil, "obstructed souls"). The trigrams of the Step of Yü also serve to create the altar of the "eight trigrams and nine palaces": Yü is also linked, via the River Chart and the trigrams, to the magic square (Granet 1968, 145–174).

This story also explains why Taoist priests, today as in the past, always "hold a tablet" (plates 1, 26). The explanation usually given is that it makes of them officials in the court of the Jade Emperor and so, like officials in the court of the Chinese emperor, they carry such a tablet. But why does an official in the earthly court hold such a tablet? Everything in Chinese court etiquette is symbolic in the first place, functional in the second: is it not more likely that it is the official in the terrestrial who is modelled on his counterpart in the celestial bureaucracy?

The second and third stages of the altar, earth and heaven, must be treated together, just as both are measured by Yü's tablet. Having saved the world from the flood of evil—the rituals of the three Days of Origin are rituals of confession—Yü, and the priest, must now create a new heaven-earth, a new universe. This he does by setting up on the two upper stages a total of five tables. They correspond to the five directions and elements, and also to the five True Writs with which, even today, the altar is constructed during the Nocturnal Invocation (*su-ch'i*) ritual. The construction of the altar during the *su-ch'i* occurs immediately after the Altar-sealing (*chin-t'an*) combat of Chang Tao-ling with the tiger demon. In other words, it occurs in the same sequence as the entry of the priest onto the altar.

The fact that four of these five tables are "on earth" and the central fifth one is "in heaven" is also extremely revealing. The four tables (directions, writs) are like the four generals with whom Chang Tao-ling made his new covenant; they hold the earth in place. But it is the center, which is of celestial origin, that holds everything together. It gives a point of reference for the four directions on the horizontal plane; it is itself, running as it does from top to bottom, the axis of the vertical. Put another way, it is the vertical (celestial) that holds the horizontal together. The vertical axis in Taoist ritual is likewise the central priest, the one of High Merit (*kao-kung*), around whom all turns, on whom all depends. He is the heir of Chang Tao-ling, who was the One who made the contract with the four generals.

The five writs without which there is no altar were, like the trigrams, revealed to Yü. In TT 388 *Ling-pao wu-fu hsü* (1.4a), a text from the third or fourth century A.D., we read how the mythical emperor Ti-k'u received the five True Writs from Heaven. Not understanding them,

> Ti-k'u sacrificed to the Emperor of Heaven on the altar of the Northern River and buried [the texts] on top of Bell Mountain (in the northwest), sealed in a case of green jade, there to await a future saint of merit and virtue, who would *deliver them from their obscurity and obstruction* (italics mine).

This future saint of High Merit who delivers the dammed up waters of new life from obstruction proves to be none other than Yü. Having discovered them, he brings them (in from the Gate of Heaven) to Yüeh in southeastern China, at the Door of Earth. The modern priest of High Merit is thus imitating Yü each time he enters the altar from the northwest.

Chüan 3 of the *Ling-pao wu-fu hsü* describes the banquet (*chiao*) to be prepared for these writs. It involves setting out five tables for the five emperors, the lords of the writs. The writs, written in red on green paper—the format imitates the "case of green jade" in which were sealed the original "red writs"—are exposed (*lu*) on these tables. This is the reason the altar must be "open-air" (*lu-t'an*), so that the emperors in heaven will be drawn, as by a magnet, to the corresponding symbolic writs, the writs which symbolize the configuration of the energy (= the emperor) of the five directions (= phases).

A sixth table—doubling the center?—is set out for Yü himself. A Ling-pao text cited in the *Wu-shang pi-yao* (Lagerwey, 127) prescribes seven officiants for Taoist ritual, but the standard number, through the ages, has been six. These are the *kao-kung* (high merit), the *tu-chiang* (chief cantor), the *shih-ching* (servant of the scriptures), the *shih-hsiang* (servant of the incense), the *shih-teng* (servant of the lamps), and the *chien-chai* (inspector of the fast). (See, for example, TT 508 *Huang-lu ta-chai li-ch'eng yi* 16.17a-b; this text, edited by Chiang Shu-yü in 1223, is based on the "old method" inaugurated in the fifth century by Lu Hsiu-ching and used throughout the T'ang dynasty). In southern Taiwan today, the usual number of priests is five: the *kao-kung*, the *tu-chiang*, the *fu-chiang* (assistant cantor, = *shih-ching*), the *yin-pan* (leader of the troupe, = *shih-teng*), and the *chih-hsiang* (keeper of the incense, = *shih-hsiang*).

Having analyzed each of the three stages individually, we must now try to apprehend the altar as a unit. Like other altars, it represents the natural universe composed of heaven, earth, and water. Is that all? The answer is no, and once again it is to the myth of Yü we must turn to show this. In *The Annals of Wu and Yüeh* (*Wu-Yüeh ch'un-ch'iu*), a second century A.D. text describing the fifth century B.C. struggle between the states of Wu and Yüeh for the hegemony over the other states (the Nine Provinces, the magic square), an entire chapter is devoted to Yü, Yüeh's founding father. (Yüeh is said to have been victorious because it occupied the place corresponding to *ssu*, the Door of Earth, while Wu occupied the other southeastern Branch *ch'en*.) When Yü died, he was buried under a mound (*fen*) composed of *three stages* of pounded earth (2.7a). In a parallel passage in the *Yüeh-chüeh shu* (8.65b), a text which is probably earlier than the *The Annals of Wu and Yüeh*, this same three-stage mound is described, but it is called not a *fen* but a *t'an*, an altar!

Still today, in traditional communities in Taiwan, a village is protected against the demonic forces of the universe by Five Camps (*wu-ying*). Jordan (50–51) describes them this way:

> Bao-an village is not merely a collection of people. It is a physical place, with legal boundaries and with ritual ones. Four enormous trees located near the four corners of the village represent forts manned by supernatural soldiers, and a fifth fort is located immediately opposite the temple at another tree. There is nothing about these trees in normal times that distinguishes them from other trees in the eyes of human visitors. But they are the first line of defence against undesirable supernatural forces.

These five camps are to the village what the five sacred peaks are to China as a whole, and what the five organs (*wu-tsang*) are to an individual. Every entity, whatever its size, must be held in place by five such receptacles, in which dwell the Five Emperors. This necessity is described with great clarity already by Ssu-ma Ch'ien in the first chapter of *The Records of the Historian* (*Shih-chi*, ca. 110 B.C.). The central—celestial—receptacle is, naturally, the one which holds the community together. In the charge of the Yellow (earth) Emperor, the central "fort" is quite simply the palace of the god of the soil, always marked in ancient China by a tree and a mound. As we have already seen Yü was in Han times, when both *Yüeh-chüeh shu* and *The Annals of Wu and Yüeh* were written, the god of the soil of all China. Is his grave mound not the model for the Taoist altar?

But we must push our analysis still further. Apart from one extremely precious indication that the celestial writ enables one to "enter the mountain," the *Wu-shang pi-yao* does not further describe how the priest is to "enter the mountain." But in the thirteenth century, in a chapter on the "*su-ch'i*, old style," which he claims goes back to Lu Hsiu-ching (406–477), Chiang Shu-yü describes that entry as occurring in three stages: first by the *tu-men* (Gate of the Capital), then by the Door of Earth, and last by the Gate of Heaven (*Huang-lu chai li-ch'eng yi* 16.2b). We have already mentioned the fact that the high priest normally enters the altar by the Gate of Heaven; it appears here that this entry from Heaven presupposes two prior entries. That through the Door of Earth does not surprise, but what is the Gate of the Capital, which, according to Chiang, gives access to the "outer" (*wai*)—as opposed to the "inner" (*nei*)—altar?

According to Chiang himself (2.3b), the outer altar is to be entered via the southern gate (*li*☰). He does not explicitly identify this gate as the *tu-men*, but a kindred text, TT 466 *Ling-chiao chi-tu chin shu* by Lin T'ien-jen, completed in 1303, does. In the Altar-sealing ritual, the officiant, having first "burned the symbols for summoning the gods of the eight directions" (Lin T'ien-jen, 22.4a) and then purified each of the directions in turn, "goes through the Gate of the Capital to the middle stage" (22.6a). The gate of the "outer stage" which thus gives access to the middle stage is elsewhere said by Lin to be on the south side of the altar (1.13a).

Situated on the south side of the altar, the Gate of the Capital is nonetheless fundamentally "northern" by virtue of its association with the outer, aquatic stage of the three-stage altar. Thus it is that we read in yet another text of the twelfth or thirteenth century that the capital to which the Gate of the Capital gives access is none other than Feng-tu. "Feng-tu," reads a note in the text, "is in the rear of the aquatic section, between the spinal column and the kidneys" (TT 407 *Ling-pao ta-lien nei-chih hsing-ch'ih chi-yao* 2a).

Feng-tu is also a place, a hill along the Yangtze, in the province of Szechuan, where Chang Tao-ling got his start. Its many temples of hell are now being restored. When, in the fourth and fifth centuries, it first appears in Taoist texts, it is said to be in the northeast: "that is why the northeast is the Gate of Demons and the source of the energies of the dead" (Lagerwey, 75). Feng-tu, in other words, is the land of the dead, of "obstructed souls," of demons. As such, it is governed by the Lord-emperor of the North, who rules from one of its six palaces (ibid., p. 102). (Writing circa 480, Yen Tung, TT 87 *Tu-jen ching ssu-chu* 2.30a, identifies these palaces with the six demonic heavens whose reign Chang Tao-ling overthrew.) According to *The Book of the Three Origins* (*San-yüan ching*), finally, Feng-tu is also called Northern Feng, and it is where the names of those who do not follow the fast attentively will be reported by the "divine soldiers of the Five Emperors" (Lagerwey, 167). These people will lose their right to enter, literally, to "mount upon, go up to" (*teng*), the Hall of the Fast (*chai-t'ang*).

It will be recalled that the sixth priest, absent in modern rituals, is called the inspector of the fast; that the god of the soil is in the first place an inspector, a heaven-sent censor; and that Yü, god of the soil in the Han dynasty, is the sixth emperor at the banquet described in *Ling-pao wu-fu hsü* (TT 388): is it not to the founding father that a community must ultimately "render an account"? Medieval Taoist ritual, in any case, is always addressed to the great master of methods who inspects the fast (*chien-chai ta-fa shih;* see Chiang Shu-yü, 2.10a).

The third altar described in *Wu-shang pi-yao* (*chüan* 54) is constructed for the Yellow Register Fast (*huang-lu chai*). As this came to be the most typical altar construction used in medieval ritual (Chiang Shu-yü, 2.1a–7a), we do well to take a glance at it before presenting the altar used today. The plan is based on descriptions in *Wu-shang pi-yao* (shown on following page). There are twenty-two gates—the ten of the ten directions on the inner altar, the four of heaven, earth, sun, and moon of the central stage, and the eight of the trigrams on the outer altar. All are marked by 32″ × 24″ placards attached to nine-foot poles, to "accord with the celestial norm" (54.2a).

Having discussed earlier the numbers 9 and 24, we need consider here only the number 32, which also appears in the measurement of the central stage. Thirty-two refers to the 32 heavens first detailed in the late fourth century in *Chu-t'ien nei-yin* (TT 97). Chiang Shu-yü explicitly states that the flags (*fan*) of the 32 heavens are to be placed on the central altar (2.1b). The 32 = 4 × 8 heavens: four, as we have seen, is associated with the terrestrial stage, and we have here, as in the *Chu-t'ien nei-yin*, eight heavens for each of the four directions. 4 × 8

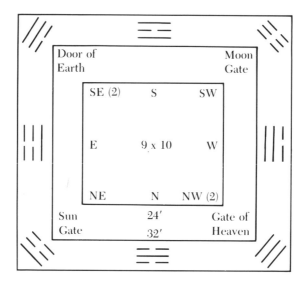

is thus a number of horizontal totality, as 3×8 is of vertical. The 24-foot side of the first altar above is thus to be found here as the length of a side of the inner, celestial altar.

As far as the gates are concerned, the only novelty here is the ten gates of the inner altar: the eight directions plus the top (NW: Gate of Heaven) and the bottom (SE: Door of Earth). In accord with this shift from 9 to 10, we have a total of 90 lamps and 10 burners prescribed for the heart of the altar, where the ritual as such, after the conclusion of the entry rites, is performed.

A SOUTHERN TAIWAN ALTAR

In the third altar above, the inner stage of the three-stage altar is the equivalent of the square altar of the Fast of the Three Sovereigns, the first altar. This fact prepares us to examine the altar used in southern Taiwan today. The plan is given on following page.* This is the ideal form of the altar, known as the "altar of the eight trigrams, the nine palaces, and the ten directions." To all appearances the modern altar is but a replica of the "altar of the spirits" used in the Fast of the Three Sovereigns. But appearances here are just as deceiving as there, and a

---

* This drawing and the next are based on the seminar given by Master Ch'en Jung-sheng during the spring term of 1977 at the Ecole Pratique des Hautes Etudes, Ve Section, in Paris. Master Ch'en had been invited by K. Schipper.

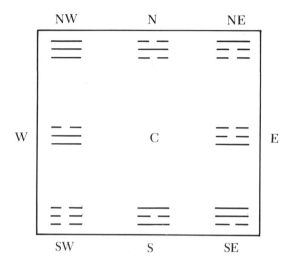

three-stage vertical dimension—there linked to the Three Sovereigns, here to the body of the high priest—is implicit and must be added to make sense of the ritual. The vertical dimension is indicated here by the presence of the ten directions, that is, the eight trigrams plus the center, which is doubled into top and bottom: this central pivot, this vertical axis of the altar, is the *kao-kung* himself (cf. Schipper 1982, 129).

Next to the ideal must be set the real form, outlined by Master Ch'en as follows:

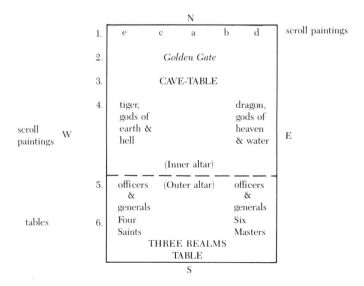

Before commenting on the altar item by item, we must note that, like the previous plan, the directions are placed in the positions to which we are accustomed. On a traditional Chinese map, the reader is in effect placed in the position of a king, for the king is described as one who, in order to receive the full benefit of the sun's rays, "sits facing south" (Granet 1968, 301). If the south is on top, the east, the land of the rising sun and hence of life, is necessarily on the left, and the land of the setting sun and death on the right. Why, then, are the directions of the modern Taoist altar placed like those on Western maps?

The first answer is, they are not, they only seem to be. This may be seen from the ranking of the five scrolls along the north wall: as the letters a-e indicate, the order goes out from the center to stage right. The right being the "negative" (*yin*) side, it is clear we must view the altar from the lofty perspective of those who preside over it if portrait "b" is truly to be "above" portrait "c." The second answer, therefore, must be that the directions *are* inverted, but only from the human point of view. On the map of the altar the human is subordinated to the heavenly point of view. This means, first of all, that the human beings on the altar are in the position of servants, and that is precisely how the high priest normally refers to himself, as the "servant of the Way." But it also means that the altar is heaven, for the celestial center is in the north, the Pole Star, "which remains in its place while all the lesser stars do homage to it" (*Analects of Confucius* 2.1). It means, finally, that when the high priest enters the altar by way of the Gate of Heaven, he is truly bringing in his own person new life from heaven. The description which follows discusses the altar level by level, from north to south.

1. On the north wall are hung portraits of the presiding deities. In Master Ch'en's scheme, there are five:

a. Heavenly Worthy of the Primordial Beginning (Yüan-shih t'ien-tsun)

b. Heavenly Worthy of the Numinous Treasure (Ling-pao t'ien-tsun)

c. Heavenly Worthy of the Way and its Power (Tao-te t'ien-tsun)

d. Supreme Sovereign, Jade Emperor (Yü-huang shang-ti)

e. Great Emperor of the Purple Empyrean (Tzu-wei ta-ti)

The three central scrolls represent the Three Pure Ones (plates 2,14), origin of heaven (a), earth (b), and man (c). They correspond to the Three Energies, both in the universe and in the human body, and therefore also to the three levels of the universe, the altar (plate 23), and the high priest's body, as well as to the Three Caverns of which the Taoist canon is composed, that is, the revealed writings of the Three Sovereigns. The Jade Emperor, head of the "popular pantheon," comes only in fourth place; he has been there for no more than a millennium (see Chang Jo-hai, 14b, for the oldest mention of the Jade Emperor as the recipient of Taoist ritual, and Chiang Shu-yü, 16.4b-5a, for a criticism of this practice). The Emperor of the Purple Empyrean is associated with the Pole Star and the northern center of the heavens. The name of the palaces inhabited by each of these five supreme representatives of the order of the universe is indicated by an inscription above the "gates" giving access to their portraits.

As many as nine portraits may be hung along the north wall if there is room (Ofuchi, 202). If the temple is very narrow, the Three Pure Ones will preside on the north alone, and the two emperors will be shunted off into the corners. The table above which rise the three central palaces is called the Table of the Three Pure Ones.

2 and 3. The table around which the priests normally stand is called a "cave-table" (*tung-an*; plate 7). The standard gloss of *tung*, cave, in Taoist texts is *t'ung*, to communicate: the altar is a mountain, that is, a cave, within which communication occurs by way of the defile of the Golden Gate. According to TT 22 *Wu-lao ch'ih-shu ching* (1.5a-b), it is at the threshold of the Golden Gate that the Heavenly Worthy of the Primordial Beginning transmits the five True Writs used to construct the altar. The *Sheng-hsüan ching* informs us that this gate is beyond the Three Realms (*san-chieh;* Lagerwey, 115), that is, it is in the supreme heavens where, when the world is inundated, the Queen Mother receives the "elect" (ibid., 74). This place of ultimate safety is also called the Mountain of the Jade Capital (Yü-ching shan) and is situated in the supreme Ta-lo Heaven. In this magic mountain there is a Celestial Terrace of the Seven Treasures (Ch'i-pao hsüan-t'ai, referring to the seven stars of the Big Dipper, whose bowl points to the Pole Star), to which returns, at the time of the final cataclysm, the literature of the Three Caverns (ibid., 115). This literature had originally been revealed by the lords of the Three Treasures, that is, the Three Pure Ones (ibid., 104).

We have come full circle. The Three Pure Ones, who preside over the Taoist altar, are the alpha and the omega of the Taoist scriptures, and it is by using the revealed scriptures of the Three Pure Ones that one comes to participate in their cycle of emergence and return. In other words, just as the Jew, by his participation in the Seder, reenacts and so actualizes the Exodus, just as the Christian by his participation in the Eucharist, takes part in the death and resurrection of Jesus Christ, so the Taoist priest, in reciting the scriptures of the Three Caverns and in acting them out in ritual form, relives their revelation and so renews their capacity to save.

Put another way, the ritual of redemption will be a repetition of the original revelation:

> For seven days and seven nights, the sun, the moon, the planets, the constellations, and the Big Dipper ceased to turn. The divine wind hushed and fell silent; the seas and the mountains hid their clouds. The heavens were free of floating shadows; the air in all directions was clear and luminous. The entire land—mountains, rivers, and forests—became level, and there ceased to be a distinction between high and low. All the earth was as green jade: there were no other colors. The multitude of the perfected stood in waiting on the throne, and the Heavenly Worthy of the Primordial Beginning, seated astride a five-colored lion that floated in space as though suspended, uttered the scripture one time. (TT 1 *Wu-liang tu-jen ching* 1.1a)

The Heavenly Worthy utters this *Scripture of Unlimited Salvation* ten times in all, causing the divine powers of the ten directions to gather and thus causing the blind to see, the lame to walk, and the dead to rise (1.1b). In this text too, the Tao explains that "whoever recites this scripture ten times" will not only save his ancestors but will himself "be enabled, when his merit is sufficient and his power achieved, to become an immortal and fly up to the Golden Gate, there to wander, banqueting, in the Jade Capital" (1.4a).

The ritual is the time when time stops; it is the time of the final cataclysm, when man—in the person of the priest—turns to the Three Pure Ones and gives back to them, by means of recitation and reenactment, their scriptures. Thus do the scriptures and the faithful get a new lease on life.

But we cannot fully comprehend this process of renewal if we do not follow up on the idea that it is the Queen Mother who receives the elect at the Golden Gate. Her full title is Queen Mother of the West (Hsi wang mu). Being Queen of the West, she is Queen of the realm of the dead; indeed, the oldest mythological representations of her show her to be a tiger spirit, the tiger being the emblematic animal of the *yin* land of the setting sun (the position in Posterior Heaven of the third daughter ☱). But as a glance at the succession of trigrams on the periphery of the altar shows, the next trigram is ☰, and it is obtained by the simple transformation of the upper line of ☱, or rather, by the pushing upward of the two *yang* lines by a third *yang* line. This is the inevitable next transformation, given that all *yin* possibilities have been exhausted and that trigrammatic change is always, like vegetal growth, an up-rising. Once again, we see why it is so crucial to be able to do the Step of Yü.

But to come back to the "golden" gate (cf. plates 14, 21). Since the Queen Mother is from the west, we are led to ask whether the gate is really "golden" or simply "metallic," for *chin,* the element of the west, has both meanings. We have already seen that, in the five phases cycle of mutual birth-giving, the most curious is the giving of birth to water by metal. How does metal give birth to water? By gestation!

The Queen Mother, after all, *is* a mother, and on (in) K'un-lun, her magic mountain in the Far West, she banquets the immortals. On what?—on fruit, say some; on books, say others. To Lao-tzu she fed fruit on Turtle Mountain in the west (Lagerwey, 77); to the Imperial Lord of the Golden Gate, Latter-day Saint of the Nine Mysteries (Hou-sheng chiu-hsüan Chin-ch'üeh ti-chün), on Man-Bird Mountain, also in the west, she transmitted a text. The Imperial Lord of the Golden Gate, though not identical with Lao-tzu himself, is clearly his latter-day manifestation—an expression of his spirit (cf. Strickmann 1981, 272). The Nine Mysteries are the Nine Heavens, products of the nine months of cosmic gestation (TT 318 *Chiu-t'ien sheng-shen chang-ching*). They are the Pure *Yang*, as opposed to the Pure *Yin* of the Nine Obscurities of hell. It is the light of the former which is used to break open the darkness of the latter in the ritual for the salvation of the souls of the dead (Lagerwey, 158-9).

This Pure *Yang* comes ultimately from Man-Bird Mountain, for it is the "source of primordial energy" (ibid, 76), and it is no doubt on this primordial energy that Lao-tzu banquets when in his mother's womb:

> I alone am different from others
> And value being fed by the mother.
> (*Lao-tzu* 20; trans. Lau, 77)

Lao-tzu dwells within the Golden (Metallic) Gate, on K'un-lun (Seidel 1969, 62, 76), and when the world looks to heaven for help, sends forth the Imperial Lord. The elect of the Queen Mother are therefore also called the "people of the Latter-day Saint" (Lagerwey, 148).

To summarize, the Golden Gate opens out on a womb-tomb, the tomb of the White Tiger, the womb of the Queen Mother. Her womb is the womb of the Tao, and when the high priest penetrates, via the Golden Gate, into the land of the Three Pure Ones, he is, at the end of time, returning with the red scriptures to their place of origin, the Mountain of the Capital of (green) Jade, the womb where, through the ritual reunion of the terrestrial facsmiles with the celestial originals, by means of the ritual *symbolization* of their original revelation, the redemptive writs will be "born again." There, in the Western Paradise, time stops for seven days (seven is the number of the west in Taoist texts), and metal, in the fullness of time, "gives birth to water."

Metal gives birth to water. In fact the water had been raging to get out of its Ninefold Obscurity, but Kun, the father of Yü had tried to stop it with "swelling mold." For his failure, he was executed on Feather Mountain. (Is this Man-Bird Mountain? Which in turn may be the mountain of the "bird men," as Taoists are sometimes called). Kun fell off into Feather Abyss, of which he became the spirit (*The Annals of Wu and Yüeh* 2.2a). According to another early text, there is a turtle in the bottom of the abyss, inhaling and exhaling primordial energy; on the turtle's back (Turtle Mountain) is a magic square; in the central position of the bottom row of the square sits "the mother of the primordial energy of the Tao" (TT 1168 *Lao-chün chung-ching* 1.14b). From a late thirteenth century work, we find this portrayal of the figures:

上清靈寶大

The comment reads in part: "Mountain of the Western Turtle . . . the Metal Mother dwells there. . . . It is the root of the nine heavens and of the nine palaces in man('s head, i.e., K'un-lun). . . . It is in the northwestern corner of heaven, corresponding to *hai* and *tzu*. It is the birth-root of infants" (Wang Ch'i-chen, 4.38a). A little further on Wang writes,

> The smelted concentrate of primordial energy is what nourishes the celestial and terrestrial souls and produces the true essence. The true essence has its root in the right kidney. The right kidney is the Gate of Destiny; it is situated at the extremity of the spinal column. Beneath it is a large bone. The marrow in this bone enters the urinary tract. This cavity is called the Tail of the Turtle; its god is the Queen Mother. She rules facing south. When referred to in terms of the Emperor who faces it (from the east), it is called the Mountain of the Western Turtle. . . . It is called the Metal Gate because it is situated in the west. . . . The spinal column communicates with the Jade Capital: it is the main road to the Jade Capital on top of the head. That is why it is said that the Western Turtle Mountain and the Jade Capital are neighboring realms. (4.42a–b)

When he does the Step of Yü, the high priest recreates the magic square on the back of the turtle, causes the $9 \times 9 = 81$ lamps to dispel the darkness and the Old Infant to be reborn as a latter-day saint.

Lao-tzu is the key, therefore, to the whole process. Who is Lao-tzu? Lao-tzu is the third of the Three Pure Ones, that is, the third of the Three Energies, of the Three Treasures (plate 2). The Three Energies are the Mysterious (*hsüan*), Primordial (*yüan*), and Original (*shih*) energies, whose colors are, respectively, green, yellow, and white (east, center, and west). The Three Treasures are the Tao itself (the Heavenly Worthy of the Primordial Beginning), the scriptures (the Heavenly Worthy of the Numinous Treasure), and the masters (the Heavenly Worthy of the Way and its Power; cf. Lagerwey, 104). Lao-tzu is the master of all masters, the one who transmits to Chang Tao-ling, to K'ou Ch'ien-chih, to the high priest the potent treasures on which he had fed in the womb of the Mother and with which they then rescue the "seed-people" (*chung-min*) of the Latter-day Saint.

All this we can say of Lao-tzu. Of the other two Pure Ones, nothing is known. What Doolittle (1:249-50) tells us about the Taoists he knew explains the reason:

> The "Three Pure Ones," is the title of certain three idols found in temples belonging to the Tauist religion and worshiped by Tauist priests. The images are seated side by side. One of them, as some explain, represents Lö-chü, or the "*Old Boy*," the founder of that religion. Others explain that the three images refer to three different incarnations of Lö-chü. . . . Some account for the origin of this trio by the saying that "Lö-chü in one breath was transformed into the Three Pure Ones."

4. Portraits are hung on the side walls, among which we find east and west contrasts of tiger versus dragon, death versus life, hell (human "demon-gods") versus heaven. Dragon and tiger are general designa-

tions referring to the "officers" (*kuan*) of heaven and earth respectively. Earth, hell, heaven, and water are together called the Four Courts (*ssu-fu*) or the Four Spaces (*ssu-chien*). A similar quadripartite division of the universal bureaucracy is found already in the *Wu-shang pi-yao* (Lagerwey, 102; cf. 35), in the Three Officers plus the officers of the "cave-heavens" (*tung-t'ien*), where Feng-tu is located.

A minimum of two, a maximum of six such collective portraits are hung on each wall (cf. plates 8, 12), in northern as well as in southern Taiwan (Schipper 1982, 128; Liu Chih-wan 1983, 79). The order in which they are hung also varies widely, but that shown by Liu Chih-wan is most logical:

Terrestrial Court	Celestial Capital
Human Space	Aquatic Country
gods of north and west	gods of south and east

Not only does this arrangement properly pair heaven with earth and man with water, but it places the divinities of the four directions along the same walls as the True Writs of those directions (see below, p. 103).

5. Master Ch'en described the "officers and generals" as the "emissaries and agents of the priest" who "guard the altar and carry messages." In other words, the high priest, a mere servant on the inner altar, becomes a commander-in-chief on the outer altar.

The number of individual portraits of emissaries varies, as does the order of their placement. The following is a composite representation of Ch'en's practice:

Mother of Lightning (Tien-mu)	Duke of Thunder (Lei-kung)
marshals $\begin{cases} \text{K'ang (north)} \\ \text{Kao (west)} \end{cases}$	$\begin{rcases} \text{Chao (south)} \\ \text{Wen (east)} \end{rcases}$ marshals
Metal Armor (Chin-chia)	Red Robe (Chu-yi)

Ch'en's ritual title tells us that he is "in charge of the various offices of thunder and lightning" (below, p. 95f). They are instruments of exorcism in his hands (cf. plate 24). From ordination documents we learn that Marshal K'ang (plate 7) is "commander-in-chief of the heroic dead of T'ai-shan"; Marshal Chao is "chief inspector of the somber altar of Orthodox Unity" (Taoists of Northern Taiwan consider these two to be "gate gods," *men-shen*, guarding the entrance to the inner altar; note their position in Liu Chih-wan 1983, 79); Marshal Wen (plate 3) is "supreme commander of the earth spirits" (see below, chap. 14); and Marshal Kao (plate 7) is "expediter of children from the Nine Heavens" (Ofuchi, 431b, 432a, 433a).

As a group, the four marshals, by their association with the four directions, may be assimilated to the Four Potentates (*ssu-ling*) whose job it is to surround and protect the priest on his voyage of the spirit to heaven. This is why the same marshals, in the form of giant papier-maché figures astride mythic mounts, line the path to heaven for the Presentation of the Memorial (plates 17, 19).

Metal Armor and Red Robe (plate 4) are also found in an internal (scroll) and external (papier-maché) form. Metal (west) Armor (military) represents the priest as exorcist and is therefore portrayed with a sword and (usually) hung next to the Somber Warrior (see next item). Red (south) Robe (civilian) represents the priest as civil official and is therefore portrayed holding a book and hung next to Chang Tao-ling. According to the system of correspondences, Metal Armor is also an expression of the high priest's lungs, that is, his breath, and Red Robe of his heart, that is, his intentions. Taoist ritual is ultimately a form of breath-control, that is, control of the breath by the heart.

6. A table on each side is dedicated to Four Saints and Six Masters. The concepts date to Northern Sung times (Chiang Shu-yü, 2.9a-10a; TT 1220 *Tao-fa hui-yüan* 171.2a, 178.4b). The Somber or True Warrior (Hsüan- or Chen-wu: plate 5), also called the Emperor of the North (Pei-ti is the chief of the Four Saints. The Saints' table is called Wu-tang shan (the Warrior-is-the-Match Mountain), after the mountain in the province of Hupei where the Emperor (Pei-ti, Emperor of the North, or Hsüan-ti, Somber Emperor) originally "obtained the Way" and which has therefore long been the center of the True Warrior's cult and of the tradition of martial arts linked to that cult (see Grootaers). Chin Yün-chung (2.7b) identifies the Four Saints with the Four Potentates, whom Kuo Wang-feng (1.34a) instructs the priest to visualize, during the ritual, as emerging respectively from his liver (the Green Dragon, east), his lungs (the White Tiger, west), his heart (the Red Bird, south), and his kidneys (the Somber Warrior, north). An esoteric tradition I have recorded in southern Taiwan identifies these exteriorized energies of the priest's vital organs with his four limbs.

Chang Tao-ling (plate 1) is the most important of the Six Masters, and their table is therefore given the name of the mountain in the province of Kiangsi where the descendents of the first Heavenly Master lived, probably since the tenth century, Lung-hu shan, or Dragon-Tiger Mountain. The role of these two mountains on the altar will be discussed in Chapter 5.

7. On the Table of the Three Realms—the Three Realms are composed of twenty-eight inferior heavens (Lagerwey, 74)—are placed the offerings for the divinities of the people. Bleachers covered with red paper are set up behind this table, and here are deposited the divinities brought by the people from their homes, as well as the divinities of the temple in which the ritual is being performed (plate 6). The divinities thus become spectators in their own precinct.

Indeed, the whole ritual may be described as theater done for the divinities' amusement and instruction, for their re-creation. A re-presentation, as we shall see, of the origin and structure of the universe, the ritual reminds the assembled gods of their proper role as local parts of a great Whole. In a certain sense, this goal is already achieved simply by setting the gods on the bleachers, for the Table of the Three Realms is also called the Table of the Three Officers, and the gods are thus at once placed under the jurisdiction of and assimilated to the Three Officers, that is, to the deep structure—the order—of the natural universe. At the same time, the Taoist, in performing the Offering under the watchful eyes of the Three Officers, is "rendering an account" of what he has received from his masters to these inspectors of the fast and thereby progressing toward immortality.

The division into an inner and an outer altar proves thus to be at bottom a distinction between nature and culture, and a commentary on their proper relationship. There is a heaven-earth on either end of the altar, but the triad with the Human Sovereign is cultural, the one with the Aquatic Officer natural. From the dominant north side, the cultural triad (plate 14) stares serenely across the length of the altar at the natural triad and the motley crowd assembled behind it. Against this heterogeneous congregation of the spontaneous, overflowing religiosity of the people, the Three Pure Ones have every reason to be serene. Their servant is a disciple by apostolic succession of the Human Sovereign, and like Yü he knows how to channel the flooding waters along the trigrammatic "veins of the earth."

There is, then, no fundamental difference between Master Ch'en's altar and the altar described by Chiang Shu-yü and others in the 13th century. Not only are the same inner/outer, north-south polarities respected, but the Table of the Three Officers clearly represents the gateway to the capital of Feng "in the rear of the aquatic section." The Offering provides the local gods—who are none other than the "obstructed souls" of Feng-tu, the demons of the Six Heavens—with a glimpse, through this doorway, of how the Way works. Just to see it is already to be transformed, humanized, integrated. But they will get no more than a glimpse for like Marshal Wen, they are not yet ready to be enrolled on the Taoist's register (see p. 243), and in the meanwhile, the entry onto the Land of the Way is closely guarded, by the Somber Warrior on the one hand and Chang Tao-ling on the other.

The identification of the Table of the Three Realms with the Gate of the Capital implies as well that it affords access to the middle of three stages. It separates the flood waters of the lower stage from the heaven-earth of the two upper stages, which must be treated together, as noted earlier. And like the altar of the three Days of Origin, Master Ch'en's Land of the Way is divided into 4 + 1: the scrolls show it to be a representation of the entire humanized universe—composed of the spirits of the Four Spaces of heaven, earth, man, and the waters— converging on, returning to, "going in audience before the Origin" (*ch'ao-yüan*) from which they originally emerged.

Our study of the altar would be incomplete without a look at those who are to animate it, the musicians and the community representatives:

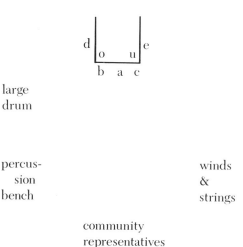

large
drum

percus-
sion
bench

winds
&
strings

community
representatives

The disposition of the five Taoist priests (a-e) shows that there are in reality two altars, for the fact that the chief cantor (b) is on the high priest's (a) left and the assistant cantor (c) on his right means that his body, too, is a source of orientation. He is for that reason also known as the "central worthy" (*chung-tsun*).

The Central Worthy, together with the large drum, represents the voice of man, the chief cantor the voice of heaven, and the assistant cantor the voice of earth. The instrument of the first is his own breath, of the second a wooden (east) drum (o), and of the third a metal (west) bowl (u; cf. plate 7). The bowl, called the "jade stone," marks the periodic transitions of the ritual. The drum, called the "golden bell," keeps its regular rhythm. The voice of the Central Worthy, often inaudible, "calls the shots."

The leader of the troupe (d) represents an extension of the military, the keeper of incense (e) of the civil persona of the high priest: the incense keeper hands him the incense to be presented to the various divinities, and the troupe leader "clears the way" for him, especially in the procession of purification at the start of most rituals and in the sword dance prior to the dispatch of an important message. Given their functions, the two acolytes would seem to be wrongly positioned, and comparison with the order of the six officiants of medieval ritual would seem to confirm this suspicion (above, p. 33). One can only conclude that the leader of the troupe has usurped the fourth position at d, properly belonging to the incense keeper, so as to be already at the head of the troupe when it sets out on its clockwise tours of the altar.

The drummer (plate 17) should be a Taoist. In a sense, he is the missing sixth officiant, and he occasionally plays a role in the ritual. The other musicians are laymen. Their positions on the altar are determined by the fact that instruments of percussion are considered *yang*, and winds and strings *yin*.

The community representatives (plates 9, 15) are the leaders of the community, those who have paid the most to make the Offering possible. Each of them is also represented by a lantern, hung from the ceiling on the south end of the altar, and by a "bushel lamp" (*tou-teng*), placed either on a table in back of the Cave-table or along the side walls. Frequently, there is such a lamp for every participating household. The name *tou-teng* refers to the Northern Bushel (Pei-tou), our Big Dipper, and its southern counterpart (Nan-tou), which are associated respectively with good fortune and longevity. Normally, a red bucket filled with rice, a purifying agent, and other objects such as a ruler, a scale, a sword, a mirror, a pair of scissors, and a saucer with oil and a wick are used to represent these "lamps of destiny" (plate 14) The oil is regularly replenished so that the wick never goes out during the Offering. According to one priest's explanation, sword and scissors symbolize the householder's personal war on evil, the ruler his desire to lead a "straight" life, the scale his awareness that he will be judged according to his merits in the tribunals of hell, and the mirror his vow to "wipe his heart clean" of the "dust of passion." Human moral effort thus takes its place within the context of stellar destiny.

PART

II

Basic Taoist Rituals

Liturgy for the Living: The Offering

CHAPTER

4

The Basic Program *

Few things could be more overwhelming than the combined density of Chinese mythology and cosmology. One thing is: Taoist ritual. Of the rituals, the Offering (*chiao*) is the basic liturgical service conducted for the living. There is no possible substitute for being present at such a ritual, and words are without doubt the worst possible substitute; one would like to play a tape, show a film, sing along, call out "look!" The vestments, the altar trappings, the offerings, the music: all is so rich and varied one hardly knows where to begin.

With the music?—it is dramatic, even menacing when the drums roll and the cymbals clang to accompany an exorcistic sword dance. It is shrill and sustained to the point of breaking when the oboes (*so-na;* plate 17) and strings accompany the bringing of new light (candles) to the Three Pure Ones. It is slow and meditative when, during the Announce-

* A chart summarizing the data of this chapter will be found in Appendix B, Table 1.

ment, the high priest "transforms his body" into the body of the Tao, and one has the feeling of being present at the beginning of time, as slowly, ever so slowly, the music gathers speed and quickly, quickly the high priest mutters under his breath, points in his hand, spins on himself, burns a cone of yellow paper, takes another giant step. The music is now of the utmost solemnity and then utterly comic, and there may be but a few drum beats to signal the shift.

This music of supple rhythms and great tonal variety, some of it perhaps as old as the fifth century, remains virtually unstudied. There is only one record of it in the public domain, and it is badly edited. Nothing is more urgent than good recordings; already in northern Taiwan, the electric organ has been introduced, with the results one can imagine.

But a Taoist ritual is not only what goes on inside the temple, it is also what goes on outside, for an Offering is a time when ordinary time does indeed stop, and the whole community engages in its own re-creation. Outside the temple there is theater, often two or three competing companies, each with the microphones turned up full blast. There are processions, of youth squadrons dressed up in military garb and making mock charges in front of the temple with staffs and halberds, of neighboring communities who have brought their gods in sedan chairs to pay a visit, of the community itself carrying its gods around on an inspection tour. There are food stands and ambulant peddlers of every kind, there are vendors of paper money and, of course, firecrackers. So much indeed is going on outside the temple that on the rare occasions when the Taoist priests do emerge from their "retreat," no one pays much attention and if someone does it is not for very long—unless it is the Universal Salvation (*p'u-tu*) ritual. This ritual ends with mounds of blessed food—cookies, breads, crackers, fruits of all kinds and sizes—thrown out into the scrambling crowd by the priests.

One could mention as well the organization of the festival: the arm-banded officials selling "stock" in the community and keeping tally on a huge bulletin board of the names of every contributor and the amount contributed; the capped-and-gowned community chiefs arguing over whether to allow a foreigner in the temple and resorting to the divining blocks to assist them in making their decision; the private rituals being performed by Taoists in front of altars erected at the gates of individual homes of the well-to-do, or by barefoot priests in the side rooms of the temple, with buffalo horns for summoning their legions and snake whips for chasing away evil. And the food!—never does one eat so well as during the three-day retreat prior to the "coming out." You are assured it is all vegetarian, but you have to take that on faith, for the bean curd is cut, seasoned, and fried to look and taste like pork and chicken, and the vegetable-and-rice balls will beat meatballs any day. Snow peas, cabbages, carrots, broccoli, cauliflower—the variety is incredible, and the rice, in huge, two-foot deep containers, plentiful. But the greatest dinner of all is the last one, after the priests have emerged from their retreat to Present the Memorial and before the Offering to the gods. Then wine and meat appear on the tables together, and the one flows in abundance, while the other arrives in bewildering variety and quantity. In the evening, after it is all over, there will also be individual banquets all over the village or neighborhood. The more guests come to such a banquet the better, for "he who has no guests is the laughingstock of all." At such meals one will eat delicacies such as one never sets eyes on in normal times, and your host will constantly refill your bowl with new treats before you have half-emptied it.

But all this excitement we will have to ignore in order to concentrate on what is going on behind closed doors, in the magic mountain of the Tao. We will take as our point of departure a detailed description of a *chiao* that was performed 19-22 November 1980 in Taitung, Taiwan, with Ch'en Jung-sheng as *kao-kung* (priest of High Merit). The entire ritual program took about twenty-five hours and included two separate Offerings which we will not describe in this volume, the one to prevent fire (*huo-pu*), the other to ensure the beneficence of the local god of the soil (*ch'ing-t'u*, literally, "congratulate the earth"). Also, interspersed throughout was a reading of the *Hsieh-tsui pao-ch'an* ("Litany for the Confession of Sins"), each of whose ten chapters is recited as a ritual unit. We have skipped as well, in establishing the "minimum program" that follows, the regular evening concert (*tsou-yüeh* or *nao-t'ing*). The Offering was undertaken to celebrate the completion of the temple and was therefore called an Offering of the Golden Register to Celebrate Completion and Pray for Peace (*Chin-lu ch'ing-ch'eng ch'i-an chiao*). Each ritual which will not be studied in detail in a separate chapter is briefly described here. The figures in parenthesis denote the time elapsed for each ritual in this 1980 ceremony. The reader is referred to Schipper (1975, 10) for a description of an ideal minimum program.

1. Firing the Oil to Drive Away Dirt (*fan-yu cho-hui*; 21:05–21:40). A wok is filled with oil and placed on top of a container of red hot coals. When the oil is bubbling, a priest, an exorcist, with a red kerchief on his head (hence referred to as a "redhead") and a buffalo horn in his hand summons the legions to drive off all evil spirits. After the incantatory portion of the ritual, a second Taoist begins to throw alcohol on the bubbling oil, and everything is passed through the resulting flames: vestments, documents, musical instruments. Even the community representatives who will stay inside to witness the ritual walk past the flame and purify themselves by swinging their arms over it. When

everything inside has been purified, the wok is taken outside and several ritual points outside are purified.

2. Starting Up the Drum (*ch'i-ku;* 23:03–23:14). This is an all-percussion concert. (On the symbolic significance of this rite in the context of the merit ritual, cf. De Groot 1884, 48-50).

Day 1 (November 20)

3. Announcement (*fa-piao;* 6:20–7:50). See Chapter 6.

4. Invocation (*ch'i-pai;* 7:52–8:49). The first invocation of the Three Pure Ones and a whole host of lesser divinities is made now. Their presence at the ritual is requested. The invocation is followed by a first "feeding" of the gathered guests with sticks of incense, three for each of the five directions. That in turn is followed by a confession, uttered by the high priest on his knees, and then a final procession with the *kao-kung* holding the crescent burner (*shou-lu,* literally, "hand-held burner"; see plate 13), and presenting it in each of the five directions. The burner is later held throughout the ritual by the head of the community.

5. Flag-raising (*yang-ch'i;* 10:03–10:22). A long, rectangular yellow banner is hoisted outside the temple, usually across from it, near the platform where the Presentation of the Memorial will take place. Its function is to attract the attention of the gods. On the flag is therefore written in red, "Assorted saints and perfect ones, supreme perfected of the Four Courts and the Three Realms of the Supreme Emperor of the Golden Gate of the Jade Capital." Above this "invitation" are drawn three circles linked together by squiggly red lines, a motif which also appears at the top of most symbols. The circles represent a constellation of six stars, called the Three Terraces, which governs fundamental aspects of human destiny. They mean here, "May the heavens give me life, sustenance, and protection" (Ofuchi, 216a).

Underneath this motif are written the personal Taoist names (*hui*) of the Three Pure Ones, each of which has the character for "rain" on the top half and three dots signifying "water" on the the bottom half. The personal names are differentiated on the right side of the bottom half: one uses the character for "vast" (*hung;* Primordial Beginning), one uses "pure" (*ch'eng;* Numinous Treasure), and one "bright" (*ming;* the Way and its Power). Between these three characters and the invitation is a circle crisscrossed with lines. The figure represents the concentration—the union—of the Three Energies which produces all the "ten thousand things," starting with the invited saints: in the world of the Way, all that is vast, pure, and bright falls, like rain, from heaven. All is "showers of blessing," all is showers of grace. After the flag is raised, the placard (*pang*), previously prepared (see Chap. 5), is pasted up on the outer wall of the temple.

6. Noon Offering (*wu-kung;* 11:31–12:35). Each priest in turn per-

forms a song and dance while "presenting"—a flower, a candle, tea, incense, fruit, and so on (plate 7). This offering is made every day and is sometimes the occasion for the high priest to display the extent of his repertoire and the beauty of his voice, or for one of the lesser priests to "ham it up."

7. Division of the Lamps (*fen-teng; 21:27–22:37*). This ritual is in fact three rituals done one right after the other. First comes the Division of the Lamps as such, then the Curtain-raising (*chüan-lien*), and last the Sounding of the Metal Bell and the Striking of the Jade Stone (*ming chin-chung chi yü-ching;* for a full description, see Schipper 1975). The Division of the Lamps, also called Request for Light (*ch'ing kuang*), represents the entry of the "light of grace" (*en-kuang*) into our world of darkness and sin. All the lights in the temple are first put out, new fire is then brought in from outside and is used to light three candles on the central table. The first candle is brought up and placed before the Heavenly Worthy of the Primordial Beginning, the second before the Heavenly Worthy of the Numinous Treasure (plate 8), and the third before the Heavenly Worthy of the Way and its Power. Between each presentation a hymn is sung. Finally, each of the five priests takes a torch, and together they light the remaining candles on the altar. The ritual as a whole is an elaborate representation of *Lao-tzu* 42: "The Tao gives birth to the one, the one to the two, the two to the three, and the three to the ten thousand things." Each of the four separate acts of lighting is preceded by a prose passage which begins with the relevant portion of the *Lao-tzu* passage.

With the light of the Three Pure Ones flooding the altar, it is time to "raise the curtain" that covers the scroll on which is written "[Golden] Gate" (plate 14) and so prepare the setting for the Land of the Way ritual the next morning. Like the Land of the Way, the Curtain-raising involves the presentation of a stick of incense to each of the Three successively, each time followed by a hymn.

The third ritual is at once a ritual of union and exorcism. Each of the acolytes in turn, from the cantor down to the keeper of incense, half-sings, half-reads a mandate (*tieh*) addressed to a general in charge of suppressing the negative (*yin*) and stimulating the positive (*yang*). Each in turn relays an order from the high priest to "strike the golden (*yang*) bell" or the "jade (*yin*) stone" a symbolic number of times. (The "golden bell" here refers not to the cantor's wooden drum—an instrument borrowed from the Buddhists—but, more appropriately, to one of the percussionist's gongs.) Thus is the morrow's communion with the Way prepared by strict observance of the laws of nature and culture, the one expressed in terms of musical numerology, the other in terms of hierarchical transmission and execution of orders.

Day 2 (November 21)

8. Land of the Way (*tao-ch'ang;* 6:28–8:18). See Chapter 8.

9. Noon Offering (11:36–12:53). The same ceremony as 6 above.

10. Floating the Water Lamps (*fang shui-teng;* ca. 16:00–16:30). A procession, led by the musicians and three of the priests and including, in principle, one member of every participating household, goes outside the village or neighborhood, beyond the boundaries of the community, to a place where there is flowing water. There, after a brief ritual, candles inside paper lanterns are lit and the lanterns set afloat. The purpose is to summon the solitary souls in the aquatic hells, especially the souls of those who have drowned, to the Universal Salvation feast to be held the next day. (In the Buddhist "masses for the dead" described by De Groot, this ritual and the summons of the soul must be done by Taoists (1884, 48-51, 87-88).

11. Invocation of the Masters and Saints (*ch'i shih-sheng;* 16:55-17:40). Two separate, successive rituals are carried out in preparation for the major rituals later that evening. The name notwithstanding, the first invitation is addressed to the Four Saints of Wu-tang Mountain, the second to the Six Masters of Lung-hu Mountain. These are the Four Saints and Six Masters whose tables stand in the outer altar.

12. Sealing the Altar (*chin-t'an;* 20:32–21:28). See Chapter 7.

13. Nocturnal Invocation (*su-ch'i;* 21:33–22:52). See Chapter 7.

Day 3 (November 22)

14. Renewed Invocation (*ch'ung-pai;* 6:43–7:52). Repeat of no. 4.

15. Scripture Recitation (*nien-ching;* 8:30–8:50). *The Scripture of the Jade Pivot* (TT 16 *Yü-shu ching*), *The Scripture of the Big Dipper* (TT 622 *Pei-tou ching*), and *The Scripture of the Three Officers* (*San-kuan ching*). Normally, the recitation of scriptures is allotted more time than on this occasion.

16. Presentation of the Memorial (*chin-piao;* 9:30–10:26). See Chapter 9.

17. Noon Offering (11:00–11:30). The same ceremony as 6 above.

18. Orthodox Offering (*cheng-chiao;* 16:30–17:44). The ritual begins, facing north, with a renewal of the opening rites of the Land of the Way (see Chapter 8). Then, while each of the four acolytes in turn invites a portion of the pantheon, the high priest leads the community representatives in a series of bows that starts facing south and makes its way gradually up through the hierarchy to the Three Pure Ones. After a presentation of incense to the Three Pure Ones, there is some clowning as the chief cantor insists on changing robes with the leader of the troupe, and this touches off a general inversion of roles involving all but the high priest. The priests now turn around and go in procession before the Table of the Three Realms.

A huge black banner has been strung up near the ceiling. Running the length of the altar, it is higher on the northern end where the portraits of the Three Pure Ones hang than on the southern end. It is the Celestial Bridge (*t'ien-ch'iao*), used by the divine guests first to descend to our world, the world of the Three Realms, and then to return to heaven. On either side of it is pasted a whole series of two by six inch slips of paper. All are marked "celestial officer" (*t'ien-kuan*) and have the sketched images of six such officers. They are of two colors, purple (heaven) and yellow (earth), and are pasted alternately on both sides of the bridge.

The leader of the troupe and the keeper of the incense take seats on either side of what has become, since the priests turned to face south, the rear of the altar. Each is holding a pennant of black paper bordered with scalloped orange paper. On one of these pennants is written "Heavenly Worthy Who Commands Demons and Captures Dirt," on the other "Heavenly Worthy Who Cleanses the Ten Directions." The three other priests, who are on their knees in front of the Table of the Three Realms, invite anew the $(6 \times 3) = 18$ supreme divinities first invited during the Invocation, and then again just before the presentation of the message during the Land of the Way. They are, however, invited here in inverse order, from lowest to highest. This ritual of the Orthodox Offering is thus at once a "thanks-dismissal" and a "return to the Origin."

After every third invitation, the kneeling priests sing a verse while the seated priests wave their flags over the bowed backs of the·kneeling community representatives, as if to chase away from them all that is demonic and polluting. The music played at this time sounds like a broken record. It is as though, with the Presentation of the Memorial, the spirit had gone out of the ritual, and it is rapidly winding down. A firecracker is set off, and the entire ritual comes to a stop. Then the music starts up again, the flags wave, the music gets stuck, another firecracker, another pause. This sequence is repeated six times, and then the pennants are put away and the priests return to the Cave-table for the rest of the Orthodox Offering.

Again it is as though the music cannot "get going." After all have gotten to their knees and made deep bows to a roll of drums, the music is renewed, and a series of three processions are made to the accompaniment of the music. This is the "banquet" part of the ritual, for first incense and then wine are presented to each of the Three Pure Ones in succession. At last the crescent burner is retrieved from the chief of the community representatives and its light "extinguished" (*fu-lu*). Having put out the light, it is time to "say goodbye": this is the dismissal part of the ritual. One by one the True Writs set out during the Nocturnal Invocation are removed, read, and burned, deconstructing the altar. Facing south, the high priest thanks-dismisses (both senses of *hsieh*) the Masters and Saints. The priests come back around to face south after a procession which moves counterclockwise. The *kao-kung* writes with his seal and sprays southward the purifying symbol-water one last time, and then exits. The Offering as such is now over. There still remains, after supper, the ritual of Universal Salvation.

19. Universal Salvation (*p'u-tu;* 18:50–21:00). This final ritual is conducted for the appeasement of homeless souls. A white flag has replaced the yellow flag raised at the beginning of the *chiao*, "lest the solitary souls be scared away." The huge placard (*pang*) that had been posted on the temple wall is torn down to be burned. The scrolls that had defined the limits of the altar and had made of it a world of the gods are taken down as the high priest begins the introit. Almost immediately, the priests go outside, where they see stretching out before them row on row of tables piled high with food: breads, special red cakes, fruit, stacks of canned fruit and bottles of beer, even "food sculptures," all of it prickly with burning sticks of incense glowing in the gathering twilight. But the most characteristic spectacle is that of the huge pigs: slit down the middle of the belly from throat to tail, they lie sprawled over entire tables, a green orange in the mouth, and a stick of incense stuck in the orange. Their bristles have been scalded and scraped away, and their whitish pink bodies covered with red stamps. Like so much lace, their intestines have been draped over their backs.

The priests go up and down the aisles, blessing the mountains of food. Finishing with the field in front of the temple, they move across the alley to a second field, larger than the first, and when they have made the tour of the second field, they go out in back of the temple, up and down the streets of the neighborhood. It is 19:30 before they come back to the temple to stand at the foot of the theater platform, already used that morning for the Presentation of the Memorial. After a song, the high priest goes up onto the platform and picks up from the table the crown of the Heavenly Worthy Who Saves from Distress (Chiu-k'u t'ien-tsun). He shows it to the crowd, and all bow. Then the four other priests come up onto the platform. One of them unfolds a huge yellow sheet, an explanation of the ritual written in black characters. At the beginning of the sheet, which is addressed to the lost souls, one huge character circled in red says, "Be it known," and at the end several medium-sized characters read, "Let the solitary souls take notice of what is written on the right" (that is, "above"). Then, in red, is written another large character, "EAT!"

Now begin the mudras, the special positionings of the fingers and hands learned from Tantric Buddhism as a means for the transformation of things. The priests all sit down; the music continues. The high priest has both hands in a mudra while making a rolling motion out toward the people. He takes his bowl of symbol-water and writes in the air. Then, with a small yellow flower held between his index and third fingers, he writes again. Using the crescent burner, he fumigates the mounds of cookies, pancakes, and coins on the table in front of him. Further gesturing and fumigating follows. The music winds down. More mudras, another song. At last he puts on the crown, thus completing his transformation: *he* is now the Heavenly Worthy Who Saves from Distress (cf. below, p. 237).

Without musical accompaniment, the high priest recites a passage, then takes up a handful of incense sticks and places them one by one into a row of red-frosted buns, each time with an incantation. When this long process is done, he hands the sticks down to the keeper of the incense who hands them to the community representatives at the foot of the platform. The oboes begin, and all sing. The high priest lifts the long yellow tassles dangling from his crown as though they were braids. He fumigates once more, and then begins to throw the food out into the crowd. The kids call for more. It is 20:20. Slowly, the pile of food begins to diminish. The acolytes pitch in and start sailing great flat pancakes out like frisbees. The last items are thrown, and the priests come down from the platform, the high priest holding the crescent burner. The oboes accompany them in a final procession to the giant papier-maché marshals lined up two on either side of a papier-maché Mountain of Kuan-yin, the goddess of mercy who cares for all the hungry souls. The priests bow and move on, back into the now deserted temple. There they sing a final song and then come back out into the night to watch the huge bonfire made with the mountain, the marshals, and paper money. The feast is over. Final debts are being paid. That night they no longer sleep in the side rooms of the temple: their work for the community of the Palace of Compliance with Heaven (Shun-t'ien kung) is done. Tomorrow they go home to the other side of the island, to Tainan.

CHAPTER

5

Preparations

Having gone through the general outline of a *chiao*, we will now consider what goes into the making of such a ritual, especially what tasks are the duty of the chief priest. Seeing him get ready for an Offering will prepare us to understand the details of his ritual work in the chapters that follow.

Among the many reasons that may lead a community to decide to invest in an Offering, the most important in modern Taiwan are the completion or total refurbishing of its temple or the desire to avoid disasters—an epidemic, a drought, a major fire—that threaten to occur, or to avoid a second occurrence. In some communities such an Offering is made periodically, once every three years in the case of the famous *chiao* at Hsi-kang (Liu Chih-wan, 1983, 285–400). The organizing committee's first step is to invite a high priest, often the same priest as on the previous occasion, or that priest's successor. Sometimes divination blocks are used to decide between several candidates. Exceptionally, the committee will invite the area's most famous high priest.

The high priest once engaged has a good two weeks' work ahead of him to prepare the necessary documents. The most time-consuming will be the calligraphy of the placard (*pang*). Hand-written in large characters, it will be posted, as we saw, on the outside wall of the temple after the Flag-raising. The text of the placard is virtually the same as that of the memorial (*shu*), which is read at all major services. A full translation of a typical memorial is given here (cf. Schipper 1974 and Ofuchi, 405b-406b);

Hsi-ting Compound, Palace of the Rising Sun.
In the *keng-shen* year (1980) of heaven's revolution, eleventh month.
Request for Good Fortune for the Fragrant Offering of the Golden Register to Celebrate Completion and Pray for Peace.
Humble servant in charge of the various offices of thunder and lightning, the bureau of the Dipper, and the Celestial Clinic, immortal minister of the canonical register of the Covenant of the Orthodox Unity of the Most High with the Powers, possessing and practicing the ritual methods of the Divine Empyrean, Ch'en Ting-sheng, full of fear and trembling, does obeisance and kowtows; he bows a hundred times as he addresses himself to heaven. Respectfully, he memorializes on behalf of
All the people of the Palace of the Rising Sun in Hsi-ting Compound, North Gate Village, district of Tainan, province of Taiwan, Republic of China. Together, they go to the Palace of the Rising Sun to worship the Way and prepare an Offering in celebration of the completion [of the temple] and to pray for peace, protection, and prosperity.
Chairman of the Assembly so-and-so;
Chairman of the Offering so-and-so;
Chairman of the Altar so-and-so;
Chairman of the Universal Salvation ritual so-and-so;
Assistant Chairman of the Assembly so-and-so;
Assistant Chairman of the Offering so-and-so;
Assistant Chairman of the Universal Salvation ritual so-and-so;
Host of the Incense Burner so-and-so;
Chairman of the Committee so-and-so;
Assistant Chairman of the Committee so-and-so;
Members of the Committee so-and-so;
together with all the faithful, having respectfully bathed and lit incense, bow humbly and address themselves to heaven:
Majestic is the temple, firmly fixed like the mountains and rivers; luminous are the gods, living forever as companions of the Father (☰) and Mother (☷). It is because the people who belong to this incense burner [temple] have repeatedly experienced the protection afforded by its abundant merit that they think constantly how to show their gratitude. Seeing that the precious hall had not been cleaned up in a long time and that it was no longer very nice to look at, they engaged workers to rebuild it and to change the old to new. When the workers informed us they had finished, we rejoiced at having been able to bring it to fruition.
We pray that Sovereign Heaven will bless us and Lord Earth favor us: let the Green Dragon produce signs of approval and the White Tiger

go into hiding. May its broad foundations be our succor and the veins of earth our source of livelihood forever. Cause the whole area to enjoy peace and quiet and gods and men to dwell in harmony together. Allow no calamities to occur. May the students win signal honors and the farmers sing over full granaries; may the merchants make profits and the laborers obtain what they desire. Let there be abundance in fields and seas: cause the fish and crustaceans to flourish and multiply, the five grains to yield a rich harvest, and the six domestic animals to increase in numbers. May all undertakings produce the desired results and every enterprise be crowned with success. We celebrate the repair, we celebrate its completion: on the land of the Way we give thanks, we pray for peace, we make our offering. We have selected by divination this month, the 11th, 12th, and 13th days, to go, leaning on the Way, to the palace in order to set up an altar and convene the great assembly of the Fragrant Offering of the Golden Register to Celebrate Completion and Pray for Peace.

For three days and nights we will execute rituals: at an auspicious hour, we will beat the drum for the first time and then flame the oil to drive away evil. First we will dispatch a whole set of documents to inform the authorities of the Three Realms that we are reverently preparing a fragrant banquet. Respectfully, we will invite the Emperor in his chariot. We will raise the flag and post the placard so as to inform all the perfected everywhere. We will command the generals to protect the altar and prevent the entry of nefarious energies. We will recite *The Great Litany of Confession and Homage to Heaven;* we will present our marvelous offering of nine gifts. In the evening we will make a farewell sacrifice to the earth gods of the five directions so that they go far away to other regions. We will set out a libation for the Office of Earth, summon good fortune by waving the willow branch, and set in place the symbol-orders. The first night we will light precious torches so as to illumine the perfected, we will roll up the pearl screen and pay our respects to the Emperor. We will sound the golden bell so as to bring heaven and earth into harmony; we will strike the jade stone so as to bring the *yin* and the *yang* into union. Temporarily, we will close our secret canons.

The next morning, when the sky is clear and the air pure, we will add incense in the jade burner. We will mount the altar for the Land of the Way; we will present the incense three times. Again we will proclaim the scriptures; again we will make the vegetarian offering of fruit and rice and present jewels and flowers. That evening, we will light and release the water lamps so that they may illumine the paths in the darkness. We will invoke the saints and masters, worthy lords of the Great Teaching. The divine ritual of the Nocturnal Invocation is the mainstay of the Teaching: we will open the cloud covers to display the True Writs, and we will hold them in place with the four treasures of the calligrapher. We will memorialize the nine heavens and make confession to the ten extremities. Then we will take leave of the masters and loosen our belt; for a while the divine sounds will cease.

When the third morning comes and the heavens are bright, we will clean the altar area and straighten things up. Once again we will sound the drum of the law, address ourselves once again to the most venerable ones. We will present fine teas; we will open up and intone the most perfect of the marvelous scriptures. We will mount the stage to perform our teaching, and we will respectfully forward the petition, setting it forth for imperial examination. At each home we will present incense, at each gate proclaim the memorial. At noon we will make the fragrant offering and strew fine flowers all around. Having finished the canonical stanzas, we will announce this in prayer to the myriad potentates of the Three Realms. The lamps of the saints aglow, the prime stars of the root destiny of the multitude will be resplendent. We will communicate our sincerity in the Orthodox Offering, welcoming all who descend from the Jade Capital. We will sing the mighty texts of the great thanksgiving; we will pour the fine wine of the triple libation. Outside, we will prepare a small banquet to be distributed to all the solitary spirits. We will pray over the divine lamps of the five thunders and set forth the Pure Offering for Peace with the Pestilence (gods).° We will escort the ship of the immortals back to the islands in the sea; we will welcome home the felicity which enters our borders. Having completed the libations and offerings and having seen the saints off on their return journey, we will distribute by burning the money (for transmission) of the memorial to reward the officers and soldiers. We will take respectful leave of heaven's face and put the lord of this territory and the perfected back in their proper places. Having executed rituals for three days and nights, we will worship the supreme perfected on high and pray for peace and manifold blessings here below.

In the *keng-shen* year of heaven's revolution, the eleventh month, the ____ day.

Your humble servant, Ch'en Ting-sheng, bows three times and presents the memorial on high.

As already stated, the placard posted *outside* the temple is essentially the same as the memorial read *inside* the temple. There are, nonetheless, certain differences, both in the text and in its final disposal. The memorial is taken home by the priest and kept as part of his archives, so that the next time he or his successor is called on by the same community to perform an Offering, he can use it as a model. This is of some importance, for every temple community has its own traditions, its own program of rituals for an Offering. The placard, as we have already mentioned, is unceremoniously torn down, crumpled up, and burned. At the beginning of the placard the following phrase is inserted:

Having received the investiture of the Emperor, I have the use of the symbols and the seal which give me power to command the various authorities and to preside over the Offering prepared on the divine altar.

At the end on the placard, the following is added:

On this day we open up the divine altar and announce the ritual of Offering. For what precedes, we look to the officer of merits in charge

---

° This sentence and the next refer to another *chiao* which may be inserted. It is addressed to the pestilence gods (cf. Liu Chih-wan 1983, 285 ff.).

today, the great spirit who guards the placard, and the gods and keen-eared ones of this neighborhood to keep the realm of the altar clean and to sweep away all nefarious energies. We welcome with respect the chariot of the Emperor, that his light may come down to the land of the Tao and guarantee the cultic covenant. When the ritual is finished, your merit will be made clear to all. We can render a cult in accord with the Teaching only if your divine protection is not wanting. This must be posted: may its light shine everywhere, inexhaustible; let the myriad gods all pay heed.

The above placard: be it known!

In the *keng-shen* year, the eleventh month, the _____ day, issued (under the authority of)

The Perfect Lord of the Response to Tranquillity and the Manifested Aid of the Orthodox Unity, Pillar of the Teaching of the Three Heavens and Founding Master, Chang (Tao-ling).

PLACARD   (signed) Ch'en Ts'un-hsin

Once this placard has been posted, the villagers crowd around to see that their names are properly written, and also to know what is going on behind the closed doors of the temple. But if that is, so to speak, the social function of the placard, its ritual role is clearly one of announcement, not to the villagers, but to their gods. As such, it seconds the ritual of the Announcement itself, in which the high priest also goes outside the temple to dispatch his message, and in which he also makes much of the authority he has inherited from the "founding master" over the gods of the people, as well as over the gods of the time cycle in charge of the transmission of messages, the "officer of merit in charge today."

In addition to these two basic documents, the high priest has a whole host of lesser documents to prepare. Among them are two other placards, one for the Six Masters, one for the Four Saints, to be posted above the tables on the altar that represent their respective mountains. These placards assign to the masters of Mount Lung-hu the role of guardians of the integrity of the altar and guarantors of the proper transmission of all messages, and to the saints of Mount Wu-tang that of seeing to the rapid execution of all symbol-orders (*fu-ming*). In other words, the masters have a positive role as the intermediaries in communication with heaven, and the saints have a negative one in the war against the dark forces of their northern domain.

This distinction in their roles—the one civil, the other military—is further accentuated by the documents and symbols. In the Introduction it was mentioned that the first Taoists were accused of "deceiving the people by fabricating documents and symbols." These two placards, linked to two mountains which became important in Taoist history only during the Sung—and the same is true of the groups of six masters and four saints associated with them—show how Taoism, while undergoing vast and constant superficial changes, has remained impervious throughout its long history to deep structural alteration.

Indeed, inasmuch as the Six Masters are, as it were, summarized in the one master Chang Tao-ling, it would seem that essentially the two mountains at the back of the altar in southern Taiwanese Taoism are simply representative of Chang and the generals of the four directions with whom his original covenant was established. This conclusion is supported by statements of Chin Yün-chung (fl. 1225) concerning the school of the Five Offices (*wu-fu*) current in his time (Chin, 10.18b). It also calls to mind the altar of the three Days of Origin, with its distinction between the four directions of the terrestrial stage and the central direction of the celestial stage.

The high priest also prepares a certain number of "reports" (*chuang*), usually thirty-six, used to mark the "divine seats" (*shen-wei*). In southern Taiwan flat rectangular yellow envelopes are used. The divinity's name is written on the outside and a brief letter expressing allegiance to the god and announcing to him the ritual to be held is placed inside (plate 23). These are burned at the end of the ritual along with the three placards. Taoists in northern Taiwan use painted rectangular wooden tablets which are not burned and which thus constitute, like the scroll paintings and altar hangings, a part of the moveable Taoist altar kept in trunks in the home of the high priest.

The last major category of documents consists of various letters and messages. Virtually every ritual involves burning one or more letters in order to communicate with the powers of the other world. As we saw in the memorial, a whole set of documents is dispatched during the ritual of the Announcement (*fa-piao;* plate 24). These documents are described in an "announcement" (*kuan*) which is read at the end of the Announcement (cf. Ofuchi, 408b–410b):

Announcement (dispatch!): Office of the Great Method of the Numinous Treasure. This office today worships the Way and prepares an Offering to give thanks and pray for peace. Being charged with maintaining the order of the Three Heavens, the office-holder is enrolled in the ranks of the five record-keeping bureaus. The antiquity of canon law ensures that sincerity penetrates the high (heaven) and the thick (earth); the luminosity of the ritual texts makes certain that the somber heavens (water) reach both the dark (earth) and the light (heaven). All our earnest petitions must be transmitted by an honorable office-holder if they are to be executed with dispatch. Those who must receive this announcement are as follows:
—five box envelopes (*fang-han*) with invocations, invitations, and presentations are respectfully sent to:
the Golden Gate in the Jade Capital: respectfully invoked;
the gate of the Four Bureaus of the Three Realms: respectfully invited;
the Bureau of the Great Sovereign of the Office of Heaven: respectfully presented;
the Court of the Celestial Pivot in the Highest Purity: respectfully presented;
the Office of the Eastern Peak Tai: respectfully presented.

—two box envelopes with letters of presentation are respectfully forwarded to:

the offices of the Six Masters of the Numinous Treasure: respectfully forwarded;

the offices of the Four Saints of the North Pole: respectfully forwarded.

—four box envelopes with missives of offering are respectfully presented to:

the officers of merit who transmit symbols,

the various gods who assist the Way,

the gods of the soil and of the walls and moats,

the gods to whom is rendered a cult recognized by law: to each, presented.

—seven letters, cards, and notes are respectfully passed on to:

the officers, generals, clerks, and soldiers of the various offices of the thunder and lightning of the Numinous Treasure in the Court of Law of the Highest Purity;

the various officers, generals, clerks, and soldiers of the altar where gather the gods of the Three Realms in the Chamber of Spontaneity for Communication with the Perfected;

the host of the immortals who bring catastrophes during the various parts of this year;

the venerable god of supreme virtue in charge of the Great Star (T'ai-sui);

the venerable gods of the walls and moats of the district and the prefecture of Tainan;

the gods and keen-eared ones from above, below, far, and near who receive sacrifices in this neighborhood;

the six gods of the soil and directors of destiny of the incense burners of each family.

The above documents have all been duly stamped, sealed, and completed. We look to the divine powers on high to transmit them for us. Let the mounted gods gallop each in his own direction and give (his documents) to the right office, penetrating on high to the Golden Gate of the Jade Capital and below into the bright waters and dark earth. May our sincerity be communicated directly on high and a response be forthcoming. Let there be no delays: it must reach those concerned.

The above is announced to the jade lasses of the Three Heavens charged with transmission, the messengers of the roads through the clouds of the Nine Heavens, the officers of merit of Orthodox Unity, the great generals of the molten metal and fiery bells, the potent officers in charge of memorializing on this day, the clerks mounted on the flying dragons—all the gods of transmission.

In the *keng-shen* year of heaven's revolution, the 11th month, the 20th day, dispatched.

In charge of the execution of the rituals: Ch'en Ts'un-hsin (seal)
ANNOUNCEMENT (DISPATCH)

The word "dispatch" (*hsing*) at the beginning and end of this proclamation is written in red above the word "announcement"; it also means "execute, carry out." The word "seal" is written in a similar manner above the name Ts'un-hsin. Ch'en's personal seal is stamped over the date. A number of words in this announcement are marked with a red dot or stroke; they are marks made by the high priest when checking the announcement to ensure it is complete and without errors.

Ts'un-hsin, literally, "concentrated mind," is a ritual name (*hua-hao*, "flowery appellation") shared by all Taoist priests of Ch'en Jung-sheng's generation in Taiwan. By contrast, the name used in the memorial, Ting-sheng, is composed of an element which is personal, Sheng, and an element, Ting, which is generational. This name—called a *fa-hao*, "ritual appellation"—is given the high priest at the time of his ordination. Its generational element derives from the lineage poem of the Heavenly Master tradition (each separate Taoist lineage has such a poem).

The gods who are to be notified are listed in hierarchical order, and are further differentiated by the type of letter, card, or note of invitation sent and by the verb of invitation used. Only the Three Pure Ones, within the Golden Gate, are "respectfully invoked." The inclusion of the Eastern Peak (T'ai-shan or Tai) in the highest group is also worth noting: the Eastern Peak is the most important of the five sacred mountains because it is the main place for communication with both heaven and hell.

The primary hierarchical distinction is between gods who receive their invitation in a "box envelope" and those who do not. All letters of invitation are rolled up, fumigated with incense, and inserted with three sticks of incense in flat rectangular envelopes—yellow for the higher grades, white for the lower—like those used to mark the "seats of the divinities." Each envelope is individually addressed and stamped. Preparing the box envelopes is a whole technique of its own. Starting with a flat six-inch wide, two-foot long double sheet whose two long sides have been glued together, one produces from it, by folding, a rectangular box with 3-inch sides which shuts by interlapping folds on either end. The rolling, fumigating, and folding takes several Taoists at least two hours, a job they do while other members are hanging up the scrolls and preparing the altar.

Nowadays, most of the messages are printed, and only such items as names and dates are written in by the high priest. In the past, he wrote them all out. The burden of the paper work was indeed so great that warnings were issued against using apprentices to copy them out, for in their ignorance of the secret parts of the ritual the apprentices might leave words out and so undermine the the ritual work of the high priest (Lü Yüan-su, 1.11b).

CHAPTER

6

The Announcement

The ritual of announcement (*fa-piao*, "dispatch the memorial") is "modern," that is, it dates from the Northern Sung:

> The ritual of antiquity had no announcement to the god of the soil. The Announcement is the Nocturnal Invocation of the outer altar. Later generations added it and wrote texts just for an invitation and an announcement. Then they created official documents and added the technique for performing [the ritual]. Finally, those who had the position of master added hand seals and gestures, symbols and incantations, by means of which they ordered the god of the soil and the other gods to come. Probably the Announcement started in [the movement of] the Orthodox Method of the Heart of Heaven. It has by now become the norm. (Lü T'ai-ku, 9.1a)

The Orthodox Method of the Heart of Heaven (T'ien-hsin cheng-fa) is a Taoist movement whose beginnings go back to the late tenth century.

By the time Lü T'ai-ku wrote in 1201, its method for "dispatching the memorial" (*fa-piao* or *fa-tsou*) had "become the norm," and a very complicated norm at that! The "official documents" dispatched could number in the hundreds, and the ritual itself was often repeated three times before the "real fast" (*cheng-chai*): one hundred days prior (*yü-kao*, "prior announcement," or *yü-tsou*, "prior memorializing"); one month prior (*shen-tsou*, "detailed memorializing"); and one week prior (*cheng-tsou*, "real memorializing") (see TT 466 *Ling-chiao chi-tu chin-shu* 2.2a-5a).

The ritual of announcement practiced in Taiwan today is hardly as elaborate as those described in the liturgical manuals of the Southern Sung and Yüan, and it is only done once. Otherwise, Lü T'ai-ku's description corresponds perfectly to the ritual one can observe in Taiwan today. It too is carried out on the outer altar, that is, facing the Table of the Three Realms on the south side of the altar; it involves the summoning, by means of documents, of the god of the soil and "all the other gods"; it involves the use of symbols, gestures, and the "transformation of the spirits" (*pien-shen*) according to methods prescribed by manuals which are secret, in principle known only to the high priest himself.

To understand this ritual, therefore, one must have access to the secret manuals actually used by a given high priest. But even that is not enough, for a priest may well have more than one such manual and may, in actual practice, switch back and forth between them. In the descriptions which follow I am indebted to Master Ch'en Jung-sheng of Tainan for allowing me to record him, using a clip microphone, on 18 November 1981, in the Temple of the Great Man (*Ta-jen miao*), Ta-wan, near Tainan. This particular Offering was conducted in honor of the gods of pestilence (*wang-yeh*) and was a five-day *chiao* that began on 17 November and ended on 22 November. I am also indebted to Poul Andersen for lending me the manuals, reproduced with Master Ch'en's permission when Mr. Andersen was studying with Ch'en in 1979. The two manuals are entitled *Hsüan-k'o miao-chüeh* and *Lung-hu shan cheng-yi Liu-hou Chang t'ien-shih yü-chüeh ch'üan-chi*.

There are five main parts to the Announcement: purification, invitation of the saints and masters, summons, dispatch, and dismissal of saints and masters.

After an introit, the *shui-pai* ("talking over the water") rite begins. During it the high priest begins the transformation of his body and the purification of the altar. He does this while the cantor is singing the following song very slowly:

> Truly, in order to *cleanse* the universe, we must rely on the auspicious light of the nine-phoenix; to *purify* the altar, we depend on the divine water of the five-dragon. *Therefore*, in order to get rid of all that is

perverse and filthy, to activate that which is sluggish and set in motion that which is pure, and so to prepare the Realm of the Law, *making* it magnificent and perfectly clean, we must *first* invite respectfully the perfect officers who destroy filth and the clerks who get rid of the oppressive to send down auspicious light in great *abundance* to sweep away all foulness and *transform* this place of ordinary men into a land of immortals, turn this abode of dust into one of immortals, *subdue* cadavers and stale energies and hail them off to the bowl of the Dipper, so that the *auspicious* incense and lucky clouds fill the altar with fragrance. *Respectfully. . . .*(Ofuchi, 242b)

The underlined words represent the point in the song at which the high priest begins a new action. In the description of his actions below, these words are used to denote each stage of the actions that constitute the transformation.

Cleanse. At this point the priest begins by murmuring under the cantor's song:

> My Cinnabar Field opens up for communication; my heart [directs the energy] through the Three Barriers. The ten thousand spirits unite; the body depends on the tranquillity of its spirits. Quickly, quickly, in accord with the order. (ibid., 243a)

While pressing with his left thumb the point in his left hand corresponding to his "own destiny" (*pen-ming;* cf. plate 13), the priest says, "Respectfully and sincerely, your servant prays. . . ." At the same time, with his right hand, he forms the "sword gesture"—index and middle finger stiff—and places this "sword" on the left hip, near his left hand. He then presses on the point *k'an* $\equiv\equiv$ of his hand (for the map of the hand, see p. 17), which corresponds to the palace or heaven of Jade Purity in his body, and says, "The Emperor of Jade Purity orders!" He draws his "sword," raises it over his head, and makes with it a throwing motion toward the incense burner on the Table of the Three Realms: he is exteriorizing the energy of the Cinnabar Field in his lower belly and thus lighting the external incense burner. He does the same thing for the emperors (energies) of Highest Purity ("palace of the center") and Great Purity (*li* $\equiv\equiv$), which correspond respectively to his heart and his *ni-huan.* The progress from the first to the third Pure One is thus itself an exteriorization, a cosmogenesis, for it moves from his lower belly to his head and also from the base to the tip of the middle finger of his left hand.

The priest continues, at once murmuring and pressing points in his left hand (given in parenthesis below):

> The Emperor on High orders! With the sun I wash my body (*mao*); with the moon I refine my perfection (*yu*). The immortal lads bear me up

(*tzu*); the jade lasses protect me (*ch'ou*). My three celestial souls are pure and correct (*mao*); my seven terrestrial souls are quiet (*yu*). The twenty-eight constellations join forces with me (*ch'en* to *ssu*, counterclockwise). All perversity and filth (*ken*) is driven away by the water and made pure (*k'an*). My heart is in communion with the true Way (*pen-ming*): I ascend to the realm of the formless (*wu*, flick out). Quickly, quickly. . . .

According to the *Lung-hu shan* manual (p. 3), the actions here of hand and tongue should be complemented by visualizations which "realize" them: the moon is to be imagined nine inches from the face of the priest; in it is the Perfect Water with which he washes his body. In like manner, the sun provides the Perfect Fire with which he refines his body. The immortal lads are seen on the left with his left eye, the jade lasses on the right with the right eye. They are the energies of True Yang (*chen-yang*) and True Yin (*chen-yin*) respectively. These visualizations prescribed by the manual should indeed be done, according to Master Ch'en, and most Sung liturgical manuals likewise confirm the need for such accompanying visualizations (see especially TT 547 *Ling-pao yü-chien* 7.14b ff.)

Purify. Having thus gathered all his forces and ensured himself of adequate protection, the high priest is ready to "enter the maelstrom." This he does by spinning once on himself, clockwise, performing a "circle of the Great Ultimate" (*t'ai-chi ch'üan*). With this he enters the "palace of the center," and in this magic circle which symbolizes the endless transformational creativity of the body of the universe, he can now perform the ritual. He raises both hands to the level of his eyebrows, grits his teeth five times, and pronounces the "incantation for the transformation and purification of his body":

> Heavenly Worthy of the Primordial Beginning, pray transform my body that it be no longer the body of an ordinary mortal: my head is like a cloud of ink, my hair like the scattered stars. My left eye becomes the sun, and my right the moon. My nose is like a mountain; my mouth is the Gate of Heaven. My teeth are like a forest of swords; my tongue is the Golden Bridge. My breath is like poisonous vapors, my ears like bells of fire. These ten fingers of mine are like the ten officers of merit who snag [wrongdoers]. My left ribs are the Lord of Mount Lu, my right the Lord of Mount Mao. My left foot becomes the General of Thunder, my right the General of Lightning. My spinal column is Mount T'ai. My body is transformed and purified. On my left is the green dragon, on my right the white tiger; in front of me is the red bird, behind me the somber warrior. The thirty-six celestial birds and twenty-eight mansions are all found in my body. Quickly, quickly. . . . (*Hsüan-k'o*, 19; cf. Ofuchi, 249a)

A text virtually identical to this chant is given in a manual of the sect of the Orthodox Method of the Heart of Heaven. It dates at least to 1116 (Yüan Miao-tsung, 2.2b). It adds to the changes of the body two items, making the "upper lip the Master of Rain and the lower the Count of the Wind." According to Master Ch'en, this formula turns the high priest into the "lord of the religion" (*chiao-chu*), Lao-tzu.

Every line of this transformation is worth commenting on in detail. Through the transformation, for example, we see what it means to say in the memorial and on the placard that the high priest is in charge of the offices of thunder and lightning. But for our purposes, the identification of the spinal column as T'ai-shan is most revealing. Taoists have from ancient times "returned the essence to repair the brain" (Maspero, 522), and we have already seen allusion to this practice in Wang Ch'i-chen's description of the spinal column as the link between the Metal Gate and the Jade Capital. In every Chinese town of any size there was traditionally a Temple of the Eastern Peak, invariably in the charge of Taoists (Day, 119). It was the temple, with its infernal "Chamber of Horrors" (Giles, 469), where people troubled by ghosts came to seek relief, either through a medium or through a Taoist. It is already two millennia since the first emperor mounted T'ai-shan to make a sacrifice to heaven and a cosmic claim (*feng*) to the empire (Chavannes 1910, 19). The spinal column is thus the "hinge" on which the health of the body—politic, communal, familial, individual—depends. It is the conduit through which the obstructed waters of hell may be drawn off and recycled, that is, returned to heaven. There is, however, one condition: there must be someone who knows how to dance the Step of Yü on the turtle's back, and so bring order where there was disorder, light where all was darkness. The analogy of the Offering with the imperial sacrifices of investiture is all the more pertinent if we consider that its purpose is the same: by means of the cult to lay claim to the land.

But let us come back to the Announcement. With his hands still at eyebrow level, the priest pronounces the "formula for hiding his body" (*Lung-hu shan,* p. 4):

> The Big Dipper is brilliant: its bowl is in front of me, its handle behind.
> From heaven it descends to hide my person.

Dropping his hands and bringing his right hand back to join his left at the left hip, the high priest now does the "Step of the Three Terraces," that is, taps the ground in front of him with the heel of his left foot, it being a *yang* day. He touches the floor thus three times, once for each of the Three Terraces, at the Earthly Branch *wu* first, then at *wei*, and finally at *ssu*. His hands then separate, and he points into his left hand as he says:

> The Three Terraces cover my head. My celestial and terrestrial souls are calm and vigorous. Whoever transgresses my boundaries will meet with instant heaven-sent disaster. (*Lung-hu,* 4; Ofuchi, 706a)

Therefore. Both hands sweep outward, back together, and up. The priest drops the left hand only and turns once on himself. Then he brings them back together and up, and speaks:

Upper Terrace, one and yellow: it eradicates what is inauspicious. Central Terrace, two and white: it protects my person and anchors it solidly. Lower Terrace, three and green: it sweeps away filth and gets rid of evil. Everywhere the terrace stars terrify the powers and potentates. Quickly, quickly. . . . (ibid.)

Making. The priest continues speaking:

Respectfully I request the great general of the nine-phoenix who destroys filth, the great saint of the Dipper, the astral lords of the various sectors, the perfect officers who get rid of oppression, and the youths who destroy filth to heed my call and descend quickly to this altar. Quickly, quickly. (*Hsüan-k'o*, 20; cf. Ofuchi, 243b)

First. The priest makes a bowing gesture with his joined hands, then steps forward to pick up a yellow slip of paper, on which is written the "Nine-phoenix symbol for the destruction of filth." He lights it, allows it to burn almost down to his fingers, and then blows it out into the air. The name of this symbol, a model of which is given in the manual, is no doubt expressive of the purifying role of fire. The phoenix (the "red bird" the priest had visualized before him) is the emblematic animal of the south, whose number in Posterior Heaven is nine. This interpretation is confirmed by the fact that this symbol was probably first used in the "smelting" (*lien-tu*) ritual of the Southern Sung (TT 219 *Tu-jen ta-fa* 68.2a).

Abundance. Pressing the appropriate point in his left hand, the priest goes to the center of the altar, faces east, makes a rolling motion with the hands as if pulling something out of a well, and says, "Respectfully I request the green energy of the precious heaven of charity to enter my liver." At the word "enter" (literally "inhale") he "draws" the energy with his right hand down into his body and makes an exaggerated sound of inhaling. A different verb, corresponding to a different way of inhaling (or exhaling, for the energies of the north and the south), is used for each of the five directions, with the priest turning each time to face the appropriate direction. The *Lung-hu* manual calls this process "spitting out the stale and inhaling the fresh" (p. 6). It ends with the priest, who is facing north, raising his joined hands in front of his face and saying:

Lords of the living energies of the five directions, of the dominant energies of the five directions, of the power of heaven and the moon, most perfect energies of the five directions, hear my call, respond to me. (Ofuchi, 243b)

Transform. Rolling his hands clockwise three times along the left side of his head, and then counterclockwise seven times on the right side, the priest now summons his celestial and terrestrial souls (the three celestial souls are identified as from the Upper, Middle, and Lower Realms respectively). Then, with a great flail of the long yellow sleeves which extend past the wrist and hide the hands (cf. plate 20), he spins clockwise three times on himself, saying:

> One turn: heaven and earth shake.
> Two turns: gods and ghosts tremble.
> Three turns rock the Dipper.

Subdue. The priest now performs the "Walk of the Dipper of the nine-phoenix." There are two ways of doing this walk. On *yin* days, the priest starts in the south and ends in the north, and he makes each of his giant forward steps with his right foot. On *yang* days, as in the present case, he does the reverse. The path he traces is as shown (*Lung-hu,* 7; cf. Ofuchi, 244a):

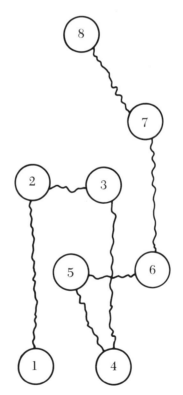

(*Lung-hu*, p. 7; cf. Ofuchi, 244a)

(An identical diagram is to be found in the early 13th century text TT 219 *Tu-jen ta-fa* 68.2a.) At each point from 1 to 8, the priest mutters a phrase and, while pressing the appropriate point (given in parenthesis) in his left hand, takes a giant step to the next station:

> The nine-phoenix soars (*yin*);
> It destroys filth on all sides (*ch'en*).
> The golden lads lead me forward (*wei*);
> The jade lasses protect my chamber (*tzu*).
> I go up in audience before the Golden Gate (center);
> In person I behold the Jade Emperor (*hsü*).
> Everything that is filthy (*shen*)
> Disappears instantaneously (*wu*).

The priest completes this step-murmur with a spin clockwise called "gathering the forces of the Dipper," that is, he internalizes the forces that have just been activated by stepping on them with his feet. Thus stepping with the feet is like pointing in the hand. He adds:

> Web of earth, net of heaven; net of heaven, web of earth. A thousand dippers and ten thousand bushels follow the movement of my hand. (*Lung-hu*, 8; cf. Ofuchi, 706a)

Auspicious. The priest now takes another yellow slip of paper, on which is written the "fiery symbol for the destruction of filth." He murmurs:

> God of the fire, god of the fire; spirit of the flame, spirit of the flame: communicate on high in the purple tenuity; penetrate below in the utter darkness. Eradicate all that is perverse and foul; do not let them interfere with my ritual. Quickly, quickly, in accord with the order of the astral lord of the virtue of fire in the south. (Ofuchi, 244a)

He then burns the symbol and blows it toward the incense burner.

Holding the "symbol of brightness and purification," he says:

> Respectfully I summon the nine-phoenix that destroys filth: may the divine water be bright and clear. Agents of the five thunders, root out every nefarious ether; subdue corpses and stale energies so that they go quickly far off and do not linger. Let this order be executed, quickly, quickly, in accord with the astral lord of the virtue of water in the north.

He then burns the symbol so that the ashes fall into his bowl of symbol-water.

Respectfully. Once again the priest turns around on himself and then "takes the energies of the three luminaries" (*Lung-hu*, p. 11). This involves pressing a series of points arrayed in the form of the Dipper in his left hand, flipping that hand, writing with the right hand's "sword" the secret name (*hui*) of the sun, the moon, or the Dipper, pronouncing a corresponding formula of pseudo-Sanskrit syllables, flipping his left hand once again, and then patting the bowl of water with it. This process is repeated for each of the three luminaries. The pseudo-Sanskrit goes back, once again, to texts of the Orthodox Method of the Heart of Heaven (Teng Yu-kung, 1.2a–4a; Yüan Miao-tsung, 2.11b-12a). These texts make clear that the formulae serve to summon up the energies of the three luminaries, energies which are then used by the priest to write efficacious symbols. In the manuals we are following, the symbols all have the rain radical on top like the personal Taoist names of the Three Pure Ones.

Having thus transformed the already purified water into "symbol-water" (*fu-shui*), the high priest takes up a real (ritual) sword in his right hand and the bowl of symbol-water in his left hand. He turns to face the Gate of Demons in the northeast, dips the sword in the bowl, points it toward the northeast, calls out "Death to you, filthy energies!" fills his mouth with symbol-water, and sprays it along the blade. He then returns to the Table of the Three Realms to put down sword and bowl and take up his court tablet. The "talking over the water" has lasted a full ten minutes.

Until this point, other than the slow singing of the cantor, usually accompanied by the other acolytes, there has been in the background only the most desultory form of percussion. Long intervals of instrumental silence are interrupted by occasional beats on the big drum, followed by blows to the various gongs. Now suddenly the horns peep several times, like birds waking up, and then their sustained wail announces the "text for entry in the cave." While the acolytes sing a brief version of this text—a version found already in the manuals of the Orthodox Method (Yüan Miao-tsung, 8.9b)—the priest mutters a more complete version (Ofuchi, 244b):

In the dark emptiness of the cave is born an energy;
Luminous is the Great Nothingness which controls the myriad potentates.
The mighty gods of the eight directions separate to the left and to the right,
Enabling me, spontaneous, to go in audience to Highest Purity.
With the symbol-orders of the Numinous Treasure at my belt,
I announce the myriad potentates throughout the Nine Heavens.
Net of heaven, emptiness like the Great Void:
Trap the demon-seeds in the great mystery of cavernous space.
The four-eyed old man descends from heaven;
Marshal T'ien-p'eng commands the heavenly host.
The agents of the five directions let fly the rumbling thunder;
The spirits of the time cycle follow me when I move.
The great god of the flames executes my orders;
The thirty-six thunder [generals] do not tarry.
Celestial thunder, grumbling, comes down from heaven;
Terrestrial thunder, rolling, stirs heaven and earth.

Gods and officers chase away the evil ghosts;
Thunder and lightning sweep away the nefarious ethers.
The perfect officers of mountains and rivers obey my commands;
The gods of the soil and of the walls and moats come to greet me.
The perverse ghosts of all the world are exterminated;
Not one of the myriad demons survives.

No text could show more clearly that the paintings hung along the two side walls represent the exteriorized energies of the high priest's, that is, Lao-tzu's body.

The leader of the troupe now comes to kneel in the high priest's place, and then stands to receive the bowl and sword and to lead the procession for the purification of the altar. When the priests have returned to their positions and finished the song, the music stops altogether, and the priest reads from the manuscript of the ritual (Ofuchi, 245a):

> To study the Way one must seek out a teacher so as to hear the songs and practice the rites. One must go in audience to Heaven and pay respects to His face before one can act out the teaching and perform rituals.

The priest then recites a list of nine types of incense whose fragrance "fills the precious pavilion in the Capital of Jade." At this point the high priest plants three sticks of incense in the brazier on the table before him. Then, addressing himself to the officer of merit in charge of transmissions on that day and to the agents of the incense, he asks them to inform the "orthodox god and perfect officer of this neighborhood and its soil" that he is to "transmit this precious incense on my behalf." While reciting, he hands three sticks to the keeper of incense and three more to the leader of the troupe. They take them to Wu-tang and Lung-hu Mountains respectively.

On his knees now, still without musical accompaniment, the high priest begins the invocation, one by one, of the Six Masters of Lung-hu shan and the Four Saints of Wu-tang shan, together with their assistants "of the left and of the right" (Ofuchi, 245b). Incense is offered so that they will "come back and illumine" the altar with their presence. The high priest remains on his knees while the leader of the troupe (normally, it should be the assistant cantor) reads the memorial for the first time.

That done, the priest stands up to read a brief introduction to the "prior announcement": "Leave the Golden Gate far behind," he says, "come and see the sincerity of our allegiance." Accompanied by gentle oboe and plucking on a three-string mandolin, all then sing, inviting each of the Six Masters and Four Saints (the high priest is once again on his knees). The music virtually stops now. The high priest and the others then speak the following verse responsively, the first and third lines by the high priest, the second and fourth by all:

> The cloud chariot has descended;
> The team of cranes is approaching.
> When the Offering is done,
> We will see you off.

The high priest bows deeply to acknowledge the arrival of the invited guests, then stands to sing:

> Please be seated on your thrones
> While we present you with incense and tea.

The second line is sung by all, as is the refrain that follows and that will be heard many times during the course of the Offering:

> The water in the Yangtzu: spreads flowers.
> The tea of Mount Meng: fills the altar.

This refrain announces a triple presentation of wine. Each presentation is preceded by a prose section recited at breakneck speed, to regular percussion, by the high priest (normally, such recitation falls to the chief cantor). Then the lilting refrain breaks in again as the wine is presented. The first recitation concerns the Way, the second the immortal guests, and the third the ritual offering. The Way, though it is unfathomable and unnamable, nonetheless unceasingly, inerrantly produces the rhythm of the seasons. The immortals have come down to the "dusty world" and filled it with their light and their music. Rice is no offering: sanctity is the product of virtue. Flowers can be presented: ritual depends on sincerity.

> I pray the Great Way in its compassion to look down on the ritual of its humble servant. May it shed its light on all sides, like the bright moon in the sky; may it reveal its transformations without favoritism, as the green lake reflects objects. Deign to accept the sincerity of our allegiance that all may be blessed with the grace of salvation. (Ofuchi, 246a)

The cantor now calls out, "Respectfully I state my ritual rank." This the high priest does, and then kneels. He recalls his own initiation, which "opened wide the road of the cultivation of perfection" and provided him with the rituals with which to save others. Being himself thus favored, it is "incumbent upon me to present on high whatever people ask me to" (Ofuchi, 246b). At this point, a brief version of the memorial is read again. The rapid percussion, modulated by the cantor's wooden drum, continues throughout.

The priest then concludes his introductory prayer by asking again that his sincerity be observed as he makes the prior announcement. He also asks that his own "mean substance of dust," his own lack of merit, be taken into consideration. He speaks of his fear that what he announces will "have difficulty reaching the heavens," and that the officers under his orders will "detain or disobey" the documents and symbols that he will be asking them to transmit. He calls on the Masters and Saints, therefore, to ensure that "all the requests of your servant reach the heavens." The percussion stops, the high priest stands up and calls, "Teachers of the Lineage" three times, to which the others respond each time with "Heavenly Worthy, Our Guarantors." A flurry of loud gonging marks the end of the first half—the invitation half—of the ritual of Announcement.

Without a pause, the priests swing into a second introit. The announcement part of the ritual has begun. This announcement or summons is the lengthiest single portion of the Announcement ritual. The oboes join the priests on the second line of the introit, which ends with furious drumming and clanging as the high priest takes up his bowl of symbol-water to purify the altar. Dipping a flower held between the index and middle fingers of his right hand into the bowl, he murmurs a phrase, and then flicks the water out over the altar. The furious percussion continues as he takes a giant stride, swivels, dips, and sprinkles again. The percussion stops. Facing the Table of the Three Realms from a distance, the high priest in a loud voice orders the "oppressors" of heaven and earth to go back where they came from, and the oppressors of men and ghosts to disappear (boom-boom, clang-clang, a blow on the metal bowl of the assistant cantor):

> When they hear my ritual water, let them all go back to their proper places. Whoever does not, turn him over to the lads of the White Potentate of the West for beheading. . . . Heavenly Worthy of the Purification of the Ten Directions.

Boom-boom, clang-clang, a blow on the bowl. If the cantor's drum, the "voice of heaven," may be compared to the sun in that it determines the basic rhythm, the assistant cantor's metal bowl, the "voice of earth," is like the moon in that it marks the intervals. Together they form the rhythmic context within which the "voice of man" renders the ritual text. Let all "oppressors go back to their proper places," says the voice of man, and it is natural they should listen to words measured out in cosmic rhythms. The high priest concludes: "Heaven and earth become dustless when I use the divine water of the Three Lights" (Ofuchi, 247a).

Without a pause, still uttering his words with great emphasis, the voice of man moves directly into the presentation of incense:

> The perfect incense of a hundred harmonies diffuses, the auspicious smoke billows, and this ordinary place is transformed into a realm of immortals.

While the high priest murmurs now over a fat stick of incense which has been lit at both ends and in the middle, the cantor first, then the assistant cantor, and finally the two remaining acolytes in turn sing a slow incense hymn to the accompaniment of a two-string violin (*er-hu*) and a mandolin. The song describes the incense going up to the "flowery canopy" and down to the "source of potency."

> Jade lasses bring it back to the Golden Gate;
> Golden lads lead it into highest heaven.
> It takes the form of celestial seals;
> The colored clouds fly through space,
> Bearing the immortals into our cave to watch.

Incense, in other words, is not just a fragrant offering to the gods, making the altar a pleasant place for them to spend some time. It is what literally draws them to the altar, as to a magnet, and especially to the altar-body of the high priest, for the incense is in the first place a symbol of the Three Energies of his body, billowing up into the bizarre configurations of all primordial energy—"celestial seals"—and thus attracting its divine counterpart, its "other half" into the cave. This explains why the fat stick of incense, burning at three points, must be murmured over by the high priest as follows:

> One stick of incense of the Way and its power
> Goes straight up through the Nine Heavens.
> All the generals and marshals in outer space
> Come down directly into the imperial burner.
> Quickly, quickly, in accord with the order of the living energies of the Great
>   Mystery.

Having thus assured himself of divine assistance, the high priest is ready to begin issuing his orders. He removes the "flame" (*yang*)—a precious stone set in a gold-painted metal halo fixed on a flexible metal stem—from the metal crown on top of his black skullcap, takes up his "five-thunder seal" (cf. plate 24), and prays that "Heaven will not deal lightly with those who go against me":

> The imperial order assists me. I wish to assist you, and you wish to assist me. One [blow to the] table: heaven is clear. Twice to the table: earth is potent. Thrice: the officers and generals reveal their true form forthwith. On the day of merit, your names will be written in Highest Purity.

He stamps the table with his seal three times during this speech.

By this time, the assistants have finished their song, and all call out, "Heavenly Worthy of Constant Purity and Cleanliness." After responsive shouting—the words concern the "coagulating smoke of the precious tripod (the incense burner) forming auspicious clouds in the Realm of the Law" (Ofuchi, 247b)—the high priest adopts the "*ting*-character stance" (cf. Ofuchi, 217a, and plate 24). Facing right, his thunder-seal held firmly in outstretched hands at eye level, he summons the Duke of Thunder, the Count of the Wind, the Master of the Rain, and various marshals (cf. plate 19). Then shifting to face left, he summons the spirit of the nine-phoenix, the generals of his register, and various agents of transmission. He again strikes the table with his seal three times, now to summon the officers of merit of the Three Realms (Ofuchi, 248a), and then he hands the seal to the leader before summoning the local gods. Throughout this summons there is neither music nor percussion, except when all join to call out an occasional word. The priest now replaces his flame in his metal crown. Still without accompaniment, he introduces the second high point of the ritual of Announcement, the dispatch of the documents, with a prose recitation. In this recitation, he gives a summary description of the celestial bureaucracy: the Three Pure Ones, the Jade Emperor, the nine categories of saints and immortals, the sun, the moon, and the Dipper. It is a long road that leads to the purple empyrean:

> Hard to go up there without a phoenix-team or a crane-mount; no way to get there unless you ride the mists and clouds. (Ofuchi, 248b)

As for the immortals of the five peaks and ten caves, the three islands and nine isles, and all the ghosts and gods of the nine springs and the six caves, all gods, from the rulers of the Nine Heavens down to the most humble earth god, all play their part in controlling the changes that occur and all "wield the scepter of fortune and misfortune." Therefore, they must be informed whenever there is an "expression of sincere prayers." There are offices of transmission in the Three Realms, there are masters of time, and their presence too is ardently hoped for. He, the priest, will be using a symbol to make his announcement, and he hopes that they will "come as soon as they hear his call." The ritual is hardly lavish, but they should accept it because of the sincerity of officiants and community alike.

Towards the end of this reading, one begins to hear very tentative snatches from the two-string violin. It now accompanies the high priest as he sings, in a long, drawn-out manner, the title of a song, "Incantatory Hymn of the Golden Light." Like the first great hymn of the Announcement, the song itself will be sung very slowly by the cantor while the high priest carries on the work prescribed in the secret manuals.

Using red ink, he completes the red symbols on two documents called "Symbol-order to Open Heaven" (*k'ai-t'ien fu-ming*; Ofuchi, 409b). One will serve to open the gates of heaven during the Presentation of the Memorial; the other is draped over a two-tiered paper tray piled high with the documents about to be dispatched (plate 24). The text that accompanies the symbol, known already from TT 219 *Tu-jen ta-fa* 41.4b (early thirteenth century), is written in ordinary black ink and calls on the "agent in the symbol" to deal with the "stellar winds," which block communication, and in this way to ensure that "heaven's law" be respected. The priest also completes the red-ink symbol on the "Symbol-order of the General Summons" (*tsung-chao fu-ming;* already in the early thirteenth century TT 547 *Ling-pao yü-chien* 8.3b; Ofuchi, 410a).

When the priest has finished filling in and verifying all three documents, all of which are on large sheets of yellow paper, he folds the general summons diagonally twice and, holding up the resultant lozenge with both hands, turns to face north and recite once again the formula for the transformation of his body (see p. 71). He then turns once on himself and, with his hands still held high, recites the *yang* version of the "unicorn walk incantation" as preparation for the walk itself:

> Heaven and earth are fixed in their places;
> *Yin* and *yang* unite their forms.
> My left agent Li Ang
> Pushes open the Gate of Heaven.
> My right agent Wu Fang
> Reaches the Way and communicates with the perfected.
> To the jade chambers in the Golden Gate
> I now hasten.
> Inside the confines of my fine dust
> I communicate with the perfected and the potent.
> Illumine my body on the inside,
> Protect it on the outside.
> The red infant [newborn] ascends,
> The myriad gods pay heed.
> Quickly, quickly. . . . (Ofuchi, 249b)

Pointing into his left hand to the appropriate points and murmuring at each step the name of one of the seven stars of the Big Dipper, he now performs the "unicorn walk" (see next page; cf. *Hsüan-k'o*, 29, and Ofuchi, 249b). Having "walked the Dipper," the high priest then goes outside to declaim the general summons.

We will follow him there in a moment, but let us first examine what has just happened. We may observe, first of all, that in the early twelfth century texts of the Orthodox Method of the Heart of Heaven, the ultimate sources of the process here described, the walk of the unicorn is done after, not before, the dispatch of documents (Teng, 6.9a). By tracing out the *yang* version, going from north to south, the Orthodox Method priest carried the burning documents up to heaven; by the *yin*

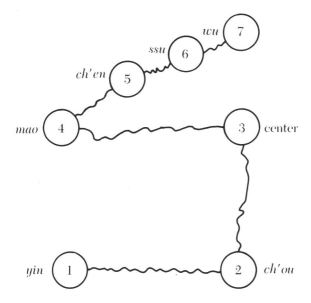

version, he brought back the "response" (cf. Saso, 22). From this we may conclude that the dance is to be seen not as an elaborate exit rite, but rather as an ascension.

According to the incantation which prepares for the walk, the ascension is, in fact, made by the "red infant" within the "confines of my fine dust," that is, within the transformed body of the high priest. Teng Yu-kung's text once again makes this very clear. In his text, the symbol for opening heaven is called "Symbol for Opening the Heart" (6.5b), and it is ingested by the priest, not spread out over the documents to be dispatched, as here. Thus the message comes in the form of primordial energy—the red infant—from the priest's lower belly (*yin*, the trigram *ken*, which corresponds to the right kidney, the Gate of Life) and goes up to his heart (*wu*), that is, the body's heaven. In Teng's text, this "silent audience before the Supreme Emperor" is prepared for by the ingestion of four additional symbols—those of the "Three Pure Ones and the Three Realms" and that for "Putting the Spirits in the Body to Work" (that is, "myriad gods")—and realized by means of a series of visualizations, starting with that of the generals T'ang, Ko, and Chou, who are the message-bearers (Teng, 6.5b-8b).

That something from the early twelfth century procedure does survive in Ch'en's practice may be seen not only from the text of the General Summons that will be discussed next, but also from the fact that he follows up his Dipper walk with the visualization of a message-bearing general (Ofuchi, 249b; *Lung-hu*, 15). Another point made clearly in Teng's text, namely, that the Announcement ritual is essentially a replica of the ritual for the Presentation of the Memorial (Teng 6.9b), is also of some importance for our understanding of the shape of Ch'en's ritual. For it is only in these two rituals that he goes *outside* the temple and then *up* onto a raised structure, a table in the case of the Announcement, a theatrical stage in the case of the Presentation. The Announcement is thus a kind of prefiguration of the Presentation, a preface addressed to the Three Realms as the Presentation is a postface addressed to highest heaven.

Let us now follow Ch'en outside. In front of the table he performs yet another star-walk, called the "Constellation of the Eight Trigrams" (Ofuchi, 250a; *Hsüan-k'o*, 53).

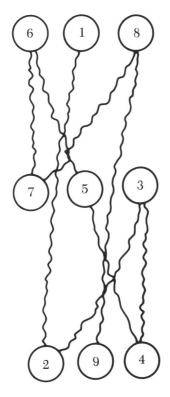

At each step, he murmurs one of the following lines:

1. I carry heaven's generals on my head.
2. I command heaven's soldiers.
3. I sound heaven's drum.
4. I broadcast heaven's voice.
5. I strike heaven's bell.
6. I hurl the flaming chimes.
7. I lay my hand on the astral murderers.
8. I set in motion my primordial essence.

9. Officers and generals of the various bureaus, come quickly to the altar.

The title of this walk in the *Lung-hu* manual (p. 20)—"Constellation for Summoning the Generals"—indicates clearly its function. When he has completed it, the high priest climbs up onto the table and, holding up his five-thunders seal, orders these generals to "hurry and show their real form." "I am on the altar, waiting for an answer." Then at last it is time to declaim the General Summons:

> Jade Purity: announces the alliance with the Three Realms: to control the myriad potentates: summoned by the symbol, they come immediately. As soon as the symbol arrives, it is executed, in accord with *The Book of Summons of Nü-ch'ing*.
>
> General T'ang of the Upper Realm drives out the demons of heaven. General Ko of the Central Realm beheads the fiends of earth. General Chou of the Lower Realm chases away the evil spirits of the waters. Whoever dares disobey will be hailed off to hell. Let the myriad gods pay heed and not dally. The symbol summons the myriad potentates to show their true form forthwith. Here on this altar I am burning incense and sending off the symbol, summoning respectfully the celestial soldiers and generals of the Court of the Celestial Pivot in Highest Purity, the divine soldiers and generals of the Court for the Expulsion of Perversity in the North Pole, the thunder soldiers and generals of the Court of the Five Thunders in the Jade Bureau, the agents in charge of symbols in the Three Realms, the officers of merit in charge of the jade writs of the four temporal units, the gods of the soil and of the walls and moats, and all the sundry gods: join in the alliance of this announcement. Let all the gods come quickly with this symbol and make this announcement with me. Follow the symbol immediately: you must not dawdle.
>
> Order of the Jade Emperor: the bearer of this symbol will execute it in accord with the command. Transmitted by the post of wind and fire. (cf. Ofuchi, 410b)

Dated, stamped, and signed, it is issued, like the two symbols for opening heaven, in the name of Chang Tao-ling, founding master. Clearly, the Announcement is also a renewal of the alliance Chang made with the generals, who know how to put the demons in their place.

The priest now refolds the summons, lights it with a burning yellow paper rolled into the shape of a cone, holds it on three fat sticks of incense until completely burned, and then blows the remains out into the air. Paper money, meanwhile, is set afire in a wok on the ground in order to pay for the transmission. The high priest now takes up his bowl of symbol-water and his seal and calls:

> Symbol-order of the Three Heavens,
> Command the presence of the myriad potentates.
> Let those who obey the symbol live
> And those who disobey die.

> Golden Register, White Account Book:
> Let me live forever.
> Quickly, quickly . . .
> Heavenly Worthy Who Responds as Shadow to Light.

He spins rapidly on himself, writes the word "orders!" in the air with his seal, describes seven circles with it (as he had earlier circled the trigram *li* when filling in the symbol on the General Summons), sprays symbol-water over the wok, and calls: "Celestial energies! Let there be no foul ethers in heaven!" Firecrackers are set off to expel any such ethers, and the high priest goes back inside the temple. The summons is completed.

The entire process, from the filling in of the symbols to the return to the temple, has taken about twelve minutes, more than enough time for the cantor to have finished the "Hymn of the Golden Light":

> Mysterious ancestor of heaven and earth,
> Root of the myriad energies.
> Widely practiced for eons:
> Guarantor of my spirit-communication.
> Within the Three Realms and without,
> I alone am the honored one:
> Its body gives off a golden light
> Which envelops and illumines my person.
> Neither visible to the eyes
> Nor audible to the ears,
> It contains heaven and earth
> And nourishes all life.
> Having sung this ten thousand times
> My body becomes luminous,
> The Three Realms wait upon me,
> The Five Emperors welcome me.
> The myriad gods pay homage before me;
> I put the thunder and lightning to work:
> Demons and fiends lose courage,
> Imps and sprites disappear.
> In it dwells the thunder,
> The thunder god who appears and disappears.
> Universal wisdom interpenetrating,
> The five energies soar on high.
> Golden light, appear quickly:
> Cover and protect the Perfect Man.
> (Ofuchi, 248b)

The best commentary on this hymn comes from instructions for the internal presentation of the memorial given in the early thirteenth century text *The Great Method of Universal Salvation* (TT 219 *Tu-jen ta-fa*). We read there that "without the light of the perfect wisdom of the numinous treasure, it is impossible to destroy the stellar winds" (41.1a). What is this light?—the answer is given (41.7a-b):

The purple chariot turns the axis of the earth, whose white energy, coming from the lower Cinnabar Field, goes straight up into the *ni-huan*. Shortly, it is seen entering the Golden Gate, and then, behold!—ten thousand rays of golden light illumine your body. Next, visualize a light of white jade issuing from the top of your head: it merges with the golden light, they interpenetrate, and then they entirely surround your body, which becomes utterly luminous within and without.

The golden light is thus the light of the "honored one," the "root of the myriad energies": the Heavenly Worthy of the Primordial Beginning. It is by marrying the light of his own incense burner, the Cinnabar Field, to this golden light that the priest achieves the "universal wisdom" which will protect him from the stellar winds as he goes on the "distant journey" to heaven's gates.

Now back in the temple, the high priest turns several times on himself and then, with his seal held high in his right hand, sprays south, and calls out:

> Heaven vast in its purity;
> Earth vast in its potency:
> Order the officers and generals to come
> And show their true form forthwith.
> Quickly, quickly.
>
> (Ofuchi, 250b)

All join, to the sound of gongs: "Heavenly Worthy of the Rapid Descent of the Powers." Again the priest recites alone: "Now I've called you, be gracious enough to come. Take your places at the feast: we have tea and wine." He sings: "Respectfully, we make the first offering." All join in on the refrain as the music picks up:

> The smoke rises from the burner on the Cave-table: flowers spread.
> Incense of non-action of the Way and its power: the altar fills.

This wine is for the generals and soldiers.

The priest reads a brief passage about the proper separation of *yin* and *yang,* the living and the dead, and then an acolyte reads from the memorial. The priest recites again: he is made of "ordinary stuff" and therefore relies on the "most potent" to transmit the announcement for him: hence the offerings. The second offering is for the officers of merit (Ofuchi, 251a).

The cantor calls, "Respectfully, I announce my title," which the high priest does. He then recites a third passage without accompaniment. It describes him as possessing the "mandate of the Emperor and wielding the seal and symbols that empower him to command the various bureaus" of the Three Realms. His job is to announce, theirs to transmit. He calls on the officers of merit to serve as his eyes and ears, to be his legs, for then no region of the universe will be out of his reach: "I pray your cloudy mounts will linger awhile in this fragrant land." The third offering is for the agents of the symbols.

Now at last comes the time for the dispatch of the documents. After a brief introduction read by the high priest, an acolyte declaims the "announcement" (translated p. 65). This is followed by another passage read by the priest without accompaniment: the announcement has been read; now money and horses will "assist its journey through the clouds" (Ofuchi, 251b). May all the powers contribute to its transmission on high to the phoenix-gate, below to the abode of the turtles. When the ritual has been successfully completed, their names will be reported to the Jade Emperor.

A responsive reading recapitulates the role of the agents in charge of the symbols of the Three Realms, who are temporarily to leave the world of men and go up to the Golden Gate to report on the "good deeds" being done so that "all the gods will come to the assembly."

The stack of documents and a paper horseman is given to the community representatives to carry outside. The priest removes his flame, and all go out to dispatch the documents, singing a traditional verse for the burning of paper money. Documents and horsemen are put in a wok, over which the priest sprays symbol-water while holding his seal up on his right (plate 24). Firecrackers are lit at the same time as the documents, and as they burn the high priest pronounces an incantation for the "dispatch of the generals": come down into the flames to fetch the documents and carry them to the offices of heaven, earth, and water; don't be slow; bring any troublemakers ("stellar winds, energy storms") to the Heavenly One at the Northern Peak for punishment; I am waiting here for a response (Ofuchi, 252a).

The priests return to the temple, singing the "precious name" of Chang Tao-ling (Ofuchi, 703a) and weaving in and out in figure-eights as they go. The high priest puts his flame back in as the cantor calls on him one last time to recite his title. One last time he does so, and then kneels to "thank-dismiss" (*hsieh*) the Six Masters of Lung-hu shan and the Four Saints of Wu-tang shan. He rises to recall the purpose of the ritual. An oboe breaks in. All join in increasingly rapid staccato chanting as they send off, one by one, the Saints and Masters. This ends with a responsive verse concerning the same "cloud chariot" mentioned in the invitation part of the ritual (see p. 78):

> The cloud chariot moves on;
> The team of cranes cannot be retained.
> Hereafter when we make an offering,
> Respectfully, we shall invite you again.
> (Ofuchi, 252b)

The four musicians produce a veritable blast of music as the priests turn around and go to the Cave-table on the inner altar. The high priest kneels before it while the leader of the troupe retrieves the crescent burner from the chief of the community representatives. The high priest stands, removes his flame, and presents it with a curtsy. The ritual ends in a flurry of oboes, gongs, and drum as the high priest exits by the same Gate of Heaven through which he had originally entered and goes up before the Three Pure Ones to take respectful leave of them. In two minutes the Invocation will begin.

CHAPTER

7

Sealing the Altar and Nocturnal Invocation

In the program outlined in Chapter 4, which reflects present practice in southern Taiwan, the Altar-sealing and Nocturnal Invocation are performed on the second evening and come after the Land of the Way, performed on that morning. Historically, however, the order has always been the other way around. In the *Wu-shang pi-yao*, for example, a fast consists usually of three rituals performed in the following order: the Nocturnal Invocation, the Walking the Way (*hsing-tao;* that is, Land of the Way), and the Statement of Merit (*yen-kung*). In spite of the gradual proliferation of rituals that occurred in the T'ang and Sung dynasties, and the inevitable redundancies which resulted, this logical order—construction of the altar, followed by its use, and finally the declaration to the Three Officers of the merit obtained by its use—was always followed. It is, moreover, followed to this day in northern Taiwan, and was in southern Taiwan until the beginning of this century, according to Schipper's informants (1975, 11). As our primary interest in this essay is less to give a complete description of actual practice—that would require a full book on each major ritual—than it is to analyze the deep structure of that practice, we will give priority here to the more logical order of traditional practice.

SEALING THE ALTAR

The ritual of Sealing the Altar seals the altar area against demonic disruption so that the altar may be constructed. The oldest extant text of the ritual is associated with the name of Tu Kuang-t'ing (850-933). One version of the ritual is given in Chapter 19 of the early thirteenth century text of Chiang Shu-yü (TT 508), and another, more elaborate version in Chapter 7 of a collection originally compiled by Lü T'ai-ku in 1201 (TT 1126). Both versions, however, clearly derive from a rite described already by Chang Wan-fu (fl. 712) in his "Offering for the True Writs and the Five Methods of the Three Caverns, a Ritual of the Register of the Covenant of Orthodox Unity with the Powers" (TT 1212, *Chiao san-tung chen-wen wu-fa cheng-yi meng-wei lu li-ch'eng yi*, 5a-6a).* The purpose of this rite, to be performed at the beginning of all Offerings, prior to the rite of "entry onto the altar," is to "get rid of all old energies and enrich the true potentates so that within and without communicate in purity and gods and men alike become responsive" (5a).

Lü T'ai-ku (1b) attributes to Tu Kuang-t'ing the statement that the ritual should be done by a "black-capped, red-robed" priest, whom Lü identifies as the chief cantor. Chiang Shu-yü (1a) adds:

> When the invitation of the masters has been completed, a procession to the hymn Hua-hsia goes once around the altar and stops at the Door of Earth. The ritual master stands there while performing the prescribed visualizations. Then he selects a black-capped, red-robed ritual master of Orthodox Unity (*cheng-yi*) to do the altar-sealing ritual. It is also acceptable for the one of High Merit to perform it himself.

Master Ch'en invariably performs this ritual himself, and he performs it in the yellowish-orange Taoist robe (see Appendix A). It is, however,

---

* Chang's offerings were briefer affairs, basically a single ritual, of which the sealing was a rite.

in southern Taiwan, quite unusual for the high priest himself to do the Altar-sealing, and in northern Taiwan, where all Taoists are most insistent on their identification as Orthodox Unity Taoists, it is usually a younger priest, one who has a special reputation for the agility the ritual requires, who seals the altar, and he does so wearing the red robe specified by Tu Kuang-t'ing. The black cap is worn by all Taoists in Taiwan who perform Offerings.

It may be added that the dramatic sequence we shall be describing below, in which the demon, in the form of a tiger, erupts onto the altar to steal the incense burner, appears to be a southern specialty. It has the merit of accentuating still further the exorcistic character of the altar-sealing and thereby making clear why the ritual should be done by Orthodox Unity priests. They have always been closest, among Taoists in general, to the purely exorcistic "redhead" tradition (above, p. 53). Indeed, many of the Taoists of northern Taiwan consider their real work not to be the Offerings done for whole communities but the exorcisms done for individuals. All of this encourages us to look for the origin of the altar-sealing in the "search and summons" (k'ao-chao) rituals which Yüan Miao-tsung identifies as being of Orthodox Unity origin (7.1a). These, in turn, are related in both function and method to the Fast of the Three Sovereigns whose altar as recorded in *Wu-shang pi-yao* was examined in Chapter 3.

The Altar-sealing is embedded in the Nocturnal Invocation, whose introit and purification hymn precede it and whose invocation proper follows it. After the purification procession, the priests, rather than return to their places for the usual presentation of incense, continue to weave in and out, clockwise and counterclockwise, in front of the altar, with the keeper of the incense carrying a small metal incense burner wrapped in paper thick enough to avoid burning the hands. Then the reed mat covering the floor is rolled up by one of the musicians, and the altar area is left to the leader of the troupe. To furious drumming and clanging, he sprays symbol-water out along the blade of the ritual sword, spins on himself, writes—or rather pretends to write—with the sword, sprays again, stabs into the air, leaps across the altar, walks rapidly in a circle, spinning the sword like a baton, takes a mouthful of water, swivels, writes, sprays, stabs, and passes bowl and sword to the master of High Merit.

The high priest, facing south, begins by tapping out the Three Terraces with his right heel. He then performs his own sword dance, during the course of which he sprays both south (earth) and north (heaven; plate 9). This is followed by the "Constellation for Getting Rid of Filth" walk (plate 10):

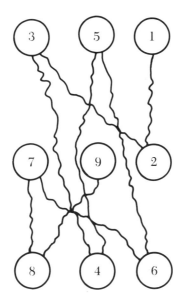

With each step he says one of the following lines:

1. I hold my precious sword, whose name is Dragon Source;
2. Flashing as I unsheathe it, it illumines the Nine Heavens.
3. With the roar of a tiger, it comes through space;
4. It mounts on high to the Great Void.
5. Sun and moon, wind and clouds emerge on either side;
6. Auspicious clouds of energy carry the Eight Immortals.
7. When ordinary mortals see it, calamities disappear;
8. When perverse demons hear it, they go down to the Nine Springs.
9. The Most High gave me these secret instructions:
   Walking the constellation, I circumambulate the altar.
   Heavenly Worthy Who Responds as Shadow to Light.
   (*Hsüan-k'o*, 1; Ofuchi, 283b-284a)

Note that this dance, like the high priest's entry onto the altar in the Fast of the Three Sovereigns, starts in the northeast corner, called here the Road of the Demons (*kuei-lu*), across from the Gate of Man. Prior to each giant step, Master Ch'en points with his sword in the direction he will take next and calls out the appropriate line. From "sun and moon" on, the formula is sung. Afterwards Ch'en circles the altar clockwise and turns several times on himself.

Let us pause a moment to compare this beginning with those recorded by the earlier ritual experts. According to Chang Wan-fu, the priest should start by going to the Door of Earth, "that is, outside the altar" (Lü T'ai-ku, 1a)—Ch'en facing south. There he should "first [use] the sword, and then the water. Each [act] should be separated by three steps—the step of the Three Virtualities—and a prayer." This step would seem to correspond to Master Ch'en's step of the Three Terraces, the use of sword and water to his sword dance and sprayings.

Chang Wan-fu's priest next performs a series of visualizations: visualizations of his Three Masters, in the west; of the generals of the Three Realms of heaven, earth, and water, T'ang (to the left), Ko (to the right), and Chou (in front); of a Real Man, "clad in red, astride a nine-phoenix, and walking the Dipper as it approaches the altar to gather up the filth"; finally, of the seven stars of the Dipper, its bowl covering the officiant's head and its handle pointed forward "without obstructing his vision." The priest then opens his eyes and summons the Four Potentates, after which he adopts the *ting*-character stance and repeats a formula. As the full formula is not given in Chang's text, we will follow that of Lü T'ai-ku (7.3a-b):

> I have summoned the Four Potentates (Chang: "the hundred spirits"), and they have gathered. With the sun at my belt and the moon under my arm, I shall now travel through the nine provinces [i.e., the altar]. The sixteen spirit generals of [the Astral Lord of the Great One] cause the officers of heaven, earth, and the waters to join their forces to mine.

Although what we have seen of Master Ch'en's ritual is quite different from what is recorded in Chang and Lü, the early texts do help us understand Ch'en's ritual, for Ch'en's nine-step "Getting Rid of Filth" walk is clearly related both to the Dipper-walking of the red-robed Real Man astride his nine-phoenix and to the *ting*-step voyage through the "nine provinces." The link becomes even clearer when we see that Ch'en, after completing the "Filth" walk, circles the altar clockwise and then turns several times on himself at the south end of the altar. These concluding turns, which "gather the forces of the Dipper," correspond in sense to the above concluding formula of the early rituals, especially in Chang Wan-fu's version, which affirms "I have summoned the hundred spirits, and they have gathered." Thus, even though the visualizations and the summoning of the Four Potentates have disappeared from Ch'en's ritual, the segment of it examined so far clearly represents the preparatory portion of the Altar-sealing: the gathering of the forces for the attack.

Still at the south end of the altar, Master Ch'en now sprays northward, then turns to face south and says:

My water is not ordinary water: it is the water of the perfect energies of the five dragons. My sword is not an ordinary sword: it is the sword with which the Heavenly Master beheaded the perverse ones; it is hard as steel smelted a hundred times, and it bears [the image of] the Dipper. I control the Dipper; I crouch under its bowl. The living water of the Celestial One penetrates everywhere in the four directions: in purity (i.e., heaven) there is no excess of water; in thickness (earth) there is no surfeit of filth. In heaven it forms the rain and the dew; on earth it produces the springs and the sources. In spring it flows, in winter it congeals; it runs at *k'an* (N) and stops at *ken* (NE). It is round or square, depending on the place; it is cold or warm, depending on the time. Here it is in my bowl: when I spray heaven, heaven becomes pure; when I spray earth, earth becomes potent; when I spray man, he lives forever; when I spray demons, they disappear. One spray: like frost. Two: like snow. Three sprays and four: the hundred perversities are eliminated, malicious demons swept away, and natural catastrophes subside. Long Life of the Southern Dipper; Longevity of Sun and Moon. (Ofuchi, 284a)

This incantation is interrupted several times by clockwise circumambulations (three in all) and sprayings (four, as indicated in the above text; according to Ofuchi, Ch'en sprays the community leaders after saying, "I spray man"). It is followed by a brief formula about the water "spat out by the five dragons."

This segment of Ch'en's ritual appears to be a somewhat corrupted conflation of what we find in the earlier texts. The same long chant and short formula are given in both Chiang Shu-yü (19.2b-3a) and Lü T'ai-ku (7.3b-4b), but in reverse order, and the brief formula is associated, as in the *Lung-hu shan yü-chüeh* (pp. 54-5), with a similar formula for the sword. Furthermore, in their long incantation, before the line on the "water of the perfect energies of the five dragons," the dragons of the five directions are invited, each in turn, "with its symbol in its mouth, to descend with its perfect energies into my water." Chang Wan-fu, by contrast, has these energies enter the priest's own body. Chang mentions four sprayings, but he does so in connection with the water formula—he has no separate formula for the sword—which precedes, as in Chiang and Lü, the invitation of the five dragons. Lü likewise mentions sprayings, but in the context of the long formula, and adds that his authorities—Tu Kuang-t'ing, Yang Chieh (*chin-shih*, 1059), and Chang Shang-ying (1043-1121)—omit the phrases, "I spray heaven, etc."

To return now to Master Ch'en's practice. Still facing south, he calls next on the divinity T'ien-p'eng—one of the Four Saints in texts of the Orthodox Method of the Heart of Heaven—to see to it that no "perverse energies, filth, or foulness" interfere with the proper transmission of the various documents. This formula seems to be a truncated version of a separate rite given only in Lü T'ai-ku's version, where each of the Four Saints in turn is addressed, each in a different corner (7.5a-7a). These incantations, it should be noted, are attributed to an Orthodox Unity text on "search and summons."

Since the chief of the Four Saints is none other than the Somber Warrior (plate 5), it should prove worth our while to enquire here a bit more closely into his place on Ch'en's altar. According to legend, the Somber Warrior is the incarnation of the heraldic animal of the north, the tortoise, and the charge he receives from the Jade Emperor is to "hold the north in place" (TT 775 *Chen-wu pen-chuan* 2b, 3b). At the same time, however, Wu-tang shan, the mountain whose name means the Warrior-is-the-Match (for it) and on which the Somber Warrior practiced the Way for forty-two years before "ascending to heaven in broad daylight" (3b), this mountain, described as an "outpost and assistant of the Central Peak," is located far in the southeast (Liu Tao-ming, 1.1a). It was Yü himself, according to yet another text, who decided to make this mountain which controlled the Door of Earth—the door through which he had first led the waters into the Great Abyss so that they might "return to the Origin" for recycling—the center of the Somber Emperor's cult (TT 958 *Hsüan-t'ien shang-ti ch'i-sheng lu* 1.19b). The same text describes the Somber Warrior as a "transformation of the Celestial One of the Great Yin ☲ , the Five Potent and Somber Elders of the Energy of the Beginning of Anterior Heaven" (1.1b). He therefore lives in the Palace of the True Felicity of the Celestial One (1.11a).

Clearly, the "living water of the Celestial One" which is evoked in Master Ch'en's Altar-sealing is the Somber Warrior's water, as the sword is Chang Tao-ling's. This is why the Altar-sealing and Nocturnal Invocation are preceded by the Invocation of the Masters and Saints who dwell on the two mountains of the outer altar. But, as the fact that the Somber Warrior's mountain is the "outpost of the Central Peak" suggests, the water of the Celestial One, sprayed along the sword of the Heavenly Master, issues from the Central Peak, that is, the Central Worthy. More precisely, it issues from his heart, from the red-robed Real Man (cf. plate 4) of Chang Wan-fu's visualizations, for everything, in Taoist ritual, comes down, in the end, to this One Man.

In Master Ch'en's ritual this One Man, after invoking T'ien-p'eng, proceeds to "clean the dirt of the five directions with water". Turning first toward the northeast, he writes with his sword, sprays, and then sings, "Water cleanses the green filth of the east, the foul odor of plants and trees" (Ofuchi, 284b). Turning toward the southeast, he does the same thing for the south, then goes once around counterclockwise to the northeast corner. Facing southwest, he writes, turns once on himself, and then sprays away the filth of the west. Once again he goes around the altar, first counterclockwise, then clockwise, then turns on himself once in the southeast corner and faces northwest to cleanse the north, and then north to cleanse the center.

The oboes stop, and there is once again only percussion as the high priest turns on himself, goes clockwise once around the altar, ending up on the south side, facing south, to recite a long incantation: the filth of heaven and earth, of the sun and moon, of ghosts and gods, of cadavers, of birds and beasts, cows and horses, all this filth will be eliminated by my "divine water." The four heraldic animals, the Duke of Thunder, the Mother of Lightning, the Count of the Wind, the Master of the Rain—all agents of his body, many of whom are depicted in the paintings hung to form the altar—will disperse the filth on his behalf. They are to carry the message throughout the universe so that all present and everything on the Land of the Way (the altar) will be purified. Make all the oppressors go back where they belong; turn over those who linger to the "perfectly potent lads" of the west for execution: "Heavenly Worthy of the Cleanliness of the Ten Directions."

The priest then concludes the incantation:

> Tell the local god of the soil, who is the most potent of the gods: he communicates with heaven, he penetrates earth; he merges from darkness and enters obscurity. For me he will guard the borders of the altar and execute malicious spirits. On the day of merit, his name will be written in Highest Purity. Heavenly Worthy of the Dragon Spirit Who Holds Things in Place.

This incantation, together with the cleansing of the five directions which precedes it, is clearly related to a formula used by both Chiang Shu-yü (19.3a-4a) and Lü T'ai-ku (7.7a-b), and which Lü prescribes as said in the southeast. It is not without interest that the One Man thus concludes the altar-cleansing by addressing himself to the One Dragon: it is their alliance which constitutes the Covenant of Orthodox Unity (*cheng-yi meng-wei*), and on that alliance depends the peace and prosperity which the present *chiao* ritual is designed to guarantee.

Since the *chiao* ritual is designed to guarantee the peace and prosperity of the community, it too must be protected by the alliance. Master Ch'en, therefore, now asks the "officials of the Offering" to get down on their knees and "receive my orders":

> Your bodies receive the primordial energy;
> On your heads the potent rays arrive.
> The six male spirits of the time cycle stand in waiting on the Real Man;
> The six female spirits follow his agents.
> Perverse demons dare not attack;
> Mountain sprites turn heel and run.
> The water of wisdom and supreme goodness
> Cleanses the filth of your bodies.

> Purified, you enter into non-action;
> Communing with the perfected, you live forever.
> Those who are soaked by the water of the law
> Live long and obtain the distant vision.
> Heavenly Worthy of Extended Life and Added Years.
> (*Lung-hu*, 58; Ofuchi, 284b-285a)

All this is chanted with a rapid rhythmical lilt. The comparable formula in Lü T'ai-ku's text (7.9a) includes the passage on water—"I spray heaven, etc."—Master Ch'en chanted earlier.

The next incantation in Lü's ritual is virtually identical to what Master Ch'en now says, in a voice close to ordinary speech:

> Respectfully, I order you, officials of the Offering, heads of the assembly, and all the faithful: the five viscera and six organs of your body, the seven governors and nine palaces, the skin and the blood vessels, the sinew, the bones, the marrow, and the brain, the nine orifices, the blood, and the energy, the twelve spirit-houses, the three celestial souls on the left, and the seven terrestrial souls on the right, the twenty-four spirits of the three levels and their eight rays, the twelve hundred shadows of the body, the twelve thousand projections, the 360 articulations, the 84,000 pores—let them all receive my spirit-water.
>
> I am the son of the Most High, the grandson of the Original Sovereign. On my head I carry the Three Terraces (Lü, 9b: "the Red Bird"); underfoot I tread the Somber Warrior. To my left I straddle the Green Dragon, on my right I bring the White Tiger to heel. After I shall have freed you from oppression on this day, may your hearts no longer admit perversity, your livers illness, your gall bladders fear, your lungs disturbance, or your stomachs filth; may your eyes no longer suffer dimness, nor your energy interruption. May your whole body be purified, and the myriad perversities leave you unharmed. I have the divine incantation of long life, which will help you overpower the potentates. It goes: "Heavenly potentates, orderly and resplendent, protect me that I may live long. Unity of the Great Mystery, guard my true form. Divine lords of the five organs, stay quiet and content. Quickly, quickly, in accord with the order." Heavenly Worthy of Long Life and the Protection of Destiny. (*Lung-hu*, 58-9: cf. Ofuchi, 285a)

The community representatives are now told to get up and listen to the reading of the "Letter for the Destruction of Filth," one of the white missives rolled up and inserted in a long, flat white envelope. It is addressed to the Nine-phoenix of the South, the General Who Destroys Filth. It asks the general to come down to the altar and cleanse it with incense and the "water of the law of the five planets" (Ofuchi, 413a).

Meanwhile, two pots have been set on the floor in front of the community representatives, one on either side of the burner wrapped in paper that the keeper of the incense had carried during the purification procession at the start of the ritual. The one on the west side contains vinegar: its fumes, breathed in by the community representatives, purifies them within. To the sound of gong and drum the letter which has just been read is rolled up, put back in its envelope, and burned in the pot on the east side. Master Ch'en writes over the burner with his sword, then sprays, first over the incense burner, then over the earthern pot containing the ashes of the letter. He then begins to sing three formulae of purification which, in Lü T'ai-ku's ritual, appear just before the incantations addressed to the Four Saints. They are the formulae for the purification of heaven and earth (said in the southwest, according to Lü), the "pacification" of the god of the soil (NW), and the purification of the altar (NE). As Master Ch'en sings, he walks around the altar and sprays, first northwest, then southwest, and then again northwest. When he has finished, his four assistants, in black robes, lead the community leaders in straddle-stepping over the three pots. Having gone then once around the altar, the acolytes and community representatives retire to the sidelines.

Now occurs the dramatic sequence with the demon-tiger. To furious gonging and drumming, the high priest rushes onto the altar. With bowl and sword in left and right hand respectively, he takes giant steps across the altar, then swivels and sprays north (cf. Lü T'ai-ku, 7.11b-12b). Several strings of firecrackers are set off, and then, to piercing oboes, the devil, barefoot and dressed in tiger-striped rags, rushes from the northeast corner onto the altar. The priest makes way for the demon, who runs from one end of the altar to the other, doing somersaults and looking under the altar hangings, up a foreigner's pants, sniffing, looking, then sniffing some more. Suddenly he smells what he is after, but the smell is so powerful it nearly knocks him over. He snatches up the incense pot and runs away with it.

The high priest comes after him and charges him several times with his sword, nearly running him through. When that proves insufficient, he glowers and sprays at him, and at last succeeds in driving him into the northeast corner. Once again, Chang Tao-ling's successor has won the war with the demons of the Six Heavens and forced them to go back where they came from, and he makes a jaunty circumambulation of the altar to show just how proud he is about it.

Now at last, in Ch'en's ritual as in Lü's, it is time to "seal the borders." Facing east, his sword held high, he calls:

> Now I close off the border to the east. This is the sector of the Heavenly Trunks *chia* and *yi;* it corresponds to the green dragon. Riding the virtue of wood, the year star destroys filth and summons the green lads. Green clouds pile up and fill the vastness of space. Pennants are arrayed in ranks; light illumines the Palace of Fu-sang. Walking like Yü on the Dipper, I tread the palace of *chen* $(\equiv\!\equiv)$. The Road of the Demons in *yin-mao* is closed to traffic.

> Respectfully, I request the Green Emperor of the East, the Green Dragon-lord, the officers in his suite, and the agents of his symbol to mount the perfect energies of the year star of the virtue of wood in the east and descend through space to come near to the altar.

At this point, the high priest turns once on himself counterclockwise and then writes with his sword as he sings:

> Set your symbol to work for me, spread its energy; capture the germs of perversity, drive away demons and evildoers. Do not pardon wrongdoers.

Again he spins on himself counterclockwise, sprays a mouthful of symbol-water eastward, and calls:

> From the east to the southeast corner, I seal the border so that all demons there cease to operate. Quickly, quickly, in accord with the order of the Celestial Lord of the Nine Energies of the East forbidding access to the altar. (*Lung-hu*, 60-1; *Hsüan-k'o*, 5-6; Ofuchi, 285b)

He cries, "Celestial Lord of the Nine Energies of the East" once again and, turning counterclockwise while the oboes play, faces southeast, writes with his sword, sprays, walks to the southeast accompanied by percussion alone, pauses briefly, and then moves to the south. He bows and launches into the incantation for the south (sprays S and SW), then the west (W and NW), the north (N and NE), and the center (N and S). The incantations are an inflated form of the texts given by both Chiang Shu-yü (19.4a-5b) and Lü T'ai-ku (7.12b-14a; Chang Wan-fu, 6a, also mentions these formulae). Their texts, however, read more precisely, "I seal the border from the northeast to the southeast corner," and so on. Lü calls the step the "*ting*-character step"; Chiang calls it, as Ch'en does, the "step of Yü." *The* Step of Yü, we might add: the step by which he saves the world from the flood, that is, from the "obstructed souls," the demons.

The sealing of the altar completed, the high priest swings once around the Cave-table, re-enters the altar area with his sword aloft, and begins to sing:

> I am done now closing off the bounds;
> One more time I'll make the tour of the altar.

He comes around into the center of the altar to sing, first, "I am the Worthy Great One inside the cave" and then, while tapping out with his right foot the Three Terraces (points 1-3), "I carry the Three Terraces on my head." Singing, "I walk on the Four Potentates" he moves to point 4, and then begins to work his way around the altar, starting in the east at *chen* ☳ and ending up in the northeast at *ken* ☶. The pattern of his steps is given below (*Hsüan-k'o*, 11; Ofuchi, 286b):

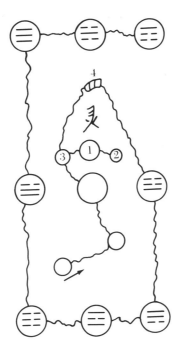

The song Ch'en sings as he makes his way clockwise around the altar to the Gate of Demons shows clearly where he is at each moment:

In the position *chen* (☳) I wield the precious sword:
I do not allow evil energies to rise on the inside or the out.
At the Door of Earth, the palace of *sun* (☴), I must close the border;
By way of *li* (☲) I go quickly straight to *k'un* (☷).
I walk like Yü in the palace of *tui* (☱) and go to *ch'ien* (☰) and *hai;*
From afar I gaze at the Celestial Palace and visit the Imperial Lord.
From *k'an* (☵) and *tzu* I go straight across the top
And arrive at the palace of *ken* (☶) to seal the Gate of the Demons.
(Ofuchi, 286b)

And that is what remains to be done: to seal the Gate of the Demons (cf. Lü T'ai-ku, 7.15a, and Chiang Shu-yü, 19.6a). On the table in the northeast corner, a bucket of rice (a purifying agent) has been placed, and in it is the mask worn but a short while ago by the tiger demon. The bucket symbolizes a "metal well" (cf. DeGroot 1910, 6.1259). The priest begins the process of "fixing" the demon there by writing with his sword the character "demon" in the rice and saying:

> If any perverse demons disobey me, they will be seized, put to the sword, and turned into fine dust. I have received the orders of the Emperor on High of the Primordial Beginning. (Ofuchi, 287a)

He pronounces another formula concerning the "water of earth that flows against the current into prison," and then traps the demon in the rice by drawing with his sword five horizontal and four vertical lines (for a month of 30 days; four horizontal and five vertical lines are used in a month of 29 days):

According to Lü and Chiang, the demon(s) are thus caught between "the stretched-out net of heaven and the web of earth."

The priest now "presses" the demon down in this pit by tracing with his sword a symbol composed of the character for "demon" under that for "mountain" (*Lung-hu*, 66). Then, pronouncing yet another incantation, he "fixes" the demon by planting his sword upright in the rice. After two final incantations, using the "sword gesture," he writes the character "quickly" in his left palm, claps his hands together, stands back, fills his mouth with symbol-water, locks his hands into the "ram gesture," turns on himself counterclockwise, taps out the Three Terraces, and sprays and thrusts at the prison all in one motion.

Three sticks of incense and two candles are planted in the bucket as the priest removes his flame. His seal of authority is added to the weights keeping the demon in (plate 11). There is a peal of oboes as the high priest goes out and a wokful of paper money is set afire in the corner near the bucket. The tiger-demon has been vanquished. Better, he has been "converted" into a guardian of the altar's most vulnerable corner.

NOCTURNAL INVOCATION

With the altar area sealed off against demonic disruption, it is now time to construct the altar itself. The Nocturnal Invocation is the ritual which accomplishes this. As with the altar for the Fast of the three Days of Origin, this is essentially done by placing one of the True Writs in each of the five directions. Taoist priests in southern Taiwan no longer actually write these writs out. Prior to the ritual they set out five pots of rice, each of which contains the "four treasures" of the calligrapher, namely, an inkstone, a brush, a stick of ink, and a pad of paper (plate 12). When it is time to "place the writ" of a direction, the priest whose function puts him in correspondence with that direction simply sings a brief, staccato chant. The implication is that the "masters are being asked to write the True Writ" with the four treasures at their disposal.

The actual placement of these writs is preceded by the planting of three sticks of incense in each of the burners of the five directions, the consecration of the crescent burner, the invitation of the divinities, a prayer of confession, and an expression of homage to the heavenly worthies of the ten directions. Both the incense-planting and the expression of homage are done in procession, the first while singing the Mi-lo fan (see p. 114), accompanied by a tremulous oboe and slow plucking on the mandolin, the second without music. The homage and the double confession which follows are both found also in the Land of the Way ritual.

Then, to emphatic drumming and light percussion, a staccato song is sung describing the emergence of the cosmos from the Three Energies: "Before the jade sounds were broadcast, the celestial writings had not been corrected." At last the energies of heaven congeal sufficiently to form characters ten thousand meters square (Ofuchi, 290a; this text is based on TT 97 *Chu-t'ien nei-yin* 3.2a, where the characters are only one meter square). "They were the quintessential potency of the Three Energies, the very flower of the Five Phases." Further remarks follow, familiar from Six Dynasty texts, concerning the transformation of the five writs into the five planets which stabilize the heavens, the five peaks which stabilize earth, and the "five constant" (virtues) which stabilize man. Hence with them one can "protect the state and bring peace to the family, give support to what is straight and get rid of what is crooked" (Ofuchi, 290b).

Now the writs are placed. This is done in the order east (done facing northeast), south (SE), west (SW), north (NW), and center (N). Each time, the high priest calls out the name of the celestial lord of the energies of the direction. The east has nine energies, the south three, and so on, as shown here:

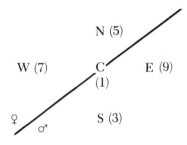

$(S + E) = (N + W)$: $12 + 12 = 24$, the number of "segmental energies" (*chieh-ch'i*) in the year. They are grouped around that which holds them together, the upright "1" of the central pivot, Chang Tao-ling and, by way of "apostolic succession," the present one of High Merit. Note that like the altar for the Fast of the Three Sovereigns, the altar is here viewed as a womb, that is, as a heaven-earth "di-verse" from which emerge all 24 "segmental energies" or "governances." The division of the directions that thus emerge from the celestial center is that of Anterior Heaven.

After the high priest's invocation of the celestial lord, the appropriate priest calls out: we take refuge in "the Celestial Lord of the Old Man" (the Emperor) of the direction. Each priest takes a direction: cantor (E), assistant cantor (S), leader of the troupe (W), keeper of the incense (N), high priest (C). And all five sing the brief, staccato songs which are simply an oral version of the writs themselves. These songs go back to TT 352 *Ch'ih-shu yü-chüeh ching* (1.8a–16a), that is, to the late fourth or early fifth century.

The central writ is placed in the north. The priests then move on around the altar one and a half times while continuing to chant in the same manner used for the texts of the writs:

> When the perfect energies descend at the five cardinal points,
> Ten thousand blessings come spontaneously to welcome them . . .
> The Stabilizing Planet of the Great One:
> (In it) the Three Energies merge to perfection.
> Superior light of the womb-house,
> Mysterious Father, Primordial Mother:
> Give birth to my five organs;
> Hold my essence and spirits in place.
> Having collected the jade sap below,
> Let it go in audience to the *ni-huan* above.
> In the evening refine my seven terrestrial souls;
> In the morning harmonize my three celestial souls.
> On the left command the flower of jade;
> On the right order the spirit of metal.
> Enable me to ascend to immortality,
> To have the gods and potentates do my bidding.

May profit and pleasure be ours forever;
May we soar up into the ten heavens:
We wish to obtain eternal life.

(Ofuchi, 291a-b)

The remainder of the ritual is given over largely to a sequence of hymns like those described in the Land of the Way ritual (see Chapter 8, pp. 126 ff.) and to the dispatch of a message addressed to the Bureau of Correspondence with the Origin of the Nine Heavens and its Heavenly Worthy of the Universal Transformation by the Voice of Thunder. An "announcement" (*kuan*), addressed to the transmitting agents of the "one energy of Anterior Heaven," accompanies the message. The letter's dispatch is also done in much the same manner as the "Presentation of the Message" (*ch'eng-tz'u*) portion of the Land of the Way. The ritual here concludes with the expression of a series of wishes and the "Extinction of the Burner" (again, as in the Land of the Way).

The Nocturnal Invocation as such is now over. There remains, however, a brief ritual action to accomplish: it is a kind of postface, as the earlier invitation of the Four Saints and Six Masters was a preface to the Invocation. The invitation had opened a parenthesis in time; now the dismissal must close it. This is signified by a procession which moves *counter*clockwise around the altar. The priests sing the name of the Heavenly Master as they walk around to the south to "enter the Masters' altar." All kneel, and the cantor reads aloud a summary of the ritual and a final prayer for good fortune while the high priest murmurs a brief confession. They stand up to sing the name of the Somber Emperor the lord of Wu-tang shan, and then kneel for a parallel confession and prayer, read this time by the assistant cantor. They stand and turn, first north and then south, to announce the end of the Invocation.

CHAPTER

8

The Land of the Way

The *tao-ch'ang*, "Land of the Way," is the most important of all the rituals that compose an Offering. It is the ritual for which all of the others exist, around which they are grouped, to which they point. This primacy is no longer as clear as it was in the fifth and sixth centuries when, as already mentioned, a fast consisted in the Nocturnal Invocation, the Walking of the Way (*hsing-tao*), and the Statement of Merit. A long process of ritual proliferation—the Walking of the Way itself came in the Sung dynasty to be repeated as often as nine times—has obscured the centrality of the Land of the Way. Another factor has been the more recent displacement of the ritual to an illogical position on the morning before rather than after the Nocturnal Invocation.

Nonetheless, the Land of the Way clearly remains the central ritual, because it is the ritual in which the high priest goes in audience before the Way. There again, however, changes have occurred which make this less clear than it was originally. Originally, one "walked the Way" in order to go in audience before the Way and present one's "petition" (*chang*). It was, in fact, the only ritual in which such a petition was made. The other two rituals had their own purposes. The Nocturnal Invocation was originally for the swearing in, so to speak, of the officiants, and the "proclamation of the prohibitions" to be observed during the period of the fast; in Sung times it also came to be for the construction of the altar with the five writs. The Statement of Merit, it is true, was for the dispatch of letters, but the letters were sent to the Three Officers, not to the Way. During the modern Land of the Way a message is still sent, to the Three Pure Ones, but the ritual for the Presentation of the Memorial has to some degree supplanted the Land of the Way as the ritual of audience.

But again, we must soften this judgment, for a bit of ritual archaeology will demonstrate that the Land of the Way remains, in spite of modifications, the ritual of all Taoist rituals, the pivotal ritual around which the other rituals revolve and on which, to a large extent, they are modelled. Virtually all the individual rites—introit, purification, incensing, invocation, dispatch, offering—common to the various major rituals are found in the Land of the Way as well, but in a more complete form or in a more precisely defined context. A simple example is the use of a sequence of hymns in the Nocturnal Invocation (see p. 105). Not only is the sequence shorter in the Nocturnal Invocation than in the Land of the Way, its situation in the overall structure of the ritual is not clear. Its basic function, as in the Land of the Way, is to express gratitude to the Three Pure Ones for the central ritual event which has just been accomplished, in the case of the Nocturnal Invocation the placement of the five writs. But as there is still to come in the Invocation a message-dispatch, the sequence also becomes transitional, preparatory. It no longer performs its natural function of celebration and offering.

The message-dispatch itself, moreover, seems like a kind of afterthought in the context of the Nocturnal Invocation. This is true also of the Announcement ritual, to a different effect. When the Announcement is broken down into its component parts, we find the following times: purification (14 minutes), invitation of the saints and masters (17), summons (25), dispatch (14), dismissal of saints and masters (7). The dispatch thus occupies a relatively humble proportion of the ritual to which it nonetheless gives its name. This place is even more palpably secondary when one witnesses the ritual, for the dispatch is, structurally and emotionally, anticlimactic after the three long sequences which precede it. Especially the first and the third rites, with their slow, solemn hymns and the now mysterious, now dramatic action of the high priest which accompanies them, overshadow the dispatch. Finally, insofar as the Announcement remains a ritual of announcement, it is modelled on the ritual of audience, that is, on the Land of the Way.

If we push our analysis far enough, the entire Offering may be seen as a product of the attractive and transformational power of this one model ritual. There is, first of all, the fact that, whether or not the Nocturnal Invocation precedes it, the Land of the Way occurs on the second morning, approximately the central point of the three-day program. And when, as used to be the case, the Nocturnal Invocation does precede it, every ritual that occurs before it points forward to it and every ritual that comes after it refers back to it. This is true not only in terms of the function of the various rituals, it is also true as far as their structure is concerned. Put another way, all the major rituals, as regards their function, point to the central ritual and, as regards their structure, imitate it. We have already seen this to be true of the message-dispatch, which finds its full deployment and justification only in the Land of the Way. It is also true of the hymn sequence which follows the message-dispatch in the Land of the Way.

This sequence may indeed be viewed as the emotional highpoint and center, not just of the Land of the Way, but of the entire Offering. Why? For three reasons: their music, their positioning, and their duration. The entire hymn sequence lasts a good thirty-five minutes, and involves presentation first of incense and then of tea to each of the Three Pure Ones (normally, presentation sequences involve only tea, or only incense, or only wine). Coming immediately after nearly fifteen minutes of the dramatic stepping and spraying and the frantic gonging and drumming for the message-dispatch, the hymn sequence represents a half-hour one might almost say of ritual relief, of relaxation in the midst of the busyness. The constant shifts of rhythm, attention, and action that characterize all the other rituals and the rest of the Land of the Way as well is here suspended.

This impression of relaxation, almost of time stopping, is reinforced not only by the fact that it lasts long and that it comes after, rather than before the dispatching of the message (in contrast with the Nocturnal Invocation), but also by the fact that the same sequence of recitation, procession, and song is repeated three times, with appropriate variations which prevent the reassuringly familiar from becoming monotonous. To all of this must be added the sheer beauty of the hymns. If one tape could somehow be inserted into these pages, it would be of those hymns. All these factors together make of this half-hour sequence a truly privileged moment in the twenty-five hours of ritual that compose an average Offering.

There is yet another way in which the rite of Offering of Incense and Tea (which includes the hymns) clarifies the pivotal role of the ritual of the Land of the Way. As mentioned, the rite pays homage to and thanks the Three Pure Ones, to whom the message of this ritual, and this ritual alone, is addressed. This being so, every other triple presentation—of wine, of incense, of candles—may be seen to be a transformation of this triple presentation, at once deriving from it and pointing toward it. The case of the Division of Lamps is particularly interesting, because its sequence of recitations and songs for the successive presentations of one candle to each of the Three Pure Ones is basically a replica of the triple presentation of incense that forms but an element of the Offering of Incense and Tea. This detached segment of a sequence within the larger ritual of the Land of the Way furnishes the entire substance of the Division of Lamps as well as its function, for its function—to bring new light into the world—is inseparable from its tripartite structure. In a grammatical analogy, the Division of the Lamps may be defined as an adaptation to a specific purpose of one clause of the complex sentence of the Land of the Way.

Two other facts may be adduced to establish this point even more firmly. First, in the Division of the Lamps after the *three* candles have been brought up, all *five* priests take a torch and light the "ten thousand" lamps on the altar. In like manner, the *third* presentation of tea in the Land of the Way involves *three* cups, for the "three give birth to the ten thousand things" through the intermediary of the five elements represented by the five writs of the Nocturnal Invocation.

The second concerns the relationship in the Division of the Lamps between the lighting of the altar and the ritual which follows, the Curtain-raising (see p. 55). This ritual too has a tripartite structure, being essentially a triple presentation of incense to the Three Pure Ones. Its function is to "raise the curtain" on the world of the Way to prepare for the audience to be held the next morning during the Land of the Way. But coming hard on the heels of the lighting of the Altar in which the new light which alone makes the audience possible enters the altar from on high, its presentation of incense in fact stands in the same relationship to the "message" of the candles as does the presentation of incense and tea to the dispatch of the document in the Land of the Way.

For what are the candles but the light of the Three Pure Ones, for which the priest has prayed? And what are the writs of the Nocturnal Invocation but the luminous coagulation of the energies which, before they were five were three, and after they are three become one? And what is the memorial sent to the Three Pure Ones in the Land of the Way but the energies of the community concentrated into the one voice of the high priest who, because he knows the structure of all bodies, knows how to ensure that the communication of the concentrated energies of the community elicit its counterpart, its echo, its "other half" from the body of the Way?

Put another way, the Division of the Lamps/Curtain-raising sequence, together with the Altar-sealing/Nocturnal Invocation which originally occurred on the same evening, represent, as a unit, a mirror-image of the Land of the Way. To the message of the Land of the Way, which goes from the community to the Three Pure Ones, corresponds the message of the prior rituals—first the three candles, then the five writs—from the Three Pure Ones to the community; the thanksgiving in the Land of the Way, involving first three sticks of incense, then five cups of tea, at once repeats the presentation of the Curtain-raising and adds to it one corresponding to the five writs. The Land of the Way, finally, begins with a lengthy purification which corresponds to that of the Altar-sealing. Thus do the deep structures of the rituals which have over time grown up around the Walking of the Way reveal their dependence on the central ritual at the same time that they adumbrate upon and point to it.

It is because of the fundamental importance of the Land of the Way that Master Ch'en, when he was in Paris in the spring of 1977, took it as the subject of his seminar. The description that follows is based primarily on that seminar and on the recording of a live performance, part of a three-day Offering, on the morning of 24 November 1981 at the Palace for the Protection of Perfection (Pao-chen kung) in a suburb of Tainan. The Land of the Way being the only truly self-sufficient and complete ritual, we will describe it from beginning to end. To facilitate matters for the reader, separate headings are given here for the individual rites composing the ritual:

1. Pacing the Void (*pu-hsü*)

2. Purification of the Altar (*ching-t'an*)

3. Entering the Door (*ju-hu*)

4. Invitation of the Masters (*ch'ing-shih*)

5. Consecration of the Burner (*po-lu*)

6. Homage to the Masters (*li-shih*)

7. Incantation for the Protection of the Powers (*wei-ling chou*)

8. Lighting of the Burner (*fa-lu*)

9. Reading of the Memorial; Confession (*ju-yi, ch'an-hui*)

10. Self-introduction and Invitation (*ch'eng fa-wei, shang-ch'i*)

11. Presentation of the Message (*ch'eng-tz'u*)

12. Offering of Incense and Tea (*yün-hsiang chin-ch'a*)

13. Homage to the Ten Directions (*li shih-fang*)

14. Confession (*ch'an-hui*)

15. Presentation of Incense and Tea (*shang-hsiang chin-ch'a*)

16. Final Invocation (*shang-hsieh*)

17. Expression of Wishes (*fa-yüan*)

18. Extinction of the Burner (*fu-lu*)

19. Going Out the Door (*ch'u-hu*)

In the remainder of this chapter, descriptions of the ritual will be augmented by Master Ch'en's own commentaries on the ritual. These will be marked "Notes" and set off from the text.

We begin with Master Ch'en's general comments on the ritual.

Notes: The Land of the Way is "the place where the Way is walked and proclaimed." It is the crucial ritual. It should be done after the Nocturnal Invocation and should be started at dawn ("when the golden cock announces the dawn"). To do it, one must know how to transform one's body, walk the Dipper, and execute ritual. It consists of three prayers and three offerings, a confession, a presentation of the memorial, and a walking the Way. The altar is called the "altar of the nine palaces, the eight trigrams, and the ten directions."

To oboes and the big drum, the community representatives enter the altar area and bow a total of nine times (3 × 3, since they stand up after every third bow). The keeper of the incense first plants a stick of incense in each of the burners around the periphery of the altar and on the two main tables, and then gives a stick to each of the community representatives, of whom there are about a dozen. To their chief he hands the crescent burner. The four assistant priests are dressed in the red Taoist robes, the high priest in the orange one. Under it, he wears his "apron." Now he puts on a necklace of amber beads and plants his flame in his metal crown (see Appendix A). He dresses himself in front of the third of the Three Pure Ones, murmuring a consecratory command over each item as he puts it on (Ofuchi, 241b). Then he goes before the first of the Three and salutes each of them in turn. The music continues as he enters from the Gate of Heaven (NW) with large, stately steps that take him physically to the center of the altar, symbolically to the Gate of Man (SW) or the Door of Earth (SE; see Ofuchi, 218b). There he swats with his court tablet to the right, to the left, turns on his high, boatlike shoes to face the north, and makes a deep bow in that direction. The steady tock-tock of the cantor's wooden drum is heard for the first time, then a blow to the metal bowl of the assistant cantor. The oboes diminish and then stop. Almost simultaneously, the assistant cantor strikes his bowl and the high priest begins a verse of the hymn which starts almost every Taoist ritual and which is therefore appropriately called the introit.

1. Pacing the Void (*pu-hsü*). This section of the ritual takes its name from the type of hymn with which it begins. The hymn, of which a translation follows, serves the function of an introit.

> Perfect incense of the Way and its Power,
> Of non-action and calm, marvellous and solemn
> It fills the Realm of the Law
> And spirals up to highest heaven.
> A sign of good fortune spreading through the realm of the Three Pure Ones,
> It bears within it the smoke of the Nine Energies.
> Golden lads and jade lasses
> Transmit it to the abode of the highest perfected.
>
> (Ofuchi, 271b)

At the beginning of this hymn, the keeper of the incense hands three sticks of incense to the high priest. He places them on his court tablet and murmurs as follows:

> One stick of heart-incense
> For the exclusive worship of the Three Pure Ones.
> Spirals of smoke form seal-characters
> And penetrate the void on high.
> A thousand perfected ones, ten thousand saints
> Come one and all to observe the Court of the Brazier.
> Quickly, quickly, in accord with the order of the
> Heavenly Worthy of the Seal-characters Formed by the Smoke of the Incense.
>
> (Ofuchi, 704b)

He then hands the three sticks to the leader of the troupe for planting in the burner on the Cave-table.

Notes: This is the incense of the three lives, past, present, and future. Incense is the mode of communication with the "other world." The golden lads are acolytes or angels in the heavens who burn incense, while the jade lasses scatter flowers; together they evoke a celestial dance. They transmit our request to the divinities. The high priest begins alone but all five priests sing this song, accompanied by the oboes, minor percussion, and the cantor's drum, but not the big drum, for it is a meditative song. It begins slowly and quietly, and then accelerates as the divinities assemble.

2. Purification of the Altar (*ching-t'an*). The beginning of the rite of purification merges into the last notes of the introit. The invocation, sung by all the priests as they circle the altar, is the brief version of that used in the ritual of Announcement (p. 76). To each of its four-character lines, the high priest adds, in a murmur, the three additional characters of the full version.

> When heaven and earth are spontaneous,
> Foul energies disperse.
> In the dark emptiness of the cave,

The Great Nothingness is luminous.
The mighty gods of the eight directions
Enable me to become spontaneous.
The symbol-orders of the Numinous Treasure
Are announced throughout the Nine Heavens.
Net of heaven, emptiness,
The great mystery of cavernous space:
Behead the myriad perverse spirits,
Slay the demons, trap the wicked.
Divine incantation in the mountain,
Jade writings of the Primordial Beginning:
Sung one time,
It drives off ghosts and lengthens years.
I make the rounds of the five mountains,
The eight seas are all notified.
The demon-kings bow their heads
And stand in waiting by my side.
Filth and danger are swept away,
The energy of the Way endures forever.
(Ofuchi, 704a)

Notes: The leader of the troupe carries in his left hand the bowl of symbol-water, in which have been placed the ashes of a symbol. He holds it with his little finger, index finger, and thumb, which represent the stars above the Big Dipper, a kind of canopy, the Three Terraces (cf. plates 9, 10, 24). The Dipper corresponds to the North Pole, that is, water and the number one. With his right hand he forms the "sword gesture" with his index and middle fingers, between which he holds a small willow branch. He dips it in the water and sprinkles the altar area as they proceed, writing in the air the characters for "one heart." They go once around, clockwise, then do a figure-eight in front of the Cave-table (this maneuver is called a "five-petal plum flower"). The whole procedure is called "making the rounds of the ten directions." The formula ends with an invocation of the Heavenly Worthy Who Commands Demons and Captures Filth.

To this we may add that, earlier, as the priests began the last line of the introit, the assistant cantor had struck his bowl, the drummer had begun to beat the big drum, and the oboes to slow down to a very brief pause just before the end of the introit. For a moment only the big drum and the oboes were heard and then the high priest launched the processional verse. Itself a rather sing-song chant, it is accompanied by the oboes and deliberate, almost obsessive beating on the big drum. The priests are back in their usual positions for the last few lines, and the cantor begins to tap his dry-sounding wooden drum. As the invocation comes to a close, the assistant cantor strikes his bowl once. A brief interlude of oboes and big drum, without the cantor's drum, follows. The assistant cantor then strikes his bowl a second time, bringing all music to a halt. The cantor immediately calls out: "All the Taoists set their hearts in motion, take refuge in the Three Treasures, and sing together." This marks the beginning of the rite of entry.

3. Entering the Door (*ju-hu*). The rite of entry is achieved by song and music.

Notes: Sometimes in the cantor's call the phrase "sing together" is replaced by "extinguish all wayward thoughts." They come down to the same thing, for to sing together, all thought must be extinguished. The four assistant priests now sing the "appellation" (*hao*) of the Jade Emperor while the high priest begins the entry rite. The appellation, called Chart of the Firmament (*Mi-lo fan*), is simultaneously a collection of all the epithets describing the Jade Emperor and a description of heaven. It should be sung to 108 beats on the cantor's wooden drum (= 36 heavenly constellations + 72 earthly "assassins": all the powers of the universe). The entry rite may be summarized as follows: the high priest takes a symbol, his "entry pass," and hands it to the leader of the troupe, who burns it before the Three Pure Ones and blows on it so the ashes scatter. Then he invokes the Heavenly Worthy of the Five Masters. He bows, and all begin to walk slowly clockwise until the high priest arrives in front of the Three Pure Ones. There the keeper of the incense hands him three sticks of incense. He pronounces a formula over them, they are planted in the incense pot, and then the same is done in the east, the west, and the south. When they come back then to the central table, they are at last truly "inside the door" of the altar.

Musically, the Hymn to the Firmament is one of the anthology pieces of the Taoist repertoire. It is announced by several light, rapid taps on the side of the cantor's drum as the cantor finishes the words "sing together." Then there are a few squeaks from the violin, followed by further light taps as the first word is sung, slowly and gutturally. The violin continues to scrape rather tentatively before stopping altogether; the cantor's drum becomes regular and forthright, but still infrequent; an oboe squeals briefly, and then re-enters to stay: by the end of the second word, the song is under way. At the beginning, the oboe will stay close to the voices, both in melody and breathing pauses, but as the song slowly, almost reluctantly, picks up speed, the oboe will gradually be replaced by a mandolin whose plucking, desultory at first, becomes eventually a driving force propelling the song forward. The oboe is free then to weave in and out around the melodic line. At last a single boom comes from the big drum, silent for the nearly eight minutes the song has lasted, and then another, and then a whole string of them, answered by blows to the large gong, as the song then winds down to the halt marked, as always, by the assistant cantor's bowl. The text of this hymn is given here as written out from memory by Ch'en (cf. Ofuchi, 702b; the last four lines, sung facing south, are placed by Ofuchi, 703a, in the *pao-hao*, "precious name" or "appellation," of the Three Officers):

> Highest heaven, net of the Most High;
> Realm of an abundance of mysterious perfection.
> Marvellous, the purple Golden Gate;
> Ethereal, the Palace of Jade Purity.
> Infinity of the highest saints,
> Luminosity streaming out of emptiness.

> Solitude going beyond all ancestry,
> Mysterious chart embracing the universe.
> Profound as the ocean, it is truly the highest Way;
> Vast as the desert, divine communion abounds.
> Great Heavenly Worthy, Emperor of Jade,
> Highest emperor of the somber heavens.
> Three principles of heaven, earth, and water:
> Great emperors of the Three Offices.
> Nine subdivisions of the Three Palaces:
> Great Heavenly Worthy Who Responds.

At the beginning of this hymn, while still standing before the Cave-table, the high priest murmurs:

> Four officers of merit in charge [of the year, the month, the day, and the hour], agents who communicate with the perfected, golden lads in waiting on the incense, jade lasses who transmit messages: on my behalf, inform the orthodox god, treasure of the Way, that we are going in audience this morning, and everything must be heard on high. Quickly, quickly. (Ofuchi, 705a)

Then the high priest hands the entry symbol to the leader; he receives three sticks of incense from their keeper and murmurs over them:

> The three luminaries light up the cave;
> The five masters are equally brilliant.
> Golden lads, jade lasses,
> Pray to the potentates on my behalf;
> Inform them of what is in my heart,
> That it may reach the masters directly.

He hands the sticks to the leader, who plants them in the burner on the Cave-table. The clockwise procession now begins. Up front, before the Three Pure Ones, the priest says:

> Heaven is bright, the air is clear;
> The Three Treasures are equally potent.
> Golden lads, jade lasses,
> Pray to the bright ones on my behalf,
> Inform them of what is in my heart,
> That it may come quickly before the Three Pure Ones.

Having placed three sticks of incense in the pot up front, all proceed to the right central table, the east, where the high priest prays the golden lads and jade lasses to inform the saints; then to the west, again the saints; finally to the south, the "myriad potentates": "Quickly, quickly, in accord with the order of the living energy of the officers of incense."

4. Invitation of the Masters (*ch'ing-shih*). Each of the officiants chants an invitation to one of the Masters.

Notes: "The fact that I can do this ritual is due entirely to my masters, to whom therefore I owe homage, so that I not forget my origins." Five masters are invited: the "original master," who has no distinct personality; the "heavenly master," that is, Chang Tao-ling; the "initiating master," that is, the officiant's master; the "master of registers,"; that is, the master of the initiating master; and the "master of the scriptures," that is, the master of the master of registers.

In actual fact, the Six Masters and Four Saints of the Announcement are all invited (Ofuchi, 272a). To a background of taps on the cantor's drum and plucking on the mandolin, the high priest sings, "All have respectful faith in. . . ." The cantor then sings, without accompaniment, "Perform the Offering, walk the Way," and then, to a soaring sound of oboes, "Respectfully invite the Perfect Lord and Original Master to come down to our altar." The assistant cantor strikes the bowl. The oboes continue as he now invites, with the same phrases, the Heavenly Master. His invitation ends with a blow on the big drum, several taps on the cantor's drum, and one on the bowl, as all bow. The leader of the troupe invites the masters of the scriptures, the registers, and initiation; the big drum and the bowl sound. The keeper of the incense invites the Ritual Master Who Inspects the Fast; the cantor's drum, the big drum, and the bowl sound. The oboes maintain their brilliant flare throughout. Last, the high priest invites the Four Saints: there are several blows on the big drum, taps on the cantor's; the music stops briefly at the striking of the bowl.

As in the Announcement, the invitation is followed by a "cloud chariot" verse sung responsively, with the high priest on his knees (see p. 78). The first and third lines are said rapidly by the high priest without accompaniment; the second and fourth lines are intoned slowly to the accompaniment of the cantor's drum, the big drum, and the gong, and their end is marked by the bowl.

Notes: The bell (that is, the cantor's drum) represents heaven, the stone (the assistant cantor's bowl) earth, and the (big) drum man. They must be "sounded together to welcome the chariot of the saints." Altogether they are struck a total of nine times.

5. Consecration of the Burner (*po-lu*). The high priest stands up, removes his flame, and accepts the crescent burner from the leader of the troupe, who has retrieved it from the chief of the community representatives. While he fumigates his flame over the burner, the cantor sings, unaccompanied, "Ascending the altar of the Land of the Way." To the rhythm and percussion of the "cloud chariot" verse, all then intone, "We light incense and announce." Meanwhile, the high priest murmurs:

> Thanks to the supreme Way of my masters,
> I ascend to enter the formless.

> I practice the teaching received from my masters
> And join in the perfection of the Way.
>
> (Ofuchi, 272a)

Notes: This means the priest is about to "transform his body" (*pien-shen*). At the start of a major ritual, the head of the community must be brought forward to pay his respects and show his sincerity. This is why the high priest, who is interceding on behalf of the community, takes the crescent burner to consecrate it. This burner, with its crescent-shaped handle, represents the moon, and the moon represents the Way. The fire in the burner represents the *yang* within the *yin*. Holding the burner in his right (*yin*) hand, pointing to the appropriate points in his left (*yang*) hand (cf. plate 13), the priest visualizes the addition of a pinch of incense to his own body's burner, the Cinnabar Field, then pulls it all the way up to blow it out and add it to the crescent burner. This is called "expelling the incense" (*po-hsiang*).

A responsive verse which continues the pattern of one line uttered without percussion and one sung with percussion accompanies this consecration (the points on the left hand are given in parenthesis):

> It is with the heart one studies the Way (center, *ssu*);
> The heart relies on the incense for transmission (center, *wu*)
> The hand holds the precious burner (center);
> The heart visualizes the Nine Heavens (*ch'ou, yin*).
> The perfect potentates look down from on high (center),
> Immortal companions approach from both sides (center).
> Enable your servant's announcements (*hsü*, birth date point)
> To go straight to the Three Heavens (*yin, ch'ou*, center, *wu*, and out).

During the recital of the first three lines, the high priest first points in his left hand, then describes a circle with the burner in his right. During the fourth line, he places his left hand on top of the burner and steps forward. At the word "announcements," he brings his left hand back to his hip, points, and "throws" his "birth date" energy on to the burner. He repeats this gesture three times as the acolytes sing the phrase "Three Heavens." The oboes enter during this last line and continue briefly, with percussion and the big drum, after the voices have stopped. The striking of the bowl again signals the end of the rite.

6. Homage to the Masters (*li-shih*). Regular percussion and the big drum accompany the acolytes as they sing, "Let each pay homage to his masters and visualize them as prescribed." This is sung over the high priest's murmur:

> I pray that my masters will carry out their teaching,
> That I may become immortal,
> And that my seven generations of ancestors
> May leave purgatory and ascend to heaven.

Notes: In order "not to forget one's roots," one must evoke one's three masters (of initiation, the register, and the scriptures) by thinking of their personal names.

7. Incantation for the Protection of the Powers (*wei-ling chou*). This verse for this ritual is sung responsively by the two cantors to regular percussion. The big drum enters for several beats in the last line. Each of the eighteen lines is glossed by Master Ch'en's commentary.

The five planets shine.

Notes: This invocation of the planets is linked to the five phases so that they send their agents to protect the priest's body. Here the priest evokes the cycle of "mutual generation" by pressing with his left thumb the points in his left hand corresponding to water, wood, etc., at the same time that he makes one and a quarter turns clockwise. He ends up facing east. This line refers to the action of heaven.

Their light illumines the five directions.

Notes: The priest points out the cycle of mutual conquest while making one and a quarter turns counterclockwise to end up facing north. When he reaches the end of the cycle at earth, he says *hsü, hu, k'o*, sounds of inhaling or exhaling of the Three Energies. This line refers to the response of earth.

The aquatic planet averts catastrophes.

Notes: Thunder from heaven, fire from earth, and drowning by water are the catastrophes; thumb on *k'an* ☵ and facing north.

The virtue of wood brings prosperity.

Notes: The priest moves to east in his hand and with feet, starting with left foot on *yang* days, right on *yin* days, and dragging the other behind. This is the Step of Yü.

The flaming planet douses fires.

Notes: The priest is facing south.

The great white planet repulses [metal] weapons.

Notes: The priest is facing west.

The stabilizing planet holds the others in place.

Notes: He is at the center. At the end of each of the above five directions, he makes the sound of inhaling (for east and south) or exhaling (for west, north, and center), and brings its energy into the appropriate organ; finally, he repeats *hsü, hu, k'o* for the Three Energies.

Family and state are benefited.

Notes: Thumb on Central Palace.

My name is carved on the tablet of jade.

Notes: Thumb on ☱ . The breath work just described gives him the merit that enables him to have his name inscribed on the tablet he holds before him. It serves as a screen, keeping bad breath outside from coming in and vice versa.

I am registered in the Chamber of the Emperor.

Notes: Because he has the register given him at his ordination, his name is on the register of the immortals; touches ☰ , the heavenly palace of the Jade Emperor.

I ride the dispersing rays.

Notes: Thumb on ☴ , the wind; it is used to ride the energy rays from his Cinnabar Field.

I soar up into the great emptiness.

Notes: Thumb on ☱ .

I go in and out of the void.

Notes: Points to *wu*, center, and *ch'ou*, that is, the Three Pure Heavens, ending in Jade Purity.

I wander feasting throughout the universe.

Notes: Points to all ten directions, starting with the NE, then SE, SW, NW, N, E, S, W, above ☳ —the "best place in the body"—and below ☳ . This is "nourishing the energies."

The five clouds lift the covers.

Notes: Of the five viscera. Their energies steam from the cauldron-like organs as clouds issue from the five sacred peaks. These represent the noble energies of the twenty-four governances ruled by the Heavenly Master, of which the Taoists have the charge: "We execute change on behalf of Heaven." It is these energies which enable the priest to command the generals of heaven and their troops. He touches here the five directions in turn and then his birth date point.

I summon the gods and tame the winds.

Notes: Points all the way around his hand once and flicks out from *tzu*. Using his left hand as a "sword"—placed behind the hip, in the "ordering" position—the priest takes the energies of the Three Pure Ones and throws them on the crescent burner, saying, "The Emperor on High orders!" Thus do the energies of the twenty-four governances come out of his burner, the Cinnabar Field.

The myriad potentates do my bidding.

Notes: Points to center and flicks out.

And protect the immortal one.

Notes: Touches birth date point, as it determines the governance to which he—and therefore the altar with which he was invested at the time of his ordination and which he is constructing in the temple—belongs. He absorbs this energy and sends it through his five organs so that the officers and generals will protect his body and the altar.

Visually, the sequence of movements during this incantation looks like this: after the turnings connected with the first two lines, the priest faces north and points in his left hand while describing horizontal circles with the burner in his right. After some time, he turns clockwise until he is once again facing north (lines 3-7). He rolls his hands vertically, then turns his left hand palm upwards to point. Again he describes circles, first with his left, then with his right hand. Finally, he bows, raises his right hand above his head, and draws his birth date energy slowly down past his mouth and along his chest to his lower belly.

According to Master Ch'en, the proper movements associated with lines 3–7 involve not only moving physically to the appropriate direction but also pointing with the thumb in the left hand according to the "method by means of which the five *tzu* return to *keng*." This is done before inhaling or exhaling the energy of the direction. This method of pointing consists in starting at *tzu* and pressing all the points separating, for the east, (*jen-*)*tzu* from (*keng-*)*shen*, (*wu-*)*tzu* from (*keng-*)*yin* for the south, (*chia-*)*tzu* from (*keng-*)*wu* for the west, and (*ping-*)*tzu* from (*keng-*)*ch'en* for the north; for the center, the single point (*keng-*)*tzu* is pressed. For example, the number of points touched for the south will be three because only *chi* separates *wu* from *keng*: the priest will therefore point to (*wu-*)*tzu*, (*chi-*)*ch'ou*, and (*keng-*)*yin* (the priest points only to the Earthly Branches, not the Heavenly Trunks, because the Branches alone have positions in his left hand). In this manner, a number of points equal to the number of "segmental energies" of each direction is pressed for each direction: nine for the east, three for the south, seven for the west, five for the north, and one for the center. Thus do all the newborn babes (*tzu*) return to the womb of the Queen Mother in the west (*keng*). The activation of the energies of the twenty-four governances plus the Unique Energy of the center, followed by their universal "return to the Origin," is what ultimately ensures protection for the high priest.

Master Ch'en performs a more elaborate version of this rite at the beginning of the Orthodox Offering ritual in the *chiao* (Ofuchi, 357a-b). In that ritual for each direction, while the appropriate acolyte sings out its name, the high priest simultaneously points in his left hand according to the system just described and turns to face the relevant corner for the four directions (plus the north for the center). Facing the direction, he presses the corresponding trigram in his left hand and, having made vertical rolling motions either inward or outward with both hands, he makes the gesture of one picking a flower—the "sprouts" of the direction's energies—and inhales or exhales it as the case may be. Then he bows and, before moving on to the next direction, recites one of the verses from the fifth century TT 330 *Chen-wen yao-chieh ching* 6a-7a ("Divine Incantations for the Protection of the Powers of the Five Spontaneous Writs of the Numinous Treasure"). According to Chiang Shu-yü (17.1a-b), this more elaborate version of the incantations found in the Orthodox Offering ritual belongs to the "old method for Walking the Way." Has Ch'en transferred it from the Land of the Way to the Orthodox Offering because the altar must be reconstituted after the outdoor Presentation of the Memorial? because the Orthodox Offering, being at least in part south-oriented like the Announcement, requires fuller purification and protection than the north-oriented Land of the Way? because, in principle, the altar has been hermetically sealed the night before? because, in the Orthodox Offering, it is truly time for all things to return to their Origin?

Whatever the reason or reasons, the titles given the incantations in the fifth century text *Chen-wen yao-chieh ching* make one thing clear: the rite we have just described is a miniature, esoteric version of the Nocturnal Invocation. As the Invocation created the external altar, this rite creates the internal altar, by bringing all things back to their Origin in the One Man.

8. Lighting the Burner (*fa-lu*). The end of the preceding rite is marked by one drum beat and a strike on the bowl. Without music, the cantor sings, "Sound the drum of the law." There are several squeaks from the violin, and then several drum beats as he adds, "Twenty-four times." Meanwhile the high priest, having gritted his teeth $3 \times 8 = 24$ times, visualizes the twenty-four energies rising from his Cinnabar Field to the palaces of the Three Pure Ones and murmurs:

> The celestial potentates are in the Nine Palaces;
> The Great One keeps to his chamber.
> The myriad spirits protect me;
> My celestial and terrestrial souls are in union.
> Leaving clarity to enter mystery,
> My rays blend with those of the sun.
> Long life and distant vision
> Block up and extinguish the perverse and dissolute.
> (Ofuchi, 272b)

Notes: The teeth are divided into three groups of eight, left, right, and center, corresponding to above (celestial bell), below (terrestrial stone), and middle (human drum). Gritting the teeth assembles the spirits of the body. The corporal energy of ordinary people disperses, and their mental (heart) energy diminishes, with the result that the perfect energies (of heaven) no longer respond. That is why they must be gathered together. Gritting the teeth is knocking on the Gate of Heaven (the mouth), and the divine energies respond. While he grits the teeth, the high priest concentrates on them by counting them. The bowl should be struck three times, then the gong, and last the cantor's drum as the cantor finishes singing the rubric.

Now begins the actual lighting of the burner, which takes the form of an invocation of Lao-chün, calling on him to summon forth from the body of the master the spirits named. This invocation is said by the high priest without musical accompaniment. Italicized words are those intoned by all and accompanied by taps on the cantor's drum, one or more big drum beats, and a blow to the bowl. As above, Master Ch'en's comments are given.

Three supreme heavens—

Notes: These are the three Cinnabar Fields of the body.

Mysterious,

Notes: This is the upper field. The priest visualizes a green energy.

Primordial,

Notes: Central field. Yellow.

Original—

Notes: Lower field; white.

Three Energies

Notes: By the union of heaven and earth in our bodies these energies mysteriously take form. The priest touches the corresponding points in his left hand for each energy in addition to visualizing them (going from the upper to the lower field, according to Ofuchi, 272b).

Lord Lao, Most High:

Notes: Touches *wu, ssu,* and *wei*—the uppermost segment of the three central fingers, corresponding to the Three Terraces—and "projects" these energies into the crescent burner he is still holding. (Cf. plate 13; Ofuchi: "he visualizes the Three Energies going to the Lao-chün in his body.")

Summon forth from within your servant's body:

Notes: Touches birth date point and brings its energy into the body. Now the spiritual energies within will begin to take form. As follows:

The officers of merit of the three and the five;

Notes: Ch'ou, yin; moves the burner in a horizontal circle in front of the chest to set its smoke in circulation.

The *agents* of the incense on the left and right;

Notes: Mao, yu: the hands; horizontal movements of the burner.

The bearers of the incense on the left and right of the dragon express and its dragoons;

Notes: Ch'ou, yin: the feet, a dragon and a tiger; horizontal movements of the burner.

The golden lads in charge of the incense;

Notes: Yin.

The jade lasses who transmit what is said;

Notes: Ch'ou.

The keepers of the symbols of the Five Emperors;

Notes: Touches the points corresponding to the five directions.

The agents of the incense in charge today—
In all, thirty-six *individuals, out.*

Notes: Two hands and feet, five organs, six receptacles, three celestial and seven terrestrial souls, the nine orifices: these are the "thirty-six individuals"; the spirit of the heart exits by the mouth, that of the kidneys by the ears, that of the lungs by the nose, that of the liver by the eyes, that of the spleen by the navel; this first part of the burner-lighting is thus a "transformation of the body." The priest touches the Central Palace and *wu* here, and then "throws" onto the burner.

May they go out, each and all properly attired,

Notes: They must be visualized distinctly as civil and military officers exiting in proper ritual attire.

In order to report to the correct god and perfect officer of this district's soil.

Notes: To reconfirm the alliance with the god of the soil, which act is to be visualized; touch *yin, mao, ch'ien,* and *ssu.*

That your servant today, placing himself correctly [before you], burns incense and ascends the altar to walk the Way.

Notes: At the words "your servant today," he points to the birth point and moves burner.

9. Reading of the Memorial (*ju-yi*); Confession (*ch-an-hui*). The burner-lighting is interrupted at this point by a separate rite. The high priest introduces it.

Respectfully, *on behalf of....*

Notes: The assistant cantor now reads the memorial on his knees in front of the Cave-table. It is addressed to the god of the soil, who is to relay it to heaven. The high priest goes up in front of the Three Pure Ones to murmur a confession excusing himself to his spiritual ancestors for the poor quality of his ritual.

A typical memorial has been given in Chapter 5. The confession reads as follows (*Hsüan-k'o*, 39-40; cf. Ofuchi, 300a):

> Your servant [title], acting out his religion, has lit incense and invoked the five masters of the Numinous Treasure, perfect lords without equal, as well as the myriad saints and perfected. . . . I am an ordinary, ignorant person, and I fear I may have, in my laziness, made mistakes in the memorial or gross errors of execution. It may be that my visualizations have not been perfect, or that I have falsified and obscured the intentions [of the community]. I fear I may not realize [my errors] until after the ritual is over, and that I will repeatedly break the canonical code. I can hardly decline responsibility for this, and can only pray for the compassion of the Most High and hope for the kind protection of my masters. Vouchsafe to me your gracious pardon and pour forth your favor in abundance that my sincerity reach its proper destiny. Pray, watch over me as I perform this fast. Your servant, unworthy and inferior, bows low before you to show his gratitude for your supreme graciousness. Respectfully, I say it for you to hear. Heavenly Worthy Who Blots Out Sin and Guilt.

When memorial and confession are completed, the rest of the burner-lighting formula is read:

> May the saints in the purple void and the perfected of the green expanse grant their coveted grace; mysteriously send down help from my own heaven.

Notes: The priest visualizes the saints. "My own heaven" refers to the high priest's heart, the heaven of his own body. The priest touches the birth date point and inhales its energy.

> My sincere intentions have all been confided to the *memorial*. I pray that the living energies, perfect and correct, of the ten directions of the Most High may *flow down into* the body of your servant.

Notes: While the cantor says, "I pray," the priest visualizes the ten colored energies of the directions descending into his mouth and touches, first his birth date point, then, starting in the east, the ten directional points; at the words "body of" he concentrates on his five organs.

> So that the sincere requests of your servant may come quickly *before the throne* of the most perfect, infinitely great Way, the Supreme Saints of the Three Purities, and the Emperor of Highest Heaven, the Great Celestial Worthy and Jade Sovereign of the Golden Gate in the Bright Sky. (Ofuchi, 272b-273a)

Notes: At the word "perfect," the priest touches *wu* and flicks out. "Infinitely" refers to the ancestor of the myriad energies, the source and root of heaven and earth. Before heaven and earth separate is called 'chaos,' when *ch'ien* ☰ and *k'un* ☷ are not yet distinguished. In utter obscurity, before the birth of *yin* and *yang*, of light and dark, of the sun, the moon, and the stars, one energy is coiling within.

The last words, in the Chinese text, are "before the throne," said by all. The assistant cantor strikes the bowl, and then several other supreme divinities are added in the same manner: "*before the saint. . .*," the Great Emperors of the Three Offices, the Heavenly Worthy of Universal Transformation by the Voice of Thunder, the various saints of the Four Courts, and the gods of the temple. The bowl is struck again and, without a break, the cantor's drum and the big drum enter to accompany the cantor's call, "Respectfully, I announce my ritual title." The crescent burner is returned to the community leader (cf. plate 15).

10.   Self-introduction (*ch'eng fa-wei*); Invocation (*shang-ch'i*). The high priest introduces himself to the spirits by his official title.

Notes: The priest's title, composed of $3 \times 9 = 27$ characters, has four distinct segments. The first gives the priest's relative rank (*p'in*) in the celestial bureaucracy. This is "immortal minister of the canonical register of the Covenant of the Orthodox Unity of the Most High with the Powers." This is the second rank from the bottom, just above "Immortal Officer." The second part of the title gives the priest's position (*wei*), "possessing and practicing the ritual methods of the Divine Empyrean." The third is his specific charge (*shih*) or function (*chih*). He is "in charge of the various offices of thunder and lightning, the bureau of the Dipper, and the Celestial Clinic." His function is thus that of healer, fate-calculator, and exorcist.

The priest, who has put his flame back in his crown and stood in most dignified fashion while stating his title, now kneels for the invocation, which he recites rapidly to regular percussion.

Notes: He first invokes nine supreme divinities, namely, the Three Pure Ones, four masters of the constellations and heavenly bodies (the Jade Emperor, the Emperor of Purple Tenuity, and the Celestial Sovereign, all linked to the northern center of the heavens, plus the Emperor Who Protects Life, the Director of Destiny, that is, the sun and the moon together), and two mothers (the Empress of the Earth and the Saintly Mother of the Unique Energy of Primordial Heaven). Next he invokes nine "ancestral energies," the source of transformation, longevity, mystery, good fortune, rain, lightning, thunder, compassion, and the various ritual methods.

This second group of nine appears in the text of the ritual as the Emperor of Long Life (Ch'ang-sheng ta-ti), the Heavenly Worthy of Universal Transformation by the Voice of Thunder, and the Emperors of the Seven Stars of the Divine Empyrean (the Dipper).

At the end of this list, with the big drum adding its presence to the ongoing percussion, all intone, "Come back and illumine." The bowl marks the transition.

Notes: After the high priest invites the eighteen divinities of Anterior Heaven, the cantor invites those of Posterior Heaven, from heaven, earth, the waters, and the mountains (cf. Ofuchi, 273b).

The names of the local gods are usually added to the list given in the manuscript of the ritual. This segment ends like the last, with the call to "come back and illumine."

11.   Presentation of the Message (*ch'eng-tz'u*). Still on his knees, the priest recites the introduction to this part of the ritual. The rapid, light percussion continues throughout. The passage summarizes the capacity to save of "the cloud-seals of the five directions" and "the bright rituals of the Three Caverns." Above they maintain the orderly movement of the stars; below they save the people from disaster. They prolong life and improve fortunes. "Whoever renders a sincere cult is guaranteed an efficacious response." Having had the good fortune of inheriting the way of the Orthodox One, it is the officiant's job to present the desires of the community.

The percussion stops as he sings out, "Respectfully presents." The big drum is struck once, then the bowl, and the priest gets up. Without accompaniment, the cantor sings a couplet, and then the assistant cantor another:

> Majestic is the great chart,
> Magnificent the tradition of the immortals.
> I take refuge in, I cast myself upon
> The supreme Way.
>
> (Ofuchi, 301a)

A strike on the bowl marks the end of each couplet.

There is no break as the high priest calls out, "Let the message be proclaimed in its entirety" (Ofuchi, 301b). One blow is struck on the drum, and then the assistant cantor reads the message, which is simply a brief summary of basic information concerning the Offering: time, place, type, community chiefs, officiant, and duration (Ofuchi, 414a-b).

Notes: Normally a "green writ" is used, that is, the message is written in red, the color of fire, blood, and earth, on green paper, the color of heaven, the liver, and wood: "open the liver, bleed." (The liver corresponds to the east and is therefore associated with the color green.) It should be one foot two inches long from top to bottom, corresponding to the twelve months of the year, and there should be a top margin of three inches for heaven, earth, and man. The top is "pure," the bottom "impure"; the two are heaven and earth.

In practice green paper is used today only when a five-day ritual program is performed, with three audience rituals done on the third day. Then green paper and envelope are used for the Morning Audience, red for the Noon, and black for the Evening Audience. In three-day programs, the ordinary yellow box envelopes (*fang-han*) and letters are used. We have already seen that the message is the only one sent to the Three Pure Ones. While it is being read, the high priest stands before the Heavenly Worthy of the Primordial Beginning. He makes an occasional bow, but he does not make the confession prescribed in the secret manuals.

After the reading of the message, a brief poem is recited responsively without accompaniment:

> Limpid, the correct energies ascend;
> The vital spirit is quiet and respectful.
> All the demons of heaven provide perfect protection,
> And we receive great blessings for generations on end.
> (Ofuchi, 301b)

The cantor sings: "The high priest presents the message as prescribed." The drum sounds once, and then another responsive verse is read out:

> Smoke of the five colors
> Carries the message to heaven.
> Energies of the five colors
> Brings the message to the Emperor.
> Stale energies of the inferior officials
> Must not cause untoward interference.
> Agents of the symbol, officers of merit,
> Transmit it with all due haste.

During this verse, the high priest, who is on his knees and holding the box envelope on a white paper tray, dips a short willow branch or a flower in the symbol-water and sprinkles the envelope. The verse ends with a triple invocation of the "immortal officials who bring the message up to heaven." Cantor's drum, big drum, and gong accompany the end of the third invocation. All yell, "Heyyy!" and the bowl is struck.

Notes: The priest recites rapidly here several phrases from the *Tu-jen ching:*

> My souls are pure;
> My myriad energies are in order.
> I am fearless, I have protection.
> When my merit is complete,
> I will fly off to Great Purity.

The cantor now invites all to "go out and present the message as prescribed." Three priests move around the Cave-table clockwise, the other two counterclockwise. Chanting (in staccato fashion, to drum and gong, and ever more rapidly) their "allegiance to the Three Treasures" (cf. Ofuchi, 301b), they cross paths in front of the triad's portraits, pause briefly for the high priest to bow when he arrives in front of the Heavenly Worthy of the Primordial Beginning, and then move on around to form two small circles in the area between the Cave-table and the community representatives. The two assistant priests on either side continue to turn in these circles while the high priest passes back and forth from one to the other. As one circle turns clockwise and the other counterclockwise, the high priest is in effect doing figure-eights. This motion represents an ascension. They end up facing the Table of the Three Realms.

After a "sword dance" (*wu-chien*) by the troupe leader, done as always to furious gonging and drumming, the high priest takes over from him the sword and the bowl of symbol-water and does the star-walk of the Constellation of the Eight Trigrams (*pa-kua kang*). As he had done the *yang* version of this walk the day before during the Announcement, he now performs the *yin* version:

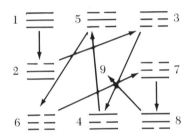

At each step, he says the following:

══ : original, successful, useful, persevering.

══ : gives rise to fierce soldiers.

══ : seals the Gate of Demons.

══ : rides the wheels of fire.

══ : water produces waves.

══ : swallows the axle of earth.

══ : thunder grumbles.

══ : wind moves mountains.

My energies hold the Central Palace in place:
The generals appear in their true form.

(Ofuchi, 249b–250a)°

Notes: Having the reached the Central Palace (9), the priest spins on himself three times, gathering into a ball all the forces of the "constellation," unifying all the spirits of his body, and thus protecting himself.

The high priest now repeats the sword dance of the troupe leader. He first sprays south, then north, and then turns again toward the south, raises his sword, and calls out:

I respectfully summon the ten thousand meters of green in the east, of red in the south. . . Step by step, I line up my essence-soldiers; inch by inch the swords and halberds are aligned: whoever dares transgress my boundaries will be smashed to smithereens by the splitting thunder. Heavenly Worthy Who Responds as Shadow to Light. (*Hsüan-k'o*, 42; cf. Ofuchi, 302a)

Then, to drumming and gonging, he turns to each of the corners in succession (NE, SW, SE, NW), each time stopping to write a symbol with his sword, spray out along its blade, and sing: "Water liberates the ten thousand meters of green in the east," etc.

This sealing and purification completed, he summons the Four Potentates (*chao ssu-ling*), who are the emblematic animals of the four directions. They are summoned in the order east (facing northeast), west (SW), south (SE), north (NW). Facing northeast, for example, he calls:

I respectfully summon the green dragon of the east: it belongs to my liver; it responds to my every thought. Lord of spring in the Palace of Thunder $\equiv\equiv$, it is by nature strong and resolute. It exhales clouds and spews mist; there is no task it cannot accomplish. Fly down, green nebulus: come support me on my left. (Ofuchi, 302a)

All then call out, "Celestial Lord of the Nine Energies of the East."

When the nine energies of the east have been thus summoned to his left, the seven of the west to his right, the three of the south in front of him, and the five of the north behind him, to gonging and drumming he turns to face south and says:

We have respectfully summoned the Four Potentates, and they have assembled as they should: with the sun under the arm and the moon on the back, go throughout the nine provinces and rally the myriad potentates; lead the thirty-six thousand soldiers and generals to do my bidding. Celestial Officer of the Upper Prime, Terrestrial Officer of the Middle

---

*This step is not performed during the Morning Audience (Ofuchi, 302a); the *yin* version will be done again during the Nocturnal Invocation (ibid., 293b), the *yang* version during the Presentation of the Memorial (ibid., 339b). The version performed is determined by the day, odd-numbered (*yang*) or even-numbered (*yin*).

> Prime, Aquatic Officer of the Lower Prime, enter all into this perfect receptacle. (Ofuchi, 340a)

The "perfect receptacle" is the priest's body. Clearly, the Four Potentates summoned, leaders of the entire heavenly host, are comparable if not identical to the four generals with whom Chang Tao-ling made his original covenant. Similarly, the sequence Step of Yü followed by summoning the Four Potentates is equivalent to the priest's entrance onto the celestial level of the altar of the three Days of Origin by passing through first the aquatic and then the terrestrial stage (see pp. 30 ff.). The two comparisons lead to the conclusion that the "perfect receptacle" is the One who made the contract with the four generals.

While the high priest is addressing the Four Potentates, the leader of the troupe has gotten out the paper horse and paper rider who will be the visible bearers of the message. The horse and rider are but a material representation of the energies inside the high priest's body, which are the true messengers. Horse and rider must nonetheless be given wine before they go, and this is what the next rite now acts out. Still facing south, sword in the right hand and bowl in the left, he calls out:

> Divine wind, driving rain: a letter flies to the nine-layered heavens. Racing on the clouds, generals and soldiers cross thousands of miles of stellar winds. Here on the altar it is time to summon [drumming and gonging] the two great marshals Hsieh and Pai who memorialize to the Three Heavens, together with all the immortal officials who will help carry the message on high. Pay heed to my summons, come quickly to the altar. Let the clear wine be respectfully presented. (Ofuchi, 302b)

Once again the gong and the drum sound together as the cantor tells the community representatives to kneel. Their chief is given a wine cup. Then, tapping the bowl with his sword, the high priest begins to chant rhythmically while the leader of the troupe rocks the horse back and forth in imitation of a gallop:

> A beaker full of bamboo leaf wine, the color of a peach ·blossom, it reflects the eyes. With it we make a fragrant offering: our hearts are not devoid of respect. We bow our heads to the military powers and present the first cup of wine.

As the incense keeper pours the wine, the troupe leader calls, "The first cup is for the officer standing by the horse." The horseman is now placed on the horse, and again the high priest chants while the leader rocks:

> Incense burns in the precious tripod; wine overflows the golden cup. When the gods shall have tasted this proof of our sincerity, felicity will gather spontaneously. We bow our heads.

This second cup is for "the officer of merit mounting his horse." The third time, the priest chants:

> Wine has been poured into a hundred pitchers; the three libations have been swallowed. In this manner we show our sincere respect and bring to a conclusion the rite of the triple offering.

The third cup is for "the agent of the symbol as he sets his horse in motion." This time the horse also drinks.

"The triple libation is done," says the high priest. "Now the announcement must be read." The leader of the troupe removes a white writ from a white envelope and declaims it. Issued in the name of the Bureau of the Great Methods of the Numinous Treasure (Ling-pao ta-fa ssu), that is, in the name of the office to which the high priest belongs, it is addressed to the marshals Hsieh and Pai, as well as to the immortal officials carrying the message. It announces the Offering underway and the letter that is being sent to the Court of the Celestial Pivot (T'ien-shu yüan) for transmission to the palace of the Three Treasures. See to its proper transmission! the priest urges (Ofuchi, 415a). According to the *Lung-hu* manual (p. 73), the Court of the Celestial Pivot is to be found just inside the high priest's metal crown, and the Hall of the Three Pure Ones is located in the very center of that Court, at precisely the point of the top of the head and the base of the high priest's flame.

The white writ is now rolled up again and set in the wok on the floor, together with the horseman and the message. Paper money is added, and the whole is set on fire. The priest, gesticulating with his sword, incants over it:

> Celestial potentates, immortal potentates, combat soldiers of the three and the five: soldiers move in response to my seal, generals obey my orders. Officers of transmission, go quickly and return the same way, do not tarry: I await you here on the altar with my sword at the ready. (Ofuchi, 302b)

This incantation ends in drumming and a bit of gonging, and all the priests sing the traditional song that accompanies the burning of paper money (see p. 212).

Notes: In a full ritual at this point, the priest will now "support the petition" (*fu-chang*). First, while the acolytes are singing the Hymn of the Golden Light (see p. 86), he "expels the incense" (*po-hsiang*) three times, once for each of the Three Pure Ones. Next he "transforms his body" into the body of Lao-tzu; as in the Announcement, the aim of this transformation is to "gather his souls" and purify his body. That done, he "walks the Dipper back to the altar," that is, to the Cave-table. There he "gathers the forces of the Dipper," kowtows 3 × 3 = 9 times and then, on his knees with his back arched so as to bring his head close to his knees, in the "position of the turtle" (plate 22), he prepares to bring the message to heaven by exteriorizing his energies and visualizing a voyage to heaven on a chariot. With the leader of the troupe standing on one side of him, holding the crescent burner out to purify his person, and the incense keeper on the other with the sword held in a vase to "kill the turtle," the high priest first makes a confession to Chang Tao-ling for any errors of composition or execution and then visualizes his audience in the capital of the Jade Emperor and his deposit of the message at the Court of the Celestial Pivot. In this "position of the turtle," the high priest "carries 9 on his head and treads on 1; to his left is 3, to his right 7." At the same time, adds Master Ch'en in an apparent contradiction, his head is in ☰ (1) and ☲ (9) is behind him.

According to Schipper (1982, 134), the high priest begins by visualizing a newborn babe (*tzu*) in his lower belly (the Cinnabar Field). Then he shifts his attention to his heart, where the babe has become a Real Man robed in red (cf. plate 4), flanked by two generals. Together the three, followed by a whole host of lesser generals, ascend by way of a twelve-story tower (the trachea) into the mouth (the lower Cinnabar Field of the microcosm of the head, *Lung-hu shan chüeh*, 75), pass through the nose (the middle Cinnabar Field), the gates of the sun and the moon (the eyes), to reach the point between the eyes, which is the third vital center of both the body and the head. Crossing the head, they arrive at last before the Golden Gate, inside the metal crown, at the foot of the flame. When the message presented there by the Red-robed Real Man has been accepted, he and his followers repeat the voyage in reverse. (According to the *Lung-hu* manual, p. 77, Red Robe stops off along the way to visit each of the Immortal Officers of the Three Origins. Is it to report his merit?). "But the voyage to the summit of the universe," concludes Schipper, "has transformed him. He has now the appearance of a venerable elder (*lao*), the Great Lord of Long Life, as he descends slowly to his origin in the Cinnabar Field." Clearly, it is through long practice of this voyage of the spirit that the one of High Merit will achieve at last complete resemblance to the origin and end of his religion: the Human Sovereign, the Old Infant.

But what are we to make of the "position of the turtle"? The complete version of the verse recited by Master Ch'en is found in the *Hsüan-k'o* manual (p. 56):

> He carries the 9 on his head and treads the 1 underfoot;
> To the left is 3, to the right 7.
> 2 and 4 are his shoulders,
> 6 and 8 his feet.
> I (5) dwell in the center:
> The truth is in the belly.

I have included "5" in the translation not to indicate a preferred reading of the text, but to show that the personal pronoun "I" and the numeral "5," homophones in classical Chinese, are interchangeable here. The version in TT 1343 *Tung-chen huang-shu*, a text which may date as far back as the fourth century, supports such a reading: "Five is in the central palace: give priority to a full belly" (3b). The diagram which accompanies the text (4a) arrays these numbers according to the magic square which we have seen is associated with the King Wen arrangement of the trigrams, Posterior Heaven:

4	9	2
3	5	7
8	1	6

This magic square corresponds very well to the content of the verse in the *Hsüan-k'o* manual, but strange to say it corresponds to neither of the dances which in the *Hsüan-k'o* manual accompany the verse (like other "Star-walks" we have dealt with, these magic-square based dances require of the priest that he recite a line of text at each station, from 1 to 9; the book of Lo [*Lo-shu*] and the River Chart [*Ho-t'u*] are the names of a famous pair of magic squares [see Granet 1968]):

Book of Lo (yin)

2	9	4
7	5	3
6	1	8

River Chart (yang)

8	1	6
3	5	7
4	9	2

However, a relationship does emerge if we examine these squares more closely. We see that both involve partial inversions with respect to the King Wen square—the horizontal outside pairs in the Book of Lo are reversed, and the vertical pairs in the River Chart are reversed. In addition, in this pair one square is a total inversion of the other. Might these two diagrams, taken together, not in fact be a recipe for union with the Tao by means of a hierogamy? Like the magic squares of Anterior and Posterior Heaven, their superimposition gives the same sum in each of the nine cells, in this case, 10. This interpretation is at least partially confirmed by the fact that in the *Hsüan-k'o* manual, next to the trigrams of each square are written the corresponding trigrams of the other version. Thus, in the *yin* model, although ꠸ (9) is on top and ꠸ (1) on the bottom, we also read that ꠸ is the head and ꠸ the feet. This is the same juxtaposition as in Ch'en's explanation of the "position of the turtle." To this we may add that the magic square of the *Tung-chen huang-shu* serves as the basis in the earliest period of organized Taoism for a ritual of sexual union and initiation to be found in TT 1294 *Huang-shu kuo-tu yi* (10b).

Some such hypothesis is clearly necessary if we are to explain the strange gesture of the incense keeper putting the sword in a vase, not to mention the even stranger designation of this act as "killing the turtle." What is it to "kill the turtle"? The sexual symbolism of the turtle is well known. The symbolism of the keeper's gesture would seem to be self-evident: he is forcing its phallic head back under its magic carapace and so obliging this master of the breathing practices that lead to longevity to recycle its excited seminal essence—equivalent to ☰, that is, to the message—to repair the brain, that is, to go in audience in the Capital of Jade (cf. below, p. 233, the term "creation in a vase"). Put another way, the keeper holding the sword in the vase is the "true form" of Metal Armor, whose portrait hangs in the outer altar: he is channeling the flood waters of seminal essence via the Metal Gate into the womb of the Queen Mother.

The term "support" in "support the petition" must also be understood in this context. The word *fu,* "support," refers to a prostrate position: does it not occur at the point when the high priest, who has until then only walked on the turtle's back, becomes the turtle itself, that is, becomes the altar? Carrying the message to heaven, putting ☰ in the place of ☷, requires perfect sublimation: killing the turtle.

I would suggest, finally, that it is once more to the myth of Yü that we must turn to find the mythological model of this "death unto self." It will be recalled that before Yü's success in taming the flood had come his father Kun's failure, and Kun had been executed for his ill-advised attempt to use swelling mold to stop up the holes in the earth through which the water was rushing. Need we be any more explicit? Yes: after his execution, Kun fell off Feather Mountain into Feather Abyss, of which he became the spirit. His son Yü, ancestor of the "feathered men" (birdmen, immortals, that is, Taoists), when he does his Step, is walking on his father's back. But when Yü dies, he is "gathered to his fathers," and his tomb, in turn, becomes the altar on which successive generations will "walk the Way." When the high priest "supports the petition," he becomes "one with the Way."

12. Offering of Incense and Tea (*yün-hsiang chin-ch'a*). Now begins the triple sequence of presentations whose function we discussed in the beginning of this chapter. Each of these offerings is composed of the following nine segments: introductory recitation; consecration of the incense; presentation of the incense; announcement of the presentation; expression of wishes; presentation of tea; hymn of completion; hymn to the scriptures; processional hymn. As the ritual actions and music are identical in the three sequences, we will describe completely the first presentation only and note for the second and third the points on which they differ.

a) Introductory Recitation. On his knees, the high priest recites rapidly to light percussion: the court has been cleaned, the altar prepared. Incense and "faith-money" are offered to the perfected from on high. We lay bare our inmost thoughts, we confess our faults. Earnestly, we pray heaven for its blessing. But the saints are far off, hidden in mystery; the light of the Way is in the ethereal void, beyond all imagination. Thus it is by means of fragrant incense that we enter into contact with that light, by pouring out our soul that we communicate. "Great Creator and impartial, turn back your light to shine upon us. . . . We set in motion the first offering of incense" (Ofuchi, 274a).

b) Consecration of the Incense. The priest stands up, and the cantor sings out, "The high priest goes before the master of Jade Purity to present a stick of incense of the Way and its Power." The keeper of the incense meanwhile takes a stick of incense and gives it first to a community representative, who bows with it, and then to the high priest, who does likewise. The mandolin is plucked as the high priest murmurs, "The incense goes to the cloud canopy of green energy and to the palace of Jade Purity, to which it is offered."

c) Presentation of the Incense: the priest bows again and then plants the stick of incense in the main brazier on the Cave-table. He takes a second stick on his tablet, swats with it to the right and to the left, and then bows northward. All five priests then leave their positions to line up facing each other, three—including the high priest—on the west side, two on the east. The high priest bows once and then steps across to the east in five steps, three with the left, two with the right foot. Exaggerated swats with his tablet parallel the movement of his feet. He now turns and bows toward the west, then steps across the altar a second time in the same manner. He turns to face north, bows once, and then walks up front. Before the Heavenly Worthy of the Primordial Beginning, he bows and then murmurs:

> Bright light of the sun of the Way, join your perfection to that of the Way. May all men become compassionate and strangers become one family. (Ofuchi, 274a)

Bowing once again, the high priest then plants the stick of incense. The keeper of the incense shouts, "Wheehh!" as the high priest comes back in front of the Cave-table. With a great swirl of sleeves, all the priests return to their positions—the two on the west and the high priest by turning counterclockwise, the two on the east clockwise.

d) Announcement of the Presentation. The plucking, which has continued throughout the previous segment, now stops, and the bowl is struck. The assistant cantor calls out, "The incense has been brought to the palace of Jade Purity." The cantor adds, "It forms a canopy of clouds, offered—" and the high priest continues, "To the Heavenly Worthy of the Great Net and the Primordial Beginning."

e) Expression of Wishes. All say, "May the smoke of the incense mount straight up—" as rapid, regular percussion begins again. The high priest completes the sentence, "To the palace of Jade Purity of the Great Abundance of High Heaven." All: "An offering—" High priest: To the Heavenly Worthy of the Primordial Beginning, the Great Emperor of the Purple Empyrean, the nine saints of the Cavern of the Perfected (the part of the Taoist canon corresponding to the first of the Three Pure Ones), and all the immortals of Jade Purity. We cast ourselves body, soul, and life-force upon the Great Way (he kneels). May the merit of this incense bring fortune to the reigning emperor (!). May his throne be solidly established, the country prosperous. May he lead the whole earth to pay allegiance to the Way (the first of the Three Treasures).

The very earliest Taoist rituals extant already associate such expression of wishes with the triple presentation of incense that occurs after the reading of the memorial (Lagerwey, 157, 162).

f) Presentation of Tea. The previous recitation ending with a blow on the bowl, the cantor calls out, "The high priest and the chief of the Offering go before the master of Jade Purity to make the first presentation of tea" (Ofuchi, 274b). Drums and oboes break in, there are several blows to the bowl, and a second lining up of the priests. The head of the community has meanwhile been given a laquer tray with a single cup of tea on it (cf. plate 15). He is kneeling. Again the priest steps, west to east first, then east to west. Oboes and deliberate, syncopated drumming cover the time the priest takes to go up front. The community chief moves to the priest's usual place and bows with the cup of tea, which is then brought up to the priest by the keeper of the incense. The priest receives it on his horizontally held tablet, bows, genuflects, and bows again with it, and then the leader of the troupe places it before the scroll of the Heavenly Worthy of the Primordial Beginning (cf. plate 16). There is another "Wheehh!" as the priests run to their places, in two lines facing each other, go through a rapid procession in two little circles, with the high priest turning first counterclockwise with the eastern circle, then clockwise with the western circle. Increasingly rapid drum and oboes mark this return to position musically.

g) Hymn of Completion. As the priests return to their places, the wooden fish of the cantor is heard, and then the bowl. To a peal of oboes, the cantor sings:

> Heaven of the Pure Empyrean, Realm of Jade Purity; congealed perfection of the ancestor of the Way, beyond the realm of forms. Divine energies of the celestial net, most worthy of emperors.

And then, very quickly: "Bright light of the divine rays in the realm of the void." With the oboes still sustaining their brilliant flare, the assistant cantor sings in turn:

> In the myriad heavens, eternity unfolds: going forth from being, we enter into non-being and go in audience before the nine saints. May the Heavenly Worthy descend to this Land of the Way."

And then, uttered quickly by all: "Celestial dragons and ghosts of humans alike cry, 'Felicity!'" High priest: "Great Net!" All: "Heavenly Worthy of the Primordial Beginning." The oboes stop as the last two words are shouted in a drawn-out fashion. There is a burst of percussion, followed by several simultaneous, deliberate blows to drum and gong, and then the oboes break in again for a new song, done to a background of syncopated drumming (in principle, three beats per word).

h) Hymn to the Scriptures. This hymn, which dates back to the early fifth century (TT 344 *Chih-hui pen-yüan ta-chieh ching* 7b) and betrays Buddhist influence, is sung in position:

> Rejoice in the law and take it to wife;
> Love the scriptures like pearls and jade.
> Keep the commandments, control the six passions;
> Meditate on the Way and get rid of all desires.
> Calmly, the correct energies rise;
> With reverence the soul is still.
> All the powers of heaven will respect and protect you,
> And from age to age you will be greatly blessed.
> (Ofuchi, 275a)

Toward the end of this song, all the priests raise their tablets with both hands above the left shoulder, set their left foot forward, and stand half-turned toward the west. After some time, they turn in the same manner to the right, this time with the right foot forward and the tablet above the right shoulder. The song ends with another call of the Heavenly Worthy's name, accompanied by a percussion burst, followed by three deliberate beats of the big drum and the gong. The oboes stop during these three beats, and the priests swat their tablets to the left and to the right and then bow toward the center. All kneel and bow deeply. As soon as the last drum beat has sounded, the high priest begins the processional hymn, sung to light percussion and oboes.

i) Processional Hymn. Three of the priests move clockwise, two counterclockwise around the Cave-table. They cross in front of the Three Pure Ones and pause briefly when the high priest arrives before the Heavenly Worthy of the Primordial Beginning. They then move on, cross in front of the Cave-table, and return to position—the group of three by a counterclockwise movement and the group of two by a clockwise movement. The hymn reads as follows:

> Realm of the Saints of Jade Purity,
> Heavenly Worthy of the Primordial Beginning;
> Worthy of the Numinous Treasure of the Great Way, Star of Jade;
> Most High Lord Lao,
> Heavenly Worthy of the Voice of Thunder which Transforms All;
> All heaven and earth: throw open wide the gateway of mystery.

Toward the end, one hears again the regular beat of the cantor's drum. As the song enters its last line, the bowl is struck, the big drum picks up the rhythm, the bowl is struck once more, and the oboes stop.

This brings to an end the first presentation of incense and tea. The second presentation differs only in details.

a) Introductory Recitation. The second presentation begins with a recitation describing the interdependance of ancestors, living family members, and generations still to come:

> Worried about the sins of the souls in hell, we have done all manner of rituals for their salvation. We pile up a capital of blessings in the other world so that our descendants may be protected. Today we ascend the altar to walk the Way. We set in motion the second pinch of incense.

b) Consecration of the Incense. The assistant cantor sings: "The high priest goes before the master of Highest Purity to present the incense of non-action." The canopy of clouds of Highest Purity is composed of yellow energy (cf. Ofuchi, 233, 234).

c) Presentation of the Incense. The actions are a mirror image of the first time. The high priest swats first left, then right before bowing with the second stick of incense. In the same way, he lines up this time on the east side, facing west, and eventually goes counterclockwise before the Heavenly Worthy of the Numinous Treasure. Having planted the stick of incense, he continues his way counterclockwise around the Cave-table. He returns to his position by circling clockwise with the eastern group; the two assistants on the west return moving counterclockwise.

d) Announcement of the Presentation. This time it is the cantor who calls out, "The incense has been brought to the palace of Highest Purity." It has been offered to the Heavenly Worthy of the Numinous Treasure, Star of Jade (Ofuchi, 275b).

e) Expression of Wishes. May this incense mount to the Palace of the Seven Jewels of the Purple Empyrean in the Capital of Jade, an offering to the Heavenly Worthy and the nine perfected of the Cavern of Mystery. May the merit of this incense fall to the chief of the offering and the seven generations of his ancestors. May they rise up from the dark underworld and mount on high to the bright void. May the sins of many lives be forgiven and the guilt of generations be washed away. May they soar beyond the Three Realms and be refined in the Court of Flowing Fire; let them wander feasting in the lunar forest and nourish their simplicity in the Inn of the Luminous Clouds. May sons and grandsons multiply and prosper. Cause all the relatives, maternal and paternal, to share equally in these blessings. We burn this incense to show our allegiance to the Worthy of the Scriptures (the second of the Three Treasures).

f) Presentation of Tea. This is like the presentation of the incense, except that when the high priest comes back in front of the Cave-table, he turns, first clockwise on the west, then counterclockwise on the east before turning counterclockwise on himself in the center to return to position.

g) Hymn of Completion. The first part of the hymn of completion is sung by the assistant cantor:

> Heaven of Yü's Remains, Realm of the Highest Purity; Chancellor of the Jade Star of the Great Way; perfected who assemble with the Emperor on the Somber Terrace in the Golden Gate.

Quickly: "Dragon stanzas and phoenix seals transmit the scriptural teaching."

The cantor responds:

> Salvation of the Three Sovereigns, distinction of the Five Emperors; greatness of the rituals of the golden book of the Numinous Treasure: may the Heavenly Worthy descend to the Land of the Way.

Quickly: "Dragons of heaven, human ghosts, all are liberated." "Great Saint!" "Heavenly Worthy of the Numinous Treasure!"

h) Hymn to the Scriptures. Toward the end of this song, the priests turn first eastward, then westward before swatting first right, then left. The song reads:

> Abundantly do family and state flourish;
> Greatly does the Way of the scriptures prosper.
> All men of heaven share the desire
> To be borne aloft in the Great Vehicle.
> A heart of compassion creates fields of fortune;
> Gradually, the wheel of the law mounts.
> The seven generations ascend to the Hall of Heaven;
> Myself, I go up to heaven in broad daylight.

i) Processional Hymn. The high priest goes this time with the counterclockwise group; he therefore returns to his position by moving clockwise with the group on the east when they arrive back in front of the Cave-table. The song reads:*

> The eighth generation after Chang Liang produced a sage:
> While walking in the high mountains, he encountered Lord Lao,
> Who transmitted symbols and registers and started the schools of the Way
>   and the Methods:
> Dragon-Tiger Mountain ensures an eternal spring.

(cf. Ofuchi, 276a)

The sage in the eighth generation after Chang Liang, who had himself received from Lord Lao a revelation linked to the rise of the Han dynasty (Seidel 1978, 148), is Chang Tao-ling. Thus are thrown together in the context of the second—central, yellow—presentation the fortunes of the family, the salvation of its dead, and the scriptural and ritual traditions of both the Heavenly Masters and the Numinous Treasure. Once again, the basis for these amalgamations is to be found in the fifth century Numinous Treasure texts (Lagerwey, 25).

The third presentation again differs in some emphases from the other two.

a) Introductory Recitation. The third presentation begins with a recitation attributing the "birth of all that exists" to the divisions of the "unique energy" (*yi-ch'i*). It sets the five phases in motion, it transforms and nourishes; it sets the three luminaries in the sky to shine down upon the earth. Country and family alike look up to the saints and the perfected for help. Peace and prosperity are entirely dependent on the "originating work of the Great Way."

b) Consecration of the incense. The leader of the troupe sings: "The high priest goes before the master of Great Purity to present the incense of purity and quietude." The cloud canopy of Great Purity is composed of white energy.

c) Presentation of the Incense. The high priest bows three times before handing the first stick of incense to the leader. The second stick is handled like the second stick for the first Heavenly Worthy except that it is planted before the Heavenly Worthy of the Way and its Power.

d) Announcement of the Presentation. The keeper of the incense announces that "the incense has been brought to the palace of Great Purity." It has been offered to the Five Potentates of the Somber Lord Lao, that is, to the third member of the Taoist triad in its manifestation as the five emperors who control the five phases. An offspring of the first two Pure Ones, the third Pure One produces within its western (white) womb the five energies which give spatio-temporal coherence to the transformations of the ten thousand things.

---

* The Morning Audience hymns to the second and third Heavenly Worthies sometimes replace this hymn and the processional hymn of the third presentation (thus my recording of 12 November 1983; cf. Ofuchi, 305a, 306a).

e) Expression of Wishes. May this incense mount to the palace of the Great Ultimate in Great Purity, an offering to the Heavenly Worthy of Metal Heaven, the Great Emperor of the Purple Empyrean, and the nine immortals of the Cavern of the Gods. May the merit of this incense fall to the chief of the Offering and the entire community.

> May they be marked down for long life on the green records, for increased blessings in the golden file. May the true lords of the Nine Heavens bestow their blessings, and the potent light of the Three Realms shine upon them. May purity and fortune dwell within their gates, and may their descendants be numerous and prosperous. Turn misfortune aside before it springs up; blot out all trace of their transgressions. May the dragon god where they dwell stay quietly in his place, and the perverse demons on all sides disappear. (Ofuchi, 276a-b)

This incense is addressed to the Worthy of the Masters, the third of the Three Treasures.

f) Presentation of Tea. In accord with the links between the three and the five announced in the introductory recitation of this presentation, cups three to five are presented now (plate 15; the first two were offered in the earlier presentations.) These now are offered the first to the Heavenly Worthy of the Way and its Power, the second to the Jade Emperor, and the last to the Great Emperor of the Purple Empyrean (plate 16). The movements are identical to those for the first presentation of tea.

g) Hymn of Completion. The leader of the troupe sings:

> Heaven of Great Redness, Office of the Great Purity, in charge of the Worthy of the Somber Prime of the Way and its Power: when you first sent down your energies, divided your body, and responded to the transformations—

Quickly: "—you established a teaching in accord with the needs of the time and became the chief of the immortals."

The keeper of the incense adds:

> Master of emperors, father of the Confucians and the Buddhists, you are the world's bridge and ford, you are the road to long life. May the Heavenly Worthy descend to the Land of the Way.

Quickly: "Dragons of heaven and human ghosts, all will be saved." "Great Saint!" "Heavenly Worthy of the Way and its Power!"

h) Hymn to the Scriptures. The hymn is sung much more slowly than during the first two presentations.

> The Great Way penetrates the somber void:
> Every thought there produces an opening.
> Refine the substance, ascend to immortality,

And form the body of an impenetrable one.
Transcend the hardships of the Three Realms;
There is release from the five sufferings of hell.
Let all return to the scriptures of the Most High
And in silent meditation, bow the head and pay respects.

Early in the hymn, the high priest alone faces the left, then turns to the right, and then all set out on the procession normally associated with the processional hymn (the high priest moves clockwise). Procession and song advance slowly together, one word per step. Back in position for the second half of the song, the priests sing it quickly while the high priest poses once more with his tablet aloft, but this time first toward the right, then the left, and then again the right. At last, to gonging, he kneels and bows deeply. The others remain standing, but also bow deeply. The music stops momentarily, and all call three times, "Long life." The oboes enter, and the priests proceed again in two groups—the high priest moving clockwise, as before—for the final hymn, which is done more rapidly, as if rushing to the conclusion.

i) Processional Hymn. This is the last hymn of the Offering of Incense and Tea.

The Somber Emperor was born on the third day of the third month;
For forty-two years he practiced
On Wu-tang shan,
Then mounted in broad daylight to heaven.
He anchors the northern sector;
The fruit of the Way comes quickly to maturity.

As the second presentation was associated with Lung-hu shan and Chang Tao-ling, so the third is with the Somber Emperor (=Warrior) and Wu-tang shan. In the end, there is only the Way, the high priest, and his four acolytes; or the Way, the high priest, and his four limbs, that is, the four most potent animals in the war on the forces of darkness. The triple presentation of incense and tea after the Walking of the Way, after the dispatch of the message to the Three Treasures, proves to be a veritable summary of Taoist history and a synthesis of Taoist doctrine. The Three Treasures = the Three Caverns = the Three Energies = the Three Purities = the Way, the Heavenly Master, and his four generals.

13. Homage to the Ten Directions (*li shih-fang*). The hymn of the last procession winds down as the priests return to position. The bowl is struck, and the high priest sings, without accompaniment, "Everyone reverent!" As he sings this, the priests begin once more a clockwise circumambulation of the altar. They arrive in the east as the cantor sings, "We make reverent obeissance before the infinity of the heavenly worthies of the Numinous Treasure of the Most High in the east, within

the heavens of its nine supreme energies" (Ofuchi, 306a). They move rapidly on, the assistant cantor singing the homage in the south (three of the "segmental energies"), the leader of the troupe in the west (7), the incense keeper in the north (5), and then each in turn again for the four corners ("cosmic energies," *fan-ch'i*), starting in the northeast. Finally, the high priest sings in front of the Heavenly Worthy of the Primordial Beginning, "to the infinity of the heavenly worthies of the Numinous Treasure of the Most High of the upper direction, within the heavens of its single supreme energy."

Then, to frantic gonging, drumming, and oboes, the priests begin to rush around the altar, clockwise, counterclockwise, describing figure-eights and circles, weaving in and out diagonally across the altar. After nearly two minutes of this, the oboes stop, and there is only gonging and drumming for a moment as all face south while the cantor sings a homage to the heavenly worthies of the lower direction's eleven energies. The priests return to their positions around the Cave-table and, without accompaniment, sing together this summary:

> We cast ourselves upon the heavenly worthies of the numinous treasure of the ten directions, the green east, white west, red south, obscure north, four corners, above, and below, and on all the gods, immortals, and potent officials of the ten directions in the heavens of the cosmic energies of the five potentates of the five directions. (Ofuchi, 277a)

Thus there are not four but five potentates:

$$3$$
$$9\ 1\ 7$$
$$5$$

that is, four acolytes + one Real Man. For "of all beings in the universe, man is the most potent," say the religious texts, and of all men the Real Man is most potent because he has inherited the Unique Energy of celestial origin. As for the ideal altar of the "eight trigrams, nine palaces, and ten directions," it proves itself to be an altar of $4 \times 2 = 8$ directions (trigrams) + 1 (above) = 9 heavens (or palaces) + 1 (below) = 1(0). There are, thus, two Ones, the inner and the outer Ones, the One of the top (NW) and the One of the bottom (SE: above, p. 36): the high priest and the cantor. Taoist ritual is the product (3) of their union (1).

14. Confession (*ch'an-hui*). In a sing-song manner the cantor calls out, "It is meet that the high priest make obeisance. By burning incense, we show our sincerity. Assistant cantor, confess." The bowl is struck, and then the assistant cantor recites the confession to regular percussion: Body, soul, and life-force, we turn to the Three Pure Ones, the perfected of the ten directions, and all the divinities here present. We pray for the Way's compassion, that it may shine its light upon us. It has revealed the means of salvation; according to the sacred scriptures, all who hold an

assembly to worship the Way must be perfectly sincere and confess any errors they commit. Here today we are worshipping the Way and preparing a banquet of thanksgiving, to "plant happiness" for the chief of the feast. He prepared this pure feast to thank the Way for its gracious blessings and to pray for protection and peace, for long life and happiness. We think now again of all the sins of omission and commission, throughout all our lives down to this present one, the sins of body, mind, and the passions, for which we have not confessed. Here then, on this carefully prepared altar of the spirits, this mat of the law arranged with earnestness, we rely on the concentrated expression of our sincerity to reach the perfected and cause them to be our witness: we pray our sins may be blotted out and our blessings increased; we pray for long life, abundant progeny, and peace. For all this we are dependent on the grace of the Great Way and the assistance of the gods on high. Cause all our ancestors to ascend directly to the Palace of the South; let myriad blessings be the lot of our descendants. May all misfortune hereafter sink into the earth, and fortune rise on all sides. We bow our heads in thanks to the most perfect Three Treasures (Ofuchi, 277a).

This voiced confession is paralleled by the internal confession of the high priest (Ofuchi, 277b), who is bowed deeply and on his knees throughout. He first identifies himself, then the feast. He asks forgiveness for himself and his fellow priests for any errors in dress, attitude, or execution, whether in the recitation, the singing, the visualizations, the murmurs, or the documents. "I fear the Three Officers will move their brushes and the Great One deliver documents [against me]." Therefore, I now confess all our many faults, hidden or not, and pray they may be forgiven. I beseech the pardon of the Great Way: dissipate my fears; deliver us from temptation; enable us to practice perfection successfully. Forgive our ignorance, grant us blessings. May the light of the Way shine brightly, the wheel of the Law never cease to turn. May the doors of this temple be open to prosperity, its brazier in constant use. Release those on the three paths who are still paying their debts; let the seven generations ascend to heaven, and blessings be showered on the living and the dead. May all sentient beings arrive on the Way's shore. May all the potent officers, the emissaries of the day, the officers of my register, the gods of the walls and of the soil, and all those sent to observe the feast, the god of destiny and of the year star wait reverently on the saint's chariot and transmit our sincere desires: they will be rewarded and promoted on the day for the announcement of merit. Grant your boundless protection, take care of your people forever. I also pray that the leader of this feast may be blessed, that young and old may receive your grace. Truly I have been limitlessly blessed by the Most High, who is the guarantor of the sincerity of my confession. I bow my head and strike my forehead on the ground to ask forgiveness. Heavenly Worthy Who Blots Out Sin and Guilt.

15. Presentation of Incense and Tea (*shang-hsiang chin-ch'a*). Three blows to the bowl mark the end of the confession. Without music or percussion of any kind, the high priest invokes the Emperor of the Jade Capital, the perfected of the Golden Gate, the astral lords on high, and all the powers and potentates of earth, and of this Offering in particular, to "vouchsafe to us your grace; without reserve, we cast ourselves upon you." He implores the Emperor to "ascend his precious throne." There is clanging of cymbals, and all call out, "We present tea and incense." Bowl. High priest: "On top of K'un-lun there is the Tortoise Tower." Cymbals. All: "Scatter a forest of flowers." "The marvellous flowers on that terrace bloom in all seasons." "Filling the Land of the Way." "Exalted perfect ones." "We offer" (Ofuchi, 278a). Thus, in the end, do we return to the paradise of of the Western Queen Mother.

The high priest sings, "Let all be reverent!" Together, cantor and assistant cantor say three times: "Let all be reverent, bow, and pay homage—," to which the high priest makes three different responses. The first time, he says, "To the marvellous Way of the Jade Capital," the second time, "To the perfect scriptures of dragon stanzas and phoenix seals," and, finally,"To the ancestral teachers of our tradition," that is to say, a homage to the Three Treasures one last time. All this is punctuated by cymbals, but is otherwise without percussion or musical accompaniment.

16. Final Invocation (*shang-hsieh*). The cantor's drum enters, the bowl is struck, and the cantor sings out, "Again announce your ritual rank." This the priest does, and then kneels for the final invocation of the Three Pure Ones, the astral gods, and all the powers of earth, the seas, and the mountains. The recitation, done to light percussion, summarizes once more the religious history of the cosmos: from the "emptiness of the marvellous Way" came forth the "unique energy," and from it the heavens, the earth, and man. Further diffusion of the energy of the Way gave rise naturally to the many gods and myriad things. The means of salvation were revealed; the "officers of the darkness were set up in the Northern Court, the registers of life placed in the Southern Palace." Earth and the waters shared authority over inspection; heaven was filled with immortals: thus were proper distinctions made between rewards and punishments so that evil might be uprooted and all life saved. The function of the priest, who has received the rules and a register, is to "proclaim the Way and transform men." If his requests are made with sincerity, he is sure to evoke a response.

The rest of the recitation refers to the chief of the community representatives, the *chiao-chu* ("head of the offering"), who has asked him sincerely to prepare the offering. The priest prays for the attention of the gods: grant your abundant blessings to him; forgive his sins. "May the merit of his accumulated good deeds be noted down in the Green Register of the Blossoming East and the words 'long life' be written in the Cinnabar Book of the Southern Extremity." Save his ancestors; cause his descendents to prosper. May the dragon god protect them so that they dwell in peace. And let the birds of the air and the fish of the sea, all that lives and grows, plants and animals alike, be blessed with life and nourishment. We are utterly dependent on the order of heaven and earth, on the light of sun and moon. "Let the nation be prosperous and the wheel of the law roll on, so that the great compassion of the Heavenly Worthy be manifest on high and our sincere worship be encouraged here below. Hear our earnest prayer" (Ofuchi, 278a).

Thus does the final recitation summarize what we may call salvation history and express the wish for universal salvation that is embedded in the very origin and structure of the Taoist universe. The function of the recitation is to recapitulate what has been accomplished, and thereby to thank-dismiss (*hsieh*) the gods.

17. Expression of Wishes (*fa-yüan*). The light percussion goes on without a stop; only the striking of the bowl indicates the transition to this new segment of the ritual, which is in fact a prolongation and summary of the preceding invocation. It is composed of twelve "wishes" recited alternately in sets of two by the two cantors: may heaven and earth be bright, the weather good; may saints and men live forever, and the whole world be well ordered; may heaven send down sweet dew, and auspicious vapors billow forth from the earth; may the four seasons come in their time, and all things come to fruition; may families be blessed with many filial children, and the country with talented ministers; may the officers of the Offering reap blessings, and the students of the Way become immortal.

18. Extinction of the Burner (*fu-lu*). The bowl is struck, and the cantor sings alone, without accompaniment, "Concentrate the spirit and put out the brazier." The priest meanwhile has gotten up and removed his flame and has been handed the crescent burner. Now he murmurs:

> Originally, the heart was one, and in it there was nothing: why should events disturb it? If one holds on to this mystery in action and at rest, how can goings out and comings in upset me? Quickly, quickly, in accord with the order of the living energy of the Great Mystery. (Ofuchi, 278b)

Then the high priest sings out, "Agents of the incense," and all add, "Lords of the dragon on the left and the tiger on the right." Still without musical accompaniment, the high priest half-recites, half-sings the remainder of the formula: may the potent officials in charge of the incense cause this Land of the Way to "yield golden liquors and mushrooms of green and red," that is, the nourishment of immortals. May the "hundred potentates meet and mingle in the incense burner of this Cave-table." All join in on the word "incense burner," the drum is struck once and then the bowl, and all say, "We pray." The high priest prays (with the words in parenthesis said by all): [we pray] that the Way grant its protection to the officials of the Offering; may they "receive pure blessings." May the immortal lads and jade lasses transmit my prayers directly to the Three Pure Ones of the Infinite Way of the Most High, the Jade Emperor of the Golden Gate ("before his throne"), the Heavenly Worthy of Universal Transformation by the Voice of Thunder ("before the Way"), the Great Emperors of the Three Offices ("before the saints"), the saints of the Four Courts of the Land of the Way ("before the saints"), and the god of this temple ("before the burner"). While the assistants are saying "before the burner," the high priest murmurs:

> The One Body is empty, silent: what goes out? what goes in? By means of my ritual, both inhaling and exhaling become inhaling. Quickly, quickly, according to the order of the living energies of the Great Mystery.

Finally, the high priest says three times, "Sets in Motion," and the others add, "Heavenly Worthy of the Marvellous Way" (Ofuchi, 279a).

19. Going Out the Door (*ch'u-hu*). The high priest hands the crescent burner to an acolyte, puts his flame back in his metal crown, and murmurs the "exit formula":

> I expel the *yin* and bring in the *yang*, and the myriad gods are fully deployed. I have done announcing and praying: pray, shut now the Yellow Chamber. Jade lasses who stand in waiting in the oratory, open the palace of the soul to the light. Quickly, quickly. (Ofuchi, 705b)

He then hands a symbol, his "exit pass," to the keeper of the incense, who burns it.

In the meanwhile, the cantor has launched the sing-song chanting of a short version of the appellation of Chang Tao-ling. Once the high priest has finished his exit formula, all set out on a final tour of the altar, chanting and moving counterclockwise. They pause when they arrive before the Three Pure Ones, and pause again, for a longer time, in a V-formation before the Table of the Three Realms: as in the Nocturnal Invocation, they are taking leave of the Saints and Masters.

They return to the Cave-table, where the high priest kneels briefly, and all express their "allegiance to the Supreme Way. . . . We pray for protection and peace, prosperity, and longevity. May we obtain eternal life" (Ofuchi, 279a). The high priest then stands to write with symbol-water, first toward the north, then toward the south, while all half-sing, half-chant the verse for the burning of paper money (see p. 212). Oboes and the cantor's drum are added to the increasingly frantic gonging and drumming. The music stops, and all return to the Cave-table, where the high priest bows, with his flame in his hands. There is a call and a response to the effect that the "Land of the Way is done." The priest straightens up, and to furious drumming and gonging, and to a great blast of oboes, steps with his flame in his hands between the other priests, who have fallen into two lines facing each other on the east and west sides of the altar. He steps his way up before the Three Pure Ones, puts his flame back in the metal crown, bows, plants his court tablet in the bucket of rice in front of the Heavenly Worthy of the Primordial Beginning, and then puts his flame in with it. With a swirl of sleeves, the four acolytes exit behind him. There is a final drum roll, with the gong, but without the oboes. The drum stops, there is a last blow to a higher-pitched gong, and the Land of the Way is done. The priests disrobe quickly, while the percussionist takes down the scroll on which is written the word "gate," for Golden Gate (plate 14). The audience in the court of the Three Pure Ones, in the Land of the Way, is done. The ritual parenthesis which was opened with the Curtain-raising in the Division of the Lamps has now been closed.

CHAPTER

9

The Presentation of the Memorial

The Presentation of the Memorial is performed out of doors, in front of the temple. The memorial presented is like that in the Land of the Way, except that it is addressed to the Jade Emperor. The ritual starts with the five priests at a table placed halfway between the temple and a stage set up for the theater put on during the Offering (plate 17). This part of the ritual, to be explained more fully below, is essentially an invocation of the Six Masters, the Four Saints, and the transmitting agents (plate 18). When it is completed, the four assistant priests put on clogs—the high priest already has his thick-soled shoes on—and each of the five opens a blue parasol. The clogs lift them above the earth; the parasol represents heaven: they are all going up as mediators between heaven and earth.

Each priest in turn steps his way to the stage and climbs up on to it (plate 19). The last to go up is the high priest, who does a special trigram step before ascending the stage (Ofuchi, 339a). The two cantors have taken up position on chairs placed on either side of the scroll of the Golden Gate which has been hung here (cf. plate 21). On the table in front of the Gate stands a paper doll, the Officer for the Presentation of the Memorial (*chin-piao kuan*) in a little paper gatehouse. Like heralds the cantors call out by turns, "The high priest hides his tablet! . . . straightens his cap! . . . straightens his robe!" and so on. Each time they announce an action, the high priest, who is facing outward, his back to the Golden Gate, performs it (plate 20). Soon, the cantor announces a series of kowtows. These the high priest performs, facing the Gate, together with all but the two cantors (plate 21).

At this point the cantors climb down from their chairs, and all join the high priest in the kowtow position. Three times the assistants call out, "Raise the shout!" and the high priest responds, "Long life!" Then, still in a deep bow (the others remain on their knees but are no longer in the kowtow position), the high priest says:

> All praise to the Supreme Emperor of the Golden Gate of the Jade Capital. . . . Here before his throne, in an attitude of reverence, let the memorial be read. (Ofuchi, 339b)

The memorial is then read and presented in essentially the same manner as during the Land of the Way, with appropriate modifications. Since the message sent is addressed to the Jade Emperor, for example, it is his appellation, not that of the Three Pure Ones, that is sung during the "ascension." Once the message has been burned, the ritual is essentially over; there is no following presentation of tea and incense.

The Presentation of the Memorial would seem thus to be but a pale outdoor imitation of the far more elaborate indoor audience accomplished during the Land of the Way. Little more than half as long, lacking both the elaborate entry and exit rituals of the latter, its message is addressed no higher than the Jade Emperor. This impression is further confirmed by the fact that whereas the secret manuals give separate texts for each of the summonings of the Four Potentates and for the triple libation in the Nocturnal Invocation and in the Morning, Noon, and Evening Audiences), the texts given for the Land of the Way and the Presentation of the Memorial are the same.

Such a conclusion, however, leaves one most unsatisfied, for the Presentation of the Memorial also is a particularly solemn and grand occasion, as the priests dance their way one by one under their blue umbrellas to the ladder that leads to heaven. Once they are on the platform, the community representatives come up too, carefully straddling the incense burner that has been set at the top of the ladder to fumigate them properly for their audience in the court of the Jade Emperor. Moreover, increasing the solemnity of the ritual, on rare occasions Master Ch'en performs a much fuller version of the Presentation. This not only adds the rite for "supporting the petition" from the Land of the Way (plate 22), but also includes a full version of the very ancient rites for the "exteriorization" and the "interiorization of the officers" (*ch'u-kuan; na-kuan*). The resulting ritual then takes a full two hours. Finally, and perhaps most significantly, the Presentation assumes an identity of its own if it is interpreted as a ritual reenactment of one of the most important episodes of the myth of Yü.

According to that myth, after Yü had successfully tamed the flood, he became emperor of all China:

> After three years he examined the merit [of his ministers]; within five years his government was securely established. He went on a tour of all under heaven, and when he came back to Great Yüeh, he ascended Mount Mao in order to receive in audience his subjects from the four directions and to inspect the feudal lords of the Central Province. When Oppose-the-Wind arrived late, Yü beheaded him and displayed [his head] to the multitude in order to make clear that all under heaven belonged to him. Then he held a great assembly (*hui*) to decide (*chi*) how to rule the state. Inside, he praised the merit (*kung*) of [the text found on] Mount Cauldron [by means of which he had] stabilized the land; outside, he displayed the saintly virtue (*te*) which made him a man after Heaven's heart. Then he changed the name of Mount Mao to Mountain of the Assembly (*hui*) of Accounts (*chi*). (*The Annals of Wu and Yüeh* 2.6a)

Let us assume, for a moment, that Yü is here the prototype of the Taoist high priest—he is, after all, like him in being one of "high merit"—what light does this part of Yü 's story shed on the Presentation of the Memorial?

We may note, first of all, that it is the merit (*kung*) Yü acquired by taming the waters that gave him such "saintly virtue" (*sheng-te*) as to make him "a man after Heaven's heart". His ritual action, which is divided into an "inside" and an "outside," recapitulates his real action by dividing it into the work itself (*kung*) and the results (*te*) of that work. Does that not correspond precisely to the ritual action of the high priest? Having accomplished the work of salvation *inside* the temple, by Walking the Way, by doing the Step of Yü, he now comes *outside* to report this action to heaven. His action within, moreover, also corresponds to Yü's in that it involved "stabilizing the land" by means of texts, the five True Writs of the Nocturnal Invocation.

To this we may add that the Chinese word commonly translated "ritual" is *kung-te* (literally, "merit-virtue"). Its sense is that the high priest has done work and gotten results; he has merit and virtue. Is it not to show this that the high priest goes up on the stage? Ostensibly, he has climbed the ladder in order to go in audience before the Emperor on High. In fact, he turns his back on the Golden Gate and faces the community representatives during the initial part of the

Presentation (plate 20). Is he not showing them—not the Emperor on High—that he is a "man after Heaven's heart"? When Yü is said to "display his saintly virtue," the word translated "display" is *yen*, which also means "to perform," as an actor on stage. Is Yü not also performing for others, showing them that "all under heaven belongs to him"? The parallel with the imperial sacrifices of investiture (*feng-shan*) need only be alluded to here to be immediately self-evident.

But the parallel with the work of the high priest would seem to break down here: he is not holding an assembly; he is calling no one to account. Or is he? What *is* the Presentation of the Memorial? In making the analogy to Yü's assembly we have suggested that the Presentation is fundamentally a *yen-kung*, a Statement of Merit (cf. Chen Yao-t'ing 1986). This idea is based on the fact that the usual sequence of rituals in medieval China was a sequence of three: the Walking the Way (*hsing-tao*, Land of the Way) preceded by the Nocturnal Invocation and followed by the Statement of Merit.

Let us try to give more substance to this equation between the ritual and a Statement of Merit by examining the mechanics of the Presentation of the Memorial. One of its most distinctive features, when compared with the other rituals in an Offering, is its ample use of symbols (*fu*). A whole packet of these symbols, written in red on small rectangular slips of yellow paper, is tied into the knot of one of the sets of ribbons which close the robe of the high priest. One symbol is pasted on his court tablet, another on the back of his robe, and still another, skewered on his flame, is on the top of his metal crown (plate 20). In addition, the symbols of the five directions are pasted at appropriate points on stage, that for the center being pasted on the edge of the Gate scroll itself (plate 21). When the ritual is over, and the high priest comes down from the stage, he is surrounded by community representatives and spectators, who nearly tear these symbols from his body. Why? What do they represent?

They represent—symbolize—the messengers who carry the memorial up to heaven. These messengers are in fact the vital forces of the high priest's own body, which he "invites," that is, exteriorizes at the beginning of the ritual. First he invites the various masters and saints, primarily those of Lung-hu and Wu-tang shan; then, he recites a passage concerning the presentation of the memorial, in which he refers to his own "ritual register" (*fa-lu*) and to the "potent officers" (*ling-kuan*) of his ritual register (the significance of this we will see below); finally he invites a long list of transmitting agents. Although the list beginning with the masters and saints is preceded by the verb *chao-ch'ing*, "summon-invite," the ritual action clearly corresponds functionally to a different action. It is what was called, in the earliest extant Taoist rituals, *ch'u-kuan*, exteriorization of the officers, that is, of the "potent officers of the ritual register" which the priest received at the time of his ordination (cf. Lagerwey, 157). The presence of this rite in even the short version of the Presentation of the Memorial—it does not occur in the short version of the Land of the Way—shows that it remains, counter-indications notwithstanding, a ritual, even *the* ritual of audience. In the medieval Walking of the Way, the rite of exteriorization was an essential prelude to the transmission of the message to heaven. The Statement of Merit occurred the following day and included a prayer for the proper recompensing of the messengers and for the return of the "perfect officers of the five organs" (once they had been promoted "according to their merit") to his body (Lagerwey, 158). In this early version then, the identity of the messengers with the priest's exteriorized energies was perfectly clear. From this conclusion we can see that the Presentation of the Memorial is indeed at the same time a Statement of Merit: why else would the community representatives be so eager to obtain the priest's symbols?

But what exactly are these symbols, these squiggly red lines which we have seen represent the potent officers of the high priest's ritual register? The lines are squiggly and red because they represent energy; hence, they are "potent." But the squiggles are prescribed in the high priest's manuals, not random, and they therefore represent specific configurations of energy; hence, they are "officers." Representing specific configurations of energy, they symbolize the secret names (*hui*) of those officers. They symbolize but they are not yet symbols, because to the *written* symbol (the *fu*) must be added either its aural or its mental form or both before it can become efficacious. That is, the secret name must be materialized either by pronunciation or by a visualization. The priest must know not only how to write the secret names of his potent officers, but also how to call them by name, to summon them, and to conjure them up, and to distinguish them from one another by their ritual vestments and paraphernalia (cf. Lagerwey, 91 ff.).

The emphasis on a person's potent officers is also seen in an archaic ritual of initiation like *Huang-shu kuo-tu yi* (TT 1294). Immediately after the first paragraph describing the "entry into the oratory," the visualization of these officers is described:

> Each [member of the couple being initiated] sounds the drum twelve times and visualizes the hats, jewels, and vestments of the officers of merit, the generals, clerks, and soldiers of the register he (she) carries on his (her) person. They are lined up, protecting him (her) on all sides, before and behind, to the left and to the right, and they are to bring to him (her) the living breath of the four directions, to eliminate calamities, and to dissipate misfortune. (*Huang-shu kuo-tu yi* 1b)

The "sounding of the drum" is the gritting of the teeth, which we have already seen to be a means of summoning, of assembling the spirits of the body. It is so called because the drum's voice is the thunder which in spring awakens the life forces dormant in the bowels of the earth (Kaltenmark 1948, 23-26). Inasmuch as Yü was "born in the same manner as the thunder" (*ibid*, 27), the quotation from *Huang-shu kuo-tu yi* leads us back to Yü's trail.

Indeed, all the entry rites in the *Kuo-tu yi* could be seen as a ritual representation of Yü's assembly on Mount Mao. The entry into the oratory corresponds to the ascension of Mount Mao; to the *gathering* around the person of the adept of his private army corresponds the assembly of Yü's subjects; and to the visualization of the officers of the register corresponds the inspection of the feudal lords. The next step in the ritual is a sequence of three more energy-centered visualizations. In the myth Yü executes Oppose-the-Wind, who has revealed himself to be no loyal subject but a rebellious energy, one who will, like the "stellar winds," prevent the communication that is to occur during the ritual.

Once the obstacle has been eliminated, Yü can hold his great assembly, his audience, with its division into inner work and outer display. Likewise, the adepts in *Huang-shu kuo-tu yi*, now that each has gathered his/her forces, can join in a ritual of union, which begins with an exteriorization of the officers in charge of communication and ends with a Statement of Merit. In this final part of the ritual, the adepts receive the "contract of the Yellow Book," that is, their diploma. They now belong to the "seed-people" (*chung-min*: 24b), that is, to the elect; they are now a couple "after Heaven's heart," a couple of initiates.

At bottom, the Presentation of the Memorial is just such a ritual, a ritual of union, in fact, a ritual of *reunion*. Reunited are all the forces under heaven, that is, all the forces of the high priest's register, which is the same as all the forces under heaven of the community "ruled over" by Yü's spiritual descendant, the one of "high merit." The priest is one of high merit precisely because, each time he does a public work—a liturgy—the officers of his register return from heaven with a renewed mandate and hence a higher rank. In this sense the Presentation recapitulates, as it were, the priest's ordination; it reconfirms him in his function as the community's spokesman; it reaffirms—makes firmer, more secure—his own legitimacy as the pivot around which all turns, the Pole Star of the community, its emperor. That is why he turns to face the people when he "displays the saintly virtue that makes him a man after Heaven's heart." And that is why the people are so eager to share in his merit when he comes down from the stage and try to get as many of his symbols as they can for themselves and their families.

To understand fully the implications of these underlying meanings, we must explore more thoroughly the rites of union represented by the symbols the priest wears. There is no better place to begin than with the word itself, *fu* (cf. the excellent discussion in Robinet 1979, 37–57). It has traditionally been translated "talisman" because its most characteristic use in lay religion was observed to be a protective one. Why, then, translate it "symbol"?—for the simple reason that like the word "symbol" itself in its Greek origin, *sumbolon*, *fu* meant "each of two halves of corresponding pieces of a bone or another object, which two strangers, or any two contracting parties broke between them, each party keeping one piece in order to have proof of the identity of the presenter of the other" (Liddell and Scott, *A Greek-English Lexikon*, S.V.). In China *fu* were originally made not of bone but of wood. In Taoism the two halves are the written configuration of a divine energy—and the energy itself. A legitimate line of transmission (apostolic succession) ensures the correctness, the orthodoxy of the model of the written half which the priest or the adept copies. But it is not enough just to copy it. It must also be "thrown" (*ballein*) "together" (*sum*), just as in the Greek, *sum* + *ballein* = *sumballein*, to symbolize with its other half (cf. Martelet, p. 14).

To appreciate the importance and significance of symbols, let us see how a text of the mid-thirteenth century tells practitioners to "symbolize." The procedure, which is elaborate, reveals the source of the efficacy of symbols.

Whenever you write seal characters, you must use symbol-orders. Enter your oratory in proper ritual manner and visualize the imperial masters of the Three Realms, the Sovereign of Heavenly Perfection, the True Master of the Yellow Register, and the potent officers of the symbol-register. When the incense, flowers, altar, brush, inkstone, and red ink are all ready, you must first do the method of "internal smelting" (*nei-lien*). At the sixth *yang* hour, enter your oratory and sit in the lotus position. Grit your teeth three times, hold your breath in silence, and visualize in the lower Cinnabar Field a flame the size of a pill. It turns nine times toward the left (clockwise: gestation) and mounts to the Scarlet Palace (the heart), and then gradually goes up through the twelve-storied tower (the trachea) to the Jade Chamber (a womb) in the *ni-huan* (between the eyes), where it sits lotus style, holding the sun in its right hand and the moon in its left. Its name is Worthy Emperor, Great One of the Large Cavern. Pray:

> Let my superior souls be clean and correct
> And my myriad energies remain forever intact.
> May I avoid suffering,
> May my body be luminous.
> May [the officers of] the Three Realms wait upon me
> And the Five Emperors welcome me.
> Let the myriad spirits pay their respects
> And my name be written in Highest Purity.
> When my merit (*kung*) is sufficient and my results (*te*) perfect,
> Let me fly up to Highest Purity.

Repeat this incantation three times, draw the fire up [from the Cinnabar Field] three times, swallow it, and pray again:

> The golden liquor smelts the body:
> I join my perfection to that of the Way.
> That which lights up the Three Luminaries
> Is called the Root of Heaven.
> In it is neither darkness nor crack,
> Neither beginning nor end.
> Nine Obstacles of the Prime Sovereign;
> Potent soul in the Scarlet Palace.
> Purple clouds fly in the sky,
> And I drive a team of six dragons.
> Water goes up, fire down:
> They flow into the Three Palaces.
> The spirit returns to the light,
> And the Great Way communicates spontaneously.

Repeat this incantation three times and swallow the saliva three times. After a long interval, a halo appears on top of the head, and its light illumines the ten directions. Pray thus:

> Lord of the Way of the Most High, Supreme and Mysterious Origin, summon forth from within your servant's body the correct spirits of the Three Energies, the directors of destiny, fortune, works, and judgment, as well as the two lords T'ao-k'ang and Ching-yen. Your servant is sublimating the True Principle within. Rays light up the Nine Heavens, releasing the *yang*-essence and filling with light the Nine Gates. Cause the souls of the dead to be melted down and then return to the womb to be reborn. Let all the spirits of my body marvelously unite their perfection to that of the Way.

Draw up the fiery energy and swallow it nine times. Whenever you write symbols you must first do this, and gradually the divine lights will manifest themselves.

When you are [actually] writing the symbols, set up a table with incense, face the Gate of Heaven, and spread out before you all the ritual implements. Visualize the red inkstone and the dish of water as the sun and the moon respectively, the paper as golden strips, the brush as a green dragon, and the smoke of the incense as white clouds. The clerks of the symbol are atop these clouds, and the lads and lasses, officers and generals of the symbolic method are arrayed to the right and left. When this is accomplished, form in your hand the sign of the Big Dipper, and visualize the dippers of the five directions enveloping the body. Walk the Huo-lo Dipper, press the point of the Emperor on High in your hand, and visualize yourself entering the Three Terraces and the Big Dipper. Do the dipper gesture with both hands, bow three times with your court tablet, present incense, grit your teeth, kneel down, and pray. (In the prayer, the master invokes the pantheon, recalls his mission to spread the "Great Teaching" even though he is unworthy of such a task, states that he has been asked to perform a fast by so-and-so and must therefore prepare the appropriate documents and symbols):

Knowing himself to be foolish and filthy, incapable of creating the Mysterious Origin, your servant lifts up his eyes and begs Heaven for mercy: look down on me with compassion and grant to me the correct energies of the ten directions, the marvellous rays of the Great Way. Let them flow into your serrvant's body and heart, into my every pore, and also into the red ink and the implements. Cause all knots to be untied, the root of the foetus to be clear, my meditations efficacious, and my true lights to beam. One brush stroke, one opening: unite with the Way, unite with perfection. When I use them later, let the reactions be good ones. Cause them to symbolize with (*ch'i*) the marvels of the mysteries on high and so make whole the work (*kung*) of salvation. Your servant makes bold to presume upon the heavenly powers, I who am without merit and wait anxiously for your mandate.

After this prayer, visualize the Most High in the Terrace of the Celestial Treasure, surrounded by the perfected and the immortals. The Emperor orders those in waiting to issue the signet-symbols and send them down. Next he sees the heavenly worthies of the ten directions emit a great light which flows down through space. Bearing a treasure box, surrounded by hundreds of precious rays, lads and lasses come before your table, open the box, and divulge them: *they unite with the seal characters you have written* (italics mine).

The light blinds the eyes, and you transform your body into that of the two perfect ones of the Green Mystery on the left and on the right, surrounded by lads and lasses. Only then do you [actually] enter the oratory and face east. Grit your teeth 32 times so that it is heard in the 32 heavens on high, and make 32 mental bows. Close your eyes and meditate in quiet: your body is seated on cloud-energies of three colors, green, yellow, and white. From the total darkness within and without emerge a green dragon, a white tiger, a red phoenix, and a somber warrior, who take up their positions on the four sides of your person. The sun and the moon light up the chamber, and on the back of your head appears a nine-colored halo whose rays light up the ten directions. Now pray, saying:

Lord of the Way of the Most High, Supreme and Mysterious Origin, summon forth from within your servant's body the officers of merit of the three and the five, the agents on the left and right, the jade lads in charge of the incense, the jade lasses who transmit what is said, the keepers of the symbols of the Five Emperors, and the officers of the incense in charge today, 32 individuals in all, to report what I say. On this auspicious day I am [preparing] to perform a great fast for so-and-so, with the purpose of transmitting the documents, symbols, and registers which will rescue the soul of so-and-so from the darkness of hell. I pray that what I ask may penetrate directly to the throne of the Most Worthy Emperor on High of the Primordial Beginning of the 32 supreme heavens.

Inhale (or, draw up the energy) 32 times, go to your seat, and write the symbols. . . . (Here follow incantations for the brush, the ink, the action of making the ink, the consecration of the symbols and their dispatch, and so on.) When you have finished writing the symbols, pray once again to the Most Worthy Saint of the Seven Treasures of the Golden Gate of the Infinitely Great Way of the Most High:

> I long for the compassion of the Way: may It deign to look down and observe. Your servant has heard that the Great Way, in Its compassion, opened the eight gates in order to save from distress; the Most Perfect One set forth his teaching and revealed the three registers by means of which to save men: whoever prays and makes an offering is certain to be granted deliverance. Your servant has just now, respectfully following the ritual method, written in seal characters the various perfect symbols and registers of the Most High. Although I have done so in accord with the proper method, I still fear there may have been something amiss in my visualizations, or that I have made mistakes in my incantations or gestures; or else I have relied on the hand of another, who has made errors or omissions in his strokes or, not understanding ultimate principles, has not followed the revealed rules. Once again I beg heaven's mercy: pour down perfect energies, that they may flow, penetrate, and irrigate the symbols and registers I have written. Cause what I have left out to be filled in, so that their radiance may soar heavenward and constitute the rays of this ritual (*kung-te*) which symbolize with (*ch'i*) the marvels of the mysteries on high. When your servant announces them, let them be carried out one and all: open wide for the drowned souls, that all may leave their misery behind. Above, show the power (*te*) of your love of life; below, symbolize with (*fu*) our sincerity in saving the dead. Your servant makes bold to importune the heavenly powers; with utmost humility he earnestly addresses you.

Bow three times, gather up the symbols, and put them in a box for storage. (TT 1221 *Shang-ch'ing ling-pao ta-fa* 39.1a–8a)

The above text describes the preparation of symbols (and registers) for the kind of requiem rituals that we will be studying in Chapters 10–13. It also gives a maximalist version of the rites of union required if a copied symbol is to be efficacious. The rites of priests in modern Taiwan surrounding both the consecration and the use of symbols are nowhere near as complicated or complete. Nonetheless, the principles guiding the elaborate ritual are entirely consistent with what we said earlier concerning the Presentation of the Memorial; they simply are clearer here because they are more completely worked out.

The passage makes clear, first of all, why symbols are written with squiggly lines: the lines represent clouds. Clouds are celestial energy, and symbols are therefore also seals, for "cloud-writing" is synonomous in Chinese for "seal-writing." The seal is basically a signature, a name (*hui*) signed in order to give force to an order. Thus the signet-symbols are also commands.

The second clarification concerns the act of copying these symbols.

It is clearly portrayed as a repetition, a re-presentation, a making present once again the event of their original revelation, that is, of their transmission from heaven to earth. This corresponds to our analysis of the Presentation of the Memorial as a confirmation of the high priest's ordination. Thus the ritual of redemption recapitulates that of transmission/ordination/initiation, which itself recapitulates the original revelation. As the above translated passage suggests, and as we shall have occasion to explore in the requiem rituals, the ritual for the salvation of souls "drowned" in hell consists essentially of the transmission of symbols and registers to these souls, that is, an ordination is carried out for them.

The passage shows us, finally, how entirely the symbols represent rites of union: union, in the preparatory rites, of the sun and the moon in the hands of the Great One of the Large Cavern; and union of the water (saliva) and the fire (Cinnabar Field energy) in and of the high priest's body. Twice in this part of the ritual, the phrase "unite (join) my perfection to that of the Way" occurs, a phrase we first encountered during the consecration of the burner in the Land of the Way. Then, in the actual writing of the symbols, there occurs the union of north and south—of the sun and the moon—in the mingling of red ink and water; and of west and east in the green "golden (metal, west) strips" of paper (now we see why yellow paper is used in modern ritual) and the green dragon (east) brush. The key rite of union is the renewed transmission itself. The single-mindedness with which this principle is applied may be seen in the phrases "symbolize with the marvels of the mysteries (energies) on high" and "make whole (*ch'üan*) the work of salvation." This "symbolizing with the marvels," moreover, occurs both at the time the symbols are copied and at the time they are used.

Ultimately, however, the true rite of union is the "symbolosis" of the Way's "love of life" and "our sincerity": the Taoists knew, too, that the only true offering was that of the sincere heart. It is through the sincere memorializing of the high priest that the community's participation in the Covenant of Orthodox Unity with the Powers is achieved, that its lease on life is renewed. The many symbols the priest wears as he goes up to present the memorial to Heaven symbolize that "covenant with the powers," that alliance, that *contract (yüeh)* by means of which Lord Lao bound the Four Generals and the "hundred demons of the temples and the rivers" to Chang Tao-ling and gave him and his heirs dominion over the Powers (Lagerwey, 43). That pact was *signified* (sealed) by means of a split rock: the work of thunder, the work of Yü.

Indeed, the multiplicity of both the symbols worn by the high priest and the parties to the contract with Chang Tao-ling brings us back to the myth of Yü in order to analyze the prototypical *assembly*—congregation—in which a varied crowd is transformed into "one body" composed of "all under heaven." Yü too brought order out of miscellanea. At the time Yü was about his work of channeling the waters, he was also compiling a book:

> Whenever he came to a famous mountain or a big swamp, he would summon its spirit and ask it concerning the deep structure of the mountains and rivers, about the kinds of precious stones, of birds, beasts, and reptiles found there, as well as concerning the customs of the people on all eight sides and the boundaries, soil quality, and size of the various states. He had Yi and K'uei note all this down and called it *The Scripture of the Mountains and Seas.* (*The Annals of Wu and Yüeh* 2.3b)

It has recently been suggested that *The Scripture of the Mountains and Seas (Shan-hai ching)*, an otherwise apparently heterogeneous collection of geographical and mythical information, was at least in part politically motivated (Mathieu, pp. ciii, cx). The attribution to Yü, in giving the book what might be called a spiritual unity, reinforces that interpretation.

The unity of the compilation resides in the fact that it was the product of what the "hundred demons (= gods = deep structures) of the temples (= mountains) and rivers" (= swamps, the other dwelling place of the gods in ancient China) could tell Yü about the territories under their jurisdiction. But what would Yü want with such a record of his travels if not to *use* them, once he became emperor, to help him *visualize* all these spirits? And by the visualizations to bring them into his presence on Mount Mao. He brings them there to renew their oaths of fealty, to inspect them and make sure that none had become "opposers-of-his-wind," in short, to bring them to renew their contribution to his power, to reaffirm his legitimacy as "one pleasing to Heaven." This was how, in antiquity, the one "who ruled by moral force (*te*) remained in place while all the lesser stars did him homage" (*Analects* 2.1).

But something is missing in this record of marvels, and that is the symbols of all these spirits, their secret names, by which they may be summoned (cf. Robinet [1979, 38], "During regularly held feudal assemblies, the sovereign 'united the symbols' [*ho-fu*] so as to attest to the sworn contract between him and his vassals"). Not only these symbols are missing, but also the symbols of the maps and the charts (*t'u*), the deep structure of their mountains and rivers. One version of the origins of *The Scripture of the Mountains and Seas* makes it out to be the text that accompanied precisely such *t'u*. These are the *t'u*, engraved on the famous cauldrons of Yü, which ensured the spiritual—and hence the political—peace of the empire (cf. Granet 1959, 489). Finally, there is no roster of names, no *lu*, and without it this scripture is in truth but the collection of fragments it is often said to be. Symbols, registers, and charts: all of these are missing. Which would have been most useful in giving back to this collection its lost unity?

The roster of names would be a natural first choice. It would resemble the ritual register transmitted to a high priest at the time of his ordination, which gives the complete list of the officers (spirits) over whom he has dominion and thus gives a fairly clear idea of the extent of his power. Like a table of contents, a register would give us a kind of key to the *Scripture*. This comparison with a table of contents unfortunately also reveals the inadequacy of a register to fulfill all the functions we ask of it. The register does unify, but it gives us very little idea of *what* it unifies. The words of a list do not have the evocative power of even a single symbol.

What we need, therefore, is something that at once unifies and evokes, which combines the powers of the symbol and the register. That we have in the map. But not in the map of the mountain or swamp of one spirit; no, in the map of the mountain where all the spirits congregate once every three thousand years for the banquet of immortality. Such a mountain would be equal to a temple, to an altar, to the body, and such a mountain is the Mountain of the Man-Bird shown in the *Scripture of the Map for the Mysterious Investigation of the Mountain of the Man-Bird* (5a):

We have already had occasion to mention this Mountain of the Man-Bird in connection with the Queen Mother of the West. Analysis of its map will show us that it is the symbol of all symbols, that it is the symbol of the matrix itself, of the womb of the body of the universe—of the Way—from which issue, over time, *all* the possible transformations of primordial energy. By contrast, the symbol represents but *one* possible configuration of this energy, *one* mode of its infinity of modes.

The *t'u*, it should be pointed out, need not always be a map. For example it is unlikely that either the River Chart given by the Count of the Yellow River to Yü (Granet 1959, 478), or the "Chart of the Governances of the [Twenty-four] Energies of Orthodox Unity," probably revealed by Lord Lao to Chang Tao-ling (Lagerwey, 43), was a map. Like our map here, however, these two famous Taoist "charts" are what Granet (1968, 147) called an "image of the world," that is, an image of the Whole. They bear out the primacy of *t'u*, for "scriptures were often diagrams or charts, *t'u*, before they became texts, posterior elaborations of the original figures" (Robinet 1979, 40). This is how the *Scripture* describes the map and its mountain:

> The Most High says: the innumerable heavens has each its mountain of the man-bird. Each has the face of a man and the body of a bird. Its soaring peaks and precipices are too many to mention. In its mysterious belvederes and precious halls dwell venerable gods. The birds and animals in its forests and ravines, the trees and rocks, the incense flowers and the mushroom grasses, all the various medicines, the fountains of youth and the saps of immortality cannot all be described, and to describe them would be of no use to study. Students must search earnestly to obtain the one and know the all: then they will truly know everything. In teaching one must show the titles; therefore I sketch an outline.
>
> The marvelous energies form characters; the saintly craftsman writes them. He transmits them to superior students; they are not to be divulged to ordinary people. These characters of marvelous energy are the *configuration of the mountain* [italics mine]. It is strange in outward appearance, and its contours are unusual. It is entirely the product of the transformations of the marvelous energy. By mystery-penetrating visualizations, you can see it when you close your eyes. When you have completed your investigation, you will get results from its use. Once the marvelous energy has descended, your fleshly body will be able to fly. If you refine it long enough to attain to mystery, mystery will fill you and your flesh disappear. Your flight will be that of a bird's, and you will roam in the mountains beyond the Three Realms. Your soul will be that of a perfect man, and you will go in to the feast in the Three Pure Heavens. Its general title is "man-bird." He who studies it will go from mountain to mountain, and the Supreme Way will protect and keep him forever. If you are not in utter earnest, do not set out foolishly.
>
> The Most High says: the body of the man-bird mountain is the living root of heaven, earth, and man, that from which emerges the primordial energy, that on which the marvellous transformation relies. Saints and perfected search for this place; immortals and potentates look up to its

god. Worship it with reverence; visualize it with concentration. Banquet it when you receive it, give it offerings when you wear it. Practice it earnestly; hide it prudently. If you do so without slacking for a long time, your three energies will harmonize: they will give birth to a body, to an infant, and you will become one of the elect of the Way.

Whether you stay in the world (as a priest) and practice transformation or enter the mountains to study recipes, wherever you are, you will be at ease, and the demons will not dare stand up to you. Then you will be able to bring the five peaks into your court and to have the eight seas do your bidding. You will be a follower of the Lord of the Three Heavens, and wear at your belt the essences of sun and moon. He who knows this will not die; he who practices it will live forever. He who examines it will merge with Wisdom; he who understands it will be as the gods.

On top of the mountain dwells the Celestial King of the Primordial Beginning; the multitude of saints, immortals, and the perfected live at its foot. The energy of this mountain gives birth to water of five colors: it is called the Flowing Sap of the Returning Soul. It forms a lard which is called the Incense of the Eastern Sandalwood. The Queen Mother of the West, when she first began to study the Way, went to visit the Celestial King of the Primordial Beginning. After three thousand years, having completed the Way and attained its power, she had to go back home to Mount K'un-lun. Just before she left, she went to take leave of the Celestial King of the Primordial Beginning, and together they carved an inscription in the space above Man-Bird Mountain. Each of the characters they formed was a meter square, and they hung them up in space for transmission to students of after days. They have survived to this day.

The Lord of the Capital of the Immortals, Nine Times Ancient, and the Giant of the Nine Energies drew a map of the mountain and wore it at the elbow. The Emperor of Heaven wrote down the characters in space and appended them to the body of the man-bird. Once in a hundred years it appears and is then transmitted to a perfect man. A Taoist who has the picture of this mountain and all the accompanying documents will obtain passage to immortality, to roam banqueting in K'un-lun. If you read this book ten thousand times and practice it without infringing its instructions, the Lord-Emperor of Heaven will dispatch a cloud-chariot with a feather canopy to come and fetch you. You need not take cinnabar liquor; it is useless to draw-and-pull, crouch-and-stretch. Practice earnestly without ceasing, and you will in due course ascend to heaven. (TT 434 *Hsüan-lan Jen-niao shan ching-t'u* 1a-2b).

After stating that the gymnastic and alchemical methods of ancient Taoism may now be replaced by the recitation and "practice" of this text (which is probably a T'ang rewrite of a Six Dynasties scripture), our book goes on to describe the banquet to be given in honor of the map once a year. It is placed on a metal mirror, and the mirror is set in the courtyard, exposed to the full moon (see p. 32; the Nocturnal Invocation is also called the Nocturnal Exposure; Lagerwey, p. 132). The adept purifies the area by sweeping and sprinkling it. He sets out two mats, one facing south, the other north, and between them he places the mirror on a low table. The ritual consists essentially of an invocation of the gods and the presentation of an offering of three cups of clear wine, incense, dried meat, dates, and fruit, which are arrayed around the mirror. "Worshiping the venerable gods in their presence," prays the adept, male or female, "I am filled at once with joy and fear. . . . Enable me to study the Way and obtain it, to search for immortality and achieve it" (3b).

In addition to this annual Offering (*chiao*), the adept should observe a "pure fast" of one thousand days, at the end of which he is to draw the map of the mountain, in red, on a small square piece of thin paper, and ingest it:

> Eat it once, and you'll live forever; twice, and you'll be able to fly like an immortal; thrice, and you'll ascend to a high station and become one with the Way. When the pure fast is over, pick up the map and wear it at your belt. Recite the text in the morning and evening for two years, and on an auspicious day do the ritual (i.e., the annual Offering). Make sure you end as you began. After a thousand days, you will be able, when you go wandering through the mountains and swamps, to control the gods and potentates of the five sacred peaks, the three rivers, the four seas, the eight oceans, and the nine earths: they will come out to greet you and pay homage to you. Your merit (*kung*) and your power (*te*) will flow and spread: after five years or seven, and certainly not more than nine, you will ascend to the Three Pure Heavens. (4b)

Clearly, it was just such a symbolic matrix which enabled Yü, whenever he came to a famous mountain or a big swamp, to summon its spirit. And it was just such a symbolic matrix that enabled him, after three years and five, to hold a great assembly in which he "praised the merit of Mount Cauldron," that is, the merit of the map of Mount Cauldron, which is the map of the ultimate receptacle, the founder's cauldron, the womb. And having praised the merit of the map, Yü "ascended to a high station" where, having "become one with the Way," he could "display his saintly virtue." Is this not what the high priest does in the Presentation of the Memorial? After the Nocturnal Invocation and the Land of the Way, after holding a great assembly in which he had gathered all his forces, he climbs the ladder to heaven and "displays his saintly virtue," his power as manifested by the clusters of symbols congregated about his body. The Presentation of the Memorial, we might say, is the apotheosis—the glorification, the exaltation—of the high priest.

But we must be careful here: it is precisely when the high priest is thus "lifted up" that he ceases altogether to be an ordinary man and becomes, in very truth, a "high merit" priest. This is the moment when the "transformation of his body" into the body of Lao-tzu which is part of the first ritual of Announcement truly takes effect. This is the moment when, as described in the passage quoted, the "characters in space" are "appended to the body of the man-bird" by the Emperor in Heaven. Below are translated these "characters in space"; the outer band of characters around the map of Man-Bird Mountain (words in brackets are variants taken from *Pao-p'u tzu* 6.9a-b; cf. Ware, 120-21) reads:

> The Man-Bird Mountain of the Most High is difficult to cross because it is so high. It is neither heaven nor earth, neither sunk nor soaring. Precipitous ravines reach into the distance: great peaks; mountain paths. The smoke of primordial energy rises mildly; gods and perfected ones roam there. Abundant and pure, the jade liquor irrigates without [ceasing]. The celestial courts of the 120 officers appear the one behind the other. There are the sun and the moon, the dark and the light. In a forest of black mushrooms, one scarlet tree stands out. [Its] treasures are all [extraordinary; gold] and jade are piled high. Sweet springs issue from the corners; clouds emerge, mushrooms spring up. Thunder drives away all that is evil; the trees and the birds know how to talk. Here are the divine adepts who have rolled back the years: they pick from the fragrant flow. If you can achieve it, you will be a companion of the perfected. If you do not know this way, all is dust and ashes. The Scripture of Mouth-to-Ear is called the Celestial Pavilion.

Thus the outer band of 120 characters, which begins and ends in the southwest at the Gate of Man, with the (Queen) Mother of the West ☷. The inner band on the map, composed originally of 124 characters, begins and ends in the northwest, at the Gate of Heaven, with the (Celestial King of the Primordial Beginning) Father ☰. It was he who originally transmitted this scripture directly from his mouth into the Mother's ear: transmission (revelation) is at once emission and reception, that is, it is conception, *the* rite of union. Here is the text of the inner band:

> This is the body of the man-bird: on the right side of the mountain, jade lasses are ascending. Soaring peaks recede into the distance. Purple clouds drift; sweet dew falls like rain. In their folds are pools of gold and chambers of jade. Stemless herbs never wither, be it winter or summer, for the mysterious sap restores them to life, and they are covered with flowers from top to bottom. The foolish mortal who rushes to get there will find nothing but lifeless slopes: only those who possess the Most High (adepts who possess the Way) can ascend without them shriveling up. Pick the flowing essence and swallow it, until you are flying in the heavens. Golden rays form a halo; perfect energies ride the thunder. Now close your eyes and dwell on the Eight Powers (the spirits of the trigrams). Stones give birth to divine animals. Their sounds have no beginning (and no end?—two characters are missing in this inscription), but they are hard to capture. The Unique Energy builds up mountains of earth that do not cave in. Write your name in the Celestial River (the Milky Way): it will be transmitted orally forever. This is called the 'mysterious light': you are immortal.

In the *Pao-p'u tzu* these two passages are said to describe two different mountains which "he who seeks the Way must know" (6.9a). The first is the Mountain of the Great Origin, the second the Mountain of the Long Valley. From this it would appear that the first inscription above, the outer one, refers to the Father's mountain even though it begins and ends in the Mother's corner, and the inner inscription, although it is "appended" to the Father's corner, refers to the Mother's mountain. This is no doubt why the Man-Bird Mountain is "neither heaven nor earth": it is the matrix of the Way, where heaven and earth, by "symbolizing," engender the Unique Energy which "he who seeks the Way must know." In like manner, it is when the two altar-mountains created by the respective positions of the Three Pure Ones and the high priest symbolize (see p. 47), when during the Land of the Way or the Presentation of the Memorial (plate 22) the high priest becomes the One (Turtle) Body (Mountain) by creating with his Unique Energy a "mountain of earth that does not cave in"—it is when this ultimate rite of union occurs that the high priest enters the "mysterious light" and writes his name in the eternal stream of seminal energy we call the Milky Way. If the high priest goes out of doors to perform the Presentation of the Memorial, if he appends characters to his vestments, it is to display the saintly virtue he has acquired by means of the esoteric rite of union and to transmit portions of this sanctified power to the community.

The Presentation of the Memorial, in other words, is at once a Statement of Merit—to the head of the exoteric pantheon and to the people—and a ritual of transmission. Indeed it is modelled on the ordination ceremony, which also involves symbols, an ascent to heaven, a declaration of the postulant's merit, and the transmission of the "mysterious light," his flame (cf. Schipper 1982, 95-7). The symbols in the ordination are 36 in number, and one is pasted on—"appended to"—each of the 36 steps (heavens) on the sword ladder to highest heaven. On his way up the ladder these symbols protect the postulant from wounding his bare feet on the upturned swords; on his way down the postulant removes them one by one and either throws them immediately to the people below or puts them in a cloth shoulder bag for later distribution. The Presentation of the Memorial is thus a re-presentation of the ordination, a confirmation of the high priest's initial statement of merit. But now it is he who emits a "mysterious light," and it is the community which receives it. Like Yü's Assembly of Accounts on Mount Mao, the Presentation of the Memorial is the rite of union between the community and its head.

One cannot help but wonder, moreover, whether the custom of distributing—or even throwing—symbols is not a reminiscence of the traditional Statement of Merit called "throwing the slips" (*t'ou-chien*):

The Taoists have [the ritual of] golden dragons and jade slips. The Academy of Scholars (Confucians!) compose the texts, and the documents of all the fasts and offerings performed in a given year are "thrown" into the cave-courts of famous mountains. During the *t'ien-sheng* era (1023-31), the emperor Jen-tsung, having decided it was too difficult to carry all the paraphernalia needed for the offering and the sacrifice to such remote and inaccessible places, and that this was a cause of considerable disturbance to the prefectures and districts involved, ordered the Academy of Taoist Registers to eliminate all but twenty sites. (Fan Chen, 4; cf. Chavannes 1919, 168-71)

The golden dragons were the paper horses of modern ritual. Of jade slips there were three, one for each of the Three Officers who today still "inspect the fast." (See Appendix A on the links between the "mantle of descent" worn by the high priest in this ritual and his "going public": does the Jade Emperor addressed in this ritual not simply replace the Three Officers of old?). These jade slips laid claim to the merit acquired by a fast or an offering. According to a fifth century text preserved in part in the *Wu-shang pi-yao* (Lagerwey, 165) and more completely in the manual of Chiang Shu-yü (35.9a), merit was claimed by hanging one "jade letter" on a high cliff (heaven), burying another under the altar (earth), and submerging the third in a river. Thus only one of the three was actually "thrown": can it be purely accidental that it was the mediating element water which was chosen to symbolize the ultimate act of "throwing together"?

Liturgy for the Dead: The Ritual of Merit

CHAPTER

10

The Basic Program*

The rituals of the Offering (*chiao*) are but one of the many types of service a Taoist priest performs. However fundamental these rituals may be in the life of a community, alone they suffice neither to feed a priest and his family nor to create a social bond of any significance between the priest and his "parishioners." In the Taoist canon itself, moreover, such rituals occupy a relatively modest place. For example, in the largest liturgical manual in the canon (largest in terms of chapters, not pages) TT 466 *Ling-chiao chi-tu chin-shu*, compiled in 1303 by Lin T'ien-jen, there are programs for more than twenty different types of rituals, all of which resemble, in outline, the Offering we have described, but none of which is specifically designated as an offering for the inauguration of a temple.

The basic distinction between types of ritual in this manual is

---

* A chart summarizing the data in this chapter will be found in Appendix B, Table 2.

nonetheless one between rituals for the living and rituals for the dead. The rituals for the dead as a group are called *k'ai-tu chai*, "fasts for opening and crossing over." The gates of hell must first be opened to the light of heaven before the souls obstructed in hell can cross over on the bridge of light to heaven. The rituals for the living as a group are called *ch'i-jang chai*, "fasts of request and exorcism." Exorcism (literally, "chasing away") of locusts, for example, and requests for posterity, longevity, good fortune, or good weather are among the purposes of these fasts. This category includes "thunder and lightning fasts," whose function is exorcistic, as well as rituals involving the stars, especially the Dipper, which have to do with life and luck in the broadest sense. Fasts are performed for Securing the House (*an-chai*), for Initiation (*ch'uan-tu*), and for Protection against Illness (*pao-ping*). Among the rituals for the dead, we find the Pure Offering (*ching-kung*, also known as *p'u-tu*), the Lake of Blood (*hsüeh-hu*, for women who die in childbirth), and the Tenfold [Recitation] for Salvation (*shih-hui tu-jen*), all of which are still practiced today in Taiwan.

Rituals of this sort have always represented the most important occasions of contact between the general populace and the Taoist priest. Their performance also provides the priest with his chief source of income, for these rituals are carried out at all times. It happens frequently that in the course of a temple Offering, one of the assistant priests will disappear for half a day or even a full day in order to perform a ritual of merit or an exorcism. Simple exorcisms need last no more than half an hour, and a priest whose family has officiated in a given village or urban district for several generations and has developed a virtual monopoly on "business" may well have, day in day out, four or more such "consultations." Such monopolies are not rare in contemporary Taiwan; on the contrary one has the impression they are the norm. In any case most Taoist priests I have met in both northern and southern Taiwan belong to the one Taoist family of their village or district.

Even the most humble family can afford a half-hour exorcism for a sick child, or a briefer consultation concerning his fate. The latter involves calendrical calculations based on the almanac and usually ends with the writing and consecration of a symbol, which the client then keeps on his person or in his house. The day-to-day interactions between a Taoist priest and his neighbors take place on this level, whether in the temple with which the priest is affiliated, in the client's home, or in a room of the priest's home which constitutes his permanent *t'an* or altar.

Rituals of Merit for the dead, *kung-te*, with which Chapters 10-13 are concerned, are not an everyday occurrence. A family usually has one celebrated only once in a generation, normally, when a father or grandfather dies. (Other deceased members of the family may then be associated with him, as we shall see.) A Ritual of Merit is also performed when a mother dies in childbirth, or when a person dies in the prime of life, for such a death represents an immediate danger to the family. Such persons, because they have not lived out their normal life span, will inevitably become not just "obstructed souls" but "resentful souls," that is, troublemakers. The family will therefore have a Ritual of Merit service performed that is in essence an elaborate exorcism. But since Rituals of Merit are normally performed out of doors (briefer versions are also regularly done indoors in the Taoist temples called Temple of the Eastern Peak), and since the whole neighborhood participates in the ritual of Universal Salvation which is also usually a part of the program, the Ritual of Merit is also an important point of contact between the Taoist priest and the general populace.

We must point out here, however, that not all Taoists perform Rituals of Merit. Northern Taiwanese Taoists, for example, do not. They say that as Orthodox Unity Taoists, they serve only the living. In their view, Rituals of Merit should be performed by Buddhists, for Buddhism is the religion of death, as Taoism is the religion of life. Asked why then the Taoists in southern Taiwan do perform such "Buddhist" rituals, they reply, like northerners everywhere it seems, that their southern colleagues are ignorant purveyors of a corrupted tradition. "They're Numinous Treasure Taoists," say the northerners with obvious contempt.

The northern Taoists have a point. The distinction they make is made explicitly already in the fifth century TT 1205 *San-t'ien nei-chieh ching* (1.3a), a text which also insists that adepts of its "correct method of the Three Heavens" not engage in "illicit cults" (*yin-ssu*) and not worship their ancestors more than five times a year (1.6a). The appearance of Numinous Treasure texts in the late fourth or early fifth century clearly represents a Taoist accommodation with the ancestor cult, and it is in Numinous Treasure texts that one finds the greatest influx of Buddhist terminology (Zürcher 1980).

The distinction between Taoists who do and Taoists who do not perform rituals for the dead seems to have become blurred in the T'ang dynasty, but it re-emerges with force in the Sung, when it acquired essentially the form visible in Taiwan today. The two most important types of Taoist initiation in Sung times were those of the Orthodox Method of the Heart of Heaven (T'ien-hsin cheng-fa) and of the Numinous Treasure (Ling-pao ta-fa). The latter specialized in the ritual of Universal Salvation and the various rituals for the salvation of the ancestors; the former, who represented a new form of Orthodox Unity Taoism (Chin Yün-chung, 43.16b), dealt with the souls of the dead only in an exorcistic context. Numinous Treasure Taoists were as likely as not to be monks living in a hermitage (*kuan*), and Heart of Heaven priests to be "country" priests.

In theory at least the Numinous Treasure initiation assumed initiation into Orthodox Unity, and Numinous Treasure Taoists were therefore of higher rank and could do both types of ritual (Chin Yün-chung, 7.17a). This may explain why Taoists in southern Taiwan, who agree entirely with their northern colleagues that their services for the dead are less dignified than those done for the living, nonetheless continue to perform them without feeling in any way diminished by the fact. It is also true that Taoists who do such services have to compete with Buddhists for clients, for Buddhists traditionally have done and still do both Rituals of Merit and of Universal Salvation. Indeed, important elements in these Taoist rituals are clearly of Buddhist origin, the paintings of the ten hells which line the side walls of the altar during these rituals, for example, and the dates after death at which the Ritual of Merit should be done (see p. 190). There is considerable overlap between Buddhist and Taoist Rituals of Merit, more even, at least in Taiwan, than De Groot's esssay on "Buddhist Masses for the Dead at Amoy" (1884) would suggest. The only real difference, a Taoist priest once told me, is that the Buddhists bring the soul to a paradise in the west, the Taoists to one in the east! And even this distinction would seem to be contradicted by the soul-banner inscription used by Master Ch'en which places paradise in the west.

For our purposes, however, the most important point is that the distinction between rituals for the living and rituals for the dead is not an absolute one, and that for two reasons. First, the exorcistic powers of the Taoist priest are even more in evidence in the Ritual of Merit than in the Offering. Virtually every ritual in the Merit sequence requires that the priest sort out the powers of darkness from those of light. This exorcistic aspect of the Ritual of Merit is even clearer when the soul of the deceased is a potentially troublesome one, for example, the soul of a mother who died in childbirth, or of someone who died by accident or committed suicide. Even northern Taiwanese Taoists will then perform a "Red[-head] Ritual of Merit" (*hung kung-te*), that is, a merit ritual which is an exorcism.

The second reason for the indistinct division between rituals for the living and for the dead, closely related to the first, is that the aim of the Merit Ritual is identical to that of the Offering, namely, to bring all things—here, the souls of the deceased; there, the gods of the living—back to their Origin in the Way. In the context of the Ritual of Merit, this means that the souls are to linger no longer in the "world of the living"; they are henceforth to dwell in the "blessed plots" (*fu-ti*) governed by the god of the soil. As in the Offering, Taoism thus boils down to the covenantal relationship between the Taoist priest and the "correct god of the soil."

But let us leave these general considerations for a description of actual practice. Once again, we shall be describing the ritual practice of Master Ch'en of Tainan, and basing ourselves on observation, manuscripts, and a second seminar given by Ch'en in Paris in 1977. Comments by Master Ch'en from this seminar will be placed, as earlier, in separate paragraphs marked "Notes." We begin with an outline of a program of a ritual observed on 24–25 November 1980 in the city of Tainan, performed for a recently deceased father and three other family members. It was a ritual of the type known as a Fast of the Tenfold [Recitation] for Salvation (*shih-hui tu-jen*) named after the multiple recitations of the *Ming-wang pa-tsui pao-ch'an* which forms one part of the ritual.

Notes: The shortest form of Ritual of Merit, called a Presentation of Treasury Money by the Coffin, is done without the construction of an altar area and contains only the rituals Opening a Road and Filling the Treasury. Any version more substantial requires the construction of an altar, whether it is a service which lasts "a noon and a night" (*wu-yeh chin-shu*, Golden Book of a Noon and a Night), one day, or one day and two nights (a Fast of the Ninefold Darkness, *chiu-yu chai*). If the fast includes the recitation of the *Ming-wang pao-ch'an*, it is also referred to as a Return of the Soul by Ten Revolutions (*shih-chuan hui-ling*). A full two-day service includes a Nocturnal Invocation and may include an Offering and a Presentation of the Memorial; it is called a Fast of the Yellow Register (*huang-lu chai*).

The ritual observed, which lasted a day and a night, is thus one of medium length. Its altar was constructed on an open hilltop about one hundred yards from the house of the deceased person, which was in an extremely narrow alley.

The altar for the Ritual of Merit is fairly large (about twelve feet by twenty-four feet), and is made of a frame of bamboo poles lashed together and overlaid by blue-and-white striped canvas tarps on the top and on three sides. The back (north) wall is essentially the same as for the Offering except that, starting in a space not encumbered by the immovable objects of a temple, the priests are able to stagger the height and distance of the five paintings from the Cave-table, so as to give a three-step appearance. The Cave-table is not one but two tables set side by side across from the single Table of the Three Realms (plate 23). Two other tables were set up on the east and west, bringing the number of tables to five. Five of the paintings of the ten hells, numbered one through five, were hung up along the east wall (plate 25) and five, numbered six through ten, along the west. In the southwest corner, at the entrance to the altar, stood a paper statue of the god of the soil, dressed in a blue paper costume with white mottling (plate 24). In the corresponding place in the southeast stood a red-clad paper statue of the "old man-spirit of the hills" (Shan-shen yeh). The two statues protect the altar (*hu-t'an*). A green Medicine King and a yellow Officer of Pardon (plate 26) were also prepared. There were, finally, eighteen "seats of the gods" (*shen-wei*), marked by the same long flat yellow envelopes used in the Offering (plate 23). Distributed six to all sides but the south, they indicate that the ritual was addressed to the Three Pure

Ones, the Heavenly Worthies of Universal Salvation by the Voice of Thunder and of the Great One Who Saves from Distress, as well as to the Great Emperor and Charitable Saint of the Eastern Peak, the kings of the ten hells, the god of the soil, and the officers and generals of the various bureaus.

The complete program, glossed by Master Ch'en's comments ("Notes"), is outlined below (see also Appendix B). The time and duration of each ritual is given in parenthesis.

DAY 1 (NOVEMBER 24)

1. Announcement (*fa-piao*, 12:58–13:19). The function of the Announcement is the same as in the Offering. As its brevity indicates, however, here it is a much simpler ritual. After the introit and procession of purification, the high priest consecrates the thick stick of incense, which has been lit at both ends. Immediately thereafter (cf. Ofuchi, 477b), he summons the various marshals on his right and left, holding up his five-thunder seal as in the Offering. Then, following a recited passage, the document of announcement (*kuan*) is read, and the priests go to the far side of the Table of the Three Realms to burn the tray of invitations. Wine is poured all around the burning documents. The high priest, who has removed his flame, writes "quickly" over it with his seal, sprays a mouthful of water (plate 24) and says, "Go carry this message. You will receive merit." Wine is poured again, and the priests return in procession, singing the appellation of the Heavenly Worthy Who Saves from Distress. They return to the Table of the Three Realms only to pick up their instruments and then move on to the Cave-table. The high priest puts his flame back in and states that the Announcement is finished.

Notes: After the burning of the thick stick of incense, which is for the officers and generals, incense is offered to the Officer of Merit (*kung-ts'ao*) in charge of transmissions on that day. The high priest must put on the expression of one giving orders when summoning the officers and generals, for he is in fact replacing Chang Tao-ling and is like an emperor summoning his ministers. At the end of the list of officers summoned, the high priest puts his flame back in his crown and lays down his seal to invoke the gods of the walls and moats, of the soil, and of the mourners' family altar. The high priest should wear his big square robe, the "mantle of descent" (*chiang-yi*; see Appendix A), with an apron underneath which is an expression of modesty before the gods. When he wears this robe, the others wear the red "robes of the Way" (*tao-p'ao*), whose chief characteristic is the eight trigrams embroidered on the sleeves, the back, and the front. When the high priest wears this red robe, the others wear the black robes called "sea-blue" (*hai-ch'ing*).

2. Invocation (*ch'i-pai*, 13:20–13:53). As in the Offering, in the Invocation here the priests take turns inviting the various divinities. As in the Offering the first eighteen are invited by the high priest: the Three

Pure Ones, the Jade Emperor, the Emperor of the Purple Empyrean, the Heavenly Worthy Who Saves from Distress, the Empress of the Earth, the Heavenly Worthies Who Save Lives on the Red Mound and Rescue from Sin in the Nine Obscurities, and the nine "ancestral energies" (Ofuchi, 483b). Among the other gods invited are those on the following lengthy list: various real persons of "great compassion and mercy"; various astral lords; the Three Officers, Six Masters, and Four Saints; the buddhas and bodhisattvas of the entire universe; the emperors of Feng-tu and the Five Peaks; the saints and immortals of the seventy-two "blessed plots" (*fu-ti*) and the thirty-six "cave-heavens" (*tung-t'ien*) of the Earth-court; the perfect lords of the Ten Halls of the Earth-court (these are the hells depicted on the ten paintings hung along the side walls); the Emperor of Fu-sang in the Water-court; the dragon-kings of the Four Seas; the gods and immortals of the rivers, lakes, and marshes; the officers of the time cycle and of the high priest's own register; the two great generals of the Divine Tiger, Ho and Ch'iao; the agents who catch the souls of the three sections (of the body); the great gods of the Five Roads of T'ai-shan; the officers of the Twelve Treasuries; the local god of the walls and moats and all the officially recognized gods, far and near; the clerks of the symbols for destroying hell and rescuing the soul; the local gods of the soil; the gods, saints, and buddhas worshiped on the domestic altar of the mourning family; its gods of the hearth and of the soil; and the gods of time and space who "hold the flag and lead [the souls]" from hell (Ofuchi, 483b-485a).

Notes: Special rituals, such as the Lake of Blood ritual for women who die in childbirth, require the invocation of special divinities (cf. Ofuchi, 484b). Last to be invited are the ancestors of the family. Each category is visualized by the high priest, who is on his knees. At the end of the list of divinities of the Three Realms, the high priest stands up to invite the officers and generals himself. Then the chief cantor invokes the officers of the hells and the administration of the Celestial Treasury. Next the memorial is read, and after that the divinities are offered tea. A poem is sung during this presentation, and the priests walk in procession, saying, "We give you tea. In this world here below there is nothing we can give you: hence, flowers, incense, tea." Two or three "tea songs" are sung as the procession continues in a circle. At each cardinal point, the keeper of the incense passes two sticks of incense to the high priest. The ritual ends with a prayer for the salvation of the soul of the deceased.

Ofuchi (485b-486b) describes a somewhat more complex conclusion, involving, first a presentation of incense, then a declaration of allegiance to the Three Treasures, followed by a confession, and finally the presentation of tea.

The gods having been invited, it is time to summon the soul. Led by the high priest, who is carrying a crescent incense burner, the priests and mourners go down the alley to the house of the dead man. In front of the house the family members get down on their knees to bow and then stand again as, in succession, the high priest and the two cantors sing a request to the Three Pure Ones to "ride forth from the Gate of Heaven" to hear the confession of the deceased. After further singing, in which the Three Pure Ones and the Heavenly Worthies Who Save from Distress and Who Transform Universally are invoked as the "incommensurable ones," the high priest summons the soul. Taking up the soul-banner (*ling-fan*), he first waves it in the direction of the domestic altar and then turns to wave it on either side of the mourners. Then, to a great clangor of gong and drum, he goes inside the house while the mourners all kneel in the alley. Inside the house, he stands in front of the family altar, on which has been placed the portrait of the deceased, and invokes the Heavenly Worthy of the Precious Flag Which Draws Forth and then invites the various soul-catchers. After he has read a short version of the memorial, wine bowls are given to each of the mourners, who make a triple libation while the high priest waves the flag from side to side, beckoning the soul to come (cf. Ofuchi, 487b). Having summoned the soul, he takes back the crescent burner, goes outside the house, turns to fumigate it, goes back in before the domestic altar to bow with the burner, and then returns to the main altar.

Notes: While the triple libation is being made, the mourners should go around the bier on all fours. (However, in the ritual observed on this occasion, the deceased had already been buried.) This is followed by the singing of a hymn and the burning of paper money (Ofuchi, 487b-488a). After the summons, an offering of soup with rice balls—like those eaten on the fifteenth day of the first month,—but white, the color of mourning—is set out in seven bowls (the number of terrestrial souls). At the same time, the priests light the three wicks—representing the celestial souls—that have been placed in each of seven shallow saucers (the terrestrial souls). These soul-lamps, filled with oil, stand on a tray under the house altar (cf. plate 25). A bucket of water with twelve coins in it is emptied into a larger container, for water and money are the two necessities of life.

The soul-banner, also called the "banner of the Way" (*tao-fan*), or even the "Buddha-banner" (*fo-fan*), is composed of eight two-yard strips of white (the color of mourning) cloth, seven thin, one wide, which are attached to a lantern-like cylinder made of yellow (earth, female) or green (heaven, male) paper. They form in this way a parasol, to protect the soul coming up from the dark underworld into the too-brilliant sunlight. This parasol with its strips of cloth in turn dangles from a four- or five-foot bamboo branch which still has its leaves (plate 25). On the narrow strips are written the names of the seven terrestrial souls. The wide strip is the real soul-banner; its inscription calls on the Savior from Distress to save the "correct soul(s)" (*cheng-hun*) of the deceased from hell and to ensure its passage to the Garland of the Law (*fa-hua*) paradise in the west. Similar flags may be seen in the Sung liturgical manuals (e.g., TT 547 *Ling-pao yü-chien* 4.7a).

3.   Scripture Recitation (*nien-ching*, 14:00–ca. 14:30). Next is the

recitation of the first part of *The Scripture of Salvation* (TT 1 *Tu-jen ching*).

Notes: The *Tu-jen ching* is recited in three parts; after each part, one of the three chapters of *The Litany of the Three Origins* (San-yüan pao-ch'an) is recited. Then a symbol-order (*fu-ming*) is read (for its text, see Ofuchi, 663b); it is attached to a paper crane, and priests and mourners go to visit the soul (*yi-ling*). The chief mourner carries a "tray of contrition" (*ch'an-p'an*), on which have been placed a mandate (*tieh*), a paper flower vase, a piece of white tissue, and a red cake in the form of a turtle with a stick of incense planted in it. There are three priests, one in red, holding the crescent incense burner, and two in black, the one who recited the litany and a second who is carrying a paper crane. When they arrive in front of the house, they recite a "recollection" (*hsiang-lai*) of the recitations just completed and then enter the room—the Chapel of Filial Piety and Grace (Hsiao-en t'ang)—where the domestic altar stands. There they sing a series of songs. Then the mourners get down on their knees while the mandate is read. This mandate is to be borne off by the soul of the deceased as proof of the Ritual of Merit held on his behalf; it is therefore burned in a basin on a table in the chapel. The reading should be followed by a triple libation, after which the priest with the crane dances very slowly, making the form of the *t'ai-chi* (the Great Ultimate, which is symbolized by ☯). Normally, this priest sings as he dances, and the verses describe the steps of Buddha's awakening, or the story of Mu-lien, or the cycle of seasons. These songs, sung either in a literary or a popular manner, may be followed by jokes. Finally, a priest says, "Now then, soul of the deceased, in this life you were a man. Now you will become a god. We will put up a spirit tablet (*ling-wei*) for you with offerings. We do these rites and make this music to facilitate your going up to paradise." Paper money is burned, a verse sung, and then they return to the altar area to burn the crane and the symbol-order, reprise the ritual just performed, and invoke the Three Pure Ones and the Heavenly Worthy Who Saves from Distress.

The dance is referred to in the memorial of the Ritual of Merit (see p. 191) as "greeting the immortal and activating the crane." The immortals, among whom are the famous Eight Immortals (*pa-hsien*), are symbol-bearing officials who use the cranes as mounts for their voyage to heaven. In using the phrase "activating the crane" to refer to the dance of the Great Ultimate, that dance is thus also designated a crane dance. One cannot help wondering whether this dance of the cranes has anything to do with the one described in the *The Annals of Wu and Yüeh* (1.34b; cf. Granet 1959, 222) in connection with the extravagant farewell to the dead prepared by King Ho-lü of Wu for his daughter, who had committed suicide. He filled her tomb with precious objects, and then

> [he] had white cranes dance in the marketplace of Wu and had thousands of people go along to watch. Then he had young men and maidens go with the cranes into the grave chamber, released a catch to shut them in, and so sent his dead [daughter] off with living [servants].

4. Opening a Road in the Darkness (*k'ai-t'ung ming-lu*, 15:00–15:19). See Chapter 11.

5. Recitation of Litanies (*pai-ch'an*, 15:42–16:32). The first three chapters of *The Precious Litany of the Shade-Kings Who Save from Sin* (*Ming-wang pa-tsui pao-ch'an*) are chanted. After each chapter, three priests go with the mourners to "visit the soul," as in the Scripture Recitation ritual. The symbols are written in red on a yellow pennant, which is attached, together with the crane, to a short stick; thus the priest is able to "wave the flag" ("activate the crane") when he dances. A text is written on the pennant in black to the left of the symbol:

> On the right is the symbol telling the infinite worlds [of the direction] to rescue the souls of the deceased [the names of the four deceased family members are written here] that they may go forth from the Long Night, see the light, and be saved. The heavens rejoice when [here are written in the infirmities associated with the direction in the *Tu-jen ching* and the cure effected by the recitation of this text]. In accord with the announced order, let the immortal transform and the crane transmit. Communicated on [date] to the officiant in charge of the ritual [name], who, having received the order, executes it [by means of] [here is given the particular Heavenly Worthy of the direction] and the Heavenly Worthy Who Saves from Distress, the Great One of the Green Palace of the Eastern Extremity. (Ofuchi, 665a-b)

The recitation of the ten chapters of this litany (the remaining seven are chanted in the next Recitation, see number 10) gives its name to the ritual program as a whole (The Fast of the Tenfold [Recitation] for Salvation). The reason is now clear: each chapter corresponds to one of the ten salvific recitations ascribed at the start of the *Tu-jen ching* to the Heavenly Worthy of the Primordial Beginning. There each recitation is associated, as here, with a specific direction and with salvation from a specific infirmity (of the feet for the north, of the eyes for the south, etc.). In addition to a symbol and a mandate (*tieh*), each chapter of the *Ming-wang pao-ch'an* is provided with its own announcement (*kuan*), addressed to the "bearer of the symbol [of the direction], the immortal officer who rides the crane." The announcement, written out, is burned with the symbol and an appropriate amount of paper money after the priests return to the main altar. The mandate is left on the altar in the house.

6. Dispatching the Writ of Pardon (*fang she-ma*, 16:50–17:40). See Chapter 12.

7. Attack on Hell (*ta-ch'eng*, 18:50–20:20). See Chapter 13.

8. Division of the Lamps (*fen-teng*, 20:54–21:44). The same ritual text is used here as for the Division of the Lamps ritual in the Offering, and the same sequence of three rituals is performed.

DAY 2 (NOVEMBER 25)

9.   Land of the Way (*tao-ch'ang*, 8:02–8:58). Structurally, this ritual is identical to the ritual of the same name in the Offering, except that, like the Division of Lamps, it ends with a visit to the house altar (cf. Ofuchi, 510b and 525a). Textually, it contains some of the same hymns, especially in the triple presentation of incense and tea. The recitations, however, are completely different, as may be expected, and the formulae for lighting and extinguishing the burner are addressed only to the Jade Sovereign of the Golden Gate and the Heavenly Worthy Who Saves from Distress. The ritual observed on this occasion was abbreviated at several points, containing, for example, no special rite for the dispatch of the message.

10.   Recitation of Litanies (9:18–10:00, 10:35–11:15). Chapters 4-7 and 8-10 of the *Ming-wang pao-ch'an* are recited.

11.   Noon Offering (*wu-hsien*, 11:24–12:02). After the usual introductory rites—introit, purification, invocation—the crescent burner and sticks of incense are retrieved from the mourners. While a song is sung, all the offerings are passed down the rows of kneeling mourners so that each can present them one by one. Then new sticks of incense are distributed to the mourners, the Flag of the Way (the soul-banner) is given to the chief mourner, a tray with coins, bracelets, and other precious objects contributed by the family members is given to the second in rank, and, carrying the burner, the high priest leads a procession down the alley to the house. Once again, the sticks of incense are collected from the mourners and the offerings presented by each of the family members, after which they again receive new incense. After a song and a recited passage, the memorial is read. Another song accompanies the pouring of wine into 12 glasses. Each of the mourners makes an offering of wine while the high priest sings, and then the mourners remove their hempen mourning garments. The priests take turns dancing and singing, and then all return in procession to the main altar.

Notes: Normally, the appellations of the Three Pure Ones and the Heavenly Worthy Who Saves from Distress are sung on the main altar before the retrieval of the crescent burner. The visit to the soul has a special name in this ritual: the Offering to the Ancestors (*chien-tsu*). It includes a formula for the destruction of hell, a chant involving the Heavenly Worthy Who Saves from Distress, and the presentation of 12 bowls of wine, 12 pairs of incense sticks, 12 large bowls of vegetarian food, a large bowl of rice, and so on, that is, the presentation of the noon meal. The symbol of all of these offerings is the bowl of rice, which is handed to the high priest. The priest takes a branch dipped in the symbol-water and purifies the bowl, and then he takes chopsticks and writes in the air the characters *wan-p'in yi-chi,* "the ten thousand items form a single sacrifice." He traces a circle around the bowl with the sticks and then uses them to pick up some grains of rice and throw them into the air, an action he performs three times. He then veils the bowl and his face with his sleeve and pronounces a secret formula for transforming the food so that it can be consumed by the deceased. He plants the chopsticks in the bowl and hands it to the leader of the troupe, who removes them and sets the bowl on the table in the first row of offerings. After the reading of the memorial, the acolytes chant a refrain inviting all the ancestors of the family to come down to the banquet, beginning with the founder, then the most recently deceased; each time the mourners make a libation. That done, the priests invoke the Savior from Distress once more, and then each sings a verse commenting on the passage of time, the harshness of life, and similar themes. These songs are interspersed with brief exchanges: "Within the bowls the whole universe is to be found," "How great are heaven and earth: our offerings will go on forever." All this has occurred in the chapel itself; the priests now go outside, invite all souls to the banquet, and sing a series of three *nan-kuan* (southern pipes) songs. As they sing, they move in circles and figure-eights, slowly at first, then faster and faster, doing more and more figure-eights, arms flung out, laughing like drunken immortals, as the music switches to *pei-kuan* (northern pipes). The priests collide with each other, and there is a moment of general confusion. Finally, the leader of the troupe stops in the southeast part of the altar (the Door of Earth), where he raises his hand to signal the end. There is a brief final song "so that the deceased can proceed to paradise."

12. Scripture Recitation (14:25–14:50). This ritual consists of the recitation and singing of *The Precious Scroll of the Savior from Distress* (*Chiu-k'u pao-chüan*). Two black-robed priests, one with the cantor's drum, the other with the assistant cantor's bowl, sit facing each other across a small table set up in front of the house. After reciting the various entry formulae which always precede the "opening of a scripture," the first priest recites the passage from *The Scripture of Salvation* (*Tu-jen ching*) which describes the celestial assembly which is gathered by the tenfold recitation of this scripture. The second priest responds:

> At that time . . . the Heavenly Worthy of the Primordial Beginning uttered the ten great unimaginable Rituals of Merit (*kung-te*) and recited *The Marvellous Scripture of Limitless* [*Salvation*]; he transmitted the real instrument of salvation. . . . This ritual of merit can be offered (*chien*) to the soul of the deceased (*ling-yi*) so that it may ascend to the Realm of Happiness. We look to the Taoists to perform it for us respectfully.
> (Ofuchi, 603a)

The rest of the *Chiu-k'u pao-chüan* is composed of these "ten great unimaginable rituals of merit," each of which contains one or two hymns and passages, and are here recited in turn by the two priests. The recitation in particular is done at breakneck speed, and interspersed with joking. The songs are accompanied by a single oboe and the large drum.

After this ritual, on this occasion a show of acrobatics and stunts was put on for a half hour for the amusement of the souls of the deceased. Paper statuettes which represent the dead had been made and set out on a table across from the main altar area, and one of the family members held an umbrella over their heads to protect them from the rays of the sun which, now that they belong to the underworld, they cannot bear. The stunts, the work of hired specialists, is said to represent the marvellous powers of the eighteen arhats of Buddhist folklore. They are collectively called *nung-nao*, "playing with the cymbals," after the main stunt, which consists of spinning a cymbal atop a bamboo pole (De Groot 1884, 77–78; as De Groot notes, pp. 74 and 108, theatrical performances may also be given).

13. Exorcism (16:08–16:28). The green paper figure of the Medicine King (Yao-wang, originally the Buddhist Bhaisajyaguru, but identified by the Taoists with Shen-nung, Chinese patron of medicine) has been set out on a table in front of the house. Four black-robed and one red-robed priest perform the ritual facing outward, that is, with their backs turned on the family altar. The purpose of the ritual is to "master and expel the evil spirits (*sha*) so they go far away to another place." Sometimes a number of eggs, "medicine for the ill," are placed on the table next to the king, and there is always an earthenware pot containing mushrooms, which also symbolize drugs. The ritual begins with an "opening to the light" (*k'ai-kuang*), that is, with the animation of the paper king, using blood from the crest of a white cock and the bill of a dark-colored duck. Carrying the two birds, the priests go in procession clockwise three times, with the exorcist's horn marking the beginning and the end of each procession. The statuettes of the deceased are given tea to drink. The birds are flung by their bound feet to the side, firecrackers are set off, the high priest swats all around, first with a broom and then with a rolled mat, and then the teapot is smashed on the ground. The priests return to the hilltop to burn the Medicine King.

14. Uniting the Symbols (*ho-fu*, 16:45–17:03). One red-robed and two black-robed priests sit down in front of the Table of the Three Realms, on which have been placed the paper images of twelve lads (*t'ung-tzu*), each of which is wrapped up in a packet of mock money and has in front of it a stick of incense planted in a banana. The ritual consists essentially of a series of invitations, issued to ten celestial divinities first (the Three Pure Ones and others), to twelve groups of ten lads each next, and finally to forty-two jade lasses. Each invitation ends with a prayer that the soul of the deceased may "leave the paths of the underworld and go to be reborn in heaven" and with an

invocation of the Most Compassionate Savior from Distress. The ritual ends with a series of recitations enumerating the categories of sins that a heavenly worthy named at the end of the paragraph is asked to "blot out," so that the soul may be removed from the blacklist (*hei-po*) and be reborn in Marvellous Joy (Miao-le, the name of a paradise). Twelve mandates (*tieh*), which have been lying on the table, are then carried down to the house, where one is read, the priest facing outward, and then, the priest facing inward, all are burned, together with the paper images of the lads themselves. (According to Ofuchi, 533a, there should be such a "house visit" during each invitation of the lads.)

Notes: This ritual derives its name, *ho-fu*, from the fact that the twelve mandates burned correspond to the twelve symbol-orders burned during the Announcement. These sets of twelve are the two halves which must be matched in order to obtain the release of the soul from the twelve hells of the underworld (cf. Ofuchi, 530a). Normally, five banners should also be prepared, one each for the four directions plus one for the Savior from Distress; these are carried by the mourners when they go in procession to the house chapel, and they are burned at the same time as the mandates and lads (cf. Ofuchi, 536b-537b). The priests should each in turn sing and dance at the house. The dance represents the trajectory of the soul through hell, where the Savior from Distress has gone to fetch him. The lads liberate the soul from the sins which "bind it," and the lasses escort the soul to heaven.

The liturgical manuals in the Taoist canon nowhere refer to the twelve hells named in this ritual. Nine of the twelve, however, are the well-known Nine Obscurities (*chiu-yu;* see for example Chiang Shu-yü, 24.7b-19a). In Chiang's ritual the high priest "transforms himself into the Heavenly Worthy Who Saves from Distress" and then "smashes" the nine hells by a combination of incantations, hand gestures, and the burning of symbol-flags (*fu-fan*). A tenth symbol-flag, a general symbol written in red on yellow paper, with an accompanying order (*kao-wen*) written in black, has been burned at the very beginning of the ritual (Chiang Shu-yü, 44.4a). It would appear then that the ritual which is practiced by Master Ch'en simply extends the principle of the combination of symbol and order used in Chiang Shu-yü's thirteenth century text for the general symbol only to each individual symbol. The general symbol is also called a "register" (*lu*), precisely because it is a general symbol for the destruction of all hells. We find reference to "golden lads and jade lasses, twelve each," in the secret instructions for the same ritual to "smash the Nine Obscurities" in TT 219 *Tu-jen ta-fa* 50.8a-b. In this passage, a flag, on which is written the name Heavenly Worthy Who Forgives Sins, is carried into each of the nine hells in turn, and the

sinners in the prison follow the flag: wherever it shines, the cangues fall away. Having gone to the root of the miseries of sin, all wake up [and recall] their Original Source. All grudges and resentments dissolve, the prison guards salute them with respect, and all cry out with joy. They look up and call upon the Heavenly Worthy, the soul-consciousness is pulled out of hell, and all go, following the light, out of the realm of darkness.

Inasmuch as the soul of a deceased person goes to a hell associated with his birthdate (ibid., 50.7a), it seems likely that Master Ch'en's Uniting the Symbol ritual has been "contaminated" by his Filling the Treasury ritual with its twelve treasury officers (see number 19 below).

15. Bath (*mu-yü*, 18:45–19:00). Inside the house, in front of the domestic altar, on which stands a portrait of the deceased, a table with offerings is prepared, and under it is placed a tray of shallow, oil-filled dishes, in each of which three wicks burn, representing the three superior souls of the deceased. Between table and altar stands a screen, set there to hide a basin of water, "so the soul can wash itself unseen." A single black-robed priest performs the Bath ritual, which begins with his singing the appellation of the Savior from Distress as the introit. After the other entry rites and a hymn called "Weeping over Hell," the priest sings out, "I have pure water here to wash the souls." Then, with his bowl of symbol-water in his left hand and three sticks of incense in his right hand, he writes in the air with the incense the character for "clean," sprinkles some water, and while saying the name of the first of the Three Pure Ones, throws the sticks over the screen into the basin. This he does three times, writing the characters "tranquil" and "washed" for the second and the third of the Three Pure Ones (cf. Ofuchi, 538a).

The next segment of the ritual, composed of alternating recitation and song, is performed to summon the soul. This is to be done by the use of the soul-banner (*ling-fan*) and the transmission of a "symbol-order of the Primordial Beginning" (*yüan-shih fu-ming*). A hymn, the "Stanza of the Dipper," describing the cosmic cycle of *yin* and *yang* and urging the soul to heed the call of the Great One and "follow my flag," is found already in Chiang Shu-yü's ritual for summoning the soul (26.4a; cf. Ofuchi, 538b). The various soul-catchers invited during the Announcement are invoked once again, together with the god of the soil, who is obviously the ultimate guardian of the souls of the dead (cf. plate 24). During this invocation, the priest waves the soul-flag and then drapes some of its white tassels over the screen (cf. Ofuchi, 539a).

It is now time for the soul to bathe, and the text indicates at this point that clothes and a towel should be burned so that the soul can dry itself and change its clothing (Ofuchi, 539b). In Master Ch'en's ritual on this occasion, a towel is draped over the edge of the basin, and clothing, a whole box of miniature clothes, set off to one side. The clothing is not burned until the Filling the Treasury ritual. The three incantations given in the ritual text concerning the bath and change of

clothing were on this occasion omitted. All three are found, in a different
order, in Chiang Shu-yü's Bath ritual (26.9a–11b) and, in the same order,
in Lü T'ai-ku's (5.21b–22a). Master Ch'en here simply sings a song after
summoning the soul, and then leaves for the main altar. The family
members, who have been dressed in ordinary clothes during the Bath
ritual, now put on their burlap mourning garments, gather up the various
ritual items—the oil saucers, the four statuettes of the deceased, the
umbrella used to shade them, the flag, and the basin—and bring them
back, accompanied by music, to the tent on the hilltop. The four images
are now placed on the Table of the Three Realms, facing the Three Pure
Ones; the tray of oil lamps is placed under their table, and the water
basin just in front. Sticks of incense are lit in front of the statues.

16. Paying Homage to the Three Treasures (*pai san-pao*,
19:06–19:28). The name by which this ritual is commonly known, Paying
Homage to the Three Treasures, is found in the body of the text; the
actual title of the ritual is "Perfect Ritual of the Most High for the Triple
Audience (*ts'an-ch'ao*) and the Issuing of the Mandate (*kei-tieh*)." The
soul of the deceased, having bathed and put on clean clothes, goes in
audience before the Three Pure Ones to pay its respects and to receive
from them its "passport to heaven."

The passport the soul of the deceased receives is transmitted to it
by the "servant" of the Three Pure Ones, that is, the priest, whose
ordination had made of him an "immortal official." In this ritual the
priest is making the soul of the deceased a Taoist initiate, an initiation
that is at once comparable to and dependent upon his own ordination.
This is very clear in the corresponding ritual in Chiang Shu-yü (chap.
28), where it is called "Ritual for the Transmission of the Commandments and Symbols for the Ascension and Passage of the Soul of the
Deceased." Chiang's ritual begins with a long sermon, followed by an
homage to the Three Treasures and the proclamation of nine commandments. A series of three documents is then read and transmitted (28.7b–
9a), of which the most important are the "golden register of long life"
(41.10a–15b)—it is the document of initiation, signed and sealed by the
three initiating masters—and the "contract for the ascension to heaven"
(41.7b–9b). The right half of the latter document is attached to the
soul-banner and the left half is sealed in an envelope addressed to the
Officer of Merit of the day. Last to be read is the "Ritual of Merit
mandate" (*kung-te tieh*). A detailed description of the ritual program,
it will be carried to heaven by the soul of the deceased as proof, "so
that the officers of earth may strike it forever from the register of
sinners, the courts of the underworld detain it no longer, and gods and
men be transformed and promoted according to their fruits" (28.9b).

The Homage ritual performed by Master Ch'en is a good deal

simpler than Chiang Shu-yü's, but it is in essence the same ritual. The soul is summoned to the Land of the Way in an introit sung to violin, mandolin-plucking, and percussion. A single priest waves its flag while standing first in the southeast corner and then in the southwest corner. He curtseys toward the southeast (the Door of Earth), puts the flag down, and goes to the Cave-table to call out:

> With utmost respect and sincerity, everyone bows his head and gives thanks to the King of the Law of the Primordial Beginning, to the most perfect Celestial Treasure. (Ofuchi, 540b)

Singing, "Supreme joy in the Realm of Triple Purity," the priest walks back to the Table of the Three Realms, where he tips the statuettes forward one by one to signify their homage. He then comes back before the Cave-table to sing a hymn of "allegiance to the Treasure of the Way." The sequence is then repeated for the other two Treasures. At last he comes back and picks up the statuettes. He brings them forward to bow, three times each, to the north (Treasure of the Way), to the northeast (Treasure of the Scriptures), and to the northwest (Treasure of the Masters; cf. Ofuchi, 541a). He goes back then to the center of the altar to bow north one more time, and then at last puts the statuettes back on the Table of the Three Realms. All this has been done to gonging and strings.

The priest now reads in turn a mandate for each of the four souls. After each mandate, he puts the letter back in its long white envelope, folds the envelope in half, and places it, with a "contract for the purchase of land" for the new home of the deceased in the other world, behind the appropriate statue. This done, he recites a confession for the soul, states a series of wishes, and concludes the ritual with a brief summary.

The mandate "issued" reads as follows (cf. Hou, 51–52 and Ofuchi, 662a–b):

LAND OF THE WAY OF THE THREE TREASURES
TO SAVE THE DEAD: TODAY,

> [address of the family home], we worship the Way by performing this ritual for the deceased. By reciting litanies, rescuing them [from hell], and filling the treasury, the living generation pays its debt of gratitude: [names of the mourners], together with all the filial family members, express our grief and think with pain of the deceased [name], one correct soul,° who was originally born in the auspicious year [filled in]. Having respectfully borrowed, at the time he received his life, ten thousand strings of underworld cash from the various officers (*ta-fu*) of the general treasury of the Internal Court of the Bureau of Heaven, he was born in

---

°That is, a soul who will regularly and legitimately receive sacrifices from his descendants; *cheng*, "correct," also means "orthodox," as in "orthodox unity."

the Middle Land [China]. He had not yet had time to reimburse the treasury when he died unexpectedly [date]. We fear his celestial souls will return to the Court of the Underworld and his terrestrial souls to the earth. Without a ritual of salvation, it will be difficult for him to escape the sea of suffering. Having selected an auspicious day in this month, we have engaged a Taoist to come to the mourning household to reimburse the debt for him by means of this Ritual of Merit (*kung-te*). Having already memorialized the Bureau of Heaven, covenanted with it, rendered a cult to it, and begged it to send down its gracious light to rescue him, we register these paired (*ho-t'ung*) mandates: one is to be verified by the officers of the general treasury of the internal court of the Bureau of Heaven; the other is for the deceased, who is to hold it as proof of this assembly.

The text of the "paired mandates" is identical to this point. The one read in this ritual—addressed to the deceased—concludes:

On the right is the mandate to be given to the deceased [name], one correct soul, that it may hold it as proof. The debt having been paid in its entirety, show this to the underworld court when they draw up the original account in the Bureau of Heaven. When you have been stricken from their record books, pray that you may ascend to human heaven, where you can use this as proof when you come into the presence of the Saint. Therefore, we adjudge for transfer to the treasury [amount], which has been verified twice.
    [date]   [name of the deceased]
MANDATE   in charge of the fast, Ch'en Ts'un-hsin.
with gratitude, [name of grandson, if any] adds his own treasury money [amount] to be given to the deceased [name] for his personal use.

The second mandate of the pair, addressed to the treasury official, is read in the Filling the Treasury ritual. It says:

On the right is the mandate for the underworld money for the gift of life, so many thousands [amount], not counting the packet of spares: it is herewith turned over to your honorable treasury. We pray you to instruct those in charge of money to draw on the capital and transfer it into the treasury. Check the names and strike them from your record books. We presume on the divine powers and await your gracious response. Respectfully, we mandate the transfer to the treasury [amount], which has been verified twice.
MANDATE   in charge of the fast, Ch'en Ts'un-hsin.
                        (cf. Ofuchi, 662a–b)

The mandate issued to the soul of the deceased is placed behind the statuette which represents him. On the envelope is written, "The mandate on the right is given, on the Land of the Way of the Three Treasures to Save the Dead, to the soul of the deceased [name], one correct soul, to hold as proof." Mandate, envelope, and statuette will all be burned, together with the paper house made for the spirit, at the end of the entire service. The envelope of the mandate to be read and burned during the Filling the Treasury ritual reads, "The mandate on the right is given . . . to the various officers of the general treasury of the internal court of the Bureau of Heaven." The high priest's seal has been affixed to these two envelopes as to a single entity, with half the impression on each envelope.

These "paired mandates" are not identical to any of the three principal documents issued in Chiang Shu-yü's ritual, but they share characteristics with all three. Insofar as they are issued at this point in the ritual under the authority, according to the mandate, of a "Taoist engaged to reimburse the debt" for the deceased, they mark in fact the culminating point of the ritual and, as such, constitute the soul's "passport," that is, his "register of long life." Insofar as half is attached to the soul's image and half sent to an officer in the celestial bureaucracy, they fulfil the function of a "contract for the ascension to heaven." Insofar as they serve as proof of the acquittal of the deceased's debt and his corresponding acquisition of merit, they correspond to the Ritual of Merit mandate. Most important, however, is that the paired mandates reveal not only that continuity in the performance of rituals for the dead over more than seven centuries is more basic than change, but also that the foundation of all Taoist ritual, whether for the living or for the dead, is indeed the rite of union. Initiation by means of and into—the medium is the message—symbolization is the secret heart of Taoism.

17. Untying the Knots (*chieh-chieh*, 19:28–19:55). From start to finish, the aim of the Ritual of Merit is redemption and deliverance. The soul of the deceased enters the ritual imprisoned in darkness, sick, dirty, caught in a tangled web of sin, debt, and unfulfilled longings; he will leave the ritual liberated, enlightened, healed, cleansed, forgiven, free of debt, in a word, detached. Each ritual within the Ritual of Merit symbolizes one or another of these aspects of salvation. The ritual Untying the Knots, which follows without break the Homage to the Three Treasures, represents salvation as "detachment." Its full title is Untying the Knots and Dissolving Sins (on the origin of the term "untying the knots," see Robinet 1979, 213 ff.).

The ritual is composed basically of seven identical segments. Holding a knotted skein of string in his hand, the officiant invokes the Heavenly Worthy of General Passage by the Bridge of the Law and then, facing the statuettes, sings a verse describing a category of sins to be "dissolved" as he makes a rolling motion with the skein of string (cf. Ofuchi, 542b). Returning to the Cave-table, he invokes the Heavenly Worthy Who Undoes Resentments and Loosens Knots and reads a brief document summarizing the purpose of the ritual. He comes back before the statuettes to recite a series of seven wishes and then, while a summary song is sung, lights a cone of "old money," writes with it, and throws it in a basin on the south side of the altar. He goes through this entire sequence seven times, expressing in all $7 \times 7 = 49$ wishes, one for each day of the main mourning period after the death of a parent. At last he undoes the knot altogether and gives it to another priest to be burned. He receives a large bunch of newly lit sticks of incense and bows with them as he sings the names of four heavenly worthies of "great compassion and mercy" (Ofuchi, 546a). Sticks of incense are passed to the mourners, who bow with them and then return them to be planted in the burner. The ritual ends with a procession to the house and an offering of song.

18. Recitation of Litanies (20:00–20:33). The three chapters of *The Precious Litany of Compassion* (*Tz'u-pei pao-ch'an*) are recited. As usual, a visit to the soul, consisting of the reading of a mandate and a dance with it, follows the recitation of each chapter. There is, however, only one mandate, and a single priest makes the visit with the family members while a second priest launches directly into the recitation of the next chapter. The mandate is to be "presented to the soul of the deceased so that it may be reborn in the Realm of the Immortals."

19. Filling the Treasury (*t'ien-k'u,* 21:00–21:47).° In preparation for this ritual, a huge circular wall of paper money has been neatly stacked equidistant from the house and the altar, at the foot of the hill. Six white paper figures and one blue have been prepared, representing the Officer of the Treasury (*k'u-kuan*), his clerks and porters. Their function, according to Hou (p. 53), is to ensure that the contract for the purchase of land in the other world set out earlier is kept and that the money is duly transferred. A box of the deceased's clothing has been set out, together with much miniature clothing; both will be thrown on the fire during this ritual. The soul-banner has been brought back from the house altar, where the candle in front of the portrait of the deceased has been extinguished. The family forms a circle around the pile of money, holding with both hands onto a rope, which both links the living family members together and prevents wandering souls from taking the money.

As the family takes its place along this rope, the bonfire is lit. The priest sprays symbol-water on the fire and then on a table which has been set up, in principle, to the north of it. The entire administration of the Celestial Treasury is invoked, and then a triple libation of wine performed. After the third libation, the mandate for the treasury official is read (see p. 186). In addition to the mandate for the "general treasury," there are as many separate mandates for specific treasuries as there are sons in mourning. (The year of their birth determines to

---

°For a translation and study of this ritual, see Hou, 49-60.

which of the twelve treasuries—one for each year in the twelve-year cycle—they belong and how much they must pay [Ofuchi, 547b].)

As these mandates are read, the clothes are thrown onto the bonfire. After the final libation, the priest enters the circle to spray the fire with symbol-water once again; the treasury officials are also thrown into the flames. The mandates are put in a smaller fire of paper money by the table where the priest had been reciting, and where he now sits down to sing the "Ballad of Pregnancy" (*Huai-t'ai ko*), also called the "Ballad of the Flowery Womb" (*Hua-t'ai ko*). This song describes the "ten months"of pregnancy—nine plus one, for the month of birth—as well as early infancy, weaning, education, and what the individual must now do to repay all he has received. It is basically a eulogy to filial piety. After every two lines of verse, the drummer sings the refrain, an invocation of the Heavenly Worthy Who Saves from Distress.

By the end of the Filling the Treasury ritual, the priests and musicians who are not participating have nearly finished taking down the scrolls and altar hangings. The Ritual of Merit is now essentially over. Often at this point the large paper house, which is to become the dwelling place of the soul in the other world, is taken out and set up facing the still-burning bonfire. After the final ritual, it will be set aflame separately, and all the paraphernalia used during the Treasury ritual—the table, the wine glasses—will be put on the bonfire, together with the oil saucers used to represent the souls of the deceased. Everything is burned; nothing may remain.

20. Crossing the Bridge (*kuo-ch'iao*, 21:50–21:56). Outside the family house, a small paper bridge has been set up, and next to it is placed the tray of oil-filled saucers. (Like several other rituals performed in the alley outside the house, this ritual is normally done inside the house, in front of the domestic altar; in the present case, this room was too small.) The chief mourner has the soul-banner, the others the four paper statuettes. The priest takes the flag and waves it over the bridge as he sings a song and then steps over the bridge and the saucers, followed by all the mourners, each of whom is carrying something. This is done three times, and then all go inside. The green and white hangings over the door are torn down and set on fire with the bridge. Thus ends a ritual program which has lasted nearly thirteen hours, excluding the Universal Salvation banquet prepared late in the afternoon by the neighborhood, in which the Taoist priests take no part.

Notes: The final ritual, involving the burning of the paper house, should be done by a Taoist priest from the neighborhood, even if the rest of the ritual has been done by invited priests. The mourners should not be present for the first part of this ritual, the Removal of the Soul (*ch'u-ling*) from the Hall of Filial Piety. It is an exorcism, using oil mixed with salt as a purifying agent, a large kitchen knife, which is planted in the table used in the house altar, a rolled-up mat, a broom, and other items, all of which contribute to expelling the bad energies associated with death. The exorcism should then be followed by a procession to a place outside town, carrying the paper house, the table, the paper images, and all the other objects. The area where all this is to be burned should be swept, then fruit, tea, and other offerings are set out for the god of the soil, and finally the house is positioned in accord with the day and with the principles of *feng-shui* ("geomancy"). In front of the house are placed the images of the deceased, the sedan chair in which the statuette of the principle deceased was brought out, the paper porters, and money; behind it are set up a Mountain of Filial Piety prepared by the young men of the family and mountains of gold and silver prepared by the young girls. When all is installed, the mourners remove their hemp garments, purify them, and give them back to the burial association.

Next comes a *yang* rite, Entering the House (*ju-chia*). Red cakes and New Year's cakes are set out, and red votive lamps hung up; the women put paper flowers in their hair, as when a baby is born. All make obeisance, and then call urgently on the soul to enter the paper house prepared for him. The sedan chair is set aflame. The Taoist priest recites some formulae to "see him off" and then removes his vestments. The mourners take a teapot and walk three times around the bonfire, pouring tea.

This ritual should be done forty-nine days after the death, corresponding to the first seven courts of hell. It should be repeated one hundred days after the death, then again after one year, and a last time after three years.[*]

Back home, the mourners should put on a small Offering to welcome back the gods and the ancestors. The gods are placed once again in the middle of the family altar, the ancestral tablets on their right, with the tablet of the new ancestor on the outside. All the family members put on new clothes. They make a lantern of the Dipper with seven flames, or a Dipper of rice with seven red candles. They may even invite the local god of the soil and perform a ritual of Settling in Place (*an-wei*), complete with triple libation. Finally, the Taoist priest goes throughout the house with symbol-water to purify it, and the men and women go in groups to offer incense in the local temple.

We may conclude our general survey of the Ritual of Merit with a translation of the large yellow wall placard (*pang*) which is the petition (*chang*) of this ritual:

PETITION FOR THE SUPREME FAST OF ASCENT, FRUIT OF THE TENFOLD
RECITATION FOR SALVATION

Ch'en, in charge of the various offices of thunder and lightning, the bureau of the Dipper, and the Celestial Clinic, immortal minister of the

---

[*]The soul is thought to be judged successively in each of the ten courts of hell. Judgment occurs one week after death in the first court, two weeks after death in the second, and so on through the seventh court on the forty-ninth day. Brief versions of the Ritual of Merit, consisting essentially of recitations of scriptures and confessions, should be performed to coincide with each judgment, and the full version should be done on or around the forty-ninth day. Brief versions are again to be performed in conjunction with the three final judgments, after one hundred days, one year, and three years.

The same time periods are given in TT 215 *Ti-fu shih-wang pa-tu yi*. The earliest mention of the 49- and 100-day periods of mourning in a Taoist text is found in TT 336 *Yeh-pao yin-yüan ching*, 8.6b, a scripture which probably dates to the late sixth century and is heavily influenced by Buddhism (cf. also De Groot 1884).

canonical register of the Covenant of the Orthodox Unity of the Most High with the Powers, possessing and practicing the ritual methods of the Divine Empyrean: bowing and kowtowing a hundred times, the above-named servant addresses himself on high and respectfully memorializes on behalf of the auspiciously placed household in the northern sector of Tainan [full address], which worships the Way and performs a fast to make confession, rescue from hell by the tenfold recitation, and fill the treasury. These living family members repay the kindness [of their parents]: the filial sons [names]; their filial wives [names]; the filial grandsons [names]; the filial granddaughters [names]; his mourning wife [name]; the filial daughters [names]; the filial sister-in-law [name]; together with the filial grandsons of the two associated grandparents [the names of the sons repeated]; as well as the nephews of the other associated soul [same names].

These filial family members, respectfully displaying their grief and their sincerity, now importune the Mysterious Creator (*hsüan-tsao*), setting forth our sorrowful purpose and praying you will deign to rescue [the deceased]. Majestic is the Great Way: it saves the living and gives passage to the dead. Great is the Somber Office: it can free the upper souls and release the lower souls. Rapidly, they arrive on the [other] shore: the methods of the Way have no limits. With grief we think of our illustrious father [name], now deceased, for whom this ritual is offered in the first place: he originally received life at a fortunate hour of a fortunate day of a fortunate month in the year 1918 and died and left this world, alas, at the *yin* hour of the 17th day of the 9th month of 1980. We also offer it for the souls of his illustrious father [name], born at the auspicious time [not filled in], and his illustrious mother [name], auspicious time [not filled in], as well as for his deceased brother [name], whose auspicious time of birth and death were [not filled in].

With pain we think of the correct souls of these four parents: their celestial souls have returned to the court of the underworld (*yin-fu*), and their terrestrial souls have entered the realm of roots (*nan-k'o*). As long as we have not made this offering (*chien*) for their rescue, it is difficult for them to go to the land of the living.

Having selected by divination the 17th and 18th of this month, we go, leaning on the Way, to the House of Mourning to set up an altar and perform a two-day and one-night Fruit of Merits (*kung-kuo*) and Pure Fast of the Supreme Tenfold Recitation for Salvation. At an auspicious hour, we will start up the drum and respectfully dispatch the Announcement documents inviting the Great Way and informing all the perfect ones. We will visit the soul to explain the ritual, express our grief, and present our offerings. We will recite *The Scripture of Salvation* and pay homage in audience with *The Precious Litany of the Shade-Kings*. We will greet the immortals and activate the cranes; by ten recitations we will bring the soul back [to the Origin]. Toward evening, we will promulgate the Document of Pardon of the Chancellery of the Three Heavens, ordering the earth-prisons of Feng-tu to release the souls of the deceased. We will destroy the Citadel [so they may] ascend to life. The first night we will divide the lamps, roll up the screen, sound the golden [bell], and strike the jade [stone].

The next day we will mount the altar for the Land of the Way and present incense three times. We will recite *The Precious Scroll of the Savior from Distress* and prepare a special Noon Offering, which we will present to our forebears that they may ascend on high. Facing the hells, we will unite the symbols that their sins may be forgiven in accord with the laws. Outside will be spread a small feast for distribution to all the solitary souls. Thrice we will summon the souls of the deceased, who will bathe and change their clothing. We will bring them thrice before the audience halls of the Three Treasures, where we will utter with our mouths the wishes of their hearts, give them instruction concerning sin and guilt, and issue to them their mandate. We will reimburse the treasury and give the deceased money for their own use. We will transform their bodies and sublimate (*lien-tu*) them. We will lead the souls of the deceased over the bridge to the land of eternal life. When all is done, we will take leave of the altar and see the saints off on their return journey. We will burn money for the memorial and then prepare a banquet in honor of the Compassionate Worthy, beseeching him for universal salvation.

We pray the Compassionate Worthy of the Eastern Extremity to emit the auspicious light that draws [the souls] forth and the Perfect Elder of Southern Cinnabar to color the cloud-road purple that they may soar along it. May the deceased ascend to heaven, those in mourning obtain good fortune, and all sentient creatures mount on high to the shore of the Way. Your servant has prepared the memorial as he was told to. With utmost respect he memorializes concerning everything above to the Heavenly Worthy Who Saves from Distress, the Great One [written in red], to whom he looks up with reverence.

LET THE ABOVE MANDATE BE KNOWN [in red, on top of these four characters is the word "execute"]. In the *keng-shen* year of heaven's revolution, the 10th month, the 17th and 18th [in red] days: your humble servant bows low three times as he presents this memorial on high to the Most Compassionate and Charitable One of the Green Palace of the Eastern Extremity, the Heavenly Worthy and Great One Who Hears Prayer and Saves from Distress.

PLACARD   Hung up in Front of the Altar

In the last line, the term "Hears Prayer" means literally "seeks out voices" (*hsün-sheng*), for the Savior from Distress goes in search of those who call upon his name. Note that he, who is from the orient, is associated in this memorial with the Perfect Elder from the south; east and south are the two *yang* directions of Anterior Heaven.

The Sublimation (*lien-tu*) ritual, mentioned in the placard also requires a brief comment. At the end of the manuscript text of the Bath ritual, the priest is told that "if there is to be a *lien-tu*, he should bring the souls to the area for sublimation." In Southern Sung times, when this Sublimation ritual appears for the first time—and when it becomes a ritual of the utmost importance—it is normally placed between the Bath and Paying Homage to the Three Treasures (e.g., Chiang Shu-yü, chap. 27). In Master Ch'en's ritual practice it is performed as a kind of theatrical dialogue leading up to and involving the Crossing of the Bridge, of which it thus constitutes an expansion. We shall incidentally see below that the association of the Sublimation with the Crossing of the Bridge goes back at least to the thirteenth century (see p. 234);

suffice it for the moment to note that in the placard it is mentioned in the appropriate place as far as Ch'en's normal ritual practice is concerned, but that it corresponds, in the ritual observed, to no specific ritual other than Crossing the Bridge.

In conclusion, the following partial translation of the memorial (*shu*)—also written on yellow (earth) paper—reveals several rather interesting variants when compared with the petition:

> With pain we think of these parents: their unique energy returns to the void; their six roots [the five senses plus consciousness] leave this world. Their celestial souls flow eastward with the rivers, their terrestrial souls go down with the setting sun. . . .
>
> We pray that the Lad of the Precious Light may grant us the grace that draws [the souls] forth and that the Real Man Who Saves from Distress may give generously of his strength to rescue so that the souls of the deceased may early ascend to the Realm of the Immortals.

The Lad of the Precious Light is the first of the 120 lads invoked in the ritual Uniting the Symbols; he is thus the leader of the first group of ten lads, associated with the east (the direction of the Savior from Distress). As we saw in that ritual, it is these lads who actually liberate the souls from the sins which bind them in hell. The "grace" (*en*) here prayed for is therefore nothing other than the "precious light" of the name of the first of the lads. It is, in other words, the symbol-flag he carries into hell as a rallying point and a source of light for the benighted souls. The Real Man Who Saves from Distress is obviously related to the Heavenly Worthy of the same name: we might express the relationship as that of potential energy (the Heavenly Worthy) to kinetic energy (the Real Man). Another identity, however, may be proposed for the Real Man. Potential to kinetic is precisely the relationship that obtains between the Heavenly Worthy and his "humble servant," the priest who addresses his memorial to the Heavenly Worthy but executes the ritual "in his place." Furthermore, the tradition of the Great Method of the Numinous Treasure followed by Master Ch'en was said to have been founded by one Ning Ch'üan-chen (1101–1181), whose alias was Real Man Who Saves from Distress (Lin T'ien-jen, Preface, 6a). Considering these contexts, it seems most probable that the Real Man here is the high priest himself.

The memorial also contains a description of a sequence of rituals which, unlike the placard, does not correspond to the ritual as it was carried out. But as we shall have occasion to refer to it later, the translation is given here:

> That night we will promulgate the Order of Pardon of the Great Method of the Three Heavens, announcing it to the eighteen earth-prisons of Feng-tu. We will summon the souls to bathe, change their clothing, and

purify their bodies. We will strew flowers and untie the knots. We will express with our mouths the wishes of their hearts and reimburse the treasury for the gift of life of those now deceased, turning the money over to the appropriate officials. When this transfer has been completed, we will lead them thrice before the Three Treasures and issue to them their mandates. We will transform their bodies and sublimate them, we will deliver the deceased into the land of the living, we will lead the souls over the bridge. We will remove them from their places and pronounce formulae as we present them ritual food. When all is done, we will see the saints off with a triple libation.

CHAPTER

11

Opening a Road in the Darkness

When the Ritual of Merit is composed of only the two rituals Opening a Road and Filling the Treasury, then a brief invocation and the summoning of the soul are added to the Opening a Road ritual, just after its introit. The Road-opening itself occurs entirely on the main altar. The tray of soul-lamps, its wicks extinguished, is placed underneath the Table of the Three Realms; the statuettes of the deceased are placed on it. A single, red-robed officiant begins by singing an introit which calls on the Savior from Distress to "ride forth from the Gate of Heaven on his lion and come to save the soul of the deceased" (Ofuchi, 473a). Then, after purifying the altar, he prepares to "turn on the light" (*k'ai-kuang*) in the statuettes by invoking the Heavenly Worthy of the Light of the Lamps.

195

To do this, he sings a hymn about the "scriptural teachings uttered by the Heavenly Worthy" (473b), and takes a brush dipped in red ink and points with it, first toward the open mouths of each of the standing mourners and then toward the heavens. Having thus mingled the energies of the family members with that of the sun, he "dots the eyes" (*tien-yen*) and other vital points of the paper figures while he and the musicians recite responsively a series of wishes:

> May the eyes forever see the jade light;
> May the ears forever hear the sounds of the law;
> May the nose forever smell the divine incense;
> May the tongue forever praise the supreme Way;
> May the body not be contaminated by perverse and deviant ways;
> May heart and mind remain forever orthodox and faithful.

The responsive enumeration of wishes goes on—for the salvation of the deceased, for the compassion of the Jade Emperor—as the priest takes a cone of "old money," writes the characters *hsien-lao* ("illustrious") in the air above the paper figures, circles it three times, and then drops it on the floor. According to Ofuchi (473b), the aim of this action is the purification of the statuettes.

The priest now takes the soul-banner and goes to the middle of the altar with it to sing, facing north, the following responsive hymn:

> The teachings of the Heavenly Worthy form a bridge:
> I lead the souls of the deceased into the Land of the Way.
> With jade pendants jingling, we go in audience before the Emperor;
> In shining garments of cloud, we join the celestial incense
> And take refuge in the treasures of the Way, the Scriptures, and the Masters,
> And sing the jade stanzas of the Spacious Cave.
> With composed demeanor we go in audience before the Jade Emperor:
> In due time we shall ascend to the Southern Palace.

While singing line two of this hymn, the priest bows with the soul-banner, and the mourners do the same. All bow again, three times, north, northeast, and northwest, at the mention of the Three Treasures. A final bow is made to the north during the last two lines, which are sung twice, and then, without any pause in the music, the priest turns south to face the statuettes and dips the banner in their direction while singing allegiance to the Three Treasures and the name of the Heavenly Worthy Who Saves from Distress, Great One of the Palace of the Eastern Extremity (Ofuchi, 474a).

Notes: The priest now hands the soul-banner to someone else and goes to relight the soul-lamps. The next sequence is repeated three times: the priest faces north to invoke the Heavenly Worthy of the Light of the Lamps, then south to burn a cone of "old money" and sing a hymn concerning the lighting of the first (second, and third) lamp, and finally north again to sing the soul's allegiance to the Treasure of the Way (of the Scriptures, and of the Masters). Each time, the "old money" is placed for burning on two chopsticks laid across a basin of water in the northwest corner of the altar. At the same time the mourners are burning "gold paper money" for the god of the soil. Each time this is done, the soul makes a part of its journey out of the underworld. The soul's progressive ascension is symbolized by the fact that each hymn of allegiance is sung a tone higher than the preceding one. At the end of the third lamp-lighting, the soul receives its mandate, and the water with ashes is poured out of the basin so that it goes down to the underworld.

The transition to this lamp-lighting segment is marked by a brief interlude of percussion. Then very rapidly the priest says, "I have summoned the soul of so-and-so. Now the road in the underworld opens, and it can see the light. It looks to us Taoists to call sincerely upon: Light of the Lamps!" The oboes break in as the percussionists sing, "Heavenly Worthy of the Brightly Shining [Light of the Lamps]." Percussionists and priest then together sing the first lamp-lighting verse: may the Heavenly Worthy of the Brightly Shining Light of the Lamps take pity on the soul of the deceased and rescue it from "evil paths."

Returning to the Cave-table, the priest recites:

> You who contain all things in your womb, save the soul of the deceased. On the mountain of the Capital of Jade the true religion is preached; the marvelous methods are transmitted in the forest of the Seven Treasures (the Big Dipper). [The soul] takes refuge in the omni- and ever-present Treasure of the Way. Here on this limitless altar, in the realm of the palace of Jade Purity, the souls of the deceased salute and bow a hundred times as, respectfully, they go in audience before the Most Worthy One.

Mourners and officiant bow as the latter sings of the soul's allegiance to the Treasure of the Way:

> Take refuge in the Treasure of the Way: in utter tranquillity, preserve the spirits [of the body] and recycle the spermatic essence to repair the brain. When the lower sort hear of this, they laugh aloud; average persons are not sure it is true; but the best of persons practice it assiduously and live forever without aging.

The second sentence is a paraphrase of *Lao-tzu* 41, as the first is a summary of Taoist practice, for to take refuge in or pay homage to the Way means to walk it.

This sequence of recitation and song is repeated for each of the Three Treasures. We will translate only the two final songs of homage, as they provide a summary of what exactly it is that lights up the dark road that leads out of the underworld:

> Take refuge in the Treasure of the Scriptures: *The Numinous Book of the Primordial Beginning, The Perfect Declaration of the Jade Emperor.*

Recite the scriptures four times to get rid of chronic illness; recite it ten times to obtain eternal life; recite it a thousand times, and all the powers of heaven will be yours.

Take refuge in the Treasure of the Masters: they open [the door] to transformation and to communication with Heaven; they are the mainstays of the Origin, the embodiment of the Way (this last is also part of Chang Tao-ling's title). It is the Golden Real One who developed the teaching and revealed the golden rituals which save from distress and deliver from ignorance. We beseech you to draw near, that we may share in the marvellous fruits [of your teachings]. (Ofuchi, 474b)

The triple lamp-lighting rite completed, the priest brings the paper figures forward so that the souls of the deceased can thank the Three Treasures for their deliverance from dark hell. When this is done, he returns them to their place on the southern table, where they face north, and announces the reading of the "Opening a Road mandate":

OFFICE OF THE GREAT METHOD OF THE NUMINOUS TREASURE

[The mourners] think with pain of the deceased [name]. Fearing that, the Hall of Heaven being far away and the Cave-court profound, the deceased will have difficulty ascending for rebirth, on [date], leaning on the Way, we have set up a Land of the Way to recite the ritual texts and thereby render a cult to the Compassionate Worthy and solicit universal salvation. Our office issues this mandate to be used as proof of the right to ascension and rebirth: should [the deceased] come to a pass, a ford, or any narrow passageway, and illicit obstacles prevent him from passing, please open this mandate and allow him to pass. (Ofuchi, 650b-651a)

The priest then puts the mandate back in its white envelope and attaches it to the soul-banner (he may, alternatively, burn it on the chopsticks over the water basin). He then makes confession on behalf of the soul:

From the very beginning of time the soul of the deceased
Has buried his true heart in unenlightened preoccupations:
He has killed, stolen, and committed adultery;
With a forked tongue he has uttered lies and flattery.
He has slandered the Great Vehicle and the orthodox teaching;
He has striven with family and friends and affiliated with enemies.
Covetousness and passion have run amok in his heart;
To the seven types of disrespect he has added anger, joy, hate, and love.
It is hard to recall all the sins of the eons;
No one can measure the karmic filth of many lives.
He casts himself upon the great compassion of the Highest Saint;
He brings everything to light, whether physical or mental, in making this confession.
May all the sins and filth of myriad eons and lives
Be all absolved by this confession.
Having worshiped the Highest Saint with this true heart,
May his sins be pardoned to their very roots.

(Ofuchi, 475a-b)

The ritual ends with a hymn, sung while the priest swings the soul-banner, first facing north, then northeast (plate 25), northwest, and finally north once more. We see from this that from first to last the Ritual of Merit is an acknowledgment of the soul's dependence on the Three Treasures for its release from the dark prison of its sins and for its passage to their realm of light. If a Ritual of Merit in its simplest form consists of just the rituals for Opening a Road and Filling the Treasury, it is because Opening a Road contains in germ all the other rituals. Already in this ritual the Savior has penetrated into hell and rescued the soul of the deceased from its distress; already its filth has been washed away, its knots untied by confession; already it has paid "homage to the Three Treasures"; already, its mandate for "escape from darkness" has been issued. All the rest is adumbration.

It is not without interest in this context to note that archaeologists have found in tombs of the Ming dynasty a document corresponding both to the mandate issued in Opening a Road and to the one issued in the ritual Paying Homage to the Three Treasures (as opposed to those named by Chiang Shu-yü; see p. 184). The document was found in a cotton bag placed on top of the cotton shroud of one Li Ying-ku (1538–1556), first wife of Chu Yi-yin (1537–1603), a prince of the royal house. The document, printed on paper, with the deceased's name and date of birth and the date of the ritual written in with black ink, had originally been placed in an envelope, and the envelope, together with the ashes of paper money—to pay for the body the soul had used during its lifetime?—had been placed in the cotton bag. The document is headed *ming-t'u lu-yin*, literally, "dark path road-puller," that is, a device, like a flag, for pulling the soul along the road that leads out of the underworld. It is issued in the name of the Heavenly Master of the Great Method of the Three Heavens, Chang (Tao-ling), and is addressed to the Savior from Distress, whose image appears between the end of the text and the title of the Heavenly Master (*Wen-wu* 1982.8, p. 21; cf. Ofuchi, 472b).

Textual evidence also leads us to the conclusion that Opening a Road is the key ritual in the Ritual of Merit sequence. There is, first of all, the fact that it is, as we have seen, a lamp ritual, in which the statuettes are metaphorically lit, the wicks of the soul-lamps are lit, the Heavenly Worthy of the Light of the Lamps is invoked, and the soul's "letter of credit" is attached to the soul-banner. The very earliest Taoist ritual for the salvation of souls in hell is precisely such a lamp ritual, in TT 1411 *Chiu-yu yü-k'uei* (early fifth century; cf. Lagerwey, 158–59). It begins with the Lord of the Great Way of the Most High asking the Heavenly Worthy (of the Primordial Beginning) whether there exists a "ritual (*kung-te*) for delivering (*k'ai-tu*) the souls of the dead from the Nine Obscurities of the Long Night." One does exist, and its very explanation (revelation) will cause all the stars in heaven to shine. This light will then penetrate the Nine Obscurities and enable all the souls in hell to see the "root of their lives" (*ming-ken*). This will cause them to "wake up," to wish to do good, and to desire to leave hell.

The ritual begins with the lighting of nine lamps so as to illumine the Nine Heavens and the Nine Obscurities, that is, illumine all heaven—insofar as heaven represents birth (the nine months of gestation)—and earth, insofar as it represents death. Thus does light—the light of heaven, of revelation, of the stars—reunite what was separated. The lamps lit, the priest goes to each of the ten directions in turn to declare his allegiance to its heavenly worthy. For the first nine directions he prays that the ritual may illumine the heavens, for the last—down below—that it may illumine the Nine Obscurities. He then makes confession for the sins of the ancestors of all men and prays that the light of the lamps will enable them to leave hell and ascend to the Blessed Hall (*fu-t'ang*).

The same Sung liturgical manuals that provide us with examples of soul-banners very much like the one used in Opening a Road (e.g., TT 547 *Ling-pao yü-chien*) also provide examples of lamp rituals which are even closer to those performed in modern Taiwan than the one just described. One Sung ritual in particular, by virtue of its name, would seem to be the immediate ancestor of the modern ritual. This is the ritual for "opening up the five roads" (*k'ai-t'ung wu-lu*); these are the roads of the "great gods of the Five Roads of T'ai-shan" who are among those invited in Ch'en's opening Invocation. In his introduction to the diagram for the placement of the lamps for this ritual, Wang Ch'i-chen (late thirteenth century) says that "whoever prepares a major fast must first open up (*k'ai-t'ung*) the roads [so as to] liberate the souls of the deceased" (34.14b).

A related text of the early thirteenth century gives not only the same diagram, but adds complete instructions for the incantations and the banners of the great gods who, at the head of their respective hosts, "open up the underworld roads (*ming-lu*) in the five directions" (TT 547 *Ling-pao yü-chien* 29.11b; cf. 5.13a-14a, 29.8a-13b). The author describes these gods as "like the Fang-hsiang-shih" (29.8a), the famous "demon impersonator" of Han exorcism (Bodde, 77). Bodde cites the relevant passage from the Classic, the *Chou-li*:

> When there is a great funeral, he [the Fang-hsiang-shih] goes in advance of the coffin, and upon its arrival at the tomb, when it is being inserted into the [burial] chamber, he strikes the four corners [of the chamber] with his lance and expels the Fang-liang. (Bodde, 78-9)

Few remarks can better help us to understand both the fundamental importance of Opening a Road and the perenniality of the Ritual of

Merit than this twice-millennial statement from the *Chou-li*. The Ritual of Merit is an exorcism, not only of all that which still causes the soul to remain attached to this life, but also of any evil spirits which might make him unhappy in his new home, the tomb. The tomb, indeed, together with its tumulus, is often called a *fu-ti*, a "blessed plot" (cf. Blessed Hall, heaven as a return to the womb-tomb). That this exorcism is indeed still the goal today may be seen in the fact that a "visit to the soul" of a special kind is performed after Opening a Road is done. At that point the priest gives the statuettes and the tray of oil-filled saucers to the family and, carrying the soul-banner, leads them to the Hall of Filial Piety. There each in turn presents the tray of burning lamps. Normally, the priest will then sing several hymns (in the particular ritual observed, he did not). This simple ritual is called "settling in place" (*an-wei*) and prefigures the Settling in Place which concludes the Ritual of Merit.

That concluding ritual involved inviting the god of the soil only, for once the Ritual of Merit is done, the "correct soul" is in the keeping of the "correct god of blessings and virtue," or, as we might now translate, the "correct god of the blessed and the virtuous," that is, the god in charge of the properly installed ancestors of the family. These ancestors, being properly installed, will continue to assist their living relatives, that is, ensure them blessings. We have already seen a link between the ancestors' Plot of Land and the god of the soil in the story of *the* god of the soil and *the* Plot of Land, that is, the story of Yü and his tomb-altar, the Land of the Way. We see now that one of the ways in which the "correct god" performs his work of ensuring the happiness of the descendants of the "correct souls" confided to his care is by "opening up the five roads" to these souls, by "striking at the four corners" of their new home. The text accompanying the "true symbol for opening up the five roads" in TT 547 *Ling-pao yü-chien* (29.10b) invokes in the same breath the local god of the soil and the five great gods who are "like the Fang-hsiang-shih." Indeed, we find elsewhere documents which consider these gods identical, documents addressed to the "offices of the gods of the soil of the Five Roads of this neighborhood" (Lin T'ien-jen, 304.14a). Clearly, here the five great gods are simply the local god of the soil in his spatial manifestation as the gods of the "offices of the Five Roads," the "five forts" (see p. 33). Thus through its linkage to these gods of the soil, Opening a Road also reveals the intimate relationship between Taoist ritual and what is usually called "popular religion."

CHAPTER

12

Dispatching the Writ of Pardon

According to the text for the ritual Dispatching the Writ of Pardon (*fang she-ma*) the ritual should begin in the regular altar area with an introit and a presentation of incense. An introduction follows in which the priest asks that "the order of pardon of the Three Heavens be sent down":

> I pray that the grace of the heavens will be everywhere abundant, the power of the Saint boundless. When the order comes down from the Three Heavens, it will dissipate all suffering in the Yellow Springs; when grace overflows the Nine Earths, all names will be stricken from the Blacklist.... Here on the altar, respectfully we request the writ of pardon, the symbols, and the letters [needed for this ritual]. (Ofuchi, 497b)

This beginning—introit, incense, and prayer—was omitted in the ritual observed by the author; according to Master Ch'en, it is very rarely done nowadays. Nonetheless it is of considerable importance for a proper understanding of the ritual of pardon. In a manual of the late thirteenth century we find a suggestion of the significance of the request the priest makes here. The passage reads:

> Whenever you wish to proclaim and execute the various symbols and orders—all the seal characters written by ordinary hands—you must first request their descent: only then can you announce and execute them. The rite for requesting their descent consists of placing the symbol-orders in front of the Table of the Emperor on High. You present incense, bow thrice, and petition on your knees. With both hands you expedite the "ten heavens gesture" to the Court of Heaven. Expedite in like manner the "gesture of Jade Purity," grit your teeth silently seven times, and send the light of your two eyes, the sun and the moon, racing up to the Court of Heaven. This wheel [of light] shines down on you: in the revolving light of sun and moon the Sovereign of the Void of the Primordial Beginning appears, indistinguishable from the ball of light. Now send forth a beam of light from between your eyes: when it has united with the light of the sun and the moon, state your full ritual title and petition the Primordial Beginning. Insist on the sincerity of your fast; beg him to open the jade case of purple *yang*, declaim earthward (*chiang*) such-and-such a symbol, and give it to his servant to declaim and execute. . . . Visualize the Emperor on High emitting beams of light of a hundred colors, all of which penetrate the precious seal characters. (Wang Ch'i-chen, 54.22b-23b)

It can be seen that the rite of union here prescribed is a simplified version of the rite for symbol-writing in general (see p. 155). Such a rite in one form or another clearly lies behind the priest's request for a writ of pardon, the portion of the ritual which is omitted nowadays. At the end of the prayer, immediately after the priest's "respectful request" for the writ of pardon, what is in effect a new ritual begins. It is called "Welcoming the Pardon" (*ying-she k'o*). There is a new introit, and then an invocation of the Heavenly Worthy of the Jade Emperor Who Forgives Sins. Only then do the priests leave the main altar and go in procession outside to a special area set up for "welcoming the pardon."

The ritual of Dispatching the Writ of Pardon which was observed begins at this point, with the mourners carrying out the paper figures in a procession accompanied by music to the outside altar. The statuettes are set down on a table behind which sits one of the mourners holding a blue parasol over the figures to protect them from the rays of the sun. This table faces another one which has been set up on top of benches on the far (north) side of a fairly large open area. The five priests, four in red, the high priest in his "mantle of descent," bow once on their knees and then climb up on the benches, their backs turned on the mourners and their statuettes. On the table in front of them stands a yellow-clad paper figure, the Officer of Pardon, waiting to receive the pardon (plate 26). We may note here that Lin T'ien-jen in 1303 writes that the priest, once he has "received directives [from Heaven] to proclaim and execute it (the pardon), must go up onto the Terrace for Welcoming the Pardon" (2.6a; the words for "go up" and "welcome" in the text should be reversed, as here).

Incense is now lit and placed before the Officer. The priests begin the incense presentation by singing:

> Limitless palaces of Jade Purity fill the realm of the saints as we light incense for the announcement of the symbols in the ritual for welcoming the pardon. Respectfully, we invite the Heavenly Worthy of the Great Net of the Primordial Beginning: stoop to save the soul of the deceased, that it may early ascend to roam rejoicing on its way to rebirth in the Realm of Heaven.
>
> Limitless palaces of Highest Purity fill the realm of the perfected as we light incense for the visit to the soul in the ritual for welcoming the pardon. . . .
>
> Limitless palaces of Great Purity fill the realm of the immortals as we light incense for the confession in the ritual for welcoming the pardon. (Ofuchi, 498a)

Thus, even without the prior "request for the writ of pardon," the celestial origin of this writ is clear enough. The divine origin of the ritual for welcoming the pardon is clear as well from the fact that, in the priests's song, each of the Three Pure Ones is invited in turn to preside over one aspect of the ritual that is to follow.

After the sung invitation, a responsive verse is chanted:

> The symbol-order of the Three Heavens is hid in the Somber Capital:
> Primordial breaths in the celestial net which marvelously take shape.
> May heaven's grace flow and open the gate of forgiveness;
> Let its rays open the earth–prisons and the souls see the light.
> The couriers of the curled dragon penetrate the Court of the Springs;
> The golden horse races to inform the Fortress of the Demons.
> The officers of merit and the postal clerks hear the summons;
> With one voice respond quickly to our prayers.

A long recitation follows:

> By burning incense we report to and summon the agents of the symbols for the destruction of hell, for the rescue of benighted souls, and for the nine dragons, the officers of merit of the terrestrial road, the postal clerks of the golden horse, the great gods of the Five Roads of T'ai-shan, and the correct gods of the soil along their path.

Having identified the ritual and its beneficiaries, the high priest makes "respectful request for the redeeming grace of the jade symbols which are to be announced in the Court of the Labyrinth of Springs in Feng-tu." Then all sing a verse about the presentation of "incense water" (*hsiang-shui;* Ofuchi, 498b). The recitation continues:

I have heard that the Heavenly Worthy of the Primordial Beginning emitted a powerful light which illumined and destroyed the Nine Obscurities. The Most Compassionate One made a great vow for the universal salvation (*p'u-tu*) of living creatures. He proclaimed the dragon stanzas of the jade coffer and issued the phoenix seals in the precious box. A single missive of ten columns descended, and all in the Ten Directions and the Three Realms submitted to it. Without the help of the potentates, how could we get the message through? Therefore we present this libation of clear wine to assist you on your journey in the clouds. Execute them [the symbol-orders] quickly: we offer wine three times.

The high priest names again the beneficiaries of the offering, the officers of merit, the messengers of the "golden horse," the gods of the Five Roads, and the gods of the soil "along the way." Then he begins a sequence for the proclamation of the three symbols mentioned in the long incense recitation.

The sequence consists each time of the announcement of the text which accompanies the symbol, followed by the invocation of an appropriate heavenly worthy and then by an incantation. The first text is half-sung, half-declaimed by the cantor, the second by the assistant cantor, and the third by the leader of the troupe. The incantation is chanted responsively while the symbol-order is burned and is punctuated by blasts on the exorcist's buffalo horn. We may note in passing that these three symbols and their incantations are already associated with the Pardon ritual in the early thirteenth century (see TT 219 *Tu-jen ta-fa* 55.19b-23b). All three symbols are also found in material from the Shen-hsiao movement (early twelfth century), but only two are there associated with salvation from hell; the third, the nine-dragon symbol, is part of a ritual for requesting rain (TT 1219 *Kao-shang shen-hsiao ta-fa* 11.4b, 21a-24a, 12.22b-24b). Indeed there remains, in the Ritual of Merit, a kind of request for rain, that is, a request—to use a Western religious metaphor—for the "showers of blessing" constituted by the revelation and transmission of the divine light of the "nine commandments of the Sovereign of the Void" (*Tu-jen ta-fa* 55.16b).

After the proclamation of the three symbols, the accompanying announcement (*kuan*) is read by the keeper of the incense and then dispatched by burning. As it burns, the high priest, who has taken up his five-thunder seal and sprayed symbol-water (cf. plate 24), "dispatches the symbol-orders" with a muttered "order of the Most High." The power of the symbols—called "directives of the Way from the Capital of Jade"—to break open hell is then celebrated, first in a song sung by turns by the high priest and the two cantors, and then in a passage recited by all. The recitation ends with the invocation of the Heavenly Worthies Who Save from Distress, Rescue from Sin, and Lead [the Soul out of Hell] with the Banner. This marks the end of the sequence for the proclamation of the symbol-orders.

The ritual returns now to the writ of pardon itself. The high priest calls on the local god of the soil and on the agents of the relay of the Golden Horse of the Three Heavens to prepare to transmit the writ, which the cantor then introduces. First he sings:

> When the petition is presented, we benefit from the compassionate concern of the Three Realms; when the order of pardon is proclaimed, it descends from the Nine Heavens. Great is the mercy of the Saint, pure and mild the words of Heaven. The bariolated phoenix comes to the Cinnabar Gate carrying in its mouth a missive in seal characters; its green mate follows it to the pure altar with a purple summons in ten columns: grace, like rain or dew, falls abundantly; the power of heaven and earth is spread abroad.

Then he recites:

> Joy mounts into the cosmos; happiness overflows in the nether regions. All sentient creatures are drenched by the holy showers; all who suffered in darkness dance to the drum of the gentle wind. In the obscure prisons the cries of the tortured are heard no more; the sea of suffering ceases its restless churning. The innumerable divine lands of infinite space are all bathed in bounteous grace and soaked with rich blessings: a sealed writ of pardon from the chancellery of the Three Heavens has arrived. (Ofuchi, 499b-500a)

Having thus welcomed the pardon ritually, the Taoists usually step down from the benches and repeat the welcome in a theatrical manner. In the particular ritual observed, this interlude lasts ten minutes and involves two mimed journeys (cf. Ofuchi, 500a). It would appear from Master Ch'en's description in his seminar that this mimed repetition may either be eliminated altogether or be performed as a single journey. If eliminated, the high priest simply turns to face south for the proclamation of the writ of pardon. As Master Ch'en makes very clear the function of the mimed episode, we will preface our description with his comments.

Notes: According to Master Ch'en, it is the leader of the troupe who first mimes going on a trip to fetch the writ of pardon and then brings it back and presents it to the high priest. He says, "Here is the writ of pardon issued by the Chief of the Teaching of the Green Heaven (the Savior from Distress). We have prepared a horse, and when the firecrackers are lit, he will be off." While saying this, the leader mimes a ride on a horse. "I am the messenger, I have the order of the Lord of the Religion of the Eastern Heaven to bring you this pardon so you can take it to Feng-tu and save so-and-so. I see that today is an auspicious day. When the firecrackers are lit, it will be time for the horse to go."

He again mimes a horse and then cries out, "Look, look: we see a light before us. We hear the sound of drum and gong: it must come from the temple of the Three Treasures. I've saddled the horse and put on stirrups: it's time to go." He mimes all this, and then concludes, "The writ has arrived."

"What for?"

"I'm here on order of the Three Heavens to present the writ."
"Did you come by water or over the mountains?"
"Neither. By horse."
"What for?"
"To make a report. Please take this writ." The leader mimes the arrival of an imperial messenger and his hitching of the horse; then he circles several times the table of the deceased, ending up in the southwest corner. At this point the high priest gets down from the bench and makes several tours of the altar, as if looking for the messenger. When he arrives in the northeast corner, they see each other, bow, laugh, and move on, the high priest to the northwest, the leader to the southeast, then each back again to his starting point, where again they bow to each other. Both move to the center of the altar, the high priest on the east, the leader on the west. They bow toward each other, then turn and bow together three times toward the north. The high priest moves in front of the leader and turns south to face him. Both make a slight bow, and the leader hands the writ to the high priest, who, having received it on his court tablet, laughs. The messenger mounts his horse, whips it, and is off. The high priest makes several tours of the altar, bowing in each of the five directions. Then he gets back up on the bench, sings a hymn called "Before the Gates of Hell," and concludes, "The writ has arrived. Let the filial children kneel and listen."

In the particular ritual observed, as already stated, there are two mimed journeys, neither performed by the leader of the troupe. The first is performed by the high priest, who carries in his right hand a ritual object that looks like a horse tail (the Buddhist fly-whisk, *fo-tzu*, a sign of one who has obtained enlightenment) and in his left hand his court tablet, on which lie the writ of pardon in its long, flat rectangular yellow envelope and the accompanying announcement (*kuan*). After several bows, first east, then west, then north, and finally east again, each bow preceded by steps to the appropriate position on the altar (between the elevated table and the table of the statuettes), he begins to walk around and around the altar, flipping the fly-whisk back and forth, moving now clockwise, now counterclockwise, usually reversing his direction in the southeast corner, and finally exiting on the east (the direction of the Heavenly Worthy Who Saves from Distress).

Then comes the turn of the incense keeper (Ofuchi, 500a, attributes this journey to the cantor). Carrying the Officer of Pardon, he enters from the east with a bow, goes around to the west to bow east, makes several tours of the altar before bowing west, and so on. At last he bows northward three times and then, after several more tours, faces west and makes a gesture as if throwing something. According to Ofuchi, this is the sign the Officer of Pardon has arrived. The west, which the acolyte is now facing, represents the land of the dead, as the east does the land of the living.

The high priest, having exchanged in the meanwhile his mantle of descent for an ordinary red Taoist robe, now reenters the altar on the west side. His left foot forward, he faces the keeper of the incense, who has his right foot forward. They bow toward each other, then exchange positions and bow again. Finally the keeper comes to the south side and faces north, holding the Officer of Pardon in front of him with outstretched arms to listen to the proclamation of the writ of pardon. The high priest gets back up onto the bench to face the Officer and proclaims the writ of pardon:

CHANCELLERY OF THE THREE HEAVENS.

Mandate issued: to the masters of the earth-prisons of the Court of the Nine Obscurities in Feng-tu.

Bright heaven cherishes life; the Emperor on High loves vitality. Respectfully, we follow the directives given by the Way: formerly, in the Yen-k'ang era, the Great Way was hidden in an appearance of speechlessness. In the Lung-han era, the perfect mechanism took form as image-writing. For the first time, the Three Virtualities (heaven, earth, and man) emerged, and the ten thousand categories were differentiated. Dragon stanzas and phoenix seals revealed the secret meaning of heaven and earth; jade strips and documents established the abstruse meaning of the *yin* and the *yang*. Among men there were neither sages nor fools; all were by nature pure and peaceable. The ciphers of catastrophe had not yet sprouted; the sway of fortune had not yet arisen. But in the K'ai-huang era, the ciphers came to *chia-shen*, writings in ink proliferated, and good and evil were distinguished. Greedy for the things of this world, men drowned in the sea of suffering; their spirit-spring muddied and filthy, men drifted down the river of passion. Therefore our Most Charitable One took pity on us and opened wide the doors of pardon; the Greatly Virtuous One, in his love for life, deigned to reveal the classics of salvation. Whoever repents his wrongdoings will be able to mount on high.

Now then, on behalf of [family's address], we worship the Way and perform a fast, we recite litanies of confession and make an offering, we refill the treasury and we provide passage. The living family members [names], who wish to pay their debt of gratitude, and all filial relations in this month [date], lean on the Way as they prepare a Pure Fast of Supreme Salvation from the Nine Obscurities. It is performed as a posthumous offering for the soul of so-and-so, who was born and died at such-and-such times [year, month, day, and hour are filled in for both]. We confess all their sins and seek universal salvation. Surely the sincerity of our sentiments will elicit your compassion. Pour forth your abundant mercies; grant us all that we implore. On this account, we specially proclaim a symbol, addressed below to

[a large symbol in red]

all places under the jurisdiction of Feng-tu: forgive the souls of the named deceased. Whatever they have done in past generations or in this life against heaven or earth, all disrespect for the saintly and the wise, all disloyalty and disobedience, all inhumanity and injustice, whatever sin of the heart, the mouth, or the body, whatever fault of the eyes, the ears, the nose, the tongue, the body, or the mind, whether serious or not: pardon and remove them all. In accord with the documents of this ritual, deliver them from their suffering and, according to their fruits, cause them to mount on high. As for all the other orphan souls and obstructed souls of the six modes of existence and the four modes of birth, may they be given passage in accord with their destiny and find happiness in a new life. Let all those in charge of the infernal offices of the Long Night in the Nine Obscurities and the buffalo-headed clerks be promoted one degree in rank. Let the generals and officers who have watched over the altar, their subordinates and assistants, the agents of the symbols and officers of merit in charge at the time of the ritual also advance one grade. In future, whenever there is a great fast of salvation to rescue those in the underworld, carry out [the orders] according to the laws of the code.

Oh! the Great Way is formless: it changes as the situation requires. Rich grace is universal: all things alike are benefited. Do not linger, lest you infringe the code of heaven. Let the masters of the Court of the Nine Obscurities in Feng-tu put this order into effect. When the writ of pardon of the Primordial Beginning arrives, let it be communicated to all offices concerned, that they may carry out the order of pardon conscientiously. When the mandate arrives, orders may be given for its execution.

Hence this mandate, in the year of heaven's revolution ____, the month ____, the day ____, at an auspicious hour: dispatched. In charge of the ritual is ____, who has received authority from:

the Chancellor of Celestial Knowledge Hsü;
the Chancellor of the Celestial Mechanism Chia;
the Chancellor of the Celestial Pivot Lu;
the Heavenly Master of the Chancellery Chang;
the Divine Duke of the Undivided Yin. (Ofuchi, 655a-b)

A very similar document, containing many identical phrases, may be found in Wang Ch'i-chen's thirteenth century manual (44.21a-22b). An editorial note, at 44.24b, observes:

[This] pardon document does not belong to our method for doing the fast. It is the invention of later people. Given the fact, however, that it has been used far and wide for quite some time, it would not do to eliminate it. . . . The writ of pardon should be proclaimed at the same time as the order to pardon.

The "order to pardon," a "precious register of the Most High ordering pardon and rebirth in heaven" (44.5b-9a), is the document normally used in "our method" (cf. Chiang Shu-yü, 44.6a-7b). An indispensable preliminary (Wang Ch'i-chen, 44.1a), it must be proclaimed several days *before* the fast itself begins (54.14b). A rite of visualization is prescribed for its "descent" into the version written by the priest (44.2a). It is addressed to some of the same celestial chancelleries as bestowed authority upon the priest at the end of the writ of pardon, a practice criticized as an "imitation of court amnesties" by Chin Yün-chung (32.15b).

For us, the chancelleries constitute rather an illustration of how the Taoists conceived of the celestial bureaucracy and of their relationship to it. All four chancellors and the duke are well-known, not to say legendary, Taoist masters. First among them is none other than Chang

Tao-ling, who is also Master of the Great Method of the Three Heavens, that is, master of the issuing chancellery. This should hardly surprise us: it was, after all, Chang Tao-ling who first broke the power of the Six Heavens (of Feng-tu, in the name of the Lord Lao, that is, using the energies of the Three Heavens; see above, p. 35). The source of the writ of pardon thus confirms our original suggestions concerning the fundamentally exorcistic character of the Ritual of Merit.

It is worth translating in this context the beginning of the parallel document found in Wang Ch'i-chen. The chancellery of the title is also governed by Chang and probably refers to the north as the exorcistic center of the universe.

DECREE OF THE CHANCELLERY OF THE PROFOUNDLY SOMBER CAPITAL

> This chancellery has received the *order* [in red, a seal character] from the Chancellery of the Three Heavens, based on the petition of the high priest so-and-so, regarding such-and-such a fast, and who today, having received the directives of the Emperor, *executes them on Heaven's behalf* (italics mine). (44.21a)

This passage shows clearly the chain of command and events that has become somewhat obscured in the Pardon ritual as it is performed today. A high priest petitions the Three Heavens; the Emperor (or the Way) responds with "directives" reaffirming the high priest's authority to act "on Heaven's behalf," that is, it gives a specific "order" addressed to the Chancellery of the Somber Capital to issue a writ of pardon. The issuance of the writ of pardon—the very fact of its existence—thus constitutes a "confirmation" of the high priest's role as Heaven's agent and, as such, a *repetition* of his initiation, of his "salvation by transmission" (*ch'uan-tu*). It is by virtue of his own ordination, his initiation into the line of "apostolic succession," that he can now, in turn, initiate—save—others. That is why Wang Ch'i-chen and others prefer to transmit not a writ of pardon, but a "register of the Most High ordering pardon and rebirth in Heaven," for a register is a document of initiation.

Notes: The priest first sings a section of the writ of pardon, then repeats it in speech. When he has finished this double proclamation, he holds the document up for all to see, then rolls it up, and puts it back in its envelope. The mourners stand up for the singing of the announcement (*kuan*), which should be done by the assistant cantor standing on the ground. (In the observed ritual, it was done by one of the younger acolytes, who got up onto the bench.) After it is sung, the mourners are asked once again to kneel. The cantor holds the paper Officer of Pardon, the assistant cantor a bottle of wine, and the chief mourner a wine cup. For the first libation, the high priest says, "Here is the messenger. We pray he will accept it. You who are going to leave for hell to see the deceased—"and he motions to the assistant cantor to pour some wine in the cup, and they sing a song. The sequence is repeated three times. Each time they mime giving the filled cup to the Officer, then throw away the wine. After the third cup, the high priest laughs and mimes being drunk. Then he says, "And now we pour a libation for all beings," and the leftover wine is poured out in a circle on the ground.

Now comes an episode called "running after the horse" (*tsou-ma*). The high priest says, "The triple libation is done. Let the groom come to take care of the horse." At this point the younger priests take over. They have trussed up their sleeves and rolled their robes up to the waist, symbolizing a change from civil to military garb and making it easier to "run after the horse." They begin by doing cartwheels: this is an imitation of Monkey (the famous assistant of Hsüan-tsang, whose career began with the theft of the peaches of immortality at the trimillennial banquet of the Western Queen Mother) and a preparation for a leap to heaven. Then they run to the four corners of the altar and do a boxing movement called "pull-disperse" (*la-san*): this is to drive off those who might block passage. The leader of the troupe then mimes bringing out the horse. Starting on the east side of the altar, he performs another boxing movement called "lifting the veil," which consists of crouching low and then leaping suddenly into the air. A third movement, in which the priests do several cartwheels in a row, sometimes without using the hands, is called "beating the unicorn." All of this symbolizes martial training for the extremely perilous descent into hell.

The leader of the troupe now holds the horse while the incense keeper feeds him straw. This may be the occasion for some ritual tomfoolery; they chase after each other ("running after the horse"); they engage in an exchange which starts normally but rapidly degenerates, with comic mispronunciations, misunderstandings, and finally outright vulgarity (no one who has attended such a service can forget how all the neighborhood children who have gathered to watch the show as well as the mourners, who are sitting in relaxed manner on the ground, all burst out laughing at this point). When the clowning is over, every priest takes a torch. The leader still has the horse, and the keeper takes the Officer of Pardon, the cantor holds the writ of pardon, and the assistant cantor the announcement. They stand in a circle to sing a hymn, each priest taking his turn in the center of the circle to sing a couplet:

Bright Heaven comes full cycle and proclaims its directive;
The Great Saint opens wide the Gate of all Mystery.
The Officer of Pardon mounts his horse and flies away on the clouds.
Straight to Feng-tu to pardon the souls of the deceased.
When one sealed letter of pardon arrives from the Three Heavens,
The eighteen earth-prisons are all notified,
King Yen and the lords of heaven all pay heed;
The Buffalo-head's prison guards respectfully obey.
May the Compassionate Worthy come to the rescue
And draw forth the souls of the deceased so that they ascend quickly to rebirth.
Wishing to make an offering to all living creatures,
We have set out incense and flowers for their nourishment.
(Ofuchi, 500b–501a)

After this song, the incense keeper climbs up on the main table and leaps into hell by doing a backward somersault. The cantor sings, "We pray the Heavenly Worthy to come and save him." The Taoists begin to move in a circle. Then the acolytes change places, and all fall into line, with the high priest bringing up the rear. To a martial northern pipes air, they go marching around the altar, slowly picking up speed until they are really running. Then they begin to weave in and out, doing figure-eights and hamming it up once again. Suddenly the keeper bolts after the leader. When he catches up with him, the writ of pardon is put in a sack on the Officer's back, the announcement in his arms, and the Officer on his horse.

According to Ofuchi (501a), the visit to the soul occurs at this point, while the burning of the writ, the horse, the Officer, and the announcement all occur after the return to the altar (501b). We will follow Master Ch'en's seminar description, in which everything is burned before going in procession to the Hall of Filial Piety. As it all burns, the Taoists sing the song for the "transformation of paper" (*hua-chih chou*), an incantation derived from *The Scripture of Salvation* (TT 1 *Tu-jen ching* 1.10b):

> Behead them by the thousands,
> Hack them up by the ten thousands:
> None of the demons will dare to attack,
> There will be no perverse spirits among the ghosts.
> Three Officers, Northern Feng,
> Verify the spectral camps with a clear [mirror]:
> Don't let any of them hide from you.
> Golden horse of the postal relay,
> Make the announcement throughout the universe.
> Let the myriad gods all pay heed,
> And the Five Emperors of the Three Realms
> Line up to report in Highest Purity.

All go then in procession to visit the soul; the song sung before the house altar reads:

> The Sovereign of the Void sends down the pardon and transmits the Golden Register;
> Riding a dragon of fire, the lads transmit my words.
> Adhering to the white clouds, the body returns to nature [?];
> Gods and immortals guarantee the ascent to the Southern Palace.
> First forgive the sins of the deceased before this life;
> Then forgive the soul and obliterate its guilt [?].
> All the sins of the soul of the deceased must now be forgiven:
> Once forgiven and free of guilt, it will ascend to rebirth.
> We pray the Heavenly Worthy will come to the rescue
> And draw the souls forth to an early rebirth.
>
> (Ofuchi, 501a)

The Taoists then return to the altar to announce the completion of the ritual.

The general thrust of the Pardon ritual should by now be clear. There remains, nonetheless, the puzzle of the mimed journeys. If the acolyte's trip represents the Officer of Pardon going to fetch the writ, what is the purpose of the high priest's *prior* journey? The answer, I believe, is to be found in the cantor's introduction (see p. 206) to the proclamation of the writ of pardon. It begins with the words "When the petition is presented," and ends, "A sealed writ of pardon from the chancellery of the Three Heavens has arrived."

It will be recalled that, according to Lin T'ien-jen, the priest must first "receive directives to proclaim" the pardon before he can ascend the Terrace for Welcoming the Pardon, where he in fact does not so much welcome it as "proclaims it" in his own turn (see, p. 204). He "receives these directives" in response to a petition addressed to the chancelleries of the Three Heavens, the Profoundly Somber Capital, the Celestial Pivot, and the Celestial Mechanism. The petition presented (*chin-ch'eng*, the word normally used for the presentation of a memorial) consists of the writ of pardon itself, called "great pardon of Jade Purity," and its accompanying "letter to the Savior from Distress" (Lin T'ien-jen, 2.5b-6a).

The "great pardon of Jade Purity" may be found in a collection of "petitions and pardons," TT 316 *T'ai-shang chi-tu chang-she* 3.1a-3b, which probably had originally been part of Lin T'ien-jen's manual. The accompanying instructions (3.3b-4a) state that the word "order" (*ch'ih*), which appears two times in the document, must be written in by the officiating priest, using red ink, only after he has "received directives in response" to a petition addressed to the "Chancellery of the Three Heavens and the three other chancelleries." "Send your spirit flying up in audience to the Golden Gate, petition earnestly, and wait to receive directives in response," read the instructions.

Historically, then, it is clear that the writ of pardon becomes an "order" of the Three Heavens *after* the high priest has returned from his "voyage in spirit" to the Golden Gate. In other words, the high priest *ascends* with the writ-as-petition; the acolyte *descends* with the writ-as-order. We might go even further and suggest that originally the high priest's journey preceded the entire ritual as it is usually performed today. After requesting the writ of pardon "here on the altar" (see p. 202), the celebrants went outside (an act denoting ascension) to the Terrace for Welcoming the Pardon "to proclaim and execute it." The high priest's journey would then be very much like the one by which he ascends the stage in that other theatrical ritual, the Presentation of the Memorial in the Offering. Such an interpretation would also explain why Lin T'ien-jen uses the same verb, "presentation," for both the pardon and the memorial, for both are petitions and both must be "answered" by Heaven before the high priest can "execute them on Heaven's behalf."

Better than any other, the phrase "execute them on Heaven's behalf" defines the role of the high priest; better than any other rituals, the Presentation of the Memorial and Dispatching the Writ of Pardon show him in this role as mediator, going up to heaven and down to the people. He goes up to heaven, hence both rituals are done outside, in the open air, and both involve climbing *up* onto an elevated "stage." He comes down to the people, hence both rituals are essentially theatrical in character, and both require that the high priest wear his "mantle of descent." In both rituals the high priest is "showing off" to the community what he has brought back from Heaven, the symbols which he has worn on his trip to Heaven in the one case, the writ of pardon converted into an order in the other. In both rituals, we may say, the high priest most truly shows himself to be an emperor, "Heaven's son," one who has Heaven's ear. In them, he most entirely wraps himself in his cosmic mantle, *represents* Heaven come down to earth, becomes, in his "mantle of descent," a living liturgy, the instrument through which is channelled the liberating light of the Three Heavens. The only difference between the Pardon ritual and the Presentation of the Memorial is that from the one voyage the priest brings back symbols for the living members of the community, while from the other he brings back an order for the release of the souls of the community's dead from the Nine Obscurities of Feng-tu.

We may enrich our comparison of the two rituals by noting the comparison which was made by Master Ch'en in his 1977 seminar. When the full Pardon ritual is performed, he said, one which starts with an invitation of the gods and ends with their dismissal, both performed on the main altar (inside), then the Pardon ritual is like the Presentation ritual in the Offering. The Presentation ritual, he additionally explained, is preceded by a Renewed Invocation and followed by the Orthodox Offering, corresponding to the invitation and dismissal of the gods in the Pardon ritual. By implication, then, what is sandwiched between these parentheses is also comparable: the Presentation of the Memorial and the Dispatch of the Writ of Pardon.

An examination of one of Master Ch'en's manuals of secret instructions also proves enlightening in this regard. The *Lung-hu shan yü-chüeh* contains no instructions whatsoever for the Ritual of Merit. The *Hsüan-k'o miao-chüeh*, on the other hand, near the end provides texts for just two rites in the Ritual of Merit. One text is for the "summons of the Four Potentates in the Land of the Way or in the Presentation of the Memorial," and the other is for the confession which is done after the memorial has been presented. The summons of the potentate of the east reads as follows:

> Respectfully, I summon the essences of the green dragon and the eastern constellations. The clouds pass, the rain falls, enriching all that lives. I am going straight to Feng-tu to proclaim the pardon of the souls of the deceased: come with your host of 90,000 perfect energies and station yourself on my left. (*Hsüan-k'o*, p. 73)

The white tiger is to "tame the wild beasts and make the myriad demons disappear," the red bird is to "peck up and eat all deviant essences," and the somber warrior is to "bring the myriad potentates in to report."

When the priests's four assistants have been thus assembled,

> it is time to proclaim earthward the order of pardon, to pass through the courts of earth and rescue the souls of the deceased. Instantly, the seven generations in the Nine Obscurities will ascend on high. At the head of a host of 72,000, which I shall have at my beck and call, agents for the inspection of the fast from the Celestial Office of the Upper Origin, the Terrestrial Court of the Central Origin, and the Aquatic Realm of the Lower Origin: descend one and all into the perfect refuge [of my body]. (*Hsüan-k'o*, p. 74)

Then, holding up his thunder seal, the priest summons the three generals T'ang, Ko, and Chou, together with the officials who are to carry the memorial to heaven. After a triple libation, they are told to "hurry there and hurry back. Do not linger. *I am here on the altar waiting for your response*" (italics mine). Although these texts are for the Land of the Way or the Presentation of the Memorial, we need only replace the thunder seal with the fly whisk to make this rite correspond visually to the one observed and historically and logically to what we have seen to be the requirements of the Pardon ritual.

In conclusion, I would see the voyage of the high priest as an ascension to heaven to "welcome the pardon," that is, to receive the celestial emission, the imperial "directive" which, by uniting with what was prepared on earth according to traditional—inherited, transmitted—models, transforms the writ into an order of pardon. Once again, then, we see that the "moment of truth" in Taoist ritual is a rite of union. As such, it is also a reenactment of the original revelation of the scriptures of salvation and a confirmation of the individual initiation of the high priest. Both scripture and priest are demonstrated anew to be "correct" (*cheng*) by virtue of their power to save from the "deviant" (*hsieh*). In other words, the Pardon ritual better than any other ritual in the Ritual of Merit enables us to see that in performing services for the dead, the Taoist priest is by no means compromising Taoist orthodoxy or orthopraxy. His exorcistic power, as successor of Chang Tao-ling, his power to deliver from darkness, simply takes a specific form appropriate to the liturgical context, namely, the power to pardon and redeem.

CHAPTER

13

The Attack
on Hell

The Attack on Hell, as its name suggests, is an exorcistic ritual. It is a ritual performed by a priest whose attributes are military rather than civil. Before actually attacking the "fortress of hell" and releasing the soul of the dead, the priest wraps a red bandana around his black cap, takes up a buffalo horn, and blows on it to summon the soldiers of the Five Camps. Such military rituals are normally beneath the dignity of a civil official, whose proper role is the "worship of the Way" (*feng-tao*), and it is only by popular demand, according to Master Ch'en, that the high priest consents to do it himself.

That it is indeed a popular ritual, in both senses of the term, may be seen in a variety of ways. There is, first of all, the fact that it is frequently performed in the Taoist temples called Temple of the Eastern Peak, which are a kind of center for what De Groot calls "the war against spectres" (1976, 6:929) and whose activities contain many features of popular religion. Even more revealing is the fact that the actual destruction of hell, whether performed in the Temple of the Eastern Peak or elsewhere, is often the work of mediums. At the decisive moment they burst into the closed family circle (cf. plate 27) and either tear the fortress to pieces with their bare hands or smash it with a "divination chair." (This is a small chair held by two persons, one of whom, a medium in trance, writes "characters" with one of the chair's legs on a surface of wood or stone at the behest of a divinity who has come to "sit" in the chair and answer questions put to him; cf. Jordan, p. 64.) Sometimes the action of the chairbearers is a purely parallel one to the main ritual. They simply stand to one side, in front of another table, swinging the chair to and fro throughout the ritual and writing with one of its legs from time to time. This writing action becomes increasingly frenzied and sustained during and immediately after the destruction, as their role in such cases is less to perform the act of destroying the fortress than it is to "verify" that the priest's destruction has been successful. It goes without saying that the Taoist high priest considers such doubling and such verification superfluous and views it with disdain.

A third indication of the popular character of the Attack is its use of theatrical dialogue, as in the Dispatch of the Pardon. Like that ritual, therefore, the Attack is already in and of itself a double ritual, even when no mediums at all are involved, with half of it turned heavenward and half of it earthward. We shall explore more fully the implications of this doubling at the end of this chapter. For the moment, let us simply note that Chin Yün-chung, writing around 1225, already has reason to criticize the theatrical aspect of the ritual he calls the Destruction of Hell (*p'o-yü*):

> In recent times people have invented rituals with [theatrical] speeches in order to make the spectacle pleasing. . . . Such rituals should be done silently rather than openly. . . . The one of High Merit ought simply to concentrate his thoughts and, with utmost sincerity, implore the Great Way and pray for the favorable response of the Emperor on High. Then there need be no fear that hell not open up. (Chin, 34.7a–b)

If the ritual is popular because it is theatrical, it is also theatrical because it is popular. In it, the whole family crouches in a tight semi-circle around the paper fortress, and everyone reaches out a hand to help shake it at appropriate moments (plate 27). In other words, the ritual is popular because it involves the family members directly in a way none of the other rituals do. Spectators otherwise, now they become participants. The Attack on Hell, therefore, when it is performed, is without question the emotional highpoint of the Ritual of Merit. If the stunts of the Pardon-dispatch often lead to laughter, the tense drama of shaking the fortress often leads to tears. Clearly, to the participating family members, the Attack on Hell involves not only the soul's rescue from hell but also its departure from their midst. It is the moment when they most directly confront *their* loss and the necessity of achieving their own detachment from the deceased.

The necessity of this leave-taking is the real source of the tension that manifests itself in the Attack. An exorcism, its essential purpose is to ensure that the deceased *not return to haunt* the family. In principle, it is performed, therefore, only in the case of an "untoward death" (*wang-ssu*), that is, a death which is likely to produce, not an ancestor who will watch over the family's fortunes but a "vengeful ghost" who will trouble them. Indeed according to Chin Yün-chung, the Destruction of Hell originated in the context of the ritual for Universal Salvation (*p'u-tu*), and hence if it is done during a fast for a single individual, either all souls should be associated with it or the attack as such should be eliminated. He even goes so far as to say that "the Emperor on High will hardly send down symbols and a petition to open up all Nine Prisons for a single individual" (35.10b). A *p'u-tu* origin for the Attack would, incidentally, go a long ways toward explaining its public and popular character. The "sending down" of symbols and a petition cannot but remind us of the Dispatch of the Writ of Pardon.

Although the Attack no longer seems to be reserved exclusively for untoward deaths—the principal deceased in the ritual we have been describing had died of natural causes at the age of sixty-two—its exorcistic character is unquestionably more obvious in such cases. In the case of a Ritual of Merit observed in 1981, for example, held after the death by accident of an adolescent girl, the fortress was destroyed by the chair-wielding mediums, who then, as it were, chased the family members with the image of the deceased girl into the shop where she had lived and worked. Once inside, the family slammed shut the metal shutters that protect the shop at night, while the two barefoot men continued to swing the chair in front of the closed shop for a good half-hour, building regularly to a furious pitch that ended with their battering the shutters with the chair. The Taoist priests, who had to wait for the chair-bearers to finish before they could do the ritual Crossing the Bridge and go home, watched this spectacle with increasingly open disgust and impatience. They in fact tried unsuccessfully to stop it several times. The mediums simply went on swinging and battering, as if trying to recapture the soul they had just enabled to escape. It is worth noting that a similar conflict between the regular Taoist priests and the mediums often occurs in the context of the invitation of the equally dangerous gods of pestilence (*wang-yeh*). There, too, after a relatively brief and dignified Taoist ritual, the mediums repeat the invitation at far greater length and with considerable show of violence.

It would seem to be the presence of the demonic—the terrestrial—that provokes such ritual doubling.

Notes: Normally, the Attack is performed before a table set up in front of the house of the deceased person. The "fortress" is placed on the far side of the table, and the mourners, one of them holding the soul-banner, form a semi-circle behind it, facing the priest. A scroll with the character "gate" (cf. plate 14) (*ch'üeh*) written on it is unfurled on the north side of the altar, behind the priest. The fortress is a rectangular watchtower of paper, white under ordinary circumstances, red for unfortunate deaths (plate 27). On top of it may be paper pennants; or sometimes on the front are the paper images of two infernal gate guardians, Buffalohead and Horsehead, and on the back is the goddess of mercy, Kuan-yin, and to either side of Kuan-yin, are the gods of the soil and the city. Inside the fortress is placed the image which represents the soul of the deceased. A small basin for washing, a change of clothing, and other items are set up in front of the table so that the soul can change and get cleaned up when it gets out of the filth of hell.

The particular ritual observed began with everyone on the altar, facing south. The family members went directly outside and turned around to face north while Master Ch'en, in his black *hai-ch'ing* robe, placed incense on the main tables and then came to sing the introit before the Table of the Three Realms:

> To transcend the difficulties of the Three Realms and
> Obtain release from the five sufferings of the earth-prisons,
> All turn to the scriptures of the Most High and,
> Meditating purely, make obeissance.
>
> (Ofuchi, 502a)

The introit is followed by the Ritual of Merit formula for the purification of the altar, and then the priest sprays the fortress with symbol-water and blows his exorcist's horn. He then "opens to the light" the figures inside and outside the fortress, using the blood of a cock's comb. He sets fire to some "old money," waves it all around the fortress, blows on his horn, and pours symbol-water through it.

The triple sequence of invocations and libations that follows is entirely inaudible because of ferocious percussion and horns. Each segment of the sequence consists of a presentation of incense, accompanied by blasts on the buffalo horn, followed by an invocation, a recited passage, a song announcing the libation, and then a libation. The divinities invoked are the usual supreme divinities, plus the various heavenly worthies, divine judges, and soul-catchers of the Merit Ritual, much like the Invocation. The first recited passage—a pastiche of lines from *Lao-tzu*—concerns the cosmic workings of the Great Way (heaven), the second is a prayer for the "compassion of its Great Power" (earth), and the third gives a summary description of the ritual (man).

The opening line of the last recitation requires our attention; it reads: "The immortal staff of the bird(-man) ritual descends temporarily into the dusty world" (Ofuchi, 503b). The interest of the phrase may be gathered from the following remark by Chin Yün-chung (34.6b):

> In recent times most Taoists no longer carry it (the *ts'e-chang*, "document staff") with them wherever they go. When they want to use it, they go before the Master and ask for the staff, which they then use to destroy hell. This is not correct.

Correct or not, it is just such a practice of "asking for the document staff" at the beginning of the ritual Destruction of Hell (*p'o-yü*) and "returning it" (*na-chang*) at the end that is prescribed in Lin T'ien-jen's manual (33.3a, 18a) nearly a century later.

The phrase used by Master Ch'en would seem then to be a reminiscence of the practice of "asking for the staff," just as we have seen that his ritual for "welcoming the pardon" is a reminiscence of the "request for descent" prescribed in the liturgical manuals of the Southern Sung. The reminiscence is far fainter in the case of the Attack ritual, but it is no less illumining. It explains why a staff-like object is in fact used in the second half of the ritual;[*] more important, it explains why the ritual is composed, like the Dispatch of the Pardon, of two rituals. The first part is to "welcome" the writ or the staff, and the second is to use it. While the distinct orientation of the two parts of the ritual is not symbolized in the Attack by the priests literally turning around, turning their backs to the mourners, it is no less clear. As we have just seen, the first half of the Attack, like the first half of the Pardon, is a typical Taoist ritual involving a triple sequence of invocations and libations; the second half, as we shall see, is also like the second half of the Pardon in that it is at once theatrical and military (exorcistic). We shall see that the contrast between the two halves of these rituals corresponds at bottom to a distinction between an internal and an external ritual that is familiar in Taoist ritual generally. Suffice it to say for the moment that the introit of the (now rarely performed) indoor part of the Pardon is the same as that for the Attack. This is the only case in Master Ch'en's ritual manuscripts of a double use of an introit.

Before turning to the theatrical half of the Attack, we have to consider two other ritual acts that occur in the first half. The first is the lighting of a single candle on the table in front of the priest at the end of the first invocation and recitation. Perhaps this candle stands for the "divine light [of the Way] which carries out its transformations" (Ofuchi, 503a); it would certainly come as no surprise should candlelight

---

[*] On the Taoist history of this staff, see p. 228. It also has a Buddhist parallel in the ringed Buddhist monk's staff used by Ti-tsang to open the gates of hell (cf. De Groot 1884, 94-96).

be used to "enlighten" the benighted souls in the underworld. But why *one* candle?—why not three, to symbolize the source of all light, or nine, to symbolize its function? The answer, I would suggest, is to be found in the same ritual for the Destruction of Hell in Lin T'ien-jen's manual to which we have already referred. The ritual master (*fa-shih*), according to Lin's description,

> [first] goes before the Heavenly Worthy with a "symbol-candle," lights it by "division of the light" (*fen-kuang*), and then gives expression to his sincerity while holding it (33.2a)

The master "expresses his sincerity" by reciting a poem, then "hands the symbol-candle to the keeper of the lamps on his left" (33.2b) and goes again before the Heavenly Worthy to ask for the "document staff," which, after reciting another poem, he "hands to the keeper of incense on his right." The ritual master has thus an instrument of life on the one hand and an instrument of death on the other. Put another way, half of him is civil, the other half military, and the relationship between the two is just what it is in the Attack ritual: first the civil (celestial), then the military (terrestrial). The Taoist, even when waging a "holy war" on the "citadel of brass" (*t'ung-ch'eng*; Lin, 33.5a), is in the first place a civil official. He knows how to perform the external spectacle; he prefers to perform the internal ritual.

The second ritual act in the first part of the Attack occurs at the conclusion. When the priest has finished the triple sequence of invocations and libations, he reads the memorial, then repeats the entire list of divinities once more, this time to thank-dismiss them, and finally he burns the memorial. This first half of the Attack is thus a complete ritual in and of itself, including even a message-dispatch. The same is true of Lin T'ien-jen's Destruction of Hell ritual, in which a traditional Lamp-lighting ritual (*kuan-teng*) is completed before the Destruction of Hell begins. The Lamp-lighting is composed of the request for the candle and the staff, a recitation addressed to the Savior from Distress, the lighting of the lamps of the nine hells, a series of three invocations, each preceded by a presentation of incense, the burning of several symbols for the destruction of hell, the dispatch of an announcement, and the recitation of *The Scripture of Salvation from Distress*. The similarity of structure to this part of the Attack is striking, to say the least.

Now we begin the description of the ritual theater. The priest starts by spraying symbol-water toward the south and toward the north; then he lights a paper cone and uses it to purify a long, pronged staff and the fly-whisk. He drops the burning "old money" and steps over it. Then, as in a theater, he introduces himself by singing a verse:

> I recall that day when I was wandering in the mountains,
> I saw the tears flowing from the eyes of all mortals.

> A student of the Way on Dragon-Tiger Mountain,
> I swore my heart would not rest until I had achieved the Way.
>
> (Ofuchi, 504a)

He carries on in ordinary speech:

> I am none other than the Real Man of Marvelous Movement Who Saves
> from Distress. I come from the Mountain of the Great Net [Ta-lo, the
> supreme heaven beyond the Three Realms]. I have come down from my
> mountain this evening for no other reason than that my host has asked
> me to his home to invite the Three Pure Ones, ancestors of the Way, to
> recite the litanies of confession and compassion and to reimburse the
> treasury of the underworld. The merit of the confessions has been
> achieved, the pardon has been proclaimed, and I have received the
> directives of the ancestors of the Way to come to the fortress to save the
> soul of so-and-so. (Ofuchi, 504b)

The text indicates that at this point the officiant may "sing whatever
he wishes" (such as "Mu-lien Saves His Mother," [Ofuchi]); in the ritual
we observed, Master Ch'en walked as he sang, leaning on his pilgrim's
staff. This symbolizes the trip to hell, and therefore at the end of the
song the priest says:

> I hear before me very distinctly the sound of drum and gongs. This must
> be the Gate of the Demons in the fortress of the underworld. I'll hide to
> one side and see what hour they are announcing.

There is a great burst of percussion, which ends with a series of drum-
beats and blows to the gong announcing that it is midnight. This leads
the Real Man to sing another song:

> The first watch has been drummed,
> The drum has been beat in the bell tower . . .
> Man lives a bare hundred years,
> A hundred years that pass like a distant dream.
> Begin to practice early;
> Do not wait until it is too late.

The Real Man then goes to the gate, shakes his staff at it, and calls on
the demon general in charge that night to open up. Again there is the
sound of percussion, and again the priest sings:

> The Demon Gate before the Hall of Yama opens:
> Cangues and chains are lined up on either side.

"This is the place of judgment," he adds, "where each person gets his
just deserts."

At this point a new protagonist, the guardian of hell's gate, enters the scene. According to Master Ch'en, this role may be played either by the drummer—as in the ritual observed—or by an acolyte with a buffalo-head mask. He also begins by announcing himself:

> I have received King Yama's instructions to guard the Demon Gate. A little devil has just come in and reported that the soul of someone who has died is knocking loudly at our gate. As it is an auspicious day and the night is clear, it must be a good man or a faithful woman from the world of the living who wishes to pass through my gate. (Ofuchi, 505a)

The clerk summons the little devil, and the orchestra plays music suitable as for an audience with the Real Man. (See also Ofuchi 505b-509b for the exchange which follows.)

> The Real Man calls impatiently, "Hurry and open up."
>
> "Who's knocking so loud on my door at this hour?" the demon wants to know.
>
> "It's me, the Real Man of Marvelous Movement from the Mountain of the Great Net."
>
> "Why isn't the Real Man on his mountain studying the Way, reciting scriptures, picking medicinal plants, and subliming the elixir?"
>
> The priest explains that he has come "with directives from the ancestors of the Way" to save so-and-so. "Sorry to bother you. Hurry and open up."
>
> "So the Real Man wants to enter the gate?"
>
> "Precisely."
>
> "That's easy enough."
>
> "Then open up."
>
> "Just let me ask the Real Man whether he brought any money or any precious gifts for us devils when he came down from his mountain?"
>
> "That's no way to talk."
>
> "How so?"
>
> "I'm a student of the Way. I eat what others give me. I've come all alone ten thousand miles. How could I carry any money or gifts for you?"
>
> "You really have nothing?"
>
> "Nothing."
>
> "Then forget it."
>
> "I'll forget it. Just open up!"
>
> "Has the Real Man never heard the words of men of old?"
>
> "Say on."
>
> "From of old there is an eight-character saying about the way to open the mandarin's gate: 'No money, don't come; with money, it's open.' If you've no money, you may as well be off." The demon laughs.

The demon has no need to tell him all this, replies the Real Man, "I knew it before you said it."

"Knew what?"

"That all your talk is just to get some money."

The demon asks why else he should be losing sleep and exposing himself to the cold.

"Well, if it's money you want, my host has given me some paper money to bring along. Wait while I burn some paper money for you demons." The priest lights a paper cone and throws it at the drummer. The demons ask where the money has been burnt, and the priest replies, "At the foot of the Drum Tower." The demon doesn't want to leave his post to get it. Besides, paper money is as worthless in the underworld as it is in the land of the living; he wants "copper cash."

What about all the paper money burned on Ch'ing-ming, or in the middle of the seventh month, asks the Real Man. "Where does it all go?" The demon responds that Yama often sends "little devils into the world of the living to spy on sinners," and they need copper cash for such trips because merchants don't accept paper money. The Real Man repeats all that in the form of a question, and the demon replies, "Precisely."

"I haven't a single copper cash."

"Then forget it."

"I'll forget it. Just open up!"

"Real Man, are you aware that we judge the living and the dead according to their deeds here at the Demon Gate?" This judgment, he goes on to explain, is based on two books, one for those who have lived out their span of life, another for those who have not.

"How does your great King Yama judge someone who has done good and whose years are not yet up, but he comes before the Demon Gate by mistake?"

"Someone who has done good and whose years are not yet up?"

"Just so."

"Our great king looks in the Record of Life to see whether this person, while he was alive, worshiped the Three Treasures, was a filial child to his parents, helped build bridges and roads, took delight in good deeds, and loved alms-giving. If so, our great king sends a golden lad and a jade lass to bring him back to the other world. Such is the Great Book of Life."

"And what about the bad man, how do you clerks of Yama judge such a one when he dies and comes to the Demon Gate?" (According to Master Ch'en, the orchestra should produce a "whistling" sound here to imitate the sound made by demons.)

"Our great king sees from the Register of Death that this person, while he was alive, did not respect the Three Treasures, was disobedient to his parents, twitted his elder brother and beat his wife, killed, committed arson, and did every imaginable kind of evil deed. When he sees this, the great King Yama sends the bullheaded general with a pitchfork and the horseheaded general with chains to hail him into the eighteen prisons of Feng-tu. . . . Such is the Great Book of Death."
"So you here at the Demon Gate urge people to do good, do you?"
"That's right."
"Good?"
"Good gets a good reward."
"Bad?"
"Bad gets a bad return. Sooner or later, everyone gets what he has coming."
"But you demons don't pay back everyone."
"That's because their time hasn't come, it's not because we here at Demon Gate don't repay good and evil."
"You say it's that their time hasn't come, not that you at Demon Gate don't judge and repay good and evil?"
"Just so."
"Now that you devils have discussed good and evil so clearly, open the gate so I can go through."
"The Real Man has heard that the two great Registers of Life and Death are important here. What is important to you who study the Way?"
"For us students of the Way, when we leave home, it's the texts and teachings of the scriptures which are most important."
"Wonderful!" The demon laughs.
"Wonderful? Don't talk that demon talk!"
"No, that was a joyous 'wonderful!' from the heart. Real Man, sing us a snatch from one of those fine scriptures from the Mountain of the Jade Capital in the Great Net that saves the souls of the deceased, and when we've heard it loud and clear, we'll let the Real Man through."
"Can demons listen to scripture?"
"Even among brigands one finds bodhisattvas, so why shouldn't demons be able to listen to scripture?"
The priest tells the little devil to spread flowers and light incense and candles if he really wants to hear a song. When he has finished singing the song, he calls on the demon once more to open up, which at last the demon does. The priest says, "We fray a path with clasped hands between life and death. We do a somersault and leap through the Demon Gate" (this somersault is not actually done,

unlike the Pardon ritual). Then he sings, "The road from the Demon Gate goes right through to the Yellow Springs. I see the road is lined on both sides by the flags of the demonic host. I hear the sound of drums and gongs. It is terrifying. I must not be afraid."

(This song, according to Master Ch'en, is punctuated by the name of the god of music, sung as a refrain. Thus music presides over the passage into hell here, as laughter and clowning did in the Pardon ritual.)

After the song, the Taoist may go on to describe the horrors he encounters in hell: sinners in stocks, heads split open, pools of blood on the ground. "This is the fiery road through the Yellow Springs. It's no place for a student of the Way to linger. I had better burn some paper money." Once again he demands that the Demon Gate be opened, and once again the demon asks who's disturbing the peace at such an unearthly hour. The priest identifies himself anew and repeats the name of the person he has come to save.

"The Real Man is late."

"What do you mean, late?"

"When Yama mounted his throne, you had not yet come. You arrived just as Yama was leaving his hall. There's nothing to be done."

"Look, demon, I've come a long ways over great mountain ranges. What do you mean, there's nothing to be done because I'm late?"

"Real Man, when Yama mounted his throne, I went with him, and when he left the hall, so did I. If I let one soul go, I will be held accountable. I dare not take any such initiative."

"Demon, the proverb has it that even a heart of iron softens [if it's beaten long enough]."

"When one word doesn't hit the mark, a thousand are of no use."

"Demon, do you see the staff I have in my hand?—It's the precious defense given me by order of the ancestors of the Way. On the left it controls dragons, on the right it tames tigers. One thrust, and heaven is clear; two thrusts, and earth is potent; three thrusts, and stocks are smashed and iron locks opened."

"I don't believe you."

"Acolyte, beat the drum of the law three times and have Hsü Chia summon forth the divine soldiers of the Five Camps to smash the fortress."

Hsü Chia is Lao-tzu-s (Lord Lao's) disciple and patron saint of the "redhead" Taoists in southern Taiwan. At this point therefore, the officiant, after rattling his pronged staff menacingly in front of the fortress, comes back in front of the Table of the Three Realms, wraps a red bandana around his black cap and trusses up his sleeves: he has become an exorcist.

He begins by summoning the agents "attached to the symbols"

(*chih-fu*) of the Three Realms (Three Offices). Blowing on his buffalo horn and lighting in succession three rolled cones of "old money," he drops them in the center, then to his right, and to his left. Paper money is burned in front of the fortress. The chair-bearers, who have been swinging the chair throughout off to one side, come now in front of the fortress and swing the chair back and forth violently. At the same time, and with equal violence, the family members shake the fortress, and there is furious clanging of gongs as one by one the priest lights, lets burn, and drops in the four corners and in the center five paper cones to summon the soldiers of the Five Camps. Then he sprays a mouthful of symbol-water at the fortress and makes the same ram gesture he made at the end of the Sealing of the Altar. "Acolyte," he says, "beat the drum of the law three more times, and I'll smash the fortress." The mourners shake the fortress and call to the soul, "Come get your money, come wash." The Real Man lights the paper cones stuck on the prongs of his staff and stabs the fortress.

In the ritual observed, Master Ch'en, holding the soul-banner, now reinvites the various divinities and makes a final prayer for the soul's salvation. Then the envelope which has marked the "seat" of the Savior from Distress is burned, together with some paper money. To instructions from Master Ch'en, the head of the family drops the divining blocks over and over again, and then at last Ch'en lights a broom and swats all around the altar with it. Then, with long strings of firecrackers exploding noisily just outside the altar area, he takes up a rolled mat with burning paper cones stuck in either end, whirls it several times, and finally smashes the fortress with it. The family members quickly remove the four paper figures representing the deceased from the table and bring them back to the house.

The description of the conclusion of the ritual which Master Ch'en gave in his 1977 seminar in Paris differed somewhat from what we actually saw at this particular Ritual of Merit. His description follows.

Notes: The officiant, after breaking through the Demon Gate by using the ram gesture, grabs the image of the deceased from inside the fortress, and ties it on the back of the chief mourner. While another family member holds a parasol over the image so that it does not come in contact with or become exposed to the energies of the world of the living, which might bring it back to life and turn in into a roving ghost, the family rushes with the image to the house, where a basin of water and a change of clothing have been prepared. The chief mourner puts on a pair of sandals previously placed under the table, the priest enters just to see that all is in place, and then leaves. Shutting the door to the chapel, the family places the statuette with a burner on the table and then dresses the image with the clothing that had been set out. The priest returns to the altar to perform the exorcism with broom and mat in order to purify the ritual area. He removes the effigies of Kuan-yin and the god of the soil from the fortress and brings the latter back to its place at the entrance to the altar. Inside, both image and clothing are burned.

Mediums are often present for this rite. From outside the shut doors of the house, the *chi-t'ung* ("divining youth," the medium) is questioned about the voyage of the deceased: what does he need? Meanwhile, the remains of the fortress are given to an elderly man, who takes them to an isolated spot for burning.

We have already referred to an Attack that ended in essentially this manner in a ritual performed for a girl's early death (see p. 218); we may add here that it was also the chair-bearing mediums who on that occasion destroyed the fortress.

The Attack on Hell is unique in the repertoire of Taoist rituals both for the great variety of ways in which it may be performed and for the fact that some of those variants involve parallel ritual action by the mediums of popular religion. It is consequently a perfect point at which to begin the analysis of the relationship between Taoism and popular religion which we shall be attempting in the next chapter. As preparation for that analysis, we shall try here to define more precisely just what the Attack is from the Taoist point of view. This we shall do by means of a brief "ritual archaeology," in which will be analyzed the priest's staff, the scroll on the altar with the word "Gate" on it, and the relationship between the civil and military segments of the ritual.

According to Chin Yün-chung, the staff which the Taoist carries with him wherever he goes contains the symbols of the Five Peaks (34.1a). Chin's description of the preparation of this staff is a thirteenth century version of that in TT 352 *Ch'ih-shu yü-chüeh ching* 1.23a-24a (cf. Lagerwey, p. 136). According to this fifth century text, the Taoist who has such a "divine staff" (*shen-chang*) is protected by the "divine soldiers" of the Five Peaks:

> If you point the staff toward heaven, the gods of heaven will bow before you; if you point it at earth, the earth spirits will welcome you; and if you point it toward the northeast, the ten thousand demons will capitulate.

This triple pointing is the ultimate source of the "three thrusts" of the "staff of Lord Lao" with which we have seen the Real Man threatens the demonic gatekeeper in the Attack. It also reminds us that Lord Lao is the Human Sovereign and, as such, occupies the Demon Gate on the northeast corner of the altar. It is, then, hardly surprising that the same "ram gesture" is used in the Attack on Hell and in the Sealing of the Altar. Nor is it surprising that the "document staff," with its "divine soldiers of the Five Peaks" (Five Camps), should have come, by Chin Yün-chung's time, to be used to "open the Gateway to Obscurity (*yu-kuan*) and enable the souls of the deceased to ascend to heaven" (Chin, 34.7a).

Traditionally, the obscurity of hell was dissipated by lighting lamps (Chin, 35.1a; cf. p. 199). A Taoist who wishes to introduce the document staff into the ritual for the destruction of hell should prepare the staff for this specific use by attaching to it, not yellow cones of "old money," but a yellow flag on which are written the names of the saviors from distress of the ten directions and the ten symbols of "mysterious transformation" (*hsüan-hua;* Chin, 34.1b). The use of the staff in the ritual itself Chin explains in a paragraph headed "The One of High Merit Turns Toward the Gate to Give Thanks for Divine Grace" (35.7a-b):

> Before the acolyte begins to recite the text, the one of High Merit performs visualizations and other rites. He first prays silently to the perfected above, setting forth in detail the purpose of the fast. Then the ritual master places in his sleeve the nine symbols for the destruction of hell, each written on half a sheet of thin paper, without the [accompanying] order, but rolled together with a copy of "The Perfect Text of the Central Section" (a portion of *The Scripture of Salvation* containing a four-character phrase summarizing each of the 64 hexagrams). Holding his staff, he transforms himself into the Heavenly Worthy Who Saves from Distress and he walks the Dipper. When he emerges from the Dipper, he faces the earth-prison on the east, burns its symbol, and visualizes the three energies, green, yellow, and white, scattering with the ashes. Rays of light shine ten thousand fathoms down into earth, and he sees the innumerable officers of interrogation of that direction's earth-prison, all of them turned to face the Gate. He causes them to receive the symbol-orders which break the locks open: all the guilty souls are released, and they follow the light to the Land of the Way.
>
> When he burns the symbol, he recites the corresponding incantation. When his visualization is completed, he also burns a copy of the [True] Form of Mount Feng-tu, scatters its ashes with a puff, and then in the wake of the energies, takes the staff and lights the lamp of the prison. He sees that all is flooded with light, within and without, up to highest heaven and down into thickest earth, and that the earth-prison is completely empty. He does the same for each of the nine prisons. When he has finished, the ritual master turns around to face the Gate. He presents incense, gives thanks for divine grace (*hsieh-en*), and leaves the altar.

This passage reveals the Attack on Hell to be, in a certain sense, the primordial Taoist ritual, for Taoism, as we have seen, began with Lord Lao's creation of a pact between Chang Tao-ling and four generals (their combined forces constitute the Five Camps), enabling him, with the help of the Three Heavens (the Three Pure energies), to control the demonic forces of the Six Heavens. In what ritual do we see more clearly the Taoist in this exorcistic role than in the Attack on Hell?

This is, then, the proper moment to recall that the temple where the "war against spectres" has been carried out daily for over a millenium is a Taoist temple, specifically those temples called Temple of the Eastern Peak. It is at such a temple that one could see—can still see in Taiwan—on virtually any night of the year all the most characteristic features of Chinese popular religion: consultations with mediums to find out what ghost is troubling the family and what to do about it, burning of paper money in huge furnaces that never go out—and attacks on hell. There, in the veritable nerve-center of Chinese religion/society, one could—can—observe, working side by side, just as we have seen them in the Attack, the mediums of popular religion and the Taoists. But just as it is the Taoist, whether civil or military, who controls the Attack even when mediums are involved, so it is the Taoists who run the temples of the Eastern Peak.

Finding ourselves thus where "you too will come," as the large characters over the entrance of one of the temples of hell in Tainan threaten, we ought perhaps to ask the question why: why will we too come? why will we come to the Temple of the Eastern Peak? and why will there be, as we hope, a Taoist there to greet us? Chavannes (1910, 13) has already suggested at least a partial answer: T'ai-shan, the Eastern Peak, is in the east, the land of the rising sun, of new life, and to be at the "root of life" is also to have charge of the length of life, that is, the time of death. To this we may add that, the "anchors" of the four directions are in the corners, like the four legs of a turtle, and among them the Eastern Peak occupies the northeast, the Gate of Demons. To be reborn, to start a new cycle like the sun—nothing could be more natural, and yet nothing is less certain. It must be natural, for the sun manages it every day. But it seems hardly certain in the long winter (north) hours between midnight (north) and dawn (east). It is undoubtedly for that reason that the Chinese placed the tribunals of the underworld under T'ai-shan. It is in the wee hours of the morning that we are judged according to our merits and either "stay put"—become "obstructed souls," souls trapped in darkness who come back to haunt the living—or rise again as ancestors. We may recall here that the trigrams of the northeast (*ken* ☶) and the east (*chen* ☳) are symbolized respectively as a mountain and as thunder.

These symbols in turn remind us, first, that every body is a mountain (p. 29) and, second, that Master Ch'en's title makes him, like Yü before him, a "master of the thunder" (pp. 44, 154). That is, Master Ch'en knows how to beat the "drum of the law" (p. 121) which at once summons up the divine forces of life and drives away, channels, or converts the demonic forces of death. He knows how, in other words, to turn his body into the body of Lao-tzu or the body of the Savior from Distress, and then to "carry out changes on Heaven's behalf." By thus transforming his body, the Taoist abolishes the distinction between within and without and so affects that which is outside him by what he does inside him. This is why the internal rituals of transformation and visualization always have priority over the external spectacle. We shall therefore conclude this chapter with two descriptions of the destruction of hell which bring us ever closer to the secret heart of the internal ritual.

The first is based on Chiang Shu-yü's thirteenth century "Ritual of the Divine Lamps for the Nine Prisons" (24.7b-19a). In this account, the ritual master begins with an announcement and then, after an invocation, burns the True Symbol of Jade Purity for the Destruction of Earth-prisons. Then he "transforms himself into the Heavenly Worthy, the Great One Who Saves from Distress." The keeper of the lamps then recites an introduction to the ritual which describes the separating out of heaven and earth as the origin of hells and the need for salvation. When he has finished, the master goes before the eastern prison, points to the location of Jade Purity in his left hand, takes up his document staff in his right, grits his teeth nine times, and pronounces the formula for the destruction of hell. He then moves on to the corresponding lamp, burns its flag, grits his teeth again nine times, and silently recites the formula for "opening to the light" (*k'ai-kuang*). Finally, he takes his document staff and "follows the instructions for internal refining (*nei-lien*), visualizing the precious light of the Primordial Beginning, which illumines and destroys the obscure prison."

When he has done each of the hells in this manner, ending with the central hell,

> the master, pointing to the Numinous Treasure (in his left hand) and holding the Symbol of Green-Black (the Savior from Distress, east plus north) for the Destruction of Feng-tu (in his right), recites under his breath the formula for the transformation of his body, and then burns the symbol, together with a Symbol for Returning the Light, in the prison. He recites the formula again mentally and then visualizes the light of the lamp turning into the auspicious rays of a hundred treasures, penetrating on high to the Nine Empyreans and below into the Nine Earths. He visualizes their transformation into innumerable heavenly worthies, who go throughout the Nine Obscurities, and all the guilty souls receive absolution. The master takes the True Form of Feng-tu, touches the Jade Purity point (in his left hand), and recites a formula. . . .
>
> When he has finished the incantation, he burns it (the True Form). Then, with his tongue arched like a column to his upper palate, he visualizes the Primordial Beginning on top of his head and visualizes golden light filling his mouth. He blows the ashes northeastward and does a gesture of expelling. All sing the formulae for the Destruction of Feng-tu and for the Sweet Dew of Communion with the Perfected. As they go around the altar, the master dips a willow twig in his water bowl and sprinkles the altar. (24.18a-b)

The most interesting aspect of this description is perhaps the pointing in the left hand. He points first to Jade Purity (heaven), the source of the "golden light" which will dissipate the obscurity of the underworld; then, at the climactic moment of the "descent into hell," to the Numinous Treasure; and finally, when the "true form"—the form of all forms of hell—is to be burned, to Jade Purity once again. The final "gesture of expelling" cannot but remind us of the "ram gesture" used in Master Ch'en's Attack. As for the True Form of Feng-tu, what is it but an infernal version of the True Form of the Man-Bird Mountain?—a matrix and map of hell (Chiang Shu-yü, 40.5b):

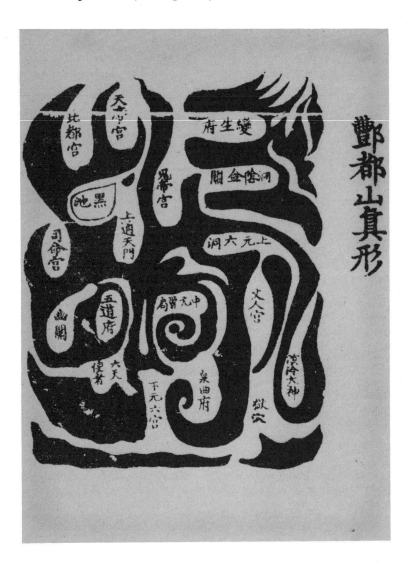

On the level of the symbol of symbols, too, the contact with the demonic provokes a doubling, and one recalls here the doubling of the Cave-table for the Merit Ritual (p. 173). That in turn calls to mind another doubling, one that occurs in the northern depths of the lower belly of the human body—the kidneys.

The kidneys in the northern depths play a very special role in the "great instructions for internal refining" which the ritual master in

Chiang Shu-yü must perform. A version of these instructions has come
down to us in TT 407 *Ling-pao ta-lien nei-chih hsing-ch'ih chi-yao*
(*Essentials for the Practice of the Internal Instructions for the Great
Refinement of the Numinous Treasure;** parenthetical explanations are
in the original):

> Facing east, bow nine times (or three times). Light incense (you can also
> light incense before bowing, and then again when you are about to
> begin). State the purpose of the ritual (at this point, in order to complete
> the explanation of your intentions, invoke all [relevant] saints, masters,
> and real persons). Bow three more times and then sit down in front of
> the table. Harmonize your spirits, regulate your breathing, and recite the
> Great Scripture nine times (*The Scripture of the Birth of the Heavens,
> The Stanzas of the Birth of the Gods*, or the Appellation of Green-Black).
> After each round, inhale once and send the energy down into your
> Cinnabar Field, (this is how the text reads; "cinnabar" should probably
> be "body," and the text read, "down into the Field of your Body," a
> field which should be filled), that is, the Aquatic Court. (*The Scripture
> [of the Internal Rays of the Yellow Court]* says, "The water kings of the
> two sections face the Gate of Life"; this refers to the aquatic section.)
> Concentrate the rays of the nine energies so as to form an infant
> (this creation occurs right at the place between the two kidneys where
> there is a spot of light). It looks like you and is seated lotus-style,
> stiffbacked, and facing outward. The rays that remain completely en-
> velop heaven and earth (this is not the universe outside the body: it is
> "creation in a vase") and the spirits of the body shine.
> Shortly, the five-colored energies of the five organs billow up like
> clouds, bearing the infant on them as in a chariot. Through the Double
> Gate at the base of the spinal column they go up into the Palace of
> Ni-huan, which suddenly turns into a pearl of great price (the grain of
> millet pearl). The infant becomes the Primordial Beginning, and the
> cloud-energies of the five organs turn into a five-colored lion. The
> Primordial Beginning is inside the precious pearl, seated on the five-
> colored lion. Trillions of precious rays light up all the heavens and all
> the earths: within and without, all is penetrated by luminosity.
> Next, concentrate on the myriad saints and real persons of the 32
> heavens: floating on space they come, and all enter the precious pearl
> and go before the Emperor, where they take the attitude of auditors of
> the law. The Primordial Beginning emits the rays of light of the white
> hairs between his eyebrows; they shine down into the Nine Obscurities
> and all the hells of Feng-tu (below the navel). Precious pearls appear
> both in the Ni-huan Palace and in the two rays [of the eyes]. The myriad
> saints and real persons of the 32 heavens appear inside these two pearls,
> at once protecting and following the Primordial Beginning. They are
> exactly like the earlier pearl of great price. In both rays you see a
> Heavenly Worthy Who Saves from Distress. The light flares up and fills
> the ten directions. Riding on the strength of the Way of the Heavenly
> Worthy, a flood of overwhelming light smashes the thick obscurity, and
> all the hells of Feng-tu turn into pure lands.

*For an annotated translation of another version of this text, see Boltz.

Now visualize the two kidneys and below: it is a place of utter darkness, *the* prison. Once the gate of the prison opens up, the Emperor of the North and all the clerks of hell and the officers of the nether world fall in rank to pay their respects outside the Gate of the Capital (Feng-tu, Feng Capital, is in the rear of the aquatic section, between the spinal column and the kidneys). When these have paid their respects, the divine kings who fly through the heavens of the ten directions, riding in dragon-chariots, surrounded by golden lads and jade lasses, and bearing symbol-orders of the Primordial Beginning, appear before the Emperor and receive from him the directives of the Way to pour light down into all the hells of Feng-tu: all the guilty souls are to be pardoned. After a while, the souls emerge from the hells and gather before the Palace of Feng-tu.

Next, visualize the Flower Pool brimming over with pure water. Visualize the myriad saints and real persons inside the precious pearl reciting the Great Incantation of Cinnabar Yang. Then visualize the Heavenly Worthy of the Primordial Beginning sending down an order to the red dragon to stir up waves on the brimming pool so that water pours down like a cascade into the Eastern Well. Visualize the tongue as the red dragon, agitating the Flower Pool. Wait until the mouth is full to overflowing with divine water, look to the left, and swallow: this is the River of Heaven, and it goes down to the Aquatic Court. Quickly visualize a boundless ocean stretching endlessly in front of the Aquatic Court: all the guilty souls enter it to bathe. An auspicious breeze and mild energies make it warm as spring. Fragrance diffuses within and without, and all are filled with rapture. Suddenly they become aware of their covetousness and their anger, and they turn in their hearts to the Correct Way.

When the bath is finished, the Primordial Beginning orders the golden lads and the jade lasses to take an incalculable amount of clean clothing to give to the guilty souls. When they have finished dressing, the myriad saints and real persons inside the precious pearl join their voices in singing the Potent Section of Hidden Words of *The Scripture of Salvation.* The heavenly worthies of the ten directions and the Heavenly Worthy, the Great One, float slowly down on the clouds to the rhythm of the recitation. The Great One sprays all souls with a ritual rain of sweet dew. They are cleansed in body and mind, and their thirst is slaked. The heavenly worthies of the ten directions, each of them with a gold basin and a jade spoon, fill the latter with the jade lard of sweet dew and strew the food throughout space. When all souls have enjoyed this food of the law and have eaten their fill, stop.

Now visualize the spinal column as the Great Bridge of the Law for the Ascent to Heaven: it reaches up to the Scarlet Palace on the Red Mound and extends below to the Aquatic Court. Bearing flags, spreading incense, strewing flowers, golden lads and jade lasses lead the souls of the deceased up along this bridge to the Court of Fire on the Red Mound. There the Great Lord of Long Life (in imperial attire), the Great God-Inspector of the Horses (in star-spangled cap and gown), the Giant Lord Han (in a cap of white jade and a blue gown with black border), the Inspectors of Destiny and Fortune, as well as the honorable spirits of longevity, career, and escape from trouble (all in star-spangled caps and gowns) inspect all souls and allow them to pass over into the melting pot.

The flames smelt them down, and all souls, as soon as they have been refined by the fire, put on celestial clothing. A hundred thousand dragons of fire pour forth light, and the flames leap up from within the melting pot, carrying the souls of the deceased upward through the twelve-story tower [the trachea]. They fly up through space, straight up into the realm of Jade Purity, where they bow before the Primordial Beginning, who brings them into his precious light. Let your own heart be obscured with a thick darkness; forget the distinction between yourself and others. Be still and do not ask where the deceased have gone. If but a single thread is left dangling, there will be no way for them to ascend. It is crucial that it remain secret. Keep your mouth shut and do it.

(This method is "creation in the vase." It is not the theory according to which you embrace heaven and earth and foolishly seek the mystery on the outside. It may not be lightly revealed to someone unfit, for fear he will doubt and be irreverent. When the disciple has a heart of unbelief, master and disciple will both meet with divine judgment. Beware! Beware!)

This is the internal ritual which, whether or not it is actually performed, underlies and gives validity to the external spectacle.

How can we be so sure? Might the external spectacle not have preceded the internal ritual? Might the mediums not have come before the Taoists? Might popular creativity not underly Taoist systematization? Perhaps. Probably. But that is neither here nor there as far as the assumptions of Taoist ritual itself are concerned. In Taoist ritual, heaven precedes earth, inside precedes outside, and civil takes precedence over military. Indeed, the whole aim of Taoist ritual—and hence the justification for its existence—is to recuperate what is outside, to recycle what is earthly, to transform what is military, to convert spectacle into ritual, Feng-tu into a "pure land," and so bring all souls back to the Primordial Beginning, back to the original matrix of the Man-Bird Mountain, before heaven and earth had separated out and hells come into existence.

The perfect illustration of this process is the Bridge of the Law for the Ascent to Heaven, which we have just seen is the visualized form of the spinal column, that is, of (the Temple of) the Eastern Peak (cf. p. 72). Did the bridge originally represent the spinal column? Do the little paper bridges used in the Temple of the Eastern Peak today, or in Master Ch'en's Crossing the Bridge represent the Eastern Peak, or is the symbolism forgotten, or irrelevant? We don't know. But what we do know is that when this bridge first appears in Taoist ritual manuals, it has already been integrated into the Taoist system, as we can see in the way it links the elements in the illustration on the following page:

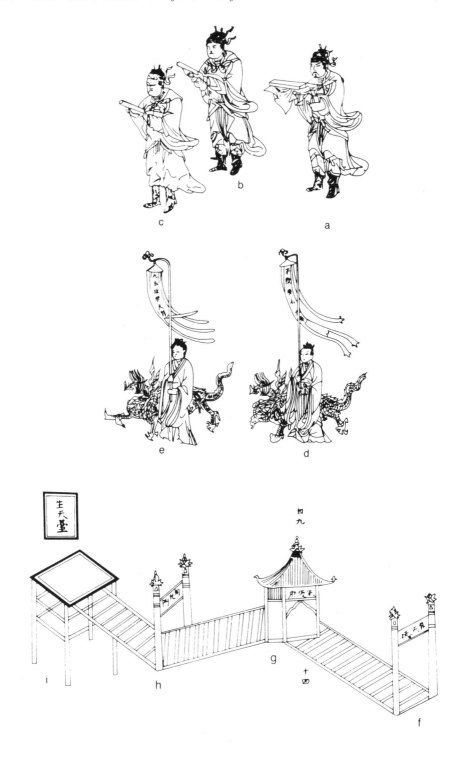

Elements of the Bridge-crossing: *a*, the ritual master, carrying a message; *b-c*, his right and left acolytes (the keeper of the incense and the keeper of the lamps?); *d*, the Heavenly Worthy Who Saves Lives on the Red Mound (corresponds to *g*); *e*, the Heavenly Worthy Who Rescues from Sin in the Nine Obscurities (corresponds to *h*); *f*, the Bridge for the Ascent to Heaven (designates the entire structure); *g*, the Court of the Red Mound; *h*, the Gate for Opening to the Light; *i*, the Terrace of Birth in Heaven. (Chiang Shu-yü, 39.16a-17b)

The bridge is constructed so that it goes up and then down before it finally goes up to heaven. We may recall that in the instructions on internal refining, it is said to "reach up to the Scarlet Palace on the Red Mound and extend below to the Aquatic Court." In *The Scripture for the Salvation from Distress* (TT 374 *Chiu-k'u miao-ching*, p. 2a), a sentence, while not explicitly referring to the bridge, reads, "It ascends to the Court of the Red Mound and goes down into the Gate for Opening to the Light." To these textual references, we may add the fact that Ning Ch'üan-chen (1101-1181)—who is the issuing authority for the symbols for the "destruction of hell" and the symbols for the "rescue of benighted souls" used in Master Ch'en's Pardon-ritual, as well as the probable founder of the Great Method of the Numinous Treasure, the name of whose office (*ssu*) appears in large characters at the beginning of many of Master Ch'en's documents—is also known as the Real Man Who Saves from Distress by Opening to the Light (Lin T'ien-jen, Preface, 6a). This may in fact be why Ch'en himself becomes a Real Man during the ritual theater of the Attack. We may even speculate further that he becomes a Real Man (Who Saves from Distress) because the Attack is performed in the context of a Merit Ritual for an individual. When he performs a Universal Salvation ritual in the Offering, by contrast, he becomes the Heavenly Worthy Who Saves from Distress.

In conclusion, we may repeat what the Taoists of northern Taiwan say, to the effect that normally Taoists ought not to perform the Ritual of Merit at all, for normally the "way of the immortals is to avoid all contact with the dead energies of that which is turbid, evil, drowned, or obstructed" (Lü Tung-yang, 16a). If the Real Man nonetheless condescends to save from distress, it is because, liturgist that he is, he has learned to "forget the distinction between himself and others" (cf. Lagerwey, p. 217). That is why, when we too come to the Temple of the Eastern Peak, we may hope to find a Taoist there to greet us.

P
A
R
T

III

Liturgical
Taoism and
Chinese Society

CHAPTER

14

Taoism and Popular Religion

In our study of the presentation of the message in the Land of the Way, we saw that Master Ch'en summons the marshals Hsieh and Pai' as his chief agents of transmission. For the same task in the Presentation of the Memorial, the *Lung-hu* manual (p. 44) prescribes the use of Marshal Wen. We have already seen portraits of this marshal, in both scroll and papier-maché form (plates 3, 19); in this chapter we shall look at his story in detail and examine what makes the difference between a god of the people and a Taoist angel (*shih*, which, like *angelos*, means "messenger").

Our source for Marshal Wen is *The Biography of Wen t'ai-pao, Commander-in-chief of the Earth Spirits* (TT 780, *Ti-ch'i shang-chiang Wen t'ai-pao chuan* 1a-13a), written in 1274 by one Huang Kung-chin. Marshal Wen's name is Wen Ch'iung and he is a native of P'ing-yang District, Wen-chou, in the province of Chekiang. His story takes place in the T'ang dynasty. His mother dreams of a "sunwheel from the south as large as a chariot wheel and making a sound like thunder" and awakes to find herself pregnant. Wen grows up to be a fierce warrior and renowned slayer of bandits and rebels. Unfortunately his chief, the famous general Kuo Tzu-yi, has a dream in which he sees Wen turn into a one-horned black snake, and Kuo, fearing this "strange man" may later cause him trouble, takes it in his mind to kill him. Sensing this, Wen flees to T'ai-shan, and at its foot he henceforth makes a living as a butcher and wine-seller.

One day, the god Ping-ling kung (Master Ping-ling), having "transformed himself into a Taoist," tells Wen that he has the "bones and energy for communicating with the gods." But, he said, for one who is destined eventually to have a cult rendered to him, it is unthinkable that he make his living as a butcher, for "this is a most serious offense against the celestial code." Wen suggests that he ought perhaps to "go up into the mountain to practice the Tao," but Master Ping-ling replies that he "doesn't have the bones of an immortal." As Wen opens his mouth to ask him what he should do in that case, Master Ping-ling suddenly disappears.

Left to himself, Wen decides the god was right and that he should give up butchering. He decides to go to the Temple of the Eastern Peak to "render service as master of transformations," that is, as chief of the mediums who communicate with the souls of the dead in the Temple of the Eastern Peak. After three years of diligent service, he once again meets a Taoist. This Taoist informs Wen that his name has been inscribed that very day "in the book of the Emperor of the Peak." He should set up a statue of himself in the temple now, to represent the position he will hold after his death as one of the mountain-court's—the temple's—*t'ai-pao* (the term is still used to refer to Taoist priests when they perform military rituals).

Wen does set up his statue, and from then on all the local *t'ai-pao* come regularly to consult with him. One day, a *t'ai-pao* by the name of Huan Ch'iu-hsiu informs Wen that "when his statue changes, he will go home to his position." Every day thereafter Wen goes to look at his statue. A temple apprentice, seeing him so earnestly scrutinizing this statue day after day, asks him mockingly whether he is afraid someone might steal it. Wen replies, "General Huan told me that when my statue changes, I would become a god. And if I become a god, you will become my foot soldier."

Thinking it all very funny, the apprentice decides to play a joke on Wen, and he and a friend paint the statue green and stick two boar tusks in its mouth. When Wen comes to burn incense, he sees that the statue has "changed into a green cap and clothing." Wen removes the boar tusks, which had turned into butcher knives, and then is "transformed on the spot." So are the two apprentices when they come to inspect the results of their practical joke.

When, by the ninth day of the fifth month, that is, midsummer, Wen's body has neither fallen over nor decomposed, an imperial order enfeoffs him as Great General of Manifest Power. The local peasants wish to build him a temple and render him a cult, but Wen informs the village head that he will burn any temple set up for him. He says, "I have received my commission from the Eastern Peak, and it is my desire to establish great merit, to rid the world of great harm, and to support the Orthodox Way (*cheng-tao*). How then could I, ignoring the fact that the Supreme Emperor loves life, crave blood and not show compassion and a desire to save?"

A year later, in accord with a memorial presented by the very god who had originally predicted Wen's glorious future, the Emperor of the Peak agrees to give recognition to his merit in refusing an imperial enfeoffment and a popular cult by installing him as Underworld Authority in the Court of the Earth. Henceforth, the registers of life and death are in his hands, and he must see to it that people are born and die at the right time.

In the year 961 a great drought occurs in Wen-chou. In response to the prayer of one Wu Ssu-ching, Wen Ch'iung sends rain, but when Wu wishes to worship him, Wen takes possession of a commoner to say that he has sworn to save people in the hope that, "in the end, the Master of the Lineage will take me into the Tao as a minor clerk at ritual assemblies. I put no stock in temple sacrifices and imperial enfeoffment. If you wish to reward my merit, please do not report it to the court. If you could report my name for me before the gates of the Somber Emperor (plate 5), then all the gods of heaven and spirits of earth will respect and serve me." The community organizes an Offering (*chiao*) to thank Heaven, and Wen's name is duly reported to the Somber Emperor.

In the closing years of the Northern Sung (1119–1125), the famous Heavenly Master Chang Hsü-ching comes on a tour to the Eastern Peak. He asks its Emperor who among the various gods in his court is most efficacious. Wen Ch'iung can be trusted, replies the Emperor. "Yesterday," responds the Thirtieth Celestial Master, "when I was checking the records of the immortal officials, there was on my register one Wen Ch'iung who did not desire blood offerings and who caused it to rain on Wen-chou. He took no glory in an imperial enfeoffment and wished above all to support the teaching of the lineage. That is why I have come here. Is this not the man?"

It is, and Wen comes forward, kowtows before the "saint," and says: "In all the years that I have held this position I have never had the chance to see heaven face to face. Today I have received your call and been allowed to come to the Cinnabar Steps." Chang Hsü-ching responds that Wen's name and merits had come to his attention as a result of a memorial presented during the Wen-chou Offering. "Here in the presence of the Emperor of the Peak, I make you Earth Deity, in charge of the symbols, incantations, and hand gestures of the Orthodox Way." Noting that Wen had "been transformed" on the fifteenth day of the third month at the *yin* hour (3-5 A.M.), Chang adds, "This is the time when wood is old and fire new. Wood gives birth to fire, which is dominant in *ping-ting* (the south). Demons are the most intelligent of all creatures, so just this seal with your true form will be sufficient." Chang forms the seal from a composite of four characters meaning "the south gives birth to a demon." He explains that, in accord with a line in *The Scripture of Salvation*, it is the role of earth spirits to "take orders from Jade Purity," and then adds, addressing his disciples, "Among all the potentates in the Department of Methods there is not one who is superior to Wen Ch'iung."

The next step in Wen's career in the subterranean bureaucracy occurs when a Taoist by the name of Wu Tsung-ching is initiated by Chang Hsü-ching into "Wen *t'ai-pao*'s secret method of the earth spirits," by which he can summon Wen Ch'iung. Its use brings Wu not only worldly renown but also the inscription of his name on the Register of Immortals of the Somber Emperor. He transmits the method to his disciple Wu Tao-hsien and sends him to Fukien to use it against the many demons and perverse spirits there who "do not worship the Tao."

Even before Wu Tao-hsien arrives, the demons, who are the servants of King Chia-lo, a Buddhist god, lay plans to do away with him. To prepare himself for the showdown, Wu practices reciting the "*Ping-ting* incantation" in front of a mirror. Nine years of this proves sufficient to invest the mirror entirely with the spirit of the incantation, and Wen Ch'iung can "exit and enter the mirror." Still not satisfied, Wu carries on his practice for three more years, adding to the Ping-ting incantation that of T'ien-p'eng, an assistant of the Somber Emperor.

Wu now feels brave enough to go to the temple, but when he gets there, he finds it so big and beautiful, so full also of the thrones of divinities, that he "is frightened and doesn't dare go into action." He leaves the temple and goes up onto a hill nearby. There, facing east, he grits his teeth, silently announces himself to the Emperor of the Peak, gets out the mirror he had "transmuted" (*lien*), and calls Wen Ch'iung to his aid. Wen leaps forth from the mirror and, brandishing his mallet, leads the attack, followed closely by thunder, lightning, wind, and rain (cf. plate 19). Suddenly there is a peal of thunder, and flames leap from the temple. Just as quickly, the storm passes, leaving behind it a heap of ashes.

Wu Tao-hsien's breathwork having vastly increased Wen's powers,

Wu can cause Wen to "ascend to heaven and enter earth, and the spirits of the Three Realms all fear and respect him." Wen's method, moreover, becomes increasingly popular, for Wu transmits it to no fewer than 532 disciples—106 of them end up in celestial bureaus as "potent officers"—and people begin to consider it an "inferior degree of the Orthodox Method" (*cheng-fa*). (That is, it now qualifies as Orthodox Taoism, but an inferior form thereof.) Unfortunately, the more people use it, the less they concentrate on it, and so Wen Ch'iung ceases to respond to their summons. But he in no wise abandons his ambition to "protect and support the Orthodox Way." Aggrieved at the rising tide of "diabolic teachings"—a form of heterodox Buddhism had gotten so far out of hand that the state itself had been obliged to legislate its suppression—Wen Ch'iung orders a Taoist by the name of Tu to report the situation to the Three Heavens.

The Supreme Emperor responds with an order which he leaves to the Emperor of the Eastern Peak to execute. The latter delegates the matter to Master Ping-ling, who summons all the forces of the Five Peaks. When they prove unequal to the task, they turn to Wen Ch'iung for help. His reward this time is a promotion to the post of Superintendent of the Temples of the Gods of the Empire. The Taoist Tu, however, following the recommendations of the Sovereign of Longevity, decides to report Wen's merit directly to the Three Heavens. The secretaries of the Celestial Chancellery, once they have gotten over their annoyance at the impertinence of "a god from the world of men, with no virtue to speak of, daring to importune the Supreme Worthies," agree to allow Wen's name to be "broadcast to all the authorities of the walls and moats in the empire" and to grant Wen the title used in his biography, "Commander-in-chief of the Earth Spirits." And his biography concludes when Wen Ch'iung reaches this eminence.

That is not the end of Marshal Wen's story, of course. As we have seen, it has not yet come to an end: he is still at work today in Tainan, "protecting and supporting the Orthodox Way" of the Taoist master Ch'en Jung-sheng, whether it be on the inner altar, when the master takes the "position of the turtle," or outside, when the high priest dances his way to heaven to "present the memorial." And not in Tainan only, but throughout northern Taiwan as well, Commander-in-Chief Wen and Chao, K'ang and Ma make up the "four great marshals" who protect the altar (Liu Chih-wan 1974, 113). In other words, it is still Taoists who are petitioning the supreme divinities, and it is still ferocious earth spirits who are devouring and decimating the demons and assorted "stale energies" who by definition die as soon as the Immortal Officer penetrates their blockade and enters into communication with the pure energies of the Orthodox Way.

Put another way, the principle will reveal itself to be one with which we already have considerable acquaintance: "Man models himself on earth, earth on heaven, heaven on the Way, and the Way on that which is naturally so" (*Lao-tzu* 25). Yü follows the "lines of the earth" in order to put an end to obstructed channels and then, having completed this public service, executes Oppose-the-Wind and displays himself as a man "after Heaven's heart" before the assembly of his vassals from the four quarters. And the Most High Lord Lao binds the Four Generals and the hundred demons of the waterways and temples to Chang Tao-ling by the Covenant of Orthodox Unity with the Powers. This is the pact whereby the Orthodox One—Chang Tao-ling as the repository of the Unique Breath of Lord Lao—joins himself to all those earth divinities who swear to follow his commands.

Wen Ch'iung's biography shows concretely what the revelation of the Unique Breath meant: henceforth, there was a clear demarcation between those principalities and powers which recognized and those which did not recognize the authority of the immortal officials of the Orthodox Way, between those who pledged allegiance to the new reign of the Three Pure Heavens and those who opposed-the-wind and became by definition "obsolete energies" of the demonic Six Heavens. Henceforth, all power in heaven and on earth was in the hands of Chang Tao-ling and his successors, and all powers had either to enroll in his ranks, that is, support and protect the Orthodox Way, join the System, perform public services, or else "go into the opposition" and so expose themselves to constant persecution, not to mention execution "according to the Black Code" of hell, as in the case of King Chia-lo. In a word, henceforth there was an Orthodoxy.

And a potent orthodoxy it reveals itself to be in the biography of Wen Ch'iung. It shows its power of moral suasion, inviting the individual, like Wen himself, to do public service without accepting public recognition; it also shows its capacity to enlist the forces of nature—wind, rain, thunder, and lightning—in the fight for the commonweal, that is, for the Orthodox Way. What is the secret of its potency? It is the whole system: mediums by definition say only what they are told to say, and they have no control over who speaks through them; Taoists, literally, "men of the Tao," are "men of means," that is, they have ways to control mediums—and hence the spirits who speak through them—and means for communicating with the Tao. Mediums are the natural foundation of most popular cults; Taoists are the natural judges of which cults "support the Orthodox Way." Throughout Taoist history, indeed, we find its representatives cooperating, as they do in Wen's biography, with the authorities in rooting out what both agree are heterodox cults (cf. Stein 1979). But Taoists also work with mediums in the Temple of the Eastern Peak, which Wen's biography reveals once again to be a privileged conduit to Heaven, the backbone of the System.

The real interest of Wen's biography lies in the detailed picture it gives of how the system of Chinese religion works. In following Wen Ch'iung's career we pass in review the successive levels of what has been erroneously called the "celestial bureaucracy." Given the fact that by far the larger part of this bureaucracy proves to be earth-bound and even subterranean, it would obviously be preferable to call this hierarchy "spiritual." No clearer illustration of this crucial fact could be found than the role of the Eastern Peak: access to heaven is through the earth; "the earth models itself on heaven." (*Lao-tzu* 25).

But let us come back to Wen Ch'iung. From the beginning, by the manner of his conception, he is identified as an individual of warlike character. His early life and subsequent career are entirely under the sign of the south, the sun, and fire. He will never be more than a military "officer of methods," an exorcist; he can never become a civil "officer of the Way," a Taoist. His job will be to wage war on "stale energies," and he will depend for his promotions on the written reports of Taoists to the Three Pure Ones. All of this information is eventually concentrated into the seal of his "true form," bestowed by the Thirtieth Heavenly Master, Chang Hsü-ching.

Chang Hsü-ching, in thus defining Wen Ch'iung's spiritual essence, reveals his knowledge of the System. Wen had "been transformed" in the middle of the third month, "when wood (spring, east) is old and fire (summer, south) new. Wood gives birth to fire." Until his transformation, Wen had "rendered service as master of transformations" in the Temple of the Eastern Peak. The Temple of the Eastern Peak is the realm of the dead, and Wen himself goes there to die. It is thanks to Chang's knowledge of the System that Wen's death in spring is transformed into a birth of fire. This transformation, however, was itself dependent on a prior transformation, namely, that of a bloodthirsty butcher into a "master of transformations." It was this transformation which had originally enabled Wen to gain the merit necessary to be enrolled in the book of the Emperor of the Peak—in his book of life, that is, as opposed to his register of death.

The first transformation, we may recall, was the result of a communication from Master Ping-ling, one of the divine assistants of the Emperor of the Eastern Peak. We are to imagine this communication, no doubt, as a kind of vision in which the god of one of the statues in the temple appears to Wen, and in fact in an account written down in the fourteenth century, this is clearly implied:

> It happened one evening that a divine man wearing metal armor and wielding a sword entered and congratulated him, saying: "You have received a nature which is not ordinary. The Eastern Peak has recommended you to the Emperor of High Heaven for the post of *t'ai-pao* in Command of All the Soldiers of the Eastern Peak. You should set up

your living image forthwith in his 'mountain,' and hereafter your soul will surely return to it." The *t'ai-pao* thanked the divine man respectfully and subsequently ordered an artisan to sculpt his image in the hall of the Moveable Palace of the Eastern Peak. Mornings and evenings he went before the Emperor and vowed that after his transformation, his soul would return to the body of clay, and he would have the power to communicate and to save on a wide scale. (TT 1220 *Tao-fu hui-yüan* 254.1a-b)

In this version of Wen's story, which serves as an introduction to his "secret method for investigating and summoning"—earth spirits, of course—his vow is fulfilled, and he becomes a particularly responsive god. One day, when the Heavenly Master Yeh Fa-shan (616–720) "borrows the troops of the peak to take the demons of pestilence into custody," Wen appears to him and offers his help. Within a month everyone in Szechuan has been healed, and Wen appears once again to Yeh, saying, "I wish to aid the officers of methods throughout the empire in capturing evil spirits and curing diseases. Here is a secret method involving symbols and their texts: I look to you for its dissemination" (254.1b-2a).

In other words, Wen, as the result of his encounter with—his vision of—Master Ping-ling, is "converted." Even before his conversion, according to this second text, he had an unusual interest in matters relating to "*yin, yang,* and the creation of transformation" (254.1a) and no interest whatsoever in the "affairs of this world." Even better, "when he grew up, he did not marry, and so did not destroy his celestial perfection." It was this very earnest young man who, ripe for conversion, naturally provoked the efficient cause of this conversion.

But it is the substance of this conversion, of this death to an old self and first step on the way to the realization of a new self—symbolized in his biography by his transformation from a butcher into a master of transformations—that interests us here. What did the "divine man" reveal to him that saved him from becoming just another medium in the Temple of the Eastern Peak? For he was thereby set on the road to becoming the greatest potentate in the "department of methods," aid of the "officers of method throughout the empire," commander-in-chief of all the earth spirits—in a word, Taoist angel. The answer is that the "divine man" gives Wen Ch'iung his first glimpse of the System when he says that being a butcher is an "offense against the celestial code." The eager Wen Ch'iung, who has not destroyed his "celestial perfection," wants immediately to go right to the top. I'll go "up onto the mountain to practice the Tao!" he declares. Not so fast, replies Master Ping-ling, you have the "bones and energy for communicating with the gods," not the makings of an immortal.

Those who communicate not with the Tao but with the gods, and that without being possessed by them, constitute a category intermediate between the medium and the Taoist. It is the category, precisely, of methods: the secret of the System is its capacity to find ways and means of saving people, to convert the raw material of revelation into a *method*. Thanks to the System, the Taoist is able to identify the essence—the spirit—of the medium's gibberish (if his god communicates orally), or to decipher the "divine tracks" (if the spirit works through the medium's hand), and then to put this unique spirit to work by situating it properly within the System. Thus we see that Chang Hsü-ching, when he has analyzed the reports on his register, identifies Wen Ch'iung and gives him a job. We see Yeh Fa-shan in one version, Wu Tsung-ching in the other, Taoists both, putting Wen's method to work. Not only do Taoists know how to make use of such new revelations, they know as well how to *transmute* them and make them even more powerful: it is only as a result of Wu Tao-hsien's breathwork that Wen finally climbs to the top of the subterranean hierarchy and so fulfills his destiny as one who has the "bones and energy for communicating with the gods."

But we have yet to discover what it is that enables Wen Ch'iung to achieve even this relative height. How does one escape the condition of medium, utterly subject, without achieving the rank of Taoist, utterly transcendent? Destiny ("bones"), determination ("vows"), and good reports (by Taoist masters) are the answers. Destiny: even before he is "converted," Wen Ch'iung, fleeing from Kuo Tzu-yi, arrives as if by instinct at the foot of T'ai-shan. The green paint which will one day provoke his transformation is already prefigured in this spontaneous flight. Determination: unlike the medium, who speaks and acts involuntarily once he is in trance, Wen Ch'iung makes his own decision—to quit butchering—and his own vows. He vows, moreover, one day to animate his own statue!

And that animation is the key to all the rest. He is but wood giving birth to fire. His method will never be more than an "inferior degree of the Orthodox Method." But because it is, already, self-expression, it will at least belong to the Orthodox Method. What is the cornerstone of this Method of all methods? The stipulation is that he must henceforth make no bloody sacrifices to the demon gods of the Six Heavens, only "pure offerings" to the pure energies of the Three Heavens. That is one reason he must stop his butchering. He may only "worship the Tao" (*feng-tao*); no other cult is legitimate. It is because Wen Ch'iung has understood this fundamental law of the System that he refuses to allow a sacrifial cult to be rendered to him, but gradually works his way up to the very bottom rungs of the ladder to heaven. But because he is—by virtue of his conception, by virtue of his bones—still so very much a man of this earth, he will be able to rise no higher than "master of transformations."

What, then, is a master of transformations? Chief of the mediums, we have said. But what gives Wen Ch'iung the capacity to control the transformations—the deaths, the trances—of mediums? The answer is clearly to be found in the "cult" he renders to his own effigy. According to the first biography, he goes daily to inspect it; according to the later version, he goes twice daily before the Emperor of the Eastern Peak to make his vow concerning it. If we compare his action with Wu Tao-hsien's practice before a mirror, we can see that both are "inspiring" an object, creating an image; but they are doing so at very different levels of abstraction, at different levels of entry into the System. Wen Ch'iung has learned to transcend the possession of his own body by a spirit and to transfer his "celestial perfection" onto a physical likeness. In this way, by rendering a cult to his true self, he manages to preserve that self from deviation and decomposition and to preserve it for its natural use within the System. He also obviates the need for becoming himself a cult object—qualifying thereby for entry into the System. We may note here that while Master Ping-ling is capable of transforming himself into a Taoist, he is incapable of being one. He can correctly identify Wen's "celestial reality"—his origin, his bones—but he is ignorant of his "real form"—his end, his use—which Ping-ling takes to become, like himself, the object of a cult.

Put another way, Wen Ch'iung succeeds, by dint of concentration on his inner essence, in not becoming yet another cult object, yet another magnetic field of power; he succeeds in determining what will become of himself after his death, and it is undoubtedly this mastery of his own "transformation" that qualifies him to become "master of transformations." But he comes nowhere near Wu Tao-hsien, who has become so entirely a "manifestation of the Tao"—that is the meaning of his name—that he is able to direct his breath, not to the image in the mirror, which could only have been his own, but to the image which is not there yet and, in so doing, utterly to transform the spirit of the method transmitted to him.

In a world replete with idols and images, Wen Ch'iung manages to preserve his identity, that is, the image of himself as he has originally been conceived. Wu Tao-hsien, who has long since become the exact image of the Tao, can now not only make use of those spirits whose celestial reality has achieved the status of true form but even augment the power of their methods by imitating the cosmic gestation of the Tao. Having thus recycled the inherited True Image, he then uses his knowledge of the System to add to the exorcistic power of "wood giving birth to fire" the power of one of the Four Saints from the north. The spirit of fire from the east thus is alchemically transformed by an alliance with T'ien-p'eng, an assistant of the Somber Emperor. This alliance reveals not only Wu Tao-hsien's general knowledge of the System but also his intimate acquaintance with the spirit he was transmuting, for Wen Ch'iung had once taken possession of a commoner to request that his rain-provoking merit be reported "before the gates of the Somber Emperor." The Taoist's knowledge, then, includes knowledge of sacred history, the history and origin of the methods used. It involves, in other words, *transmission:* the transformation of a medium-derived revelation into a method within the System implies its insertion into a lineage, and hence its subjection to the permutations of time. Over time, in the hands of new masters, the inherent capacities of the multifarious methods—including their capacity to survive, to continue to be of use—will gradually reveal themselves. And just as gradually the spirit of the method, if it succeeds in surviving, will work its way up in the hierarchy until at last it ceases altogether to have a distinct existence—form, image—and becomes once again an indistinguishable part of the "manifestation of the Tao."

In conclusion, the biography of Wen Ch'iung, Taoist angel, reveals to us that the complex world of Chinese religion is an epistemologically structured hierarchy: how do we know?—by means of an image. However subtle the graduations in the hierarchy of intelligence may be, there prove in the end to be three distinct classes of response to the basic epistemological problem posed by the ontological fact of the existence of images which mediate our knowledge. The first is the response of the medium, who, however rich he or his sponsors may become by the exploitation of his talents (cf. Elliott 1955, 67-70), will always remain the victim of an image which is not even his own and is, therefore, fundamentally alienating. Self-mutilation is the natural expression of this alienation. Mediums remain, nonetheless, a cut above ordinary man, whose only relationship with the images he worships on his family altar and in the local temple is one of mutual interest and is, therefore, not fundamentally but totally alienating. Preoccupation with self-image—with "face"—is the natural corollary of this alienation.

The first step out of spiritual alienation and into reality belongs to the second class of religious specialists, the "masters of transformation", the masters of methods. Epistemologically, as we have seen, this step consists essentially of self-realization, that is, of the realization of the vows that spring from one's celestial reality. Because this reality is the result of one's *conception*, its realization implies a *conscious* participation—starting at the time of conversion—in a system (cf. Robinet 1984, 1: 107-8, the distinction between a medium and a mystic). The degree of abstraction required for emergence on the threshold of the System, however, is just barely reached, and the master of methods remains earth-bound—bound to images, however true—and dependent on others at every step of the way for his progress. Still, he is no longer distracted by the "affairs of this world," and the mediators who help him no longer alienate him from himself but enable him to realize himself.

True and complete realization/liberation can only occur at the level of the third type of religious specialist, the *tao-shih*, or "officer of the Tao." In discussing the Presentation of the Memorial during the Offering, we have already dealt at length with this specialist's relationship to the image, which we saw to be one of "symbolosis." A lover of life like the Tao he embodies, there is in him "no place for death" (*Lao-tzu* 50), no place for alienation. Nothing is alien, all is real, and he is co-creator with the Tao.

CHAPTER

15

Taoism and Political Legitimacy *

Religious Taoism is to Chinese history what Christianity is to European history. The generalization is no sooner made than it must be qualified: Taoism set out to reform, not to replace, "paganism"; it produced no lasting ecclesiastical organization; its monks were few in number and never played a role in the civil administration; its impact on politics tended to be episodic in character. One could list the differences at some length. And yet the generalization remains valid for the simple reason that for the larger part of the last two millennia, Taoism was, like Christianity in Europe, the official religion of the state (cf. Strickmann 1981, 3-4) and the implacable enemy of "heterodox

* On this subject, see especially Seidel 1983.

253

cults" (*yin-ssu;* cf. Stein). Like medieval Catholicism, moreover, one of its techniques was to absorb and transform local cults.

Starting during the Han dynasty (206 B.C.–A.D. 220), various forms of Taoism began to interest the state as the key to successful government and, hence, to dynastic legitimacy. These forms of Taoism are collectively designated as "Huang-Lao," a term which usually is taken as a conflation of the Yellow Emperor (*Huang*-ti) and *Lao*-tzu. In the context of the first state sacrifice addressed to Lao-tzu in the year 165 A.D., however, the term would seem to designate rather a "yellow Lao-tzu," that is, a Lao-tzu of the (yellow) center (Seidel 1969, 49). Occasioned by the appearance of Lao-tzu in a dream to the Emperor Huan, the sacrifice was commemorated by an inscription in which Lao-tzu is described as

> now leaving, now uniting with the energies of Chaos (*Hun-tun*).° He ends and he begins with the Three Luminaries. Scrutinizing the heavens, he makes prophecies. He descends from and ascends to the Dipper. In his nine transformations, he follows the sun; in his waxing and waning, he is one with the seasons. He regulates the Three Luminaries; the Four Potentates surround him. . . . Since the time of [Fu-]hsi and [Shen-]nung, he is the teacher of the Saint. (*Lao-tzu ming;* cf. Seidel, 123-4)

In the term "teacher of the Saint," meaning of the Emperor, the relationship of the "founder of the religion" to the foundation of the state has received by 165 A.D. its classical definition. The next step was to bring reality into permanent conformity with the definition. That step took over four centuries, centuries which saw first the disintegration of the Han dynasty, then the fragmentation of central power (220-589), and finally the definitive reunification of the empire by the Sui (589-618) and the T'ang (618-907) dynasties. Religiously, the period is a rich one, enriched not only by the successive revelations which led to the gradual definition of the first Taoist canon, but also by the introduction of Taoism's great rival for imperial attention, Buddhism. This is the period of the Great Debates between the representatives of the Three Teachings (the third was Confucianism). The conclusion of the debates was far from foregone; not infrequently the Taoists lost. If in the end the Taoists prevailed, it was because they had a secret arm, an arm by which they regularly disarmed their opponents. "Now leaving, now uniting. . . . He descends and ascends. . . . Since the time of Fu-hsi and Shen-nung, he is the teacher of the Saint"—the secret arm in a word was revelation.

Lao-tzu comes and goes with the seasons; he emerges from and then returns to Chaos. Old (*Lao*) Infant (*tzu*), he is everlastingly new, and when men go in search of him, he appears—in a mirror, in a dream, in the mind's eye, in human form, yes, even in the form of the Buddha himself. Had Buddhism come from the West?—that was because Lao-

° On the importance of *Hun-tun* in early Taoism, see Girardot.

tzu, at the end of his life as a philosopher, had gone west and "turned into a Barbarian" in order to "transform the barbarians" (these are the two possible translations of the term *hua-hu*, on which subject, see Zürcher 1959). Buddhism is therefore just a barbarian form of Taoism. If the people or the emperor are attracted to it, it is because times are decadent, but if times are decadent, then the one who "changes with the seasons" will Come Forth Anew (Hsin-ch'u Lao-chün; cf. Stein 1979, 64) and will reveal a way adapted to the times.

This "vision of history as a succession of revelations of the Tao" (Seidel 1978, 160) inspired the authors of several Taoist histories in the canon to describe that history as the history of Lao-tzu's appearances. So it is, or so it almost is, for Lao-tzu is not the exclusive source of Taoist revelations. Revelations, however, are the exclusive source of Taoism and a key to Taoism's impact on the state. Most of these episodes in Chinese religio-political history are well known to specialists; taken together, they unveil an aspect of Chinese history which remains virtually unknown.

We have already referred on a number of occasions to the revelations vouchsafed at the origin of the Heavenly Master movement. We need only add here that these revelations actually gave rise to a state, a political organization strong enough to survive for several decades, until Ts'ao Ts'ao in 215 won the—apparently—voluntary adherence of the Third Heavenly Master, Chang Lu (cf. Seidel 1978, 164). An ecclesiastical organization of some kind nonetheless survived, for we find complaints voiced in a mid-third century text, that "ever since 231, the various [diocesan] officials are all self-appointed; the appointments are no longer derived from my (Lao-tzu's) energy (i.e., revelation)" (TT 789 *Cheng-yi fa-wen t'ien-shih chiao-chieh k'o-ching* 17a). And two hundred years later, when K'ou Ch'ien-chih received (in 415 and 423) the revelation of a "new code" from Lao-tzu, it was designed to abolish the "old code" of the Heavenly Masters.

In 423 K'ou Ch'ien-chih brought his New Code—partly of Buddhist inspiration—to the capital of the Northern Wei. There he met a Confucian in temporary retirement by the name of Ts'ui Hao, and it was Ts'ui Hao who, after he discovered his own ideas on political and moral order to be entirely compatible with K'ou's New Code, introduced K'ou to the Emperor T'ai-wu. In 425 the Code was promulgated throughout the land, and Taoist rituals began to be performed under imperial auspices. In 440, after a series of major military successes, the emperor adopted, upon K'ou's suggestion, the new era title True Lord of the Great Peace, and in 442 K'ou transmitted to the emperor the "symbols and registers" which at once legitimized his claim to the throne and made him the disciple of K'ou Ch'ieh-chih, Heavenly Master "new style."

The Taoist "theocracy," as Richard Mather calls it, did not outlive the ruler of True Lord of Great Peace, who was murdered in 452. But once again, new institutional arrangements did survive, and throughout the next five centuries emperors were regularly initiated by Taoist masters. Among the more famous instances of such initiations, we may mention that of the Emperor Wu of the Northern Chou by Wei Ching-ssu in 567 (Lagerwey, 19), of Hsüan-tsung of the T'ang by Ssu-ma Ch'eng-chen in 721 and by Li Han-kuang in 748 (Benn, 89, 91), and of Wang Yen of the Posterior T'ang by Tu Kuang-t'ing in 923 (Verellen, 244).

The legitimation of emperors by initiation into existing revealed traditions by no means put an end to legitimation by divine appearance and prophecies. On the contrary, such extraordinary events mark virtually every major new departure in Chinese political history, from the founding of the T'ang in 618 to the founding of the Ming in 1368. The founding of the T'ang is surrounded by a veritable flurry of appearances and prophecies (Benn, 24-35). The most interesting involves an illiterate by the name of Chi Shan-hsing, to whom, according to official sources, Lao-tzu made a single appearance, when he identified himself as the ancestor of the new imperial house and predicted the imminent success of its campaign to pacify the empire.

Taoist versions of this event recount a whole series of appearances made to Chi. According to one account (Chia Shan-hsiang, 5.11a-14b), Lao-tzu appears as an old man and tells Chi that the imminent pacification of the empire requires the founding of a temple with a "statue of the Tao," that is, of Lao-tzu, to be sited to the east of the capital city of Ch'ang-an. Afraid to approach the (future) emperor, Chi must be prodded by a second visit, during which he requests of Lao-tzu a "token" that will prove his good faith. Lao-tzu replies, "When you arrive in the capital, someone will present a stone turtle. Let that be your token" (5.12a). Chi now reports the appearance to the local military commander, who takes him in to see Li Shih-min, later the second T'ang emperor. Li sends Chi with a trusted general, Tu Ang, to make a sacrifice on the site of the appearance. The "old man" appears during the sacrifice to say that he "neither eats nor drinks: why make me a sacrifice?" He also confirms to Tu Ang that Chi has been given his "instructions." Tu and Chi report back to Li, who sends them on to the capital. When they arrive, sure enough one Chang Tu has just presented a turtle-shaped stone with an inscription on it reading, "The empire will be at peace, and my descendants will flourish for ten million years." The emperor then has a temple erected on the site of the appearances, and subsequent appearances of Lao-tzu occur there, before what is probably Lao-tzu's statue. In these final appearances the god is identified more explicitly as "Lord Lao, the emperor's ancestor," and he promises the Divine Ancestor's assistance to his descendants.

Appearances of Lao-tzu occurred frequently throughout the T'ang. A particularly important one in 742 led to the unearthing of a jade tablet with red characters on it promising long life and reign to the emperor Hsüan-tsung. As the inscription read, in part, "Heaven's guarantee for a thousand years," Hsüan-tsung changed the era title to Heaven's Guarantee (Benn, 198).

The Sung dynasty (960-1280) began, like the T'ang, in a blaze of revelations. Again it is a commoner—a "dullwitted" commoner at that (Wang Ch'in-jo, 1.1b) named Chang Shou-chen—who is the chosen vessel. The revelations, which begin in 960 and continue until 994, occur on Mount Chung-nan, a mountain closely associated with the cult of Lao-tzu because it was there, according to legend, that he revealed the *Tao-te ching* (*Lao-tzu*) to Yin Hsi before leaving China for the Far West. The divinity who appears to Chang, however, is not Lao-tzu but an assistant of the Jade Emperor; he eventually reveals himself to be the divine protector of the new ruling house. At first Chang Shou-chen is unwilling to serve as the god's mouthpiece. He protests that he is no "vulgar medium." But his fears are quickly allayed when the Voice says to him:

> I am a god from Heaven above, not a demon. I have [the spirits] of the Five Peaks and the Four Rivers at my beck and call. If you have a change of heart and enter the Tao, if you conscientiously render me a cult, I shall see to it that you receive a state appointment and the blessings of the True Lord. Does that put you on the same level as mediums? (Wang Ch'in-jo, 1.1b)

Chang is reassured, and he sets out an offering of meat and wine:

> Again he heard the voice, saying, "I am a god. Why do you insult me with 'meat-foulness'? I will assume it is your ignorance and will not hold it against you, but hereafter you must make offerings of perfumed tea, vegetables, and fresh fruits. I do not eat, but I will appreciate your intentions." (Wang Ch'in-jo, 1.2a)

This interview closes with the god telling Chang, "I am your master in Heaven above. You also have a master among men. You should seek out a great master and ask him to initiate you." Chang need not look far: right there on Mount Chung-nan is the oldest of Taoist hermitages, the Lou-kuan, founded by Yin Hsi when he was waiting for Lao-tzu to pass by on his way to the Far West. Chang is initiated as a Taoist by one of its hermits.

Chang's next step is to build a temple to the Northern (Somber) Emperor. In it he sets up a hall to "serve the god." Mornings and evenings he worships with utmost devotion, until the god appears again and says:

I have seen the sincerity of your heart: you are worthy to receive my instructions. An officer who is pure and chaste can drive out evil. I shall first teach you the Method of the Sword, which will enable you to exorcise evil spirits for the people. Later, I shall instruct you in the creation of an altar, so that you can pray for blessings on behalf of the state. (Wang Ch'in-jo, 1.2b)

Chang follows the instructions of the god, and the sanctuary's fame comes very quickly to the first emperor T'ai-tsu's ears. But T'ai-tsu is "not much of a believer in the miraculous" (1.4b) and, when he nonetheless decides to "give it a go," only succeeds in insulting the god by attempting to communicate with him using the shrill scream (*hsiao*) appropriate for addressing demons. The god therefore prefers to wait for the second emperor, T'ai-tsung, to come to the throne in 976 before allowing a magnificent new temple to be built in his honor. As the god had previously predicted that the Lord of Great Peace would build him a Palace of the Great Peace of Highest Purity, the temple was so named, and the era thus opened was called Flourishing State of Great Peace.

In 981 the god receives his official enfeoffment. In 994 he informs Chang Shou-chen that his tank has been accomplished:

There will be enlightened rulers one after the other, and my appointed time has come to return to heaven. You will hear my words no longer. (Wang Ch'in-jo, 1.9b)

His words will be heard no longer, but he will continue to heed the prayers of the dynasty and "vouchsafe his blessings and protection." The god's final words are for Chang himself: "Thirty-five years have gone by since you first encountered my descent, and your merit too is very great. The Emperor on High has already issued an order to name you Chief of the Five Mounds" (1.9b), that is, like Wen Ch'iung, chief among the earth gods.

So comes to a close the opening chapter in the long history of the dealings of the Sung imperial house with its divine benefactors. Equally important chapters are written during the reigns of the third emperor, Chen-tsung (998-1022), and of the eighth, Hui-tsung (1101-26). Like Hsüan-tsung of the T'ang who unearthed a tablet, Chen-tsung discovered a "celestial letter." This discovery led him to perform the sacrifices of dynastic legitimacy (Chavannes 1910, 236 ff.) and change the era title to Auspicious Symbol (Sun K'o-k'uan 1965, 72-80). The same emperor was later visited in a dream by the Heavenly Worthy Who Protects the Living (Pao-sheng t'ien-tsun) and was told that this Heavenly Worthy was none other than the Yellow Emperor, ancestor of the Chao clan and hence imperial ancestor (Sun, 83). Thus like the T'ang, the Sung acquired a famous Taoist ancestor, theirs being in the person of the other party to the Huang-Lao tandem of the Han dynasty.

As for Hui-tsung, an imperial dream-visit to the court of the Jade

Emperor led, after consultation with Liu Hun-k'ang, twenty-fifth master of the Shang-ch'ing lineage associated with Mao-shan (Mount Mao), to several discoveries. First he discovered a Taoist by the name of Lin Ling-su, and then, through Lin, he discovered his (Hui-tsung's) own divine identity as Lord-Emperor of the Eastern Efflorescence, also known as the Great Emperor of Long Life (Ch'ang-sheng ta-ti; cf. Strickmann 1978; Chin Chung-shu 1966; 338–9). Lin himself was Lord of the Religion (*chiao-chu*) of the Divine Empyrean (Shen-hsiao), yet another in the long line of new ritual codes stretching straight back to Chang Tao-ling himself.

This simultaneous apotheosis of a reigning emperor and propagation of a new form of Taoism formed the dramatic climax to the first phase of a gradual process which led to a definitive transformation of church-state relations in China. Throughout the T'ang, the Shang-ch'ing lineage of Mao-shan had been the principal religious interlocutor of the state. When emperors were initiated, it was by masters of this lineage (Strickmann 1981, 32–37). By the Yüan dynasty (1280–1368), however, Mao-shan was wholly supplanted in this role by Lung-hu shan, center of a revived Orthodox Unity Taoism. During the Yüan and Ming (1368–1644), official church-state relations were dominated, especially in southern China, by the Heavenly Masters of Lung-hu shan. The titles accorded them, and eventually accorded their wives and mothers as well, grew longer and longer, their land holdings richer and richer, and they even came to be allied to the imperial house by marriage (see TT 1463 *Han t'ien-shih shih-chia*).

This shift from one Taoist mountain to another basically reflects a shift from aristocratic, eremetic Taoism to popular, communal Taoism, for the Shang-ch'ing Taoism of Mao-shan is from the very beginning as thoroughly aristocratic and individualistic a movement (Strickmann 1977) as Heavenly Master Taoism is popular and communal (Maspero, 373–88). The Lin Ling-su episode with Hui-tsung must therefore be seen as the climax of the first phase of this shift, of this gradual rapprochement of the dynastic and local cults of the Tao.

The first substantial literary evidence of this shift is to be found in the writings of Tu Kuang-t'ing (850–933). In contrast with the refined essays on mental cultivation written by the Shang-ch'ing masters of the T'ang, Tu's collections of prayers, rituals, and tales of exorcisms and epiphanies* constitute a sudden and monumental reminder that, whatever the institutional role of Shang-ch'ing Taoism in the T'ang, its impact on belles-lettres (see Schafer) was certainly far greater than on the religious life of the people, or even of the court. As we have seen, at the beginning of the T'ang and the Sung, an illiterate and a "dullwitted commoner" respectively had determined the structure and content of the

---

*A superb study of these collections has been completed by Franciscus Verellen (see Bibliography).

official Taoist cult. Emperors were invested with Shang-ch'ing diplomas, but they gained access to divine benediction through plebeian seers—and their Taoist masters.

The contrast between individual and communal Taoism is a commonplace in Taoist texts as far back as the fifth century (Lagerwey, 24). It was stated by the founding emperor of the Ming dynasty, in his introduction to *The Standard Rituals for Offerings and Fasts of the Celestial Religion of the Great Ming* (TT 467 *Ta-Ming hsüan-chiao li-ch'eng chai-chiao yi*), dated 1374, a mere six years after the founding of the dynasty, as follows:

> Ch'an [Buddhism] and Integral Reality [Taoism] devote themselves to the cultivation of the person and the improvement of the individual endowment: they are just for the self. The [Buddhist] Teaching (the White Lotus sect?) and Orthodox Unity [Taoism] focus on salvation and lay special emphasis on filial children and compassionate parents. They improve human relations and enrich local customs: great indeed is their merit! (Preface, 1a)

A text by the third Ming emperor, Ch'eng-tsu (r. 1403–24), gives a concrete illustration of the implications of the imperial attitude, at least as regards Taoism:

INSCRIPTION FOR THE PALACE OF THE POWERFUL SAVIORS, COMPOSED BY THE EMPEROR

From of old, heroes and sages who have been famous ministers while alive, gaining prominence by their merit in succoring the people, have become luminous gods after death, assisting in the transformations of heaven and earth. . . . While alive, [the two brothers Hsü Chih-cheng and Hsü Chih-e] aided the people and the state; when they died, they were enrolled in the ranks of the immortals. Elder and younger brother were equally perfect; the stem and the flower were a single fragrance. They received appointments from Heaven on high; their brilliance was efficacious on earth below. . . .

We had not been feeling well and had tried a hundred different prescriptions, all without success. But after sincere supplication of the spirit, the potentates came to Our aid. For a brief while, we were submissive, and each supplication was answered; there was repeated evidence of divine manifestation. Use of the potent symbol, marvelous drug of the Celestial Physician, restored peace where there had been danger and caused the moribund to get up from his bed. Great is the compassion and rich the grace that brought Us back to life! The measure of Our virtue is shallow and cold: it cannot explain what We have received. We shall cherish forever the memory of the divine favor: how could We possibly forget it? Deep as the ocean, high as the mountains, it is inexhaustible.

It being the fixed practice of the state to repay merit, we hereby lengthen the official divine titles in the Book of Invocations: the elder brother will be called Perfect Lord of Boundless Grace, Protector of the State and Succor of the People. . . . The younger brother will be called Perfect Lord of Boundless Grace, Mainstay of the State and Benefactor of the People. . . . They also retain all former titles. Their temple will be entirely renewed: soaring, clean, and luminous, it will be a place fit for a god to dwell. We also order the competent authorities to keep fresh incense burning, to make sacrifices in spring and autumn, and to change their dress in accord with the seasons. We grant five households for the sweeping and cleaning as an expression of Our earnestness in response to the great goodness of the gods.

The importance of this local cult of the Hsü brothers—the "ancestral temple" had been founded in Fukien in 983—to the Ming imperial family may be surmised from the fact that the above inscription, which is dated to the first day of the fifth month of 1417, was included already in the Taoist canon of 1445 (TT 476 *Hung-en ling-chi chen-chün shih-shih* 1a–2a), and then again in the addition to that canon of 1607 (TT 1470 *Hsü-hsien chen-lu* 1.26a–27b). The former text, *The True Facts about the Perfect Lords of Boundless Grace and Numinous* Salvation, is preceded in the canon by a sequence of eight texts which together constitute a complete Taoist ritual for the cult of the two brothers. The scriptural basis of the cult, its "words of institution," is also included in the 1445 canon (TT 317 *Ling-pao t'ien-tsun shuo Hung-en ling-chi chen-chün miao-ching*). Its preface, dated to the first day of the first month of 1420, is like the above inscription by Emperor Ch'eng-tsu.

The TT 317 scripture begins with the two brothers in heaven, pleading with the Heavenly Worthy of the Numinous Treasure to "have compassion earthward and open an accessible door" to the benighted people of these "latter days." The method of my teaching, responds the Heavenly Worthy, is simple. "Loyalty, filiality, charity, and justice: practice these four, and you will dwell forever in good fortune and felicity" (1b). He then charges the two brothers with the task of descending to earth to spread this message among men. Long life, good, fortune, family peace, and the salvation of the ancestors are promised to those who regularly practice the four cardinal virtues and, on specified days, "face north, bow their heads, and in the silence of their hearts reverently meditate on" the two brothers (2a). Ch'eng-tsu's preface is a personal testimony to the efficacity of the cult, and his ordering the "printing and wide dissemination" of the scripture is a repayment of his debt to the divine brothers (Preface, 1b–2a).

The *True Facts* (TT 476) gives only the bare data on the brothers' lives. Generals during the chaotic period of the Five Dynasties (907–960), they did their heroic best to save the people under their control from the ravages of war and the depredations of rebels and bandits; they were also paragons of moral virtue who "worshiped the Three Treasures . . . and daily recited the precious name and *The Perfect Scripture of the Jade Emperor*" (3b). The grateful people of Fukien established a cult in their honor while they were still alive, saying, "They are our parents, who have brought us back to life" (4a). Shortly after, they died and went to heaven, where they received appointments as angels of the Dipper in

Charge of Water. It is in that capacity they appear in the court of the Heavenly Worthy of the Numinous Treasure in the TT 317 scripture, pleading for compassion for the people.

The text from the 1607 canon, *The True Record of the Immortals Hsü* (TT 1470), is a five-chapter collection of ritual and historical documents. They show how the cult, founded in 983 (1.6b), spread partly by "division of incense" (1.7a) and partly by creation of new but subordinate cults (1.8a), until finally in 1236 the Sung emperor Li-tsung granted the brothers their first official titles (1.5a). The emperors Ch'eng-tsu in 1417 and 1418, Hsüan-tsung in 1435, Ying-tsung in 1436, and Hsien-tsung in 1485 all lengthened these titles (1.5b–6a, 38a–43a, 3.6a–11b). Hsien-tsung announced his bestowal of additional titles in an inscription written on the occasion of the reconstruction of the temple. According to this inscription, he had personal reasons to be grateful to the brothers (3.10b), but he also had institutional obligations to their cult:

> Ever since We inherited the throne, We have rendered a cult to all the gods in the Canon of Sacrifices, but We have been particularly assiduous with respect to the two supreme emperors of the Golden and the Jade Gates. It being my imperial Ancestor (Ch'eng-tsu) who established their cult, how could I be other than especially attentive to their worship? (3.12a)

Chapters 3 and 4 of the *True Record* are largely composed of documents relating to Ch'eng-tsu's establishment of the Hsü brothers' cult in the capital. These documents state exactly what types of rituals the Taoists who were attached to the temples in Fukien and in Peking were to perform, and when. Very detailed, they even supply the names of the thirty-five Taoists in the Peking temple and the twelve Taoists in the "ancestral temple," not to mention the names of the heads of the households—twenty in the capital, sixteen in Fukien—charged with "sweeping and cleaning" (3.31b–32a, 4.17a).

The most interesting document of all, however, recounts the "establishment of the official who renders the cult," that is, the medium for the cult:

> Born Mr. Ch'en, he came to be attached to the Sun clan by virtue of his place of residence. He first took up the divine brush to determine symbols and drugs in the year 1397 in the Great Ming dynasty. [His judgments concerning] the fortune or misfortune of land patterns proved invariably accurate. Word of him reached the court, and in the year 1416 an envoy was sent to welcome the god.
>
> Whenever there was a problem, he made silent supplication. If the result was not satisfactory, greater reverence [produced] greater efficacity. On the eighteenth day of the fifth month of the year 1419, the Emperor granted him cap and belt as keeper of the temple worship, with a monthly salary of five piculs of rice. When his entire household had been assembled, apartments were prepared in the west wing of the temple, and they took up residence there. (3.30b–31a)

Clearly, Ming emperors still gained access to divine benediction through plebeian seers, but unlike their T'ang and Sung predecessors, they no longer bothered to find seers of their own: they simply borrowed them from the people. Popular religion had become dynastic religion.

The gradual rapprochement of the dynastic and local cults of the Tao which began with Emperor Hui-tsung in the Sung, reached its conclusion in the cult of the two Hsü brothers. This cult is rendered by a medium, but the "compassion" he brings "earthward" when he wields the "divine brush to determine symbols and drugs" comes through the "accessible door"—the Golden and Jade Gates—opened by the Heavenly Worthy of the Numinous Treasure, as we learned earlier from *The Marvellous Scripture of the Perfect Lords of Boundless Grace and Numinous Salvation, Uttered by the Heavenly Worthy of the Numinous Treasure* (TT 317).

Why the Heavenly Worthy of the Numinous Treasure? Because from the very beginning, the second of the Three Taoist Treasures presided over that part of Taoism which has to do with the earth, whether under it (the dead, the ancestors), or on it (the living, the Son of Heaven). Insofar as Taoism has to do with the dead, it borrowed from the "religion of death," that is, Buddhism; and insofar as it has to do with ancestors and the Son of Heaven, it absorbed the "religion of ethical relations," that is, Confucianism. Thus early in the T'ang dynasty already, Numinous Treasure Taoism begat the Way of Filial Piety (Hsiao-tao; cf. TT 66 *Yüan-shih tung-chen tz'u-shan hsiao-tzu pao-en ch'eng-tao ching* and Chin Yün-chung, 10.13b), which begat the Way of Loyalty and Filiality (Chung-hsiao tao), which now begat the Way of Loyalty, Filiality, Charity (*jen*), and Justice (*yi*).

This particular Ming synthesis of popular mediumism, Confucian ethics, Buddhist metaphysics, and dynastic propaganda reposed on two brothers who "worshiped the Three Treasures and daily recited the precious name and *The Perfect Scripture of Jade Emperor*," as we saw from the *True Facts about the Perfect Lords* (TT 476). The scripture of the head of the popular pantheon that is recited by the Hsü brothers first appears during the Sung dynasty (TT 10 *Kao-shang Yü-huang pen-hsing chi-ching*), and from then until now—for it is still a key Taoist text—it has been associated with Orthodox Unity (Heavenly Master) Taoism. No wonder, then, that one of the first miracles of the newly established imperial cult of the Perfect Lords of Numinous Salvation should occur during a seven-day fast begun on the fifteenth day of the second month—Lao-tzu's birthday—of the year 1419 and performed by over seven thousand Taoists from Chekiang, Hu-Kuang, Kiangsi, and Fukien under the direction of the Forty-fourth Heavenly Master and "lord of the religion," Chang Yü-ch'ing (*True Record*, 1.21a). Thus is confirmed, at the moment of the fusion of the popular dynastic cults of the Tao, the supremacy of the communal Taoism of Lung-hu shan over the eremetic Shang-ch'ing lineage of Mao-shan. During the alien Manchu dynasty

(1644–1911), Taoism lost its place as the religion of the state, but it remains to the present day the national religion, that is, the religion to which all the cults of popular religion belong and on which they depend.

The mediums of the popular cults, in lending their bodies to the descending gods, are so many "accessible doors," so many Golden and Jade Gates opened up allowing the Boundless Grace of Numinous Salvation to pour through. The Jade Emperor is chief of the popular pantheon because he is the ultimate Golden Gate, the last swinging door before the world of Boundless Grace itself, the world of the Three Pure Ones. It is therefore the Jade Emperor and the Golden Gate that masters of mediums approach during their ceremony of investiture (Schipper 1982, 71), as Taoists do in the exoteric ritual of the Presentation of the Memorial (see p. 150). Only Taoists, when they Walk the Way, when they transform their bodies into the Body of the Way, penetrate beyond the Golden Gate to the esoteric Land of the Way.

Crouched down like a turtle (plate 22), embodying the Way and in communion with the Way, the Taoist priest is "carrying out transformations"—opening doors, engendering gods—"on Heaven's behalf": this is the ultimate image of the cult of the Way. How could the people have accessible doors with no one to open them? How could the Son of Heaven be Heaven's Son with no one to engender him? In Chinese history as in Chinese society, Taoists occupy the position which their ritual gives them: the position of the turtle.

CONCLUSION

What is Taoism?

A certain number of propositions should no longer encounter any opposition:

Taoism is ritual; Taoism is music.

Taoism is revelation; Taoism is symbolism.

Taoism is system; Taoism is lineage.

Is Taoism mythology?

Who says ritual says grammar, structure;

Who says music says song, dance, and rhythm.

Who says revelation says mystery and its unfolding;

Who says symbolism says sign and image.

Who says system says science;

Who says lineage says transmission.

Taoism is a complex system of symbolic structures founded on revealed texts and images, expressed in ritual and music, and transmitted from generation to generation. But is it mythological? We have certainly had constant recourse to mythology—the mythology of Yü, of the Western Queen Mother, of Lao-tzu—to explain both the construction of the Taoist altar and its use. And while modern Taoists who use the Step of Yü know nothing of Yü's mythology, the conscious use of the mythology of Lao-tzu has been one of the characteristic features of Taoist history (Schipper 1982, chap. 7). But can mythology really be central in a religious system whose primary response to the universe is ritual?

According to Yehezkel Kaufmann, the answer can only be in the affirmative. As Kaufmann explains, mythology is the foundation of paganism (on the use of this term, see p. xv), ritual its supreme expression. The basic idea of paganism, he writes, is that the gods belong to, and are derived from,

> [a primordial] realm . . . , the womb in which the seeds of all being are contained. . . . The god is thus a personal embodiment of one of the seminal forces of the primordial realm. (Kaufmann, pp. 21, 22)

This "radical dichotomy" between the realms of the "divine" and the "metadivine" (p. 23) is the source of both mythology and magic. Because "each god represents only one embodiment of the forces of a universe filled with divine powers, there was room for myth-making" (p. 31). "Myth is the tale of the life of the gods" (p. 22). As for magic, it is important because "it is not the gods who redeem, but knowledge of the secrets of existence" (p. 40), knowledge of the forces which the gods derive from the primordial realm. "The gods have an important role as teachers of magical arts to men" (p. 41), but man "redeems himself through knowledge" (p. 42).

The story of Marshal Wen recounted in Chapter 14 is a perfect illustration of this. His "true form," his seal, is a composite of four characters which express his essence, the seminal force of the primordial realm of which his entire career shows him to be the embodiment. But Wen Ch'iung, as a part of the spiritual bureaucracy, only embodies this force; he is not its master. It requires the Heavenly Master himself, with his knowledge of the System, to create the seal and to teach Wen's "secret method of the earth spirits" to Wu Tsung-ching, a Taoist, who thus activates Wen's powers. Later, it is yet another "officer of the Tao" who enables Wen to reach the top of the terrestrial bureaucracy by wedding Wen's innate power to that of a compatible divinity by reciting the appropriate incantations.

Wen's story shows us that it is on the level of the mediums and their masters that we may expect to find mythology and magic. It also suggests that symbols and incantations are the basic ingredients of ritual on this level. Symbols we have already seen to be "specific configura tions of energy" symbolizing the secret names of divine forces (see p. 153). Incantations are often simply the oral form of the symbol. They therefore take the form of "orders" (*ming*), for they activate—bring to life (also *ming*)—the written symbol. But incantations can also serve, in popular religion, to "invite the god" to "descend" into the body of its medium (De Groot 1910, 6:1273). The master of a medium, as Schipper says (1982, 75), knows not just "the secret names of all the gods and the secret ways of writing their talismanic signs, he also knows their legend. He summons the gods, therefore, by reciting verses which evoke their history."

In essentially the same manner Taoist masters occasionally use combinations of sign and sound: the "Nine-phoenix symbol for the destruction of filth" and the five True Writs used to construct the altar are both good examples (see pp. 73, 103). But what is a full ritual in popular religion becomes a single rite in Taoist practice, and the mythological element disappears entirely. The gods, when it comes time to invite them, are simply enumerated, and they are called not by their names but by their titles, which distinguish them less as forces than as parts of the machinery of the universe.

As often as not, moreover, symbols are not even given a material written form: they may be written in the air by incense (above, p. 112), by clouds (p. 158), by the sword (p. 100), or by the priest's right hand in the "sword gesture" (p. 75); they may even be left unwritten (p. 103). Even when they are given an external written form, they have first been created within by a combination of breathwork and visualization (pp. 157 ff.). By visualization the Taoist creates the conditions—the order of the universe, the altar—for the renewed revelation of the symbols; by breathwork, which consists of further visualizations which set the body's energies in motion and create the gods and is followed by invocations addressed to these self-created gods, the Taoist himself "gives birth" to the symbols on the inside—in his own primordial realm of Anterior Heaven—before he reproduces them on the outside in the visible forms of Posterior Heaven.

But even symbols created with such care are not the last word in the realm of the Taoist image: that, we saw, was reserved for the chart, one form of which is the "map of the mountain" (see p. 161). It is only at this distinctively Taoist level of the image that we enter the distinctively Taoist realm of mythology, that of the Western Queen Mother in this case. In the same vein, it is at the very beginning of the ritual of Announcement—itself the first ritual—that the high priest "transforms his body" into the body of the universe, that is, of Lao-tzu (see p. 72). Thereafter, it is the "Lord Lao in his body" who will "summon forth from within his servant's body" the various forces required to perform the ritual (p. 122). As for the myth of Yü, we have had occasion to refer to it in connection both with the construction of the altar (e.g., pp.

31–34) and with the "assembly of the gods" represented by the great number of symbols attached to the priest's vestments during the Presentation of the Memorial (pp. 151–54).

Thus Taoist mythology does exist, but it exists primarily on the level of the Whole—the altar, the mountain, the body—that is, on the level of the primordial (internal) realm. And inasmuch as Taoist mythology exists for the same purpose as mediumnistic mythology, namely, to provoke a transformation of the body which prepares it to perform a specific ritual task, once the high priest has, by reference to the appropriate mythology, transformed his body into the body of the Whole, he no longer has any use for "Taoist mythology."

The differing forms taken by this mythology-induced transformation is determined by the differing tasks of the medium and the Taoist. That of the medium is passive and is provoked by his master, because his job is to speak on behalf of gods who are themselves susceptible to manipulation. They must be induced, seduced, compelled even, to "descend" into, "attach" (*fu*) themselves to, take possession of their spokesman. The transformation of the Taoist is active, self-provoked, because his job is to "enact change on Heaven's behalf." To do this, not only must he be active in the way the principles of the primordial realm are active, he must be Whole as it is whole: "By means of my ritual, both inhaling and exhaling become inhaling," says the high priest at the end of the Land of the Way (p. 147). In the same ritual, when he "supports the petition" that is made to the purest forces of the primordial realm, he again transforms his body into that of Lao-tzu and then visualizes a voyage within it (pp. 131–32). It is only when he goes out of doors to present the memorial that we can speak, as in the case of mediumnistic ritual, of "descent" and "attachment," but it is the Taoist himself who comes down from the primordial realm in his "mantle of descent," and it is the externalized agents of his own body which cling to this mandala of the Whole.

Yes, then, mythology is important in Taoism, but by no means as important as ritual. Why? What is ritual that it should be so important in paganism? "The characteristic mark of the pagan cult," writes Kaufmann, "is not its plurality of worshiped beings, but its view of ritual as automatically efficient and intrinsically significant" (p. 53). "The cult is above the gods," he continues;

> through it the gods live, create, and govern; it is *rita*, the secret and inner strength of the world. The Brahmanas represent the sacrifice as identified with the *purusha*, the primal god-man, who was sacrificed and became the stuff out of which all was created. *The priest re-enacts the moment of creation at each sacrifice* (italics mine). (Kaufmann, 55)

Kaufmann earlier describes *rita* as "the world order, the principle of pattern and regularity in all phenomena" which is "embodied in the correct cult," and concludes that "paganism here approaches a scientific and mathematical conception of the universe" (p. 33).

All this we have seen to be true of Taoism: its altar represents the structure of the universe; its ritual represents the same "world order" in time, from the combat of good with evil in the Altar-sealing (cf. Kaufmann, 56, 54) and the construction of the altar with five True Writs that first appeared at the "moment of creation" to the communication with the "metadivine realm" in the Land of the Way and the demonstration of "the intrinsic efficacy of the ritual" (Kaufmann, 59) in the Presentation of the Memorial. The high priest himself is obviously the "primal god-man": it is his own body which is sacrificed—rendered sacred—when it becomes the body of Lao-tzu; it is his own body which, when he "symbolizes with the map of the universe" and "returns to the Origin"—when he "supports the petition"—becomes "one with the Way" (see pp. 134, 166); it is from his own body, finally, that emerge the energies which are then taken home in the form of symbols by the community representatives (above, p. 152).

Of these three instances, however, it is the last which must be designated the "moment of creation":

> The theory of emanation is of particular interest, for it includes a double belief: polymorphism (or the plural element of the Godhead) and immanence. To Cabalistic theology belongs the merit of having taught, before any other school, that the theory of emanation is not foreign to the Bible.
>
> The first trace we find of it is in the very word which *Genesis* uses to designate the act by means of which God created the world, the verb *bara*. If certain authors have—wrongly—seen in this term the proof of creation *ex nihilo*, others, especially Ibn Ezra, have not left unnoticed that, quite to the contrary, it means to cut, separate, or extract from something which pre-exists. . . . [Among etymologically related words, we may mention] *berith*, pact, alliance, because of the practice of cutting the victim in half, *bar*, son, because he issues from his parents, and in Aramaic, *bar*, outside. (Benamozegh, 59-60).

It is this same "Cabala," this same "esoteric tradition," which, much to the dismay of its orthodox opponents, reappropriated the language of myth in Judaism (Scholem 1980, chap. 3). But long before that, it had found expression in Christian gnosticism, and even in the orthodox understanding and practice of the "Paschal mystery." The creation of the Church by the breaking and distributing of the body of the Christ is entirely analogous to the creation of the Taoist assembly—the animation of the Taoist body—by the "killing of the turtle," followed by the "exteriorization of the officers" (see p. 131) and the distribution of the symbols which represent the energies, the spirit, of the high priest.

Insofar as Jewish Cabala and Christian mysteries reflect pagan influences, these comparisons reconfirm our initial identification of

Taoism as paganism. But we are now in a position to affirm, with Kaufmann, that paganism, in its highest forms, is not the murderous sacrifices or the image-fetishism denounced by the Old Testament prophets. It is rituals which at once imitate and create the primordial realm; it is philosophy and metaphysics in which "salvation is no longer a matter of ritual, but of knowledge of the secrets of being and non-being, life and death" (Kaufmann, 59). At the same time, while Taoism, as we saw in the chapter on numerology, does indeed "approach a scientific and mathematical conception of the universe," it never attains it precisely because it is a "science of cosmic secrets" (ibid., 43).

That Taoism is such a science of time and space is no doubt due to the fact that it is the religion of the people of the land: a farmer's work is entirely determined by the order of the universe, determined not only by its seasons but also by the lay of the land. A peasant society naturally secretes a "religion of nature," a religion of the "high places," that is, of the mounds that serve as cult centers wherever land is cultivated. The tiller of the soil, we may add—Cain, as opposed to the shepherd Abel—is the ancestor of both musicians and metallurgists. Taoism may be described as a combination of alchemy—always closely linked to metallurgy—and music. One need only consult the table of contents of Granet's *Danses et légendes*, Part 3, Chapter 3, to get an idea of the relationship in Chinese myth between music, dance, metallurgy—and Yü. If we see no intrinsic link between these arts, it is because our tradition has largely occulted what Julia Kristeva calls the "process of the constitution of significance" by means of "pre-oedipal semiotic functions, of discharges of energy which link and orient the body with respect to the mother": "enigmatic and femine, this space underlying writing is rhythmic. . ., it is musical, prior to judgment" (Kristeva, 25, 26, 29).

Is it any wonder a religion capable of producing not only the metaphysical profundity of a *Lao-tzu* and the philosophical, narrative, even poetic brilliance of a *Chuang-tzu*, but also rich ritual tapestries woven of the very fabric of the universe should have awakened in the Marcus Aureliuses of China—men like Hsüan-tsung and Hui-tsung—spontaneous sympathy that grew into a veritable devotion? And is it any wonder that a religion based on occult magic and rites of union should have raised the hackles of the Confucians, champions that they were, like the Church Fathers, of a rational moral order? (Cf. Kaufmann, 74: "Abandoning the amoral universe of magical forces, historical monotheism conceived the idea of a moral cosmos, whose highest law is the will of God.")

But what had Taoism to do with securing the foundations of the imperium in traditional China? First of all, Taoism achieved far more than imperial recognition of local gods by the bestowal of feudal titles could ever do for local cults. Taoism, because it addressed itself to the primordial realm from which these local gods ultimately derived and on which they therefore depended, could compensate for, and to a certain extent even impose its orthodoxy on, the incoherent congery of local cults that made up the empire's religious map. Second, Taoism, because it had its feet on the ground and its head in the clouds, could offer the emperor a vision of a society like a seamless coat enveloping all, from the humblest peasant with his gods and customs to the imperial house itself, with its pressing need for an ideology of government on a cosmic level of abstraction (cf. Lagerwey, pp. 5-6, 41 and Benn, p. 5). The Confucians had to turn to the Legalists for a philosophy of government, and the Legalists themselves were profoundly influenced by the Taoists. The best the Confucians could manage regarding the cults and customs of the peasants on whose backs the whole system reposed was benign neglect.

Third, insofar as the Taoists were masters of magic and music, they had ready access to the emperor, whether he needed them to conjure up the soul of a beloved concubine who had died, to ensure progeny, to provide aphrodisiacs and elixirs of immortality, interpret dreams, produce revelations or portents, heal the sick, exorcise demons, or make the heavens rain or shine. For each of these feats, names of famous (or infamous) Taoists spring readily to mind—T'ao Hung-ching, Ch'i Hui, Yeh Fa-shan, Tu Kuang-t'ing, Lin Ling-su, Chou Ssu-te. As for Taoists' role as court musicians, it was noted in 1600 by Matteo Ricci ("To our ears they produce cacaphony"; cited by Dehergne, p. 60).

Fourth—and this is the aspect which in a sense encompasses all the others—Taoism as the science of potency was the one science a Chinese emperor could not really do without, for in the end Chinese political theory comes down to a theory of potency: the emperor was the dragon seated on the dragon throne, the most potent—not necessarily the most powerful—man on earth. Power is real, calculated in numbers of battalions and bushels of grain; potency is symbolic, and it is measured, as we have seen again and again when dealing with Taoist symbols, in drawing power, in capacity to seduce, attract, magnetize.

By Confucian standards, the emperor was supposed to rule the earth by sheer moral virtue. Moral virtue was enough, said Confucius, to enable the emperor to bring all beings into orbit around him, like the Pole Star in the sky. But was moral virtue, however necessary, sufficient? Would moral virtue produce male offspring or attract the tribute of the barbarians, not to mention the adhesion of the people? No, the first required aphrodisiacs, rituals in accord with *rita*, and calendrical science, all of which Taoism provided. The second required revelation, strategy, and conspicuous consumption, all of which were Taoist sciences, rooted in their cultivation of the art of potency (cultivating the *yang* energies).

Exorcism, in the context of paganism, requires strategy, a strategy which scorns no ruse, no ploy, no device for "stimulating the *yang* and suppressing the *yin*" (cf. p. 55). Bandits, barbarians, and rebels are alike demonic (*yin*) forces bent on destroying the Order (*yang*) of the universe. The techniques of combat, therefore, whether in love, war, or medicine, all derive from Taoist revelations, and the Taoist canon contains manuals for all three.

Conspicuous consumption is in fact one of the most important weapons in the war on the demonic. Wealth, high rank, and longevity are the three gods universally adored in traditional Chinese society; their opposites are demonic. And inasmuch as like attracts like in a symbolic system, conspicuous consumption, which obviously implies both high rank and wealth, naturally drives off destitution. When the Emperor Hui-tsung, rather than pouring money into defense against the menacing Jürchen tribes, pours it instead into fabulous construction projects such as the Mountain of Longevity (Chin Chung-shu 1967, 224-31), it is because he believes his symbolic paradise will fend off the barbarians far better than a merely human army could. From the community point of view, the Taoist Offering has the same function, and it is therefore a time when no expense is spared.

Let us pause to ask what the word longevity implies before considering the subject of revelation. Longevity is perhaps the Taoist science of all sciences, for a Taoist is one who "lives long and has distant vision" (*Lao-tzu* 59). Early Taoism taught the arts of the bedchamber not to enhance the joy of sex but to become immortal. "The basic technique," wrote Ko Hung in the early fourth century, "consists in returning the spermatic essence to repair the brain" (TT 1185 *Pao-p'u tzu nei-p'ien* 8.4a). The method is specifically attributed to Lao-tzu in the oldest extant collection of *Biographies of the Immortals, Lieh-hsien chuan* (Kaltenmark 1953, 61). Its theory is clearly stated already in the third century B.C.:

> One who daily renews his seminal energy and gets rid entirely of perverse energies, and [so] lives out his heaven[-appointed] years, is called a "real person" (*chen-jen*). (*Lü-shih ch'un-ch'iu*, 3.5b)

Longevity was much coveted by the ordinary Chinese, but to Taoists and the emperor it was a part of their very definition. Longevity alone could demonstrate that they were truly potent, entirely *yang*, "men after Heaven's heart." From the First Emperor of the Ch'in dynasty on, therefore, the chronicles are full of stories of emperors who consult Taoists (or proto-Taoists) concerning the Isles of the Immortals and solicit from them elixirs of immortality or revealed texts which show how to obtain these elixirs. Even the sacrifices of dynastic legitimacy, which are performed on that most Taoist of all mountains the Eastern Peak, are closely linked to the emperor's personal pursuit of immortality (Chavannes 1910, 224).

As for revelation, eliciting new ones at propitious times was never, as we saw in Chapter 15, a problem for Taoists, for revelation is but the publication of novel signifiers from the "eternal stream of seminal energy" (see p. 166). For the emperor, who rules over the visible world of Posterior Heaven, such new scriptures are tokens from within the Golden Gate that he has the favor of Anterior Heaven. For the Taoist, who rules over the primordial, internal realm, revelation is simply self-expression. Even the word "I" is such a signifier in Taoism. Ordinary people refer to themselves in Chinese as *wo*, a character composed of two weapons and suggesting conflict, implying that the "self" is rooted in "interhuman aggressivity" (cf. Lacan, p. 101). The Taoist term, on the other hand, is *chao* (cf. *Lao-chün chung ching* 1.5a), a character which referred originally to the divinatory cracks that appeared in a carapace of a tortoise held in the fire and which, when duly "read," enabled one to divine the future. For the Taoist, indeed, all that is visible is text, is scripture that has emerged from the Great Womb, tears in the veil that afford glimpses of the Beyond that is Within.

Ineluctably, our study of Taoism pulls us back to that inner realm which is Taoism's own. Its subterranean caverns and galleries are linked with lodes of rich ore awaiting exploitation by "future saints of merit and virtue" (see p. 32). Among them there will surely be philosophers, poets, linguists, painters, sociologists, musicians, psychologists, and liturgists, for it is in the realm of the human body, on the level of the human transformation of nature and production of meaning that Taoism has a completeness, an integrity, yes, a scientific and mathematical coherence which are inconceivable, or nearly so, in a world where the subject is subject to the Only Subject (cf. p. 10):

> Accordingly, the essential act of prophecy involves two persons: God who acts and is always outside of man, and man who passively receives his word. (Kaufmann, 99)

It is at his highest that Hebraic man is most abject, a mere medium, an instrument of the divine will. Nowhere is this clearer than at the Cross.

That this abject position was the precondition for the development of modern science and democracy, I have no doubt, for the one requires public verifiability and the other involves public accountability. In the one case, the voice of the people substitutes itself for the voice of God. In the other, the objective existence of natural laws preventing the collapse back into Chaos was guaranteed, first by the Creation—but that did not survive God's anger at man's refusal of his abject status—and then by the covenant with Noah:

And God said, This is the token of the covenant which I make between me and you and every living creature that is with you, for perpetual generations: I do set my bow in the cloud, and it shall be for a token of a covenant between me and the earth. And it shall come to pass, when I bring a cloud over the earth, that the bow shall be seen in the cloud, and I will remember my covenant, which is between me and you and every living creature of all flesh; and the waters shall no more become a flood to destroy all flesh. (Gen. 9:12-15)

Just to read these lines now, after four-hundred pages of Taoist tokens, covenants, clouds, and floods, is to realize the revolution in all the interpretive sciences that the rediscovery of Taoism must entail. But this book must stop short of tomorrow's promised land; its task has been to recover "that chapter of history which is marked by a blank or occupied by a falsehood" (Lacan, p. 21). What conclusions, however preliminary, does the recovery of this censored chapter of Chinese history suggest? What changes in our views of traditional Chinese society does it necessitate?

The first and most far-reaching change is that we must put behind us once and for all the idea that China was a haven for humanists, where Voltaire would have been safe from the "infamous" Church. The bonding mechanism of traditional Chinese society was religion, as it was of Western society. In particular, it was Taoism, which was in its very essence a system of synthesis, assimilation, and transformation. We have seen that Taoism received official confirmation in this role in North China under Ts'ao Ts'ao as early as 215 A.D., and that it played that role virtually without interruption from the early seventh to the mid-sixteenth century. It remains for future research to delineate that role not only on the imperial level, but especially on the local level where, after all Taoism was most at home.

Our second fundamental conclusion, in a sense a corollary of the first, is that Chinese political history is indeed one of an unequal contest between Confucianism and Taoism, but that contrary to what has always been said, it is Confucianism which never had a prayer, not Taoism. Confucianism represented a rationalizing, moralizing, even to a moderate degree, a secularizing influence on the Chinese state. Confucius, although he still clung to a paternalistic ideal of the state as a big family, already made moral virtue the basic criterion of political legitimacy. Mencius, in his more ecstatic descriptions of the spontaneous adhesion of the people to a ruler whose sole concern is their good, came close to identifying the "heavenly mandate" with the voice of the people. If subsequent Confucian history is also the history of factionalism and vested interests, to deny that the characteristic form of Confucian counsel to the emperor was prudence, austerity, and moral restraint would be simply to ignore the evidence. The historian Ray Huang would even attribute a major share in the blame for the declin and fall of the Ming dynasty to Confucian stubbornness in requiring of "their" emperor punctilious observation of every last detail of his moral and ritual obligations, even when such stubbornness had dire consequences for the Confucianists' own careers.

Taoism, by contrast, in spite of its lofty metaphysical principles, must be said to have encouraged and maintained the most irrational features of the Chinese polity. This is not the "fault" of Taoism, it is rather the characteristic fault of paganism. With no supremely sovereign God whose word is law—moral, cultic, political law—for all, regardless of station, there must be a ruling sovereign on earth, a "son of Heaven" who represents Heaven (cf. 1 Sam. 8). This One Man—the Chinese call him the "solitary man" (*ku-jen*)—rules by "heavenly mandate" (*t'ien-ming*), that is, by divine right, and he is the sole source of authority for all other men.

On this crucial point, Taoist theory coincided perfectly with imperial political theory: there was no order without the One Man, a man who had "never become distinct from the Great One" (*Huai-nan tzu* 14.1a; by contrast, between the One God and all men, "there is no bridge," Kaufmann, p. 77). But if political and religious theory coincided on this point, it was Taoist theory alone that was embodied in a ritual practice that enabled its realization. Little wonder, then, that at virtually every critical juncture of Chinese political history Taoists appeared on the scene to perform celebratory rituals or to discover tokens that demonstrated dynastic legitimacy. Indeed, when one considers together the diachronic and the synchronic aspects of the Taoist role, when one considers the history of Taoist relations with the throne and the coherence of its system for maintaining and increasing potency, one is inclined to think that it was the Taoists, and the Taoists alone, who had preserved the full and primeval form of Chinese kingship.

In looking back over Chinese history, one cannot help feeling that it was vitiated from the start by a tragic flaw, of which the great fault line dividing the rationalizing moralism of the Confucians from the poetic scientism of the Taoists is but one expression. The tragic flaw is the necessity—in a world without a divine arbiter, without the incontrovertible law of the Father, without his Word that "never again"—the necessity of constantly returning to the Origin. True, the fatal, the tragic flaw which not only permitted but required cosmic incest had its compensations: no angels stood guard at the entry to paradise with flaming swords, and the fruit of the trees in the middle of the garden—were they not in fact the same tree?—the peach tree in the garden of the Western Queen Mother (cf. Scholem 1980, 110)—was still accessible.

But was it worth it? Was the price paid not too great? The price is, in fact, still being paid now that Confucian moralistic rationalism has replaced imperial absolutism, and the One Party has displaced the One

Man. Imperial absolutism was irrational because it grew out of pagan subjectivism; Confucian autocracy is irrational because, like Platonism, it is a head severed from its body, an elite out of touch with the reality of the masses, and in the end not caring. Will there come a time when the One Head is reattached to the One Body? when the messages transmitted from the melting pot travel once again up the spinal column to repair the brain?

If that day is to come, Taoism must be rehabilitated, for only Taoism in China carries in its bosom the germs of science and democracy. But can Taoism go public and survive? Can the religion of the Mother symbolize with the religion of the Father? Two thousand years ago, Chuang-tzu said no: "In the age of Shen-nung, the people lay down peaceful and easy, woke up wide-eyed and blank. They knew their mothers but not their fathers. . . . This was Perfect Virtue at its height!" (Watson, 327) Must the virginal mystery of the Chinese landscape be sacrificed on the altar of modernization?

But the questions go the other way too. Can the West, obsessed with power, preserve potency? attached to the letter, can it understand the figure? hungry for the real and the really efficacious, has it room for the symbolic and the ritual? Will there come a time when symbols are not "only" and metaphors "mere"? when the self ceases to be "me"—dug in behind its weapons and its "image"—and becomes a responsible, creating "I"? when man is not all brain and analysis (Greek), not all heart and will (Hebrew), but also crucible and chaos, that is, synthesis (Taoist)?

China's characteristic fault has been to mistake the symbolic for the real, the ritual act for the real act. So true is this that the Taoist who had successfully "nourished his energies" and "repaired his brain" was called a "real man." He was truly man because he had become woman and given birth to a new self. A charming, apparently inoffensive conception, we have seen the damage done by this model, whose driving aim was to be "one with the Way," to "return to silence," to become a "solitary man." Secrecy and secret transmission, positive values in terms of the desired end, proved often in actual practice to be instruments of manipulation and germs of paranoia. The Taoist canon is full of half-methods, quarter-methods, and fragments transmitted piecemeal. And each new writer in turn pretends at last to have found the real master, the true secret. But it is all a magnificent hoax, a confidence game, for in the end the only scripture is that of "Mouth-to-Ear" (see p. 165).

In this regard, as in so many others, Taoism reveals itself to be a concentrated expression of certain distinctive cultural traits. Chief among them is the secret society, whose source of power lies precisely in its possession of "secrets." Not surprisingly, Taoist history is replete with tales, most of them cautionary, of those who seek to steal the secrets, or who spread forgeries (cf. the remarkable story of the diffusion of the Shang-ch'ing scriptures translated in Strickmann 1977, 41-62). It is the projection of this feature of Chinese social organization on to foreign societies that explains the persistence of the belief, in modern times, that China need only crib the West's "secrets," its technological tricks, and that once it has learned these, it can go back to the safe haven of the in-group.

Western history, and therefore the Western psyche, is no less flawed. Because the symbolic belonged exclusively to the Father, orthodoxy consisted of living entirely in the real, of utter submission to the revealed will of the symbolic, with the consequence that the image became purely imaginary. The total incapacity of the Hebrew prophets to understand the paganism they never ceased to denounce (Kaufmann, 7-20) is one reflection of this orthodoxy. So is the tendency to take refuge from the real in the imaginary: psychoanalysis, in denouncing the alienating character of the image-in-the-mirror, of self-image and narcissism (Wilden, 159-177), is simply carrying on the Old Testament prophetic tradition.

Even a century of symbolism in poetry and of abstraction in painting and music has not sufficed to break the hold on the Western psyche of the sterile quarrel between the nitty-gritty and the quantifiable on the one hand and the phantastic and the vacation of the mind on the other. The West has even invented an economy which develops sales and generates GNP by the advertising business' fetishistic use of the image (cf. Kaufmann, 9). The same incapacity to comprehend the symbolic is at the root of the still-unresolved debate concerning the nature of the divine presence in the elements of Christian communion: is it "real" or "only" symbolic? Calvin had no choice but to reject Catholic "realism," shot through as it had become with image-fetishism; but was the only alternative nominalism? Orthodoxy alone has preserved the original insight of Christianity, namely, that the incarnation was already the resurrection, that the Spirit-become-flesh was the Word from the Beginning which gives those who receive him "the right to become children of God" (John 1:12). The insight brought salvation from the temptation of the image by a recovery of the symbol that vivifies the flesh. To this insight corresponds the icon; to it also corresponds the place accorded music, ritual, and priestly secrecy behind the ikonostasis in Orthodox liturgy: "For now we see in a mirror, darkly; but then face to face" (1 Cor. 13:12).

The quarrel of Orthodoxy with Catholicism over the *filioque* clause has the same roots: setting the real man of history on a par with the symbolic Father is to confuse that which is manifest with that which is hidden. This too is a typically Western mistake, and all through history, down to the present day, it has had the same origin and the same consequence: excommunication of the "infidel," who thereby ceases to have the rights of a human being. Kaufmann puts it most succinctly:

> Israel devoted the enemies of YHWH to destruction; Christianity destroyed idolaters and heretics for the glory of God; Islam fought holy wars. Precisely because of its exclusiveness monotheism can be ruthless. (p. 75)

He might have added Communism to the list. "I came not to judge but to save," said Jesus, but no sooner had his followers gained power than they began to murder in his name. Even the "nominalist" Calvin fell prey to the temptation. On what grounds? On the grounds that the Truth is now public knowledge, and "no one has the right to deny the Truth." Looking the history of our holocausts squarely in the eye, one is tempted to fly to the consoling bosom of silence and secrecy.

But enough of this sorry spectacle of human greed for power, this tragic history of the human preference for half-truths. What is the root? Language, says Lacan, and we must agree with him, for the characteristic faults that we have been detailing all derive from fundamental attitudes toward language. The debate between nominalism and realism, for example, can only take place if both sides share the assumption that language is oral. It is only when language is first of all utterance that the problem of words and things becomes an unmanageable one. What is the relationship between an intangible, invisible, evanescent—and sometimes, as in ecstatic or mediumnistic speech, incomprehensible—succession of sounds, such as the Eucharistic "words of institution" and the realities which they purport to designate? Paganism had no real difficulty solving this problem: the medium's words could be interpreted by someone who knew the symbolic system, and a useful incantation made of the medium's gibberish. But when there was no such symbolic system?

> The peculiar feature of Israelite inquiry of God is that it lacks a fixed system of signs and omens. It has no science of signs or library of omens. Its ideal is the direct question to God, with a clear and simple response in return. (Kaufmann, p. 91)

But when the canon was closed, and the voice of prophecy had died out in the land? "All the rest is commentary."

Some were content to speak "in the name of." For others it was unbearable to be a "modern," perched like a little dwarf on the shoulders of the "ancients." Some set out in pursuit of the Holy Grail. Others, less romantic but far more audacious and far more determined, went straight to the Source, where they sought, by deciphering the divine name itself, to discover the key to existence, their own existence and that of all creatures (Scholem 1980, 50-7; 1983, 55-99). What is in a name? Should *Deus* be translated "Lord of Heaven" (the Catholic *t'ien-chu*) or "Supreme Emperor" (the Protestant *shang-ti*)? Or is translation treason? should it be transliterated? (The Buddhists ended up transliterating Sanskrit terms.) A small, forgotten minority wished to translate *Deus* as Tao, the Way, but no one paid any attention to them (Dehergne, 63).

The Chinese had none of these problems: for them, too, "the heavens declare the glory of God," but night unto night does not utter speech. What the Chinese saw in the night sky, in the stars wherein lay their destiny, was "celestial patterns or writings" (*t'ien-wen; wen* means "patterns," whence "writing"). All writing on earth was but a pale reflection of these primordial patterns of the stars, and Chinese writing attests to its celestial origin with its upright columns. It is hardly an accident, therefore, if civilization itself is called in Chinese "transformation by the written word" (*wen-hua*).

Human writing may be a pale imitation of the writings of Nature—not only in heaven, but also on the earth and under it, in the "patterns" (*wen*) that bedeck animals, in the "lines" (*li*) that run through jade, and in the "veins of the earth" (*mai-li*)—but it is in a relationship of direct filiation, for ordinary human writing points to natural writing. Human writing even leads the way back to its Origin by way of seals, maps, charts, painting which is calligraphy, and trigrams which systematize oracle-bone cracks. We need no longer now belabor the point that in the realm of "real writing" the Taoists are kings.

But we must ask what the Taoists' supremacy in this area implies. It implies that reality is visible, just as the primacy of speech implies reality to be audible. Eyes and ears: the chart of the universe and the name of God. We have said enough of their respective faults: what is their inner, liberating meaning?

Eric Auerbach in the first chapter of *Mimesis* draws a contrast between the heroes of Greek and Hebrew literature. Odysseus, Ulysses, and Achilles never change: no exploit, no adventure or misadventure ever alters what these heroes were at the start. They have a certain character, and that character stays constant. Contrast that with David, Auerbach suggests, or Moses, Jacob, or Jeremiah. Character is of little importance to the stories of these men; they are persons who emerge, evolve, even undergo total transformation in the crucible of life. They are the constantly changing products of what they were, of what happens, what they do, and what they are called to do, or undo. Compare David the young shepherd boy with David the old man weeping over his son Absalom; then fill in what lies between: David, the lutist before King Saul, the champion against Goliath, the fugitive, the king, the adulterer, the penitent, the psalmist. There is no plot; there is just a man, a man who sings and sins and repents and conquers and grieves. Achilles, concludes Auerbach, is to our modern sensibilities a caricature; David is a human being.

Why? Because Greek epistemology is that of the eyes, Hebrew that of the ears. The Greeks see only what meets the eye; they are prisoners of the surface, the image. But the Hebrews hear the call of God:

> The theophany to Elijah (1 Kings 19) gives this idea classic expression: wind, earthquake, and fire precede YHWH, but YHWH was not in the wind, not in the earthquake, and not in the fire. (Kaufmann, 70)

YHWH was in "a still small voice":

> And it was so, when Elijah heard it, that he wrapped his face in his mantle, and went out, and stood in the entrance of the cave. And, behold, there came a voice unto him, and said, What doest thou here, Elijah? And he said, I have been very jealous for Jehovah, the God of hosts; for the children of Israel have forsaken thy covenant, thrown down thine altars, and slain thy prophets with the sword; and I, even I only, am left; and they seek my life, to take it away.
>
> And Jehovah said unto him, Go, return on thy way to the wilderness of Damascus: and when thou comest, thou shalt anoint Hazael to be king over Syria; and Jehu the son of Nimshi shalt thou anoint to be king over Israel; and Elisha the son of Shaphat of Abelmeholah shalt thou anoint to be prophet in thy room. (1 Kings 19:13-16)

Fear and flight, yes; fatal flaws or special heroism, no, for there is nothing which sets Biblical man apart from his fellows. The only distinction between one man and another, whether Hebrew or Gentile, is between one who obeys and one who does not obey the "still small voice."

What is the still small voice? The voice of YHWH. Where is it heard? In the heart of hearts, in the holy of holies. What does it say? "YHWH," or in translation, "I am that I am," or "I will be that I will be," or "I am, because I am," or "I am who I am" (Exod. 3:14). Fearing at this most crucial juncture to commit an act tantamount to sacrilege, the editors of the 1901 American revision of the King James version of the Bible, give all these alternative translations of the divine name, YHWH, the name that Hebrew scribes wrote in fear and trembling only after ablutions and prayer. What is in a name?

> In the grammatical structure of the word Yahveh, God is not "being" alone. He is the *power* of being. The word is constructed according to the causative form of the verb *to be*. In the famous Exodus story where God confronts Moses and says that while he has been known as *El*

Shaddai (God of Power), Moses shall say to his people: "*Ehyeh* (I will be) has sent me unto you" (3:14). Both *Yahveh* and *Ehyeh* are in the future tense, implying that God should be understood in terms of both the power to be (causing to be) and the power to become. . . .

God is the power calling life into ever-greater being. In grammatical parlance, we say that the past tense is the "perfect" and the future tense is the "imperfect," in that he is the power of becoming—he is future-oriented, goal-directed, always in process, and generating the same dynamic in his creatures who reflect his image. (Spiro, p. 73)

In the end, then, the "still small voice" calls the Israelite to "reflect an image"—not the image of Narcissus, trapped in the "mirror stage," but something designated "his image." Whose image? The image of him who "calls life into ever-greater being." This is one image. The Taoists, as we have seen in the image of the Metal Mother on the turtle, have quite another: it is an image of our Origin. In Orthodox churches the Royal Door is flanked by the icon of Mary on the left and the icon of Jesus on the right. "It is like our writing," explained a priest to me, "we must go from our Source toward our End." By the same reasoning, Chinese writing moves, like Hebrew, back to its Source. But the Source of the one is not the same as the Source of the other, though the scribe is in both cases a man. Or is he? Hebrew lines lie down, like the prophet waiting passively for the Word of God; Chinese lines "stand alone," as *Lao-tzu* says of the Way:

There is a thing which forms in Chaos and is born before heaven and earth. Silent! deserted! It stands alone, unchanging; it circulates, inexhaustible. It may be considered the Mother of heaven and earth. I do not know its name; I give it the name "Way." (*Lao-tzu* 25; Lau)

The Chinese word for "thing" in this passage, *wu*, originally meant "flag." Flags, charts, pictures, characters, symbols—all are names which summon things:

Acceptable?—then acceptable. Unacceptable?—then unacceptable. A way forms when it is walked upon; things are so because they are called so. (*Chuang-tzu*, chap 2; Watson, 40)

But as the suppositional phrasing of the *Lao-tzu* suggests, there is one thing we cannot summon: "It may be considered. . . ., I do not know. . . ., I give it the name. . . ." Rather it summons us: the image in the mirror. In *The True Scripture of the Bright Mirror of the Most High* (TT 1207 *T'ai-shang ming-chien chen-ching*), Lao-tzu first explains how to hang at eye level about the adept four well-polished mirrors, and then describes a series of divinities that are to be visualized in them. The series ends with nine figures whose surname, like Lao-tzu's is Li. Each is to be visualized in turn, the first at the crack of dawn, the second at sunrise, and so on, with the eighth visualized at sundown, and the last at dusk. In this manner Lao-tzu undergoes nine transformations in his course across the sky to the bosom of his mother. Each transformation corresponds to a month of gestation and the birth of one of the nine energies (heavens) of the east (see pp. 41, 103; cf. Seidel 1969, 96 ff.) Thus is the son's cycle periodized like the phases of the moon.

In the mirror, then, we come "face to face" with the "true form" (Seidel 1969, 102) of the Old Infant. Who is the Old Infant? He is that which is born, the "thing which forms in Chaos" and "stands alone," the king, the high priest, the "I" which manifests itself on the turtle's back. This is the son. We are all sons. But this is not all:

> Here below has an Origin: consider it the Mother of here below. When you have attained the Mother, you can know her Infant. Once you know her Infant, go back and hold fast to his Mother, and to the end of your days you will be inexhaustible. (*Lao-tzu* 52; Lau)

Lao-tzu, the Infant, is "here below"; he is what "I" see when "I" have learned to look: he is the image of what I am to become when "I" become "real."

But this primordial "real man" has an Origin, for "I alone am different from others and value feeding on the Mother" (*Lao-tzu* 20). And so the Taoist adept is told to do as Lao-tzu does and return regularly before the "mirror stage" to "feed [again] on his Mother" and become thereby "inexhaustible." But where is his Mother? Through the looking brass! It is there, on the back of ancient Chinese metal mirrors—mirrors that, like the moon, reflect the rays of the son that has set—there that we find images of the magic garden of the Western Queen Mother (Hsi-wang-mu) whose fruit Lao-tzu fed upon (cf. Loewe, 83, 198, 200, 227). The ultimate symbol is the map of this matrix, which is the configuration of the mountain (see pp. 161–62).

The Taoist, like the Platonist, lives in a cave—his body—and does his best in the dark to see the light. But the one longs for the light of the sun; the other lives by the light of the moon (cf. pp. 24, 117). The one wishes to know what lies behind what meets the eye; the other turns his eyes around and "looks within" (*nei-kuan*). Taoist epistemology, like Platonic epistemology, focuses on the eyes, but the Platonist sees images on the surface and struggles vainly to escape their hold; the Taoist goes on a "distant voyage" (*yüan-yu*) through the landscape of his body (on the equivalence of the landscape and the body, see p. 289). By the light of his own sun and moon—his eyes—he learns to distinguish the entire multitude of divinities which inhabits his paradise. He learns to recognize and summon the divinities to guard his gates and carry out his commands.

How can two visual epistemologies come to such utterly different conclusions? Because the one occurs in the ontological context of the Father, the other in that of the Mother. For Platonists, Ideas are at the origin of things, and they wish therefore to abstract from things their Ideas; for Taoists, the Womb is the origin of things, and they wish therefore to feed on the Origin. In the end, "the saint is for the belly, not for the eyes" (*Lao-tzu* 12), because it is in the belly he will attain "long life and distant vision" (*Lao-tzu* 59); it is in the belly he will hear "the scripture of Mouth-to-Ear."

Is this not extraordinary? The Hebrew is led by a Voice to conform to an Image; the Taoist is led by an Image to listen for a Voice. We must modify Auerbach, therefore, and say, in the end, not the eye versus the ear, but the inner versus the outer man. All hunger for peace. But for the inner man peace is recovery of a lost equilibrium—*chai*, "fast," is glossed in Taoist texts as *ch'i*, "to equalize"—followed by communion (*chiao*, "banquet, offering"); for the outer man it is liberation from the body, followed by the beatific vision. The outer man, finding himself a prisoner of the seductive surfaces the sun's rays disclose to him, asks only to be delivered from their tyranny. All his solutions—sensualism, militarism (and its ally, sports), idealism—are therefore of necessity iconoclastic, that is, destructive of the body, which is the origin and end of the image. How impeccably this Spartiate and Platonic tradition has been transmitted may be seen in the modern totalitarian state, where ideology reigns supreme over reality, and the body is a mere instrument for Olympic performance.

By contrast both systems of the inner man find their point of equilibrium in the human heart (cf. p. 27). We need only recall the role of Red Robe to remind us of the place of the heart in Taoist ritual. For the Hebrew cult, we can do no better than to quote the psalmist (51:10-11):

> Create in me a clean heart, O God;
> And renew a right spirit within me.
> Cast me not away from thy presence;
> And take not Thy Holy Spirit from me.

If the Hebrew goes from the voice to the image and the Taoist from the image to the voice, it is because for the Taoist the written language continued to consist of written symbols—ideographs, hieroglyphs—while for the Hebrew it had become an alphabet. This meant that for the Taoist the umbilical cord tying the written language to the patterns of nature remained intact, while for the Hebrew it had been cut. The symbolic mutilation of the body called circumcision was one consequence: it cut the tie which bound man to the fertility cult of the god of the soil. The interdiction of graven images was another, for once the image had ceased to be the symbol of a living god, it became a fetish (Kaufmann, 9). The most prodigious consequence of all was the substitution of a Father for the Mother in the beginning. And all the rest is commentary, especially Hebrew messianism, for the Father, if He is now also behind remains nonetheless eternally before.

The invention of the alphabet was thus one of the most momentous transformations of human history. It is the source of the state of permanent tension and yearning which characterizes so much of Biblical literature. The Hebrew is now torn between the origin of his language and its end, between the still small voice and the "worn effigies which people pass from hand to hand in silence" (Lacan, 13; cf. Wilden, 120, "Language is a process of the degradation of the symbol into the sign"). In the world of language as speech, legalism and literalism are the natural perversions of the cult. The prophets, therefore, become ever more virulent in their denunciation of the cult-as-sacrifice (see, e.g., Is. 1:11-17) and ever more insistent on the cult of the "clean heart" and social justice, for "moral goodness makes man share, as it were, in the divine nature" (Kaufmann, 367).

In Taoism this tension and yearning are lacking because the cord was never cut:

> Take up the work of Freud again at the *Traumdeutung* to remind yourself that the dream has the structure of a sentence or, rather, to stick to the letter of the work, of a rebus; that is to say, it has the structure of a form of writing . . . which can also be found both in the hieroglyphs of ancient Egypt and in the characters still used in China. (Lacan, 30)

> Words are not just wind. Words have something to say. But if what they have to say is not fixed, then do they really say something? Or do they say nothing? People suppose that words are different from the peeps of baby birds, but is there any difference, or isn't there? (*Chuang-tzu*, chap. 2; Watson, 39)

The characters that people Taoist narratives—the immortals—are not stormy and passionate like the Hebrew prophets, but they are no less "inner men." In fact, they are entirely "inner men," for they "regulate what is within and know nothing of what is without" (*Huai-nan tzu* 7.5a). They do not preach a fiery message of moral and social transformation; they stoke the fires of their burner and transform their "inner elixir" (*nei-tan*).

But while so doing they do not abandon their fellow men, or dissociate themselves from all considerations of moral and social order. On the contrary, Taoist hagiography is full of stories of immortals saving others—from sickness, flood, locusts, bandits, hell, and self. We have seen this in the story of Marshal Wen, we have seen it in the story of the brothers Hsü, above all, we have seen it in the ritual of the one of High Merit, who "executes change on Heaven's behalf." This is not *lèse-majesté;* it is the original Chinese theory of kingship:

The saint-kings of the past perfected their persons, and the empire then perfected itself. They regulated their bodies, and the empire was regulated. (*Lü-shih ch'un-ch'iu* 3.5b)

Taoism, then, was never meant to play a "political" role, a role in the manipulation of power that came to be the state's chief characteristic once it had ceased to be led by shaman-kings or charismatic judges. But the time of the secular state was still far in the future, and desperate authorities turned to religion—the Chinese to Taoism, the Romans and Byzantines to Christianity—to legitimize their power. Was the resultant perversion of religion any worse in China than in the West? All we can say is that Samuel's judgment was more perspicacious than Voltaire's:

And Jehovah said unto Samuel, hearken unto the voice of the people in all that they say unto thee; for they have not rejected thee, but they have rejected me, that I should not be king over them. . . . Now therefore hearken unto their voice: howbeit thou shalt protest solemnly unto them, and shalt show them the manner of the king that shall reign over them.
And Samuel told all the words of Jehovah unto the people that asked of him a king. And he said, This will be the manner of the king that shall reign over you: he will take your sons, and appoint them unto him, for his chariots, and to be his horsemen. . . . And he will take your daughters to be perfumers, and to be cooks, and to be bakers. And he will take your fields. . . . And he will take the tenth of your seed. . . . And he will take. . . . And ye shall cry out in that day because of your king whom ye shall have chosen you; and Jehovah will not answer you in that day. (1 Samuel 8:7–18)

Had Voltaire lived in the twentieth century, he might have been more inclined to see things Samuel's way.

Be that as it may, the secular state has come of age. And religion? What is to be done with religion? The state has taken over its political functions, medicine its medical functions, philosophy its heuristic, and science its cosmological functions—has it nothing left to do but exit gracefully stage-left into the museum? Or is it, on the contrary, freed at last of all its historic burdens—of explaining, teaching, healing, and ruling—freed to become itself? Politicians govern us, doctors heal us, scientists mechanize us, psychologists shrink us, and philosophers talk over our heads. Who "executes change on Heaven's behalf"? Who "excels in overcoming though he does not contend, in responding though he does not speak, in attracting though he does not summon"? (*Lao-tzu* 73; D. C. Lau, 135)

What is Taoism? Taoism is non-action (*wu-wei*), that is, ritual action: Taoism is ritual action. Ritual action can be defined as "regular patterns of behaviour invested with symbolic significance and efficacy" (Wainwright, p. 8). These patterns have meaning because they are the "concentrated expression" of a "vision" of reality (ibid., p. 3); they are efficacious because they serve to regulate behavior according to significant patterns and thereby prove to be one of the chief "means by which the vision is transmitted through time" (p. 5). Such are the conclusions of a Methodist minister concerning the nature and function of Christian worship. How do they compare with Chinese and Taoist ideas of ritual?

The Taoist term for ritual is a binome composed of the words *k'o* "class, classification," and *yi*, "rite." Léon Vandermeersch defines *yi* as "the model which I embody" (p. 405), and adds, "the idea that the rites serve to model the behavior of each and all could not be better expressed." *Yi* is to human behavior, to ethics, what *li*, "deep structure" (*logos*), is to things. "It goes without saying," concludes Vandermeersch,

> that the meaning of the rites *yi* is in conformity with the meaning of things *li*. . . . The rites, which carry within them this moral meaning because they have been designed according to the order of things, are the liturgical matrices on which conduct must be—and on which it is sufficient that it be—modelled in order that law and order reign. This is why they are often compared to gauges or patterns used to determine the accuracy of measurements or forms. (p. 406)

The same character *yi* also signifies "meaning," as Vandermeersch points out, and it is closely related to a homophone signifying "appropriate."

Yi is the standard Chinese term for "rite"; in the context discussed by Vandermeersch it is also a specifically Confucian term, as can be seen from its links to ethics. The character *k'o*, by contrast, gives a peculiarly Taoist bent to the concept of ritual, for it refers less to a moral than to a cosmological order of things. Its root meaning is "a measure of grain." Another measure of grain is the "bushel" (*tou*, as in *tou-teng*, "lamps of destiny"). *K'o* suggests the measurement of time and the determination of destiny by the Northern Bushel, and hence a "classification of beings" (Schipper 1982, 92) according to their temporal and hierarchical situation in the cosmos. The fact that rank and salary in the ancient Chinese bureaucracy were reckoned in terms of measures of grain underscores the hierarchical aspect of this classification.

The binome *k'o-yi*, then, may be defined as "regular patterns of behavior that give concentrated expression to the order of things." As we saw in the story of Marshal Wen, the order of things thus expressed is one of merit, even of moral merit, and of service. But true service can be rendered, and hence moral merit acquired, only if one's action is in accord with the "order of the universe" as it is visible in the "celestial patterns" and in the "music of the spheres." The deep structure of this order is represented by the True Writs placed in five "bushels" of rice (see p. 103); its supreme expression is the hymns in the Land of the Way (see p. 134 ff.); its aim is the reclassification, that is, the promotion, of all things "according to their merit," "so that the entire world may return to its celestial, natural, and spontaneous order, in union with the cosmological system")(Schipper 1982, 92; see also pp. 63, 80, 153, 154 ff.). The fundamental measure of this order is the drum beat, which is the "voice of man" (see p. 116).

Taoist ritual is, thus, at once creational, soteriological, and eschatological in character. Insofar as it transforms the universe by humanizing it, it at once recreates and saves the world. If this recreation of the universe is in the first place a "return to the Origin," it is also a progressive amelioration of the universe which tends toward "last things" without as yet attaining them. At once a return to the beginning and an anticipation of the end of all things, Taoist ritual is every bit as much as Biblical ritual suspended in time, between an initial exodus and a final liberation.

The affinities of Taoist ritual are especially great with Christian ritual, for both depend on the sacrifice of the One Man. In the case of Christianity, it is the One Man who, by "pouring out his blood"—that is, giving up his spirit (*ruah*, "breath of God, Holy Spirit," identified by the Hebrews with the blood)—creates a new *ecclesiam* ("assembly") which at once feeds on and constitutes his resurrected Body (see especially the Epistle to the Hebrews). In the case of Taoism, it is the One Man who, having first created the conditions for communion by "sprawling out" in the position of a "murdered" turtle—that is, having first sacrificed his self in order to become the "assembly," the altar—then communicates with the Three Pure Ones on behalf of the assembly by "giving up his spirit," that is, by exteriorizing it through the summit of his head.

The sacrifice of the One Man is thus, in Taoism as in Christianity, the precondition for the communion which re-creates the One Body by the integration and amelioration of its constituents. The fundamental difference between the two religions lies in the nature of the constituency, the "people of God" in the one case, the "gods of the people" in the other. It is enough therefore to change the word "people" into the phrase "representatives of the people" and the word "God" into the word "Way" in order to convert the following description of the efficacy of Christian into one of Taoist ritual:

> Into the liturgy the people bring their entire existence so that it may be gathered up in praise. From the liturgy the people depart with a renewed vision of the value-patterns of God's kingdom, by the more effective practice of which they intend to glorify God in their whole life. (Wainwright, p. 8)

Again, we need only think of Marshal Wen to measure the truth of this statement.

Clearly, the role played by Christianity as midwife to modern science and democracy is related to the nature of its "assembly," that is, to the fact that all followers of the Christ are like him in being prophets, priests, and kings, and therefore full participants in the cult. Just as clearly, a cult based on "representative" as opposed to "direct" democracy could not create the preconditions necessary to the eventual emergence of modern science and democracy. But neither could a religion whose congregation was exclusively human, was composed of humans eager to rush through history to the New Jerusalem, neither could such a religion take the time to preserve intact, let alone recreate Nature, not in man's image, but in Hers. The Christian Church, totally preoccupied by its mission as the "people of God," the repository of God's final word in the history of "special revelation," had no time for "general revelation" (on these distinctions, see Berkouwer). It would appear that now, under the pressure of the "modern ecological crisis," theologians are turning away from "the command of Genesis 1:28 to 'subdue and have dominion'" and beginning to recognize that

> the human task is to "till the earth and *keep* it" (2:15) [italics Wainwright's], and the power to "name" the non-human creation (2:19 ff.) is less the right to exploit it than the duty to give it meaning. (Wainwright, p. 23)

But this the Taoists have been doing all along; they have been developing at once a science of the humanization, that is, the divinization of Nature, and a science of the naturalization, that is, the divinization of Man.

It is, therefore, no accident that the landscapes which are the glory of Chinese painting are of Taoist origin.

> It is only when the religious content of cosmology had been entirely integrated into the pictorial arts that they began to acquire their letters patent of nobility and that a coherent art of landscape was born. (Delahaye, p. 3)

Delahaye goes on to describe one of the first great landscapes. Painted by Ku K'ai-chih (345-406), it portrays the transmission of Taoism from its founder, Chang Tao-ling, to two of his disciples on the Mountain of the Terrace of the Clouds. This mountain is the "configuration of a mountain" drawn by energies—the clouds—which form a natural calligraphy. The notes on this painting, written by Ku himself, show clearly that the painting also represents the Taoist body, that is, an altar. But if the Chinese landscape is thus envisaged as in the image of man, we now also know that the body of man is visualized as in the image of nature.

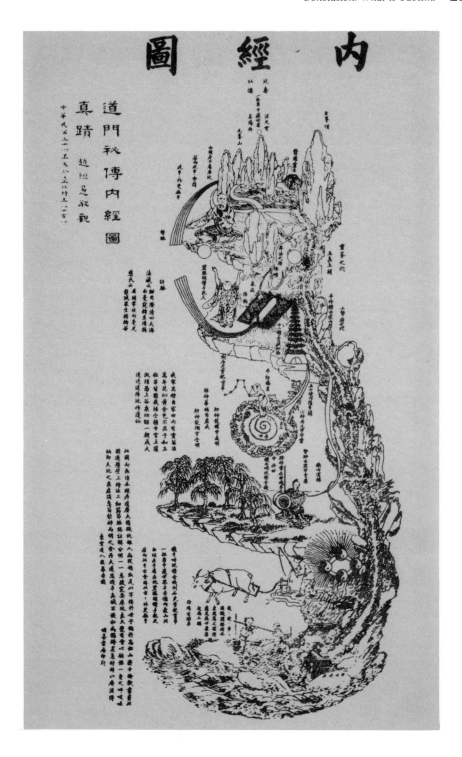

Suddenly Master Lai grew ill. Gasping and wheezing, he lay at the point of death. His wife and children gathered round in a circle and began to cry. Master Li, who had come to ask how he was, said, "Shoo! Get back! Don't disturb the process of change!"

Then he leaned against the doorway and talked to Master Lai. "How marvelous the Creator is! What is he going to make of you next? Where is he going to send you? Will he make you into a rat's liver? Will he make you into a bug's arm?"

Master Lai said, "A child, obeying his father and mother, goes wherever he is told, east or west, south or north. And the *yin* and *yang*—how much more are they to a man than father or mother! Now that they have brought me to the verge of death, if I should refuse to obey them, how perverse I would be! . . . So now I think of heaven and earth as a great furnace, and the Creator as a skilled smith. Where could he send me that would not be all right? I will go off to sleep peacefully, and then with a start I will wake up." (*Chuang-tzu,* chap. 6; Watson, p. 85)

APPENDIX A

A NOTE ON VESTMENTS

Three basic types of robe are worn, the *chiang-yi*, the *tao-p'ao*, and the *hai-ch'ing*. In Master Ch'en's ritual practice they serve at once to distinguish the high priest from his assistants and to signify the type of ritual being performed. When Ch'en wears the *chiang-yi*, for example, his acolytes usually wear the *tao-p'ao* (plate 18), and when he wears the *tao-p'ao*, they normally wear the *hai-ch'ing*. The *hai-ch'ing* ("sea-blue") is in southern Taiwan either black (plate 8) or yellowish orange, and it is used primarily, but not exclusively (cf. plate 8), in "negative" rituals such as litanies of confession, Untying the Knots, and the Attack on Hell. The term "sea-blue" probably referred originally to the plain blue robes of eremetic Taoists (cf. Yoshioka, 237).

The *tao-p'ao* ("Taoist robe") is the standard Taoist robe. Its basic color is red (*yang*, exorcism), and its basic motif is the eight trigrams (plate 18). This robe may also be yellow-orange in color. Master Ch'en often wears such a *tao-p'ao* for the Noon Offering (plate 7), the Division of the Lamps, the Land of the Way (plates 13, 16), the Orthodox Offering, and the Universal Salvation. In all these rituals, with the exception of the last, the high priest is in the position of a "servant of the Way," facing north.

As a general rule, it is when he turns around to face—or go—outwards that he wears the *chiang-yi* ("red silk robe" or "mantle of descent," depending on which character is used for *chiang*). Master Ch'en wears a *chiang-yi* in the Announcement (plate 24), the Flag-raising, the Presentation of the Memorial (plates 18, 20), and the Dispatch of the Pardon (plate 26). The *chiang-yi* being the robe in which the high priest reveals himself to the people as "Heaven's man," I have favored the variant "mantle of descent" over "red silk robe."

The "mantle of descent" is square (the symbolic shape of earth), with a round (heaven) opening for the neck. The embroidery on the back represents the three levels of the natural universe. On Master Ch'en's robe, the hem, embroidered with fish and crustaceans, represents the aquatic level. Above a green-and-white striped band separating the hem from the rest of the robe, we see first a unicorn—the magic beast of earth—and then a three-story tower representing the dwelling place of the Jade Emperor. De Groot (1910, 6:1265) describes a robe in which the earth is represented by T'ai-shan, "nominally the highest peak in the world."

In principle the mantle of descent may be worn only by the high priest. In southern Taiwan, where the ceremony of ordination involves "ascending to heaven" by means of a thirty-six-step ladder of swords it is when the postulant comes back down from heaven that the mantle of descent is first draped over his shoulders. Thus clad, he goes to kneel before his master and receive his "flame." Called a "golden flower" or a "streaming pearl," the flame is a precious stone, green or red, set in a gold-painted metal halo atop a flexible stem. Like the red "pearl" in the middle of the roof of a Chinese temple, this flame is the "exteriorized" form of the "eternal flame"—the Unique Energy—that burns in the brazier inside the temple-body (cf. Schipper 1982, 99). In the case of the high priest,

291

it is the exteriorization of this flame from his "cinnabar field" (*tan-t'ien*)—the crucible in his lower belly—that enables him to send messages to heaven. The flame is first planted in the metal crown on top of his head by his master, who has taught him to recognize and use it.

The metal crown, called a "crown of gold," a "golden lotus," or a "crown of the stars" (of the Big Dipper; cf. Schipper 1982, 98), originally served to cover the topknot that Taoists traditionally wore as a distinguishing mark (Yoshioka, p. 237). Taoists in Taiwan nowadays have short hair and therefore attach the crown to a black skullcap made of rough strands that simulate hair.

The shoes and a kind of apron worn by the high priest under his mantle of descent also deserve notice. His boat-like "court shoes" are decorated with stitched cloud-patterns symbolizing his capacity to "pace the void" and carry messages to heaven. The apron, which has an embroidered representation of the priest's cinnabar field on it, is worn as a sign of respect to the gods (cf. Schipper 1982, 97–8).

APPENDIX B

TABLE OF RITUALS IN THE OFFERING

Day 0 1. Firing the Oil to Drive Away Dirt
p.m.   2. Starting Up the Drum

Day 1 3. Announcement
a.m.   4. Invocation
         5. Flag-raising
         6. Noon Offering
p.m.   7. Division of the Lamps

Day 2 8. Land of the Way
a.m.   9. Noon Offering
p.m.   10. Floating the Water Lamps
        11. Invocation of the Masters and Saints
        12. Sealing the Altar
        13. Nocturnal Invocation

Day 3 14. Renewed Invocation
a.m.   15. Scripture Recitation
        16. Presentation of the Memorial
        17. Noon Offering
p.m.   18. Orthodox Offering
        19. Universal Salvation

TABLE OF RITUALS OF MERIT

Day 1 1. Announcement
p.m.   2. Invocation
         3. Scripture Recitation
         4. Opening a Road in the Darkness
         5. Recitation of Litanies

    6. Dispatching the Writ of Pardon

    7. The Attack on Hell

    8. Division of the Lamps

Day 2 **9.** Land of the Way
a.m.
    10. Recitation of Litanies

    11. Noon Offering

p.m. **12.** Recitation of a Precious Scroll

    13. Exorcism

    14. Uniting the Symbols

    15. Bath

    16. Paying Homage to the Three Treasures

    17. Untying the Knots

    18. Recitation of Litanies

    19. Filling the Treasury

    20. Crossing the Bridge

APPENDIX C

1. Chang Tao-ling, founder of Taoism, shown wearing Taoist vestments and riding a tiger (taming the demonic, cf. plate 11). The tablet in his hands makes him a "civil official of the Way" (*tao-shih*). This portrait is hung in the southeast corner of the (outer) altar above a table called the Dragon-Tiger Mountain (Lung-hu shan), hereditary home of the Heavenly Masters, of whom Chang is the first (cf. plates 4, 5).

2. The Heavenly Worthy of the Way and Its Power (cf. plate 14), also known as Lord Lao or Lao-tzu (Old Infant). His yellow robe links him to the central element, earth. His Taoist crown and flame recall his revelation to Chang Tao-ling of the Unique Energy by which the Taoist priest "lights the internal burner" and then, by "exteriorizing" this energy, communicates with heaven.

3. Marshal Wen (Wen Ch'iung), one of four marshals who protect the inner altar and, as agents of the high priest, help form the outer altar. Wen is the marshal-guardian of the east (cf. plate 7).

4. Chu-yi (Red Robe), representing the Taoist as civil official. His portrait is thus normally hung on the outer altar next to Chang Tao-ling's. Red is the color of the sun and of the heart, both of which aid the Taoist: the rays of the sun chase away darkness (evil), and the heart communicates with the Way (plate 22). The yellow document attached to the painting is a "symbol-order for opening heaven"; filled out during the Announcement, it is draped over the letter sent to the Jade Emperor during the Presentation of the Memorial in order to ensure its passage through the Golden Gate (cf. plate 21). The yellow envelopes beneath Red Robe contain letters of allegiance to the supreme divinities and hence represent their divine thrones. The white envelopes contain messages to be sent to lesser powers. At bottom right may be seen a paper image of Chang Tao-ling on the table representing Lung-hu shan (cf. plate 1).

5. The Somber or True Warrior, also known as the Emperor of the North, the power in whose name the Taoist carries out his military function as an exorcist. Like the exorcists of popular religion, the Emperor's feet are bare and he wields a sword. The tortoise—also known as the Somber Warrior— and the snake are the heraldic animals of the watery north. The Emperor's portrait is hung in the southwest corner of the outer altar, opposite Chang Tao-ling's and above a table called the Warrior-is-the-Match Mountain (Wu-tang shan), after the mountain in Hupei where the Somber Emperor originally "obtained the Way."

6. General view of the south (inferior) side of the altar. In the foreground, the Table of the Three Officers, whose paper images are set behind the offerings; in the background, beyond the "door gods" of the temple, the wooden statues of the gods of the people, with purple slips indicating name of owner of the statue and amount of contribution. These gods, "representatives of the people," have come to learn from the ritual how the world of the ̲n̲ ̲w̲orks and what their place in it is. The Three Officers both control access to the altar and are inspectors of the ̲n̲ ̲al universe (cf. plate 14).

7. Cave-table with candles, cups of tea and wine, and other items for the
Noon Offering. In the left foreground is the metal bowl—the "voice of
earth"—of the assistant cantor; across from it is the wooden drum—the "voice
of heaven"—of the chief cantor. The main incense burner is in the middle of
the table. The high priest is keeping the beat on a small wooden drum while
one of the four acolytes is singing and dancing. Behind him, along the west
wall, are the scrolls of the marshals Kao (west) and K'ang (north; cf. plates 3,
17, 19).

8. The leader of the troupe wearing a *hai-ch'ing* robe and presenting the third candle to the Heavenly Worthy of the Way and Its Power during the Division of Lamps. Behind him, along the west wall, can be seen portraits of the officers of the earth and the stars (for portrait of the officers of the waters, see plate 12).

9.　The high priest in Sealing the Altar. Holding the bowl of symbol-water with the "three terrace" grip, the high priest sprays water northward along the blade of his sword at the start of Sealing the Altar. He is wearing the ordinary red Taoist robe (*tao p'ao;* cf. plate 18). The community representatives are directly behind him, their gods on the bleachers to his left.

10.   Last step of "Getting Rid of Filth" walk in Sealing the Altar. The generic name for these large strides is "Step of Yü."

11. The high priest taming the demon. Having defeated the barefoot demon who had stolen the community's burner, the high priest pins him down with his sword and five-thunder seal (cf. plate 24) in a bucket of purifying rice set in the northeast corner of the altar (Gate of Demons). The tamed demon now guards this gate, and candles and incense are lit before his mask.

12. Pot of rice containing the northern of the five True Writs placed during the Nocturnal Invocation. These writs represent the divine energies of the five directions; their placement in bowls of purifying rice makes the altar a new universe firmly anchored at its five cardinal points. Along the west wall in the back may be seen two of the three portraits of the officers of the waters and the earth (the third shows officers of the stars; cf. plate 8). Balanced by paintings on the east wall—of the officers of man, heaven, and the stars—these six portraits

13. High priest touching points in his left hand in order to activate internal energies, which he then uses to "light the burner" during the Land of the Way. This hand-held burner (*shou-lu*), which will be held by the head of the community after it is lighted (see plate 15), is shaped like a crescent moon because the moon, with its phases, is a symbol of the Way. As soon as the burner is lit, the priest will put the flame of his crown, at present slipped under his skull cap, back in the metal crown on his head. The lanterns hung overhead represent the community leaders.

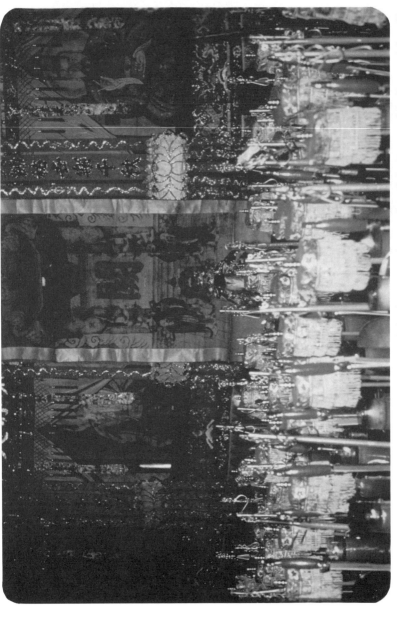

14. The Three Pure Ones in their palaces. To the left, the Heavenly Worthy of the Way and Its Power (plate 2), origin of man; to the right, the Heavenly Worthy of the Numinous Treasure, origin of earth; in the center, behind the scroll with the word for (Golden) Gate on it, is the portrait of the Heavenly Worthy of the Primordial Beginning, origin of heaven. This cultural triad on the honorable north side of the altar faces the natural triad on the south (plate 6). The entire altar is organized around the vanishing point of the central portrait and represents the universe [...] Orion." At the bottom of the Gate scroll, the high priest, in a red robe, is in a seated position, [...] of the community

15. Community representatives kneeling during the Land of the Way. The "head of the fast" (*chai-chu*) holds the crescent-shaped incense burner (cf. plate 13); a second person holds the platter with the cups of tea 3–5, which will be presented by the high priest to the Heavenly Worthy of the Way and Its Power, to the Jade Emperor, and to the Emperor of the Purple Empyrean (plate 16); all others hold sticks of incense.

16. The high priest presenting the final cup of tea to the Emperor of the Purple Empyrean. He receives the cup on his horizontally held court tablet from the acolyte on his left, curtsies with it, then turns toward the acolyte on his right, who takes the cup of tea and places it on the table beneath the Emperor's "palace" and portrait.

17. High priest in mantle of descent (*chiang-yi*, cf. plate 18), acolytes in Taoist robes, waiting for community representatives to gather behind them before starting the Presentation of the Memorial. The horn-like instrument is the *so-na*, a kind of oboe. Note also the large drum, which determines the pace of the ritual. The large paper figures lining the left-hand side of the path to heaven are, from left to right, Marshal Kao (white, west), Red Robe, and Marshal Chao (red, south; cf. plate 19).

18. High priest kneeling for invocation during the Presentation of the Memorial. He is wearing his mantle of descent. This is embroidered with a map of the natural universe composed of the heavens above (the three-storied pavilion), the earth beneath (the magic beast), and the waters under the earth (the border, decorated with crabs and lobsters). Both cantors are wearing the standard Taoist robes, *tao-p'ao*, whose chief decoration is the various arrangements of the eight trigrams. The orange robe worn by the chief cantor (red/south and yellow/center) shows him to be superior to the assistant cantor in the more typical red robe.

312

19.   An acolyte's dance during the Presentation of the Memorial. Already lifted up between heaven (the parasol) and earth by his thick-soled clogs, an acolyte dances his way to heaven during the Presentation. Behind him, left to right, are the marshals Chao and Wen (blue, east; cf. plate 3), the Count of the Wind (Feng-po), the Master of the Rain (Yü-shih), and the god of the soil (T'u-ti). In front of Marshal Chao, not visible, is Metal Armor (Chin-chia). Across from them are Red Robe, the marshals Kao and K'ang, the Duke of Thunder (Lei-kung), the Mother of Lightning (Tien-mu), and the Spirit of the Hills (Shan-shen). The portraits of ten of these agents and guardians of the high priest—all but the spirits of the soil and the hills (cf. plate 24)—have also been hung inside the temple to form the outer altar (cf. plates 1, 3-5).

313

20. The high priest, after he has danced his way to the stage which represents heaven, ascends it and turns to face the community representatives and mime the preparation for his audience with the Jade Emperor. Here, having first stuck his court tablet in his belt, he flips his sleeves back to straighten his robe. The symbols tied to his robe represent the energies of his body which, when he has "exteriorized" them, will carry the message to the Jade Emperor. He will give them to the community leaders after he comes back down from heaven. Individual protective symbols have been attached to his court tablet, to the back of his mantle of descent, and to his flame.

21. The two cantors who act as masters of ceremony. Standing on chairs on either side of the Gate scroll, they have called each gesture of the high priest's preparations (plate 20). They now announce a series of 3 × 3 kowtows, which are duly performed by the high priest and the other acolytes. Beneath the scroll, in a little gatehouse, the Officer for the Presentation of the Memorial (*chin-piao kuan*) stands waiting to receive the message, which he will then transmit to the Jade Emperor. The message is in the large rectangular envelope. The symbol attached to the scroll is the central one of five, comparable to the True Writs inside the temple (cf. plate 12).

22. High priest in "position of turtle." He is mentally carrying the message from the crucible (*tan-t'ien*) in his lower belly up to the base of the flame in his metal crown. His internal messager is the lord of his heart, Red Robe (plate 4). The acolyte holding the sword in place behind him is said to be "killing the turtle."

23. General view of north side of altar for a Ritual of Merit (cf. plate 14). The Cave-table is doubled because rituals for the dead are earth-oriented and therefore *yin* (female) and what is *yin* is symbolized by broken lines (--), hence two tables. Not being bound by the already defined space of a temple, the Taoists can build their altar as it should be, in the form of a three-stage mountain representing the same three levels of the universe as are depicted on the back of the mantle of descent. The yellow and white envelopes have the same function as in the Offering (cf. plate 4). Photograph by Patrice Fava.

24. The high priest in the Announcement of a Ritual of Merit. His feet positioned like the character *ting* ("it opens the Gate of Heaven and smashes the Door of Earth") and holding up his five-thunder seal (*wu-lei hao*), the high priest sprays burning invitations with symbol-water (*fu-shui*). With the seal he orders his agents to clear a path for the invitations; the water cleanses the same path of "stale energies" (*ku-ch'i*). At back left is the paper image of the god of the soil, one of two altar guardians for merit services. Next to him is the placard (*pang*) for the service.

25. Priest "paying respects to the Three Pure Ones" during the Opening a Road ritual. He first summons the souls with the soul-banner (*ling-fan*) he is holding, then animates the paper figure (to the right, dressed in black) representing the deceased, and finally, after lighting the soul-lamps, goes to pay homage. Five of the scrolls of the ten hells line the visible eastern wall and five are hung along the western wall. Photograph by Patrice Fava.

26. The start of Dispatching the Writ of Pardon. The Taoists have "ascended" to "welcome the pardon" coming down from the Three (Pure) Heavens. The Officer of Pardon stands on the table waiting to receive it. Next the officiants will step down for acrobatics that mime the journey to hell (Feng-tu), where the soul is waiting for its papers of release. In the background, mourners are seated holding the soul-banner. Photograph by Patrice Fava.

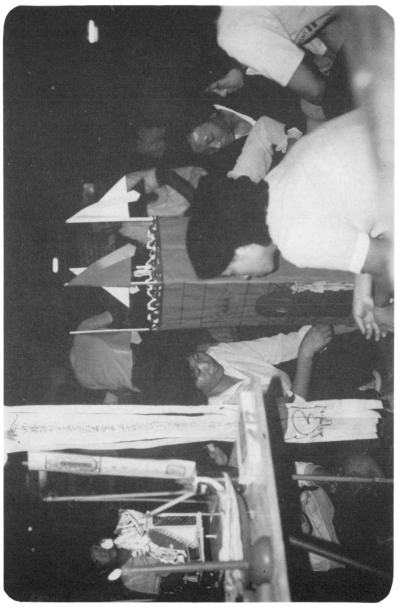

27. Family members gathered around the "fortress of hell" during the Attack on Hell. After a long dialogue with the gatekeeper, the high priest, having changed into military garb, will attack and destroy the fortress and deliver the soul from hell.

321

APPENDIX D

GLOSSARY

The following list provides the characters for all Chinese terms and for most Chinese proper names and book titles appearing in the text. Translations of terms are given only where necessary in order to distinguish homophonous terms.

an-chai
安宅

an-wei
安位

chai
齋

chai-chu
齋主

chai-t'ang
齋堂

ch'an-hui
懺悔

ch'an-p'an
懺盤

chang
章

Chang Hsü-ching
張盧靖

Chang Jo-hai
張若海

Chang Liang
張良

Chang Lu
張魯

Chang Shang-ying
張商英

Chang Shou-chen
張守眞

Chang Tao-ling
張道陵

Chang Wan-fu
張萬福

Ch'ang-sheng ta-ti
長生大帝

ch'ang-yeh
長夜

Chao
趙

chao
兆

Chao Yeh
趙曄

chao ssu-ling
召四靈

chao-ch'ing
召請

ch'ao-yuan
朝元

chen
震

chen-jen
眞人

Chen-wen yao-chieh ching
眞文要解經

Chen-wu
眞武

Chen-wu pen-chuan
眞武本傳

Ch'en Jung-sheng
陳榮盛

Ch'en Yao-t'ing
陳耀庭

cheng
正

cheng-chai
正齋

cheng-chiao
正醮

cheng-fa
正法

cheng-hun
正魂

cheng-tao
正道

cheng-tsou
正奏

cheng-yi
正一

Cheng-yi fa-wen t'ien-shih
  chiao-chieh k'o-ching
正一法文天師教戒科經

cheng-yi meng-wei
正一盟威

ch'eng fa-wei
稱法位

ch'eng-shu
成數

ch'eng-tz'u
呈詞

Chi Shan-hsing
紀善行

chi-t'ung
乩童

ch'i (energy)
氣

ch'i (symbolize with)
契

ch'i (equalize)
齊

Ch'i Hui
岐暉

ch'i shih-sheng
啓師聖

ch'i-hai
氣海

ch'i-jang chai
祈禳齋

ch'i-ku
啓鼓

ch'i-pai
啓白

Ch'i-pao hsüan-t'ai
七寶玄臺

Chia Shan-hsiang
賈善翔

chia-shen
甲申

chia-yi
甲乙

Chiang Shu-yü
蔣叔輿

chiang
降

chiang-yi
降衣

chiao
醮

*Chiao san-tung chen-wen
wu-fa cheng-yi meng-wei
lu li-ch'eng yi*
醮三洞眞文五法正一盟威籙立成儀

chiao-chu (lord of the
religion)
教主

chiao-chu (head of the
offering)
醮主

chieh-ch'i
節氣

chieh-chieh
解結

chien
薦

chien-chai
監齋

chien-chai ta fa-shih
監齋大法師

chien-tsu
薦祖

chih (governance)
治

chih (function)
職

chih-fu
值符

chih-hsiang
值香

Chih-hui pen-yüan ta-chieh
 ching
智慧本願大誡經

chih-hun
滯魂

ch'ih
勅

Ch'ih-shu yu-chüeh ching
赤書玉訣經

ch'ih-wen
赤文

Chin Chung-shu
金仲樞

Chin Yün-chung
金允中

chin-ch'eng
進呈

Chin-chia
金甲

Chin-lu ch'ing-ch'eng
 ch'i-an chiao
金籙慶成祈安醮

chin-piao kuan
進表官

chin-t'an
禁壇

ching-kung
淨供

ching-t'an
淨壇

ch'ing-kuang
請光

ch'ing-shih
請師

ch'ing-t'u
慶土

Chiu-kʻu miao-ching
救苦妙經

Chiu-kʻu pao-chüan
救苦寶卷

Chiu-kʻu tʻien-tsun
救苦天尊

*Chiu-tʻien sheng-shen
  chang-ching*
九天生神章經

chiu-yu
九幽

chiu-yu chai
九幽齋

Chiu-yu yü-kʻuei
九幽玉匱

Chou Ssu-te
周思德

Chou-li
周禮

Chu-tʻien nei-yin
諸天內音

Chu-yi
朱衣

chʻu-hu
出戶

chʻu-kuan
出官

chʻu-ling
除靈

chü
聚

chʻuan-tu
傳度

chüan-lien
捲簾

chʻüan
全

chuang
狀

Chuang-tzu
莊子

chʻüeh
闕

Chūgokujin no shūkyō girei
中國人の宗教儀禮

Chung-hsiao tao
忠孝道

chung-kuo
中國

chung-min
種民

Chung-nan
終南

chung-tsun
中尊

ch'ung-pai
重白

en
恩

en-kuang
恩光

er-hu
二胡

fa-hao
法號

fa-hua
法華

fa-lu (lighting of the burner)
發爐

fa-lu (ritual register)
法籙

fa-piao
發表

fa-shih
法師

fa-tsou
發奏

fa-yüan
發願

fan
旛

Fan Chen
範鎮

Fan Yeh
範曄

fan-ch'i
梵炁

fan-yu cho-hui
焚油逐穢

fang she-ma
放赦馬

fang shui-teng
放水燈

fang-han
方函

Fang-hsiang shih
方相氏

fang-ming
方命

fen
墳

fen-kuang
分光

fen-teng
分燈

Feng-po
風伯

feng-shan
封禪

feng-shui
風水

feng-tao
奉道

Feng-tu
酆都

fo-fan
佛旛

fo-tzu
佛子

fu (symbol)
符

fu (attach)
附

fu-chang
伏章

fu-chiang
副講

fu-fan
符旛

Fu-hsi
伏羲

fu-lu
復爐

fu-ming
符命

fu-t'ang
福堂

Fu-te cheng-shen
福德正神

fu-ti
福地

hai-ch'ing
海青

Han t'ien-shih shih-chia
漢天師世家

hei-po
黑簿

ho-fu
合符

Ho-t'u
河圖

ho-t'ung
合同

Hou-sheng chiu-hsüan
　Chin-ch'üeh ti-chun
後聖九玄金闕帝君

hou-t'ien
後天

Hsi-tz'u
繫辭

hsiang-k'o
相克

hsiang-lai
向來

hsiang-sheng
相生

hsiang-shui
香水

hsiao
嘯

Hsiao T'ien-shih
蕭天石

Hsiao-en t'ang
孝恩堂

Hsiao-tao
孝道

hsieh (thank-dismiss)
謝

hsieh (deviant)
邪

hsieh-en
謝恩

Hsieh-tsui pao-ch'an
謝罪寶懺

hsien-lao
賢勞

hsien-t'ien
先天

Hsin-ch'u Lao-chün
新出老君

hsing
行

hsing-tao
行道

Hsü Chia
徐甲

Hsü-hsien chen-lu
徐仙眞錄

Hsüan-hsüeh
玄學

hsüan-hua
玄化

Hsüan-k'o miao-chüeh
玄科妙訣

*Hsüan-lan Jen-niao shan
   ching-t'u*
玄覽人鳥山經圖

*Hsüan-t'ien shang-ti
   ch'i-sheng lu*
玄天上帝啓聖錄

hsüan-tsao
玄造

Hsüan-wu
玄武

hsüeh-hu
血湖

hsün-sheng
徇聲

hu-t'an
護壇

hua-chih chou
化紙呪

hua-hao
花號

hua-hu
化胡

Hua-t'ai ko
華胎歌

Huai-nan tzu
淮南子

Huai-t'ai ko
懷胎歌

Huang Kung-chin
黃公瑾

huang-ch'üan
黃泉

huang-lu chai
黃籙齋

Huang-lu ta-chai li-ch'eng yi
黃籙大齋立成儀

Huang-shu kuo-tu yi
黃書過度儀

Huang-ti
黃帝

Huang-t'ing wai-ching
黃庭外景

hui (secret name)
諱

hui (assembly)
會

hun
魂

Hun-tun
混沌

hung ch'eng ming
澒濙霶

hung kung-te
紅功德

Hung-en ling-chi chen-chün shih-shih
洪恩靈濟眞君事實

huo-chü tao-shih
火居道士

huo-pu
火部

jen
仁

jen-kuei
壬癸

ju-chia
入家

ju-hu
入戶

ju-yi
入意

k'ai-kuang
開光

k'ai-t'ien fu-ming
開天符命

k'ai-tu
開度

k'ai-tu chai
開度齋

k'ai-t'ung ming-lu
開通冥路

k'ai-t'ung wu-lu
開通五路

kan-ying
感應

Kan-ying p'ien
感應篇

k'an
坎

K'ang
康

kao-kung
高功

Kao-shang shen-hsiao ta-fa
高上神霄大法

Kao-shang Yü-huang
 pen-hsing chi-ching
高上玉皇本行集經

kao-wen
誥文

k'ao-chao
考召

kei-tieh
給牒

ken
艮

keng-shen
庚申

Ko Hung
葛洪

k'o
科

K'ou Ch'ien-chih
寇謙志

Ku K'ai-chih
顧愷之

ku-ch'i
古炁

ku-hun
孤魂

ku-jen
孤人

k'u-kuan
庫官

kuan (announcement)
關

kuan (hermitage)
觀

kuan-teng
關燈

Kuan-yin
觀音

Kun
鯀

k'un
坤

K'un-lun
崑崙

kung
功

kung-kuo
功果

Kung-kuo ko
功過格

kung-te
功德

kung-te tieh
功德牒

kung-ts'ao
功曹

Kuo Wang-feng
郭岡鳳

kuo-ch'iao
過橋

la-san
拉散

Lao-chün
老君

Lao-chün chung-ching
老君中經

Lao-tzu
老子

Lao-tzu ming
老子銘

Lei-kung
雷公

li (☲)
離

li (lines, deep structure)
理

li shih-fang
禮十方

li-shih
禮師

liang-yi
兩儀

Lieh-hsien chuan
例仙傳

lien
鍊

lien-tu
鍊度

Lin Ling-su
林靈素

Lin T'ien-jen
林天仁

ling
靈

Ling-chiao chi-tu chin-shu
靈教濟度金書

ling-fan
靈旛

ling-ken
靈根

ling-kuan
靈官

ling-pao
靈寶

Ling-pao ta-fa
靈寶大法

Ling-pao ta-fa ssu
靈寶大法司

*Ling-pao ta-lien nei-chih
hsing-ch'ih chi-yao*
靈寶大煉內旨行持集要

Ling-pao t'ien-tsun
靈寶天尊

*Ling-pao t'ien-tsun shuo
Hung-en ling-chi
chen-chün miao-ching*
靈寶天尊說洪恩靈濟眞君妙經

Ling-pao wu-fu hsü
靈寶五符序

Ling-pao yü-chien
靈寶玉鑑

ling-t'an
靈壇

ling-wei
靈位

ling-yi
靈意

Liu Chih-wan
劉枝萬

Liu Hun-k'ang
劉混康

Liu Tao-ming
劉道明

Lo-shu
洛書

lu
籙

Lu Hsiu-ching
陸修靜

Lu Hsün
魯迅

Lü T'ai-ku
呂太古

Lü Tung-yang
呂洞陽

Lü Yüan-su
呂遠素

Lü-shih ch'un-ch'iu
呂氏春秋

lu-t'an
露壇

Lung-hu shan
龍虎山

Lung-hu shan cheng-yi
  Liu-hou Chang t'ien-shih
  yü-chüeh ch'üan-chi
龍虎山正一劉候張天師玉訣全集

Ma
馬

mai-li
脈理

Mao-shan
茅山

Mi-lo fan
彌羅範

Miao-le
妙樂

ming (name)
名

ming (life, destiny,
  command)
命

ming chin-chung chi
  yü-ching
鳴金鐘擊玉磬

ming-ken
命根

ming-lu
冥路

Ming-wang pa-tsui pao-ch'an
冥王拔罪寶懺

Mu-lien
木蓮

mu-yü
沐浴

na-chang
納杖

na-kuan
納官

nan-k'o
南柯

nan-kuan
南管

nao-t'ing
鬧庭

nei-kuan
內觀

nei-lien
內鍊

nei-tan
內丹

nei-t'an
內壇

nei-wen
內文

ni-huan
泥丸

nien-ching
念經

Ning Ch'üan-chen
寧全眞

nung-nao
弄鐃

Ofuchi Ninji
大淵忍爾

pa-hsien
八仙

pa-kua kang
八卦罡

pai san-pao
拜三寶

pai-ch'an
拜懺

pang
榜

pao
寶

Pao-chen kung
保眞宮

pao-hao
寶號

Pao-p'u tzu
抱朴子

Pao-sheng t'ien-tsun
保生天尊

pei-kuan
北管

Pei-tou ching
北斗經

pen-ming
本命

pien-shen (transformation of the spirits)
變神

pien-shen (transformation of the body)
變身

p'in
品

Ping-ling kung
丙靈公

ping-ting
丙丁

po-hsiang
撥香

po-lu
撥爐

p'o
魄

p'o-yü
破獄

pu-hsü
步虛

p'u-tu
普度

sai kong
師公

san
散

san-chieh
三界

san-huang chai
三皇齋

san-kuan
三官

San-kuan ching
三官經

San-t'ien nei-chieh ching
三天內解經

san-ts'ai
三才

san-tung
三洞

san-yüan jih
三元日

San-yüan pao-ch'an
三元寶懺

sha
煞

Shan-hai ching
山海經

Shan-shen yeh
山神爺

shang-ch'i
上啓

Shang-ch'ing
上清

Shang-ch'ing ling-pao ta-fa
上清靈寶大法

shang-hsiang chin-ch'a
上香進茶

shang-hsieh
上謝

shang-ti
上帝

shen
神

shen-chang
神杖

Shen-hsiao
神霄

Shen-nung
神農

shen-tsou
申奏

shen-wei
神位

Sheng-hsüan pu-hsü chang
生玄步虛章

sheng-shu
生數

sheng-te
聖德

shih (charge)
識

shih (angel)
使

Shih-chi
史記

shih-ching
侍經

shih-chuan hui-ling
十轉廻靈

shih-hsiang
侍香

shih-hui tu-jen
十廻度人

shih-teng
侍燈

shou-lu
手爐

shu
疏

shui-pai
水白

Shun-t'ien kung
順天宮

so-na
嗩吶

ssu
司

ssu-chien
四間

ssu-fu
四府

ssu-ling
四靈

Ssu-ma Ch'ien
司馬遷

ssu-ming
司命

ssu-shih
四時

su-ch'i
宿啓

Sun K'o-k'uan
孫克寬

ta-ch'eng
打城

ta-fu
大夫

Ta-lo
大羅

*Ta-Ming hsüan-chiao
    li-ch'eng chai-chiao yi*
大明玄教立成齋醮儀

tai-t'ien hsing-hua
代天行化

t'ai-chi
太極

t'ai-chi ch'üan
太極圈

t'ai-hsi
胎息

t'ai-pao
太保

T'ai-p'ing kuang-chi
太平廣記

T'ai-shan
泰山

T'ai-shang chi-tu chang-she
太上濟度章赦

*T'ai-shang ming-chien
    chen-ching*
太上明鑑眞經

T'ai-sui
太歲

tan-t'ien
丹田

t'an
壇

tao-ch'ang
道場

Tao-fa hui-yüan
道法會元

tao-fan
道旛

tao-p'ao
道袍

tao-shih
道士

Tao-te t'ien-tsun
道德天尊

T'ao Hung-ching
陶弘景

te
德

Teng Yu-kung
鄧有功

Ti-ch'i shang-chiang Wen
    t'ai-pao chuan
地祇上將溫太保傳

ti-chih
地支

Ti-fu shih-wang pa-tu yi
地府十王拔度儀

Ti-kung
地公

ti-shih
帝師

Ti-tsang
地藏

ti-yü
地獄

tieh
牒

Tien-mu
電母

tien-yen
點眼

t'ien-ch'iao
天橋

t'ien-chu
天主

T'ien-hsin cheng-fa
天心正法

t'ien-kan
天干

t'ien-k'u
天庫

t'ien-kuan
天官

T'ien-kung
天公

t'ien-ming
天命

T'ien-p'eng
天蓬

t'ien-shih
天師

T'ien-shu yüan
天樞院

t'ien-wen
天文

ting
丁

tou-teng
斗燈

t'ou-chien
投簡

ts'an-ch'ao
參朝

Ts'an-t'ung ch'i
參同契

tsao-chün
竈君

ts'e-chang
刺杖

tsou-ma
走馬

Ts'un-hsin
存心

Tu Kuang-t'ing
杜光庭

tu-chiang
都講

Tu-jen ching
度人經

Tu-jen ching ssu-chu
度人經四註

Tu-jen ta-fa
度人大法

tu-men
都門

t'u
圖

T'u-ti
土地

tung-an
洞案

Tung-chen huang-shu
洞眞黃書

tung-t'ien
洞天

t'ung-ch'eng
銅城

t'ung-tzu
童子

tzu
子

Tzu-wei ta-ti
紫微大帝

Tz'u-pei pao-ch'an
慈悲寶懺

wai-t'an
外壇

wan-p'in yi-chi
萬品一祭

Wang Ch'i-chen
王契眞

Wang Ch'in-jo
王欽若

wang-ssu
枉死

wang-yeh
王爺

wei
位

wei-ling chou
衛靈呪

Wen Ch'iung
温窮

wen-hua
文化

Wen-wu
文物

wo
我

wu
物

Wu Tao-hsien
吳道顯

wu-chi
戊己

wu-chien
舞劍

wu-fu
五府

wu-hsien
午獻

wu-hsing
五行

wu-kung
午供

Wu-lao ch'ih-shu ching
五老赤書經

wu-lei hao
五雷號

Wu-liang tu-jen ching
無量度人經

Wu-shang pi-yao
無上祕要

Wu-tang shan
武當山

wu-wei
無爲

wu-yeh chin-shu
午夜金書

wu-ying
五營

Wu-Yüeh ch'un-ch'iu
吳越春秋

yang
仰

Yang Chieh
楊傑

yang-ch'i
揚旗

Yeh Fa-shan
葉法善

Yeh-pao yin-yüan ching
業報因緣經

yen
演

Yen Tung
嚴東

yen-kung
言功

yi (justice)
義

yi (rite)
儀

yi-ch'i
一炁

yi-ling
詣靈

yin-fu
陰府

yin-pan
引班

yin-ssu
淫祀

yin-yang
陰陽

ying-she k'o
迎赦科

yu-kuan
幽關

Yü
禹

Yü-ching shan
玉京山

Yü-huang
玉皇

yü-kao
預告

Yü-shih
雨師

Yü-shu ching
玉樞經

Yüan Miao-tsung
元妙宗

yüan-ch'i
元炁

yüan-hun
冤魂

yüan-shih fu-ming
元始符命

Yüan-shih t'ien-tsun
元始天尊

Yüan-shih tung-chen
tz'u-shan hsiao-tzu pao-en
ch'eng-tao ching
元始洞眞慈善孝子報恩成道經

yüan-yu
遠遊

yüeh
約

Yüeh-chüeh shu
越絕書

yün-hsiang chin-ch'a
運香進茶

BIBLIOGRAPHY

The first bibliography includes all books and articles referred to or cited in the text, with the exception of anonymous texts in the Taoist canon, manuscripts used by Master Ch'en, and a few Taoist scriptures referred to incidentally. The latter two types of text will be found in the Chinese-English Glossary. A second list here contains all books referred to that are in the Taoist canon (*Tao-tsang*, abbr: TT).

I. General Bibliography

Auerbach, Eric. *Mimesis: The Representation of Reality in Western Literature.* Translated by Willard R. Trask. Princeton, 1953.

Benamozegh, Elie. *Israël et l'humanité.* Paris, 1961; abridged edition of Paris, 1914.

Benn, Charles David. *Taoism as Ideology in the Reign of Emperor Hsüan-tsung (712-755).* Ann Arbor: University of Michigan Microfilms, 1977.

Berkouwer, G. C. *General Revelation.* Grand Rapids, Mich., 1955.

Bodde, Derk. *Festivals in Classical China: New Year and Other Annual Observances during the Han Dynasty 206 B.C.-A.D. 220.* Princeton, 1975.

Boltz, Judith. "Opening the Gates of Purgatory: A Twelfth Century Taoist Meditation Technique for the Salvation of Lost Souls." In *Tantric and Taoist Studies in Honor of R.A. Stein,* edited by Michel Strickmann, pp. 487–513. Brussels, 1983.

Chang Jo-hai. See TT 1280.

Chang Wan-fu. See TT 1212.

Chao Yeh (fl. 80 A.D.). *Wu-Yüeh ch'un-ch'iu.* Ssu-pu ts'ung-k'an edition.

Chavannes, Edouard. *Le T'ai-chan: essai de monographie d'un culte chinois.* Paris, 1910.

————. *Le jet des dragons.* Paris, 1919.

Chen Yao-t'ing. "Shang-hai tao-chiao chai-chiao ho Chin-piao k'o-yi kai-shu." Forthcoming in *Symposium on Studies of Taoist Ritual and Music of Today.* Chinese University of Hong Kong, 1986.

Chia Shan-hsiang. See TT 774.

Chiang Shu-yü. See TT 508.

Chin Chung-shu. "Lun Pei-Sung mo-nien chih ch'ung-shang Tao-chiao," parts 1 and 2. *Hsin-yang hsüeh-pao* 7.2 (1966), 324-414 and 8.1 (1967), 187-257.

Chin Yün-chung. See TT 1223.

Chuang-tzu. Translated by Burton Watson. New York, 1968.

Day, Clarence. *Chinese Peasant Cults: Being a Study of Chinese Paper Gods.* Shanghai, 1940.

De Groot, J. J. M. "Buddhist Masses for the Dead at Amoy." In *Travaux de la 6e session du Congrès international des Orientalistes à Leide.* Vol. 2. 1884.

————. *Les fêtes annuellement célébrées à Emoui (Amoy).* 2 vols. Paris, 1886.

————. *The Religious System of China.* Vols. 1 and 6. 1910. Reprint. Taipei, 1976.

Dehergne, Joseph, S. J. "Les historiens jésuites du taoïsme." In *La mission française de Pékin aux XVIIe et XVIIIe siècles*. Actes du Colloque International de Sinologie. Paris, 1976.

Delahaye, Hubert. *Les premières peintures de paysage en Chine: aspects religieux*. Paris, 1981.

Doolittle, Justus, the Rev. *Social Life of the Chinese*. 2 vols. New York, 1865.

Doré, Henri, S. J. *Recherches sur les superstitions en Chine*. 15 vols. Variétés Sinologiques, nos. 32, 34, 36, 39, 41, 42, 44–46, 48, 49, 51, 57. Shanghai, 1911–29.

Elliott, Alan. *Chinese Spirit-Medium Cults in Singapore*. London, 1955.

Elvin, Mark. *The Pattern of the Chinese Past*. Stanford, 1973.

Fan Chen (1007–88). *Tung-chai chi-shih*. Peking, 1980.

Fan Yeh (398–445). *Hou-Han shu*.

Freedman, Maurice. *Chinese Lineage and Society: Fukien and Kwangtung*. London, 1966.

Giles, Herbert A. *Strange Stories from a Chinese Studio*. London, 1916.

Girardot, Norman. *Myth and Meaning in Early Taoism: The Theme of Chaos (hun-tun)*. Berkeley, 1983.

Goodrich, Anne Swann. *The Peking Temple of the Eastern Peak*. Monumenta Serica, vol. Nagoya, 1964.

Granet, Marcel. "Le dépot de l'enfant sur le sol; rites anciens et ordalies mythiques." 1922. Reprinted in *Etudes sociologiques sur la Chine*. Paris: Bibliothèque de Sociologie contemporaine, Presses universitaires de France, 1953.

———. *Danses et légendes de la Chine ancienne*. 1926. Reprint. Paris, 1959.

———. *La Pensée chinoise*. 1934. Reprint. Paris, 1968.

Grootaers, Willem A. "The Hagiography of the Chinese God Chen-wu." *Folklore Studies* 12.2 (1952), 139–182.

Harper, Don. *The Wu Shih Erh Ping Fang: Translation and Prolegomena*. Ann Arbor: University of Michigan Microfilms, 1982.

Hou Ching-lang. *Monnaies d'offrande et la notion de trésorerie dans la religion chinoise*. Paris, 1975.

Hsi-tz'u Commentary. In *Concordance to I Ching*. Harvard-Yenching Institute Sinological Index Series, Supplement No. 10.

Hsiao T'ien-shih. *Tao-hai hsüan-wei*. Taipei, 1974.

Huai-nan-tzu. Edited by Liu An (d. 122 B.C.). Ssu-pu ts'ung-k'an edition.

Huang, Ray. *1587, a Year of No Significance: The Ming Dynasty in Decline*. New Haven, 1981.

Huang Kung-chin. See TT 780.

Jordan, David K. *Gods, Ghosts, and Ancestors: Folk Religion in a Taiwanese Village*. Berkeley, 1972.

Kaltenmark, Max. "Le dompteur des flots." *Han-hiue Bulletin du Centre d'études Sinologiques de Pékin* 3. 1–2 (1948), 1–113.

———. *Le lie-sien tchouan (Biographies des Immortels taoïstes de l'antiquité)*. Peking, 1953.

———. "Ling-pao, Note sur un terme du taoïsme religieux." *Mélanges de l'Institut des Hautes Etudes Chinoises* 2 (1960), 559–588.

———. "Notes à propos du Kao-mei." *Annuaire de l'Ecole Pratique des Hautes Etudes, Ve Section* 74 (1967), 5–34.

Karlgren, Bernard, trans. *Shu-ching (The Book of Documents)*. *Bulletin of the Museum of Far Eastern Antiquities* 22 (1950).

Kaufmann, Yehezkel. *The Religion of Israel from its Beginnings to the Babylonian Exile*. Translated by Moshe Greenberg. New York, 1972.

Ko Hung. See TT 1185.

Kristeva, Julia. *La révolution du langage poétique*. Paris, 1974.

Kuo Wang-feng. See TT 88.

Lacan, Jacques. *The Language of the Self: The Function of Language in Psychoanalysis*. Translated by Anthony Wilden. New York, 1968.

Lagerwey, John. *Wu-shang pi-yao: somme taoïste du VIe siècle*. Paris, 1981.

Lao-tzu, Tao-te ching. Translated by D. C. Lau. Middlesex, 1963.

Lin T'ien-jen. See TT 466.

Liu Chih-wan. *Chung-kuo min-chien hsin-yang lun-chi*. Min-tsu hsüeh yen-chiu so chuan-k'an, no. 22. Nankang, 1974.

————. *Tai-wan min-chien hsin-yang lun-chi*. Taipei, 1983.

Liu Tao-ming. See TT 962.

Loewe, Michael. *Ways to Paradise: The Chinese Quest for Immortality*. London, 1979.

Lü-shih ch'un-ch'iu. Edited by Lü Pu-wei (d. 235 B.C.). Ssu-pu ts'ung-k'an edition.

Lü T'ai-ku. See TT 1226.

Lü Tung-yang. See TT 399.

Lü Yüan-su. See TT 1224.

Martelet, Gustave, S. J. *Résurrection, eucharistie et genèse de l'homme: chemins théologiques d'un renouveau chrétien*. Paris, 1972.

Maspero, Henri. *Taoism and Chinese Religion*. Translated by Frank Kierman. Amherst, Mass., 1981.

Mather, Richard B. "K'ou Ch'ien-chih and the Taoist Theocracy at the Northern Wei Court, 425–451." In *Facets of Taoism*, edited by Holmes Welch and Anna Seidel, pp. 103–122. Yale, 1979.

Mathieu, Rémi. *Etude sur la mythologie et l'ethnologie de la Chine ancienne*. Paris, 1983.

Needham, Joseph, and Wang Ling. *Science and Civilization in China*. Vol. 2: *History of Scientific Thought*. Cambridge, 1956.

Ofuchi Ninji. *Chūgokujin no shūkyō girei*. Tokyo, 1983.

Robinet, Isabelle. *Méditation taoïste*. Paris, 1979.

————. *La révélation du Shangqing dans l'histoire du taoïsme*. Vol. 1. Paris, 1984.

Saso, Michael. Preface to *Chuang-Lin hsü Tao-tsang*. Vol. 1, 1–33. Taipei, 1975.

Schafer, Edward. *Mao-shan in T'ang Times*. Society for the Study of Chinese Religions, no. 1. Boulder: University of Colorado, 1980.

Schipper, Kristofer. "Taoism: the Liturgical Tradition." Unpublished manuscript. 1968.

————. "The Written Memorial in Taoist Ceremonies." In *Religion and Ritual in Chinese Society*, edited by Arthur Wolf, pp. 309–24. Stanford, 1974.

————. *Concordance du Houang-t'ing king: Nei-king et Wai-king*. Paris, 1975.

————. *Le Fen-teng: rituel taoïste*. Paris, 1975a.

————. *Le corps taoïste*. Paris, 1982.

Scholem, Gershom. *La kabbale et sa symbolique*. Translated by Jean Boesse. Paris, 1980.

————. *Le nom et les symboles de Dieu dans la mystique juive.* Translated by Maurice R. Hayoun and George Vajd. Paris, 1983.

Seidel, Anna. *La divinisation de Lao-tseu dans le taoïsme des Han.* Paris, 1969.

————. "The Image of the Perfect Ruler in Early Taoist Messianism: Lao-tzu and Li Hung," *History of Religions* 9. 2–3 (1970), 216–47.

————. "Das neue Testament des Tao," *Saeculum* 29.2 (1978), 147–72.

————. "Imperial Treasures and Taoist Sacraments: Taoist Roots in the Apocrypha." In *Tantric and Taoist Studies in Honor of R. A. Stein,* edited by Michel Strickmann, pp. 297–371. Brussels, 1983.

Spiro, Jack Daniel and John Shelby Spong. *Dialogue: In Search of Jewish/Christian Understanding.* New York, 1975.

Ssu-ma Ch'ien (145-ca. 88 B.C.). *Shih-chi.*

Stein, Rolf. "Religious Taoism and Popular Religion from the Second to Seventh Centuries." In *Facets of Taoism,* edited by Holmes Welch and Anna Seidel, pp. 53–81. New Haven, 1979.

Strickman, Michel. "The Mao Shan Revelations; Taoism and the Aristocracy," *T'oung Pao* 63 (1977), 1–64.

————. "The Longest Taoist Scripture," *History of Religions* 17 (1978), 331–54.

————. *Le taoïsme du Mao chan, chronique d'une révélation.* Paris, 1981.

Sun K'o-k'uan. *Sung-Yüan Tao-chiao chih fa-chan.* Tai-chung, 1965.

————. *Yüan-tai Tao-chiao chih fa-chan.* Tai-chung, 1968.

————. *Han-yüan tao-lun.* Taipei, 1977.

Teng Yu-kung. See TT 566.

Tu Kuang-t'ing. See TT 590.

Vandermeersch, Léon. *Wangdao ou La voie royale.* Vol. 2. Paris, 1980.

Verellen, Franciscus. "Du Guangting (850–933): un taoïste de cour." Ph.D. dissertation, University of Paris VII, 1985.

Wainwright, Geoffrey. *Doxology: The Praise of God in Worship, Doctrine, and Life.* New York, 1980.

Wang Ch'i-chen. See TT 1221.

Wang Ch'in-jo. See TT 1285.

Ware, James R., trans. *Alchemy, Medicine, and Religion in the China of A.D. 320: The Nei-p'ien of Ko Hung.* New York, 1966.

Wen-wu. "Chiang-hsi Nan-ch'eng Ming Yi-hsüan wang Chu Yi-yin fu-niang ho-tsang mu." *Wen-wu* 8(1962), 16–28.

Wilden, Anthony. *The Language of the Self: The Function of Language in Psychoanalysis.* New York, 1968.

Wolf, Margery. *The House of Lim: A Study of a Chinese Farm Family.* Englewood Cliffs, N.J. 1968.

Yoshioka, Yoshitoya. "Taoist Monastic Life." In *Facets of Taoism,* edited by Holmes Welch and Anna Seidel, pp. 229–252. New Haven, 1979.

Yü Ying-shih. "New Evidence on the Early Chinese Conception of Afterlife— A Review Article." *Journal of Asian Studies* 41 (1981), 81–85.

Yüan Miao-tsung. See TT 1227.

Yüeh-chüeh shu. Ssu-pu ts'ung-k'an edition.

Zürcher, Erik. *The Buddhist Conquest of China.* Leiden, 1959.

————. "Buddhist Influence on Early Taoism, A Survey of Scriptural Evidence," *T'oung Pao* 66 (1980), 84–147.

II. Bibliography of Texts from the Taoist Canon. (Serial numbers are from K. M. Schipper, *Concordance du Tao-tsang* [Paris, 1975].)

A. Alphabetical listing of shortened titles used in text

Chen-wen yao-chieh ching, TT 330
Chen-wu pen-chuan, TT 775
Chih-hui pen-yüan ta-chieh, TT 344
Ch'ih-shu yü-chüeh ching, TT 352
Chiu-k'u miao-ching, TT 374
Chiu-t'ien sheng-shen chang-ching, TT 318
Chiu-yu yü-k'uei, TT 1411
Chu-t'ien nei-yin, TT 97
Hou-sheng lieh-chi, TT 442
Huang-shu kuo-tu yi, TT 1294
Kao-shang shen-hsiao ta-fa, TT 1219
Lao-chün chung ching, TT 1168
Ling-chiao chi-tu chin-shu, TT 466
Ling-pao wu-fu hsü, TT 388
Pei-tou ching: TT 622
Sheng-hsüan pu-hsü chang, TT 614
Tu-jen ching, TT 1
Tu-jen ta-fa, TT 219
Tu-ming miao-ching, TT 23
Wu-lao ch'ih-shu ching, TT 22
Yeh-pao yin-yüan ching, TT 336
Yü-huang pen-hsing ching, TT 10
Yü-shu ching: TT 16

B. Numerical listing of all titles cited from Taoist Canon

TT   1 *Ling-pao wu-liang tu-jen shang-p'in miao-ching*, vol. 1 (late 4th c.).
TT   10 *Kao-shang Yü-huang pen-hsing chi-ching*, 3 ch. (10th c.?).
TT   16 *Chiu-t'ien ying-yüan Lei-sheng p'u-hua t'ien-tsun yü-shu pao-ching.*
TT   22 *Yüan-shih wu-lao ch'ih-shu yü-p'ien chen-wen t'ien-shu ching*, 3 ch. (late 4th c.).
TT   23 *T'ai-shang chu-t'ien ling-shu tu-ming miao-ching* (late 4th c.).
TT   66 *Yüan-shih tung-chen tz'u-shan hsiao-tzu pao-en ch'eng-tao ching* (late T'ang?).
TT   88 *Yüan-shih wu-liang tu-jen shang-p'in miao-ching chu*, 3 ch., Kuo Wang-feng (ca. 1250).
TT   97 *T'ai-shang ling-pao chu-t'ien nei-yin tzu-jan yü-tzu* (late 4th c.).
TT 215 *Ti-fu shih-wang pa-tu yi* (early Ming?).
TT 219 *Ling-pao wu-liang tu-jen shang-ching ta-fa*, 72 ch. (early 13th c.).
TT 316 *T'ai-shang chi-tu chang-she*, 3 ch. (early 14th c.).
TT 317 *Ling-pao t'ien-tsun shuo Hung-en ling-chi chen-chün miao-ching* (1420).
TT 318 *Tung-hsüan ling-pao tzu-jan chiu-t'ien sheng-shen chang-ching* (late 4th c.).

TT 330 *T'ai-shang tung-hsüan ling-pao chen-wen yao-chieh shang-ching* (early 5th c.).

TT 336 *T'ai-shang tung-hsüan ling-pao yeh-pao yin-yüan ching*, 10 ch. (late 6th c.).

TT 344 *T'ai-shang tung-hsüan ling-pao chih-hui pen-yüan ta-chieh shang-p'in* (early 5th c.).

TT 352 *T'ai-shang tung-hsüan ling-pao ch'ih-shu yü-chüeh miao-ching*, 2 ch. (late 4th c.).

TT 374 *T'ai-shang tung-hsüan ling-pao chiu-k'u miao-ching* (postface, 1124).

TT 388 *T'ai-shang ling-pao wu-fu hsü* (early 4th c.).

TT 399 *T'ai-shang tung-hsüan ling-pao t'ien-tsun shuo chiu-k'u miao-ching chu-chieh*, commentary by Lü Tung-yang (13th c.?).

TT 407 *Ling-pao ta-lien nei-chih hsing-ch'ih chi-yao* (12th c.?).

TT 434 *Hsüan-lan Jen-niao shan ching-t'u* (8th c.?).

TT 442 *Shang-ch'ing hou-sheng tao-chün lieh-chi* (late 4th c.).

TT 466 *Ling-pao ling-chiao chi-tu chin-shu*, 320 ch., compiled by Lin T'ien-jen (1303).

TT 467 *Ta-ming hsüan-chiao li-ch'eng chai-chiao yi* (1374).

TT 476 *Hung-en ling-chi chen-chün shih-shih* (1417).

TT 508 *Wu-shang huang-lu ta-chai li-ch'eng yi*, 57 ch., Chiang Shu-yü (1162–1223), postface by Chiang Hsi and Chiang Yen (1223).

TT 547 *Ling-pao yü-chien*, 44 ch. (early 13th c.).

TT 566 *Shang-ch'ing t'ien-hsin cheng-fa*, 7 ch., Teng Yu-kung (early 12th c.).

TT 590 *Tao-chiao ling-yen chi*, 15 ch., Tu Kuang-t'ing (850?–933).

TT 614 *Tung-hsüan ling-pao sheng-hsüan pu-hsü chang-hsü shu* (Yüan?).

TT 622 *T'ai-shang hsüan-ling pei-tou pen-ming yen-sheng ching* (Sung).

TT 774 *Yu-lung chuan*, Chia Shan-hsiang (early 11th c.).

TT 775 *T'ai-shang shuo hsüan-t'ien ta-sheng chen-wu pen-chuan shen-chou miao-ching* (early Ming?).

TT 780 *Ti-ch'i shang-chiang Wen t'ai-pao chuan*, Huang Kung-chin (fl. 1274).

TT 789 *Cheng-yi fa-wen t'ien-shih chiao-chieh k'o-ching* (3rd c.?).

TT 958 *Hsüan-t'ien shang-ti ch'i-sheng lu*, 8 ch. (early 12th c.?).

TT 962 *Wu-tang fu-ti tsung-chen chi*, 3 ch., Liu Tao-ming (preface, 1291; postface by Lü Shih-shun, 1301).

TT 1138 *Wu-shang pi-yao*, 100 ch. (ca. 580).

TT 1168 *T'ai-shang Lao-chün chung ching*, 2 ch. (2nd c.?).

TT 1185 *Pao-p'u tzu nei-p'ien*, 20 ch., Ko Hung (ca. 280–340).

TT 1205 *San-t'ien nei-chieh ching*, 2 ch. (early 5th c.).

TT 1207 *T'ai-shang ming-chien chen-ching* (T'ang).

TT 1212 *Chiao san-tung chen-wen wu-fa cheng-yi meng-wei lu li-ch'eng yi*, Chang Wan-fu (fl. 712).

TT 1219 *Kao-shang shen-hsiao yu-ch'ing chen-wang tzu-shu ta-fa*, 12 ch. (early 12th c.).

TT 1220 *Tao-fa hui-yüan*, 268 ch. (mid-14th c.).

TT 1221 *Shang-ch'ing ling-pao ta-fa*, 66 ch., Wang Ch'i-chen (late 13th c.).

TT 1223 *Shang-ch'ing ling-pao ta-fa*, 44 ch., Chin Yün-chung (fl. 1225).

TT 1224 *Tao-men ting-chih*, 10 ch., Lü Yüan-su (1201).

TT 1226 *Tao-men t'ung-chiao pi-yung chi*, 9 ch., Lü T'ai-ku (1201).

TT 1227 *T'ai-shang chu-kuo chiu-min tsung-chen pi-yao*, 10 ch., Yüan Miao-tsung (1116).

TT 1280 *Hsüan-t'an k'an-wu lun*, Chang Jo-hai (943).

TT 1285 *I-sheng pao-te chuan*, 3 ch., Wang Ch'in-jo (1016).

TT 1294 *Shang-ch'ing huang-shu kuo-tu yi* (T'ang).

TT 1343 *Tung-chen huang-shu* (6th c.?).

TT 1411 *Tung-hsüan ling-pao ch'ang-yeh chih fu chiu-yu yü-k'uei ming-chen k'o* (late 4th c.).

TT 1463 *Han t'ien-shih shih-chia*, 4 ch. (1607).

TT 1470 *Hsü-hsien chen-lu*, 5 ch. (late 15th c.).

Index

A

Altar, 16, 65, 80, 97, 120-21, 134, 143-44, 165-67, 170, 287-88
  construction of, 267-69, 308, 317
    for medieval fasts, 26-36
    in Southern Taiwan, 36-48, 173-74
    with True Writs, 103-104, 306
  inner/outer, 34-37, 44, 46, 56, 68-69, 88, 96, 105, 134, 295, 297, 299, 306, 313
  purification of, 73-77, 92-99, 112-13, 196
  rites of entry and exit, 34-35, 114, 147
  sealing of, 99-102
Ancestors, 19, 22, 40, 117, 124, 138, 144, 146, 175, 179-80, 190, 200-201, 215, 256, 258, 261-63
Announcement, document of, 65-66, 88, 131, 174, 178, 205, 207, 210
Announcement, ritual of, 51, 54, 62, 64-67, 107, 121, 131, 174, 191, 298
  dispatch of documents in, 88-89, 318
  invitation of Saints and Masters in, 77-79
  purification of altar in, 72-77
  summons of messengers in, 80-87
  transformation of body in, 69-72, 267-68
Anterior Heaven, 14-16, 20, 22, 29, 96, 104-105, 126, 133, 192, 267, 273
Assembly, 180, 186, 243, 269, 287-88
  of Yü, 151-52, 154, 159-60, 166
Assistant cantor, 33, 47, 79, 137, 301
  role in ritual, 104-105, 116, 124, 126, 136-39, 143, 149-50, 210
Attack on Hell, 178, 191, 291, 321

described, 218, 221-27
historical background of, 218, 220-21, 228-29
internal version of, 231-37
Audience, ritual of, 106-109, 127, 129, 134, 148, 150-51, 153-54, 184, 196, 213, 308, 314-16

B

Banquet, *see* Offering
Bath, ritual of, 183, 192-93, 227, 234
Bible, the, cited, 274, 280, 285
  religions based on, viii, xi, xv, 269, 273, 277-81, 287-88
Birth date, 70-71, 117, 119-20, 122-24, 183
Body, 6, 29, 72, 119, 154, 156, 161-63, 165, 230, 233, 250, 273, 282-83, 288-89
  One, 5, 21, 147, 159, 276
  transformation of, 52, 69-73, 83, 111, 117, 123, 131, 157, 164, 194, 215, 230, 236, 267-68
Breath, x, 43, 53, 244, 246, 250, 267
Buddhism, ix, xiv, 24, 58, 141, 171-72, 177, 181, 220, 244-45, 254-55, 260, 263, 273

C

Calvin, John, 277-78
Cantor, 33, 47, 79, 91, 301, 312
  role in ritual, 69-70, 81, 86, 104-105, 114, 116, 126, 136, 139, 143, 149-50, 207, 210, 315
Cave-table, 37, 39, 48, 57, 88, 100, 112, 124, 127, 137, 173, 232, 301, 317
Celestial One, 88, 95-96
Chang Hsü-ching, 243-44, 247, 249

Chang Jo-hai, 39
Chang Liang, 140
Chang Lu, 255
Chang Shang-ying, 95
Chang Shou-chen, 257–58
Chang Tao-ling, founder of religious
 Taoism, 27, 35, 43, 140, 159,
 162, 229, 246, 288, 295–96, 298
  high priest represents, 28, 32, 96,
  99, 104, 130, 174, 215
  role in Taoist ritual, 45–46, 64–65,
  85, 88, 105, 116, 132, 142, 147,
  198–99, 210, 288
Chang Wan-fu, 91 ff.
Chang Yü-ch'ing, 263
Ch'ang-sheng ta-ti, 125, 259
Chaos, 7–11, 125, 254, 273, 276,
 281–82
Chen-wen yao-chieh ching, 121
Chen-wu pen-chuan, 96
*Cheng-yi fa-wen t'ien-shih chiao-
 chieh k'o-ching*, 255
Ch'eng-tsu, Ming Emperor, 260–62
Chi Shan-hsing, 256
Ch'i Hui, 271
Chia Shan-hsiang, 256
Chiang Shu-yü, 33–35, 45–46, 91 ff.,
 121, 167, 182–85, 187, 192, 199,
 209, 230, 233, 237
Chiao, see Offering
*Chiao san-tung chen-wen wu-fa
 cheng-yi meng-wei lu li-ch'eng
 yi*, 91
Chih-hui pen-yüan ta-chieh ching,
 137
Ch'ih-shu yü-chüeh ching, 104, 228
Chin Yün-chung, 45, 65, 171, 209,
 217–18, 220, 228
Chiu-k'u miao-ching, 237
Chiu-k'u pao-chüan, 180
Chiu-t'ien sheng-shen chang-ching,
 41
Chiu-yu yü-k'uei, 199
Chou Ssu-te, 271
Chou-li, 200
Chu-t'ien nei-yin, 35, 103
Chuang-tzu, the, ix, 7, 270
 cited, 8–11, 276, 281, 284, 290

Cinnabar Field, 7, 27, 70, 87, 117,
 119, 121–22, 132, 155–56, 159,
 233, 291, 316
Confession, 32, 54, 103, 105, 110–11,
 127, 132, 135, 143–44, 200, 208
 litanies of, 62, 178, 185, 188, 222
 sacerdotal, 123–24, 132, 144, 158,
 175, 214
 for soul of deceased, 176, 185, 191,
 198, 204
Confucianism, vii, ix, xi–xii, 141, 167,
 254, 263, 270–71, 274–76
Contract, for ascension to heaven,
 184
 of Chang Tao-ling, 28, 32, 65, 130
 for purchase of tomb land, 185,
 188
 of Yellow Book, 154
Count of the Wind, 7, 71, 81, 97, 313
Crossing the Bridge, 189, 192, 194,
 218, 234–37
Cult, 22, 126, 146, 159, 166, 250, 257,
 284
 heterodox, 244, 246, 249, 253, 258
 of Hsü brothers, 260–64, 284
 pagan, 266, 268, 270
 popular, 243, 246, 261–64, 267, 271
 of the Way, 61, 65, 112, 144, 185,
 191, 208, 216, 249, 259–60,
 263–64, 286
Curtain-raising, 55, 62, 109–10, 148,
 191

D

Destiny (*ming*), 7, 9, 19, 27, 29, 70,
 156
 Lamps of, xiii, 48, 286, 308
 see also Gate of Life and
 Heavenly Mandate
Destruction of Hell, 179, 182, 191,
 205, 217–18, 220–21, 229, 230–31,
 233–35, 237
Diocese, *see* Governance
Dipper, 39–40, 48, 56, 61, 70, 72–73,
 81, 95, 113, 125, 129, 131, 156,
 170, 183, 190, 197, 254, 261, 286

walk of the, 74–75, 82–83, 94, 99,
111, 131, 229
Dispatching the Writ of Pardon, 178
compared to Presentation of
Memorial, 213–15
described, 204–208, 210–12, 320
historical background of, 203–204
Divination, 52, 62, 191, 217, 227, 273
Divine Empyrean, 61, 125, 191
Division of the Lamps, 55, 62, 109,
148, 178–79, 191, 291, 302
Door of Earth, 11, 13, 31–34, 36, 94,
96, 101, 111, 180, 318
Dragon-Tiger Mountain, *see* Lung-
hu shan

E

Earth-prison, *see* Hell
Earthly Branches, 13, 15, 17, 29, 31,
72, 75, 83, 117, 120, 123–24
Eastern Peak, 65, 67, 174, 242–45,
273
temple of, 72, 171, 216, 229–30,
246–48
Elect, the, 43, 154, 163
Emperor on High, 203, 258
Emperor of the North, *see* Somber
Emperor
Emperor of the Purple Empyrean,
38–39, 125, 141, 309–310
Emperor who Protects Life, 125, 258
Energy, 11, 70, 73, 75, 91, 127, 143,
146, 153–54, 162, 166, 196, 233,
237, 242, 245–47, 267, 272–73,
288, 306, 318
of priest exteriorized, 117, 119,
122, 130–31, 151–52, 268–69, 287,
296, 307, 314
primordial, 6–9, 11, 27, 41–43, 80,
83, 97, 162, 165, 227
segmental, 26–27, 100, 104, 120–21,
129, 142–43
Unique, 105, 120, 125, 140, 143,
145, 165–66, 193, 246, 255, 291,
296
Exorcism, 28, 45, 53, 92, 125, 170,

172, 181, 189–90, 201, 210,
215–16, 218–20, 226–27, 229, 247,
250, 259, 271, 299

F

Fan Chen, 167
Fang-hsiang shih, 200
Fast, types of, 26, 30, 35, 170, 173
defined, 283
Father, viii, 10, 15–16, 104, 125,
165–66, 275–77, 283–84, 290
Feng-tu, 34–36, 44, 175, 191, 193,
204, 206, 208, 211–12, 214, 229,
231–33, 320
Firing the Oil, 53, 62
Five Camps (*wu-ying*), 33–34, 201,
216, 226–29
Five Emperors, 34–35, 155, 157
Five energies, 73, 86, 140
Five organs, 73, 104, 118–20, 233
Five phases, 12, 33, 40, 103, 118, 140
Flag-raising, 54, 62
Flame, 80, 88–89, 102, 111, 116, 125,
131–32, 146–48, 152, 166, 174,
291, 296, 307, 314, 316
Floating the Water Lamps, 56, 62
Four Potentates, 44–45, 71, 79, 98,
142, 157, 254
summons of, 94, 100, 129–30, 150,
214–15
Four Saints, 37, 45, 56–57, 64, 66,
77–79, 88, 95–96, 99, 105, 116,
147, 149, 250
Four spaces, 44, 47
Fu-hsi, 14, 31, 254

G

Gate of the Capital, 34, 46, 234
Gate of Demons, 15–16, 28, 35, 76,
93, 99, 101–102, 128, 222 ff., 227,
230, 305
Gate of Heaven, 11, 13, 15–16, 23,
28, 31–32, 34, 36, 38, 71, 89, 111,
122, 156, 165, 318

Gate of Life, 43, 83, 233
Gate of Man, 16, 93, 111, 165
God of the hearth, 19, 21
God of the soil, 19, 21–23, 34–35, 53,
    66, 68–69, 77, 85, 97, 99, 115,
    123–24, 141, 144, 172–75, 183,
    190, 197, 201, 204–206, 219, 227,
    270, 313, 318
Golden Gate, 39–41, 43, 54, 65, 72,
    75, 77, 80, 82, 87–88, 114, 124,
    132, 134, 139, 145, 147–48, 158,
    213, 262, 264, 273, 298
    scroll used in Taoist ritual, 37, 55,
    150–52, 219, 228–29, 308, 315
Governance, 24, 27, 119–21, 162, 255
Great Ultimate, 71, 177

H

Han t'ien-shin shih-chia, 259
Heart, 23, 27, 45, 83, 96, 112–13, 124,
    132, 146, 151–52, 154–56, 196,
    198, 234–35, 237, 258, 283
Heavenly Mandate, 274–75
Heavenly Master(s), 23–24, 28, 45,
    67, 95–96, 105, 116, 119, 142,
    243, 263, 295
Heavenly Trunks, 12–13, 15, 99, 120
Heavenly Worthy of the Numinous
    Treasure, 23, 43, 54–55, 138–39,
    261–63, 308
    see also Numinous Treasure
Heavenly Worthy of the Primordial
    Beginning, 23, 38–40, 43, 54–55,
    71, 87, 127–28, 135–38, 143, 148,
    163, 165, 199, 308
    see also Primordial Beginning
Heavenly Worthy Who Saves from
    Distress, 58–59, 174–76, 178–80,
    182–83, 189, 191–93, 195–96, 199,
    205–207, 213, 221, 227, 229–31,
    233–34, 237
Heavenly Worthy of Universal
    Salvation by the Voice of
    Thunder, 105, 125, 138, 174
Heavenly Worthy of the Way and its
    Power, 23, 38, 43, 54–55, 140–41,
    296, 302, 308–309

Hell, 20–21, 35, 37, 44, 56, 67, 72,
    138, 142, 170, 182, 198, 207, 211,
    219, 227–29, 231
    descent into, 211, 226, 231
    judgment in, 190, 222, 224–25
    paintings of, 172–73, 175, 319
    see also Feng-tu and Nine
    Obscurities
High Merit, priest of, Heaven's
    agent, 37–38, 44, 47, 61, 63, 98,
    117, 119, 123, 125, 132, 143, 145,
    158, 210, 213–14, 217, 230, 264,
    268, 284
    transformation of, 59, 72, 77, 131,
    143, 157, 164, 182, 193, 222 ff.,
    229–30, 237, 269
    see also Chang Tao-Ling, Lao-tzu,
    and Yü
High priest, *see* High Merit
Ho-t'u, see River Chart
Hsi-tz'u, 9
Hsieh-tsui pao-ch'an, 53
Hsü Chia, 226
Hsü brothers, cult of, 260–64, 284
Hsü-hsien chen-lu, 261–63
Hsüan-k'o miao-chüeh, 17, 69
Hsüan-lan Jen-niao shan ching-t'u,
    163
Hsüan-t'ien shang-ti ch'i-sheng lu, 96
Hsüan-tsung, T'ang Emperor,
    256–58, 270
Huai-nan tzu, 275
Huan, Han Emperor, 254
Huang Kung-chin, 241
Huang-lu ta-chai li-ch'eng yi, 33
Huang-shu kuo-tu yi, 133, 153–54
Huang-t'ing wai-ching, 9
Hui, 54, 76, 153, 158, 160, 267
Hui-tsung, Sung Emperor, 258–59,
    270
*Hung-en ling-chi chen-chun shih-
    shih,* 261

I

Image, epistemology of, 249–52,
    279–84
    fetishism, 270, 276–77, 283

Taoist images, 38–39, 42–46, 77, 161–63, 173, 195–96, 219, 227, 232, 256, 265, 267, 281–82, 288–89
  Wen Ch'iung's, 242, 244, 247–52
  see also True Form
Incense, ritual use of, 67, 77, 80, 85, 102–103, 108–12, 114, 117, 131, 134 ff., 145–46, 155–57, 183, 204, 233, 267, 305, 309
Initiation, ritual of, 170
  of emperors by Taoists, 256, 259
Invocation, ritual of, 54, 57, 89, 174–76
  of Masters and Saints, 56, 96
  rite of, 110, 125–26
  see also Nocturnal invocation

J

Jade Capital, 39–41, 43, 54, 63, 65–66, 72, 77, 134, 138, 145, 150, 197, 205, 225
Jade Emperor, 19–20, 23, 31, 38–39, 75, 81, 85, 88, 96, 114–15, 119, 125, 132, 141, 147, 149–50, 167, 175, 196–97, 203, 257–59, 261, 263–64, 291, 298, 309, 314–15

K

Kan-ying p'ien, 6
K'an, 14–17, 27, 37, 70–71, 95–96, 101, 118–19, 132–34
Kao-shang shen-hsiao ta-fa, 205
Kao-shang Yü-huang pen-hsing chi-ching, 263
Keeper of the incense, 33, 47–48, 114
  role in rituals, 57, 104, 111–12, 132, 135, 140–41, 175, 207–208, 211, 221, 237
Ken, 15, 17, 71, 83, 95, 101, 230
Kidneys, 6–7, 27, 35, 43, 45, 83, 123, 232–34
King Wen, *see* Posterior Heaven
Ko Hung, 272
K'ou Ch'ien-chih, 43, 255
Ku K'ai-chih, 288

Kuan-yin, 59, 219, 227
Kun, 11, 41, 134
K'un, 14, 16–17, 27, 37, 61, 101, 119, 125, 165
K'un-lun, 41, 42, 145, 163
Kuo Wang-feng, 45

L

Lake of Blood, ritual of the, 170, 175
Land of the Way, 55, 57, 62, 90, 103, 105, 150, 179, 191, 196, 286, 291, 307
  importance of, 106–110, 264, 269
  offering in, 134–143, 309–10
  outline of, 110–111
  presentation of message in, 126–134
  name of altar, 46, 97, 146, 186
Lao-chün, *see* Lao-tzu
Lao-chün chung-ching, 42
Lao-tzu, ix–x, 22–24, 27–29, 43, 122, 132, 140–41, 164, 226, 230, 254–58, 263, 267–69, 281–82
  high priest becomes, 72, 77, 131
  the *Lao-tzu*, 55, 197, 219, 257, 270
  cited, 6–7, 9, 11, 41, 246–47, 252, 272, 281–83, 285
  see also Lord Lao
Lao-tzu ming, 254
Leader of the troupe, 33, 47–48, 114
  role in ritual, 57, 77, 92, 104, 112–14, 128, 131–32, 140–41, 206–207, 211, 302
Li, 14–17, 34, 37, 70, 86, 101, 119, 132–34
Li Han-kuang, 256
Libation, 62–63, 78, 87–88, 130–31, 150, 164, 174, 176–77, 179, 188–90, 194, 205, 210–11, 215, 219–20
Lieh-hsien chuan, xiii, 272
Lin Ling-su, 259, 271
Lin T'ien-jen, 34, 169, 193, 201, 203, 213, 220–21, 237
Ling-chiao chi-tu chin-shu, 69, 169
Ling-pao ta-lien nei-chih hsing-ch'ih chi-yao, 35, 233–35

Ling-pao wu-fu hsü, 32, 35
Ling-pao yü-chien, 71, 176, 200–201
Liu Hun-k'ang, 259
Liu Tao-ming, 96
Lo-shu, 133
Lord Lao, 23, 122, 138, 140, 226, 228, 256, 267, 296
  pact with Chang Tao-ling, 159, 162, 210, 229, 246
  see also, Lao-tzu
Lu Hsiu-ching, 33–34
Lu Hsün, xi
Lü T'ai-ku, 68, 69, 91 ff., 184
Lü Tung-yang, 237
Lü Yüan-su, 67
Lung-hu shan, 45, 140, 142, 222, 259, 263, 295, 298
  Six Masters of, 56, 64, 77, 88, 152
Lung-hu shan cheng-yi Liu-hou Chang t'ien-shih yü-chüeh ch'üan-chi, 69

M

Man-Bird Mountain, 41, 161 ff., 232
Mandate, 55, 177–78, 184–88, 192, 194, 198–99
Mao-shan, *see* Mount Mao
Marshal Wen, *see* Wen Ch'iung
Master of the Rain, 7, 71, 81, 97, 313
Masters, *see* Six Masters
Medium, 72, 217–18, 227–30, 235, 242, 246, 248–49, 251, 257, 262–68, 273, 278
Memorial, 61–63, 65, 68, 77–78, 86–87, 109–10, 123–24, 136, 179–80, 193, 243–44
Merit, 61, 64, 80, 132, 136, 138, 141, 146, 151, 154–55, 157–58, 164, 167, 170, 180, 186, 191, 224–25, 258, 268, 286–87
  officer of, 63, 66, 77, 81, 85, 87, 115, 122, 131, 153, 157, 174, 184, 204–205
  Statement of, 90, 106–107, 152–54, 166
  Wen Ch'iung's, 243–45, 247, 251

Message, presentation of, 105, 107–108, 110, 126–134, 150
Metal Armor, 44–46, 134, 313
Metal Gate, *see* Golden Gate
Ming-wang pa-tsui pao-ch'an, 173, 178–79
Mirror, xv, 48, 163, 244, 250, 254, 281–82
Money, paper, burning of, 19, 52, 59, 102, 148, 176–78, 212, 224, 227, 230
  to pay soul's debts, 185–89, 192, 194, 199
  for transmission of documents, 63, 85, 88, 131
Most High, 93, 98, 114, 122, 124, 138, 142–44, 156–58, 162, 165, 199, 210, 219
  Covenant of the, 61, 125, 246
Mother, 9–11, 15, 104, 125, 165–66, 270, 276, 281–84, 290
Mount Mao, 71, 151, 154, 160, 166, 259, 263
Mu-lien, 177, 222
Mutual conquest, cycle of, 13, 118
  mutual generation, cycle of, 12, 41, 118
Mythology, Taoist, 266–68
  see also Lao-tzu, Queen Mother, Yü

N

Ni-huan, 27, 70, 87, 104, 155, 233
Nine Heavens, 41–42, 44, 66, 76, 80, 81, 93, 105, 113, 117, 141, 143, 156, 163, 200, 206
Nine palaces, 16, 31, 36, 42, 121, 143
Nine Obscurities, 8, 41, 182, 199–200, 205, 208–209, 233
Ning Ch'üan-chen, 193, 237
Nocturnal Invocation, 32, 34, 56–57, 62, 68, 103–104, 106–109, 111, 121, 129, 147, 151, 163, 306
Noon Offering, 54, 56, 62–63, 179, 191, 291, 301
Northern Bushel, *see* Dipper

Numinous Treasure, 142, 231
  documents of the, 76, 113, 121,
    140, 171
  Great Method of the, 65, 131, 193,
    237
  masters of the, 66, 124
  Taoists of the, 30, 171–72
  term explained, 8

O

Offering, the, xiii, 20–21, 48, 51–52,
    164, 169–70, 172, 272, 283, 317
  a banquet, 29, 32, 57
  documents for, 61–67
  program for, 53–59
  reasons for doing, 60
Old Infant, 43, 132, 254, 282, 296
Opening to the light, 181, 195–96,
    219, 231, 237
Opening a Road in the Darkness,
    173, 177, 319
  described, 195–99
  historical background of, 199–201
Origin, 47, 156–57, 166, 198, 275,
    281–84
  return to the, 96, 120–21, 172, 191,
    235, 269, 275, 279, 308
Orthodox Method of the Heart of
    Heaven, 68, 71, 76, 82, 95, 171
Orthodox Offering, 56–58, 63,
    120–21, 291
Orthodox Unity, 44, 64, 66, 96, 126,
    162, 260, 263
  Covenant of, viii, 27–28, 32, 61,
    97, 125, 159, 191, 246
  Taoists of, 30, 91–92, 171–72, 259
Orthodox Way, 243, 245–46

P

Pao-p'u tzu, 165–66
Pardon, Officer of, 203–204,
    207–208, 210–12
Pardon, Writ of, 191
  dispatched, 210–12
  translated, 208–209

welcomed from heaven, 203–206,
    320
Petition, 107, 151, 190, 213
  internal rite for sending, 131–34
Ping-ling, Master, 242, 247–48, 250
Ping-ting, 12, 244
Placard, 29, 54, 58, 61–65, 72,
    190–92, 318
Pole Star, 12, 38–39, 154, 271
Posterior Heaven, 14–16, 20, 27,
    30–31, 40, 73, 126, 133, 267, 273
Presentation of the Memorial, 45,
    53–54, 56–58, 62–63, 81, 83–84,
    107, 121, 129, 264, 269, 298,
    311–16
  description of, 149–50
  and myth of Yü, 151–52, 159–60,
    164, 166
  use of symbols in, 152, 268
Priests, Taoist, 7, 13, 17, 21, 33, 40,
    149
  civil and military functions of, 45,
    47, 64, 221, 228–29, 235, 295,
    298–99, 321
  and emperor, 9, 272, 275, 284–85
  hierarchical order among, 47–48,
    55–56, 104, 116, 135 ff., 142–43
  and mediums, 248–52, 264, 268
  redhead, 53, 92, 172, 216, 226–27
  role of in traditional society, x,
    xiii–xiv
  and Yü, 11, 23, 29, 46
  see also High Merit
Primordial Beginning, 113, 203–205,
    209, 231, 233–35
Primordial realm, 266–71, 273
Psychoanalysis, xv, 10, 277–78, 284

Q

Queen Mother of the West, 39–43,
    120, 134, 145, 162–63, 165, 211,
    266–67, 275, 281–82

R

Real Man (*chen-jen*), 6–7, 94, 96–97,
    132, 143, 222 ff., 272, 282

Real form, *see* True form
Red Robe, **44**–45, 96, 132, 283, 298, 313, **316**
Refinement, *see* Sublimation
Register (**lu**), Academy of Taoist, 167
 of adept, **153**
 Golden, 53, 61, 184, 212
 of the Heavenly Master, 243, 249
 of Immortals, 244
 of life and death, 145–46, 184, 187, 225, 243
 of pardon, 209–10
 priest's ritual, 61, 81, 144–45, 152, 154, 161
 and symbols, 157–61, 182, 255
 Yellow, 35–36, 155, 173
Revelation, general and special, 288
 importance of in Taoism, 27, 38–39, 200, 246, 249, 254–57, 264, 271–73
 and redemption, 39, 41, 208, 215
 and transmission, 251, 267
 to Yü, 31–32
Ritual, Taoist, essence of, xiii, 45–46, 285–87
 importance of, viii, xiv–xv, 6, 39, 255–56, 263, 269–70
 as theater, 46, 55, 62, 152, 159, 166, 206–207, 211–15, 217, 220–27, 230, 235, 314, 320
Ritual of Merit, documents for, 178, 185–86, 190–94, 198, 208–209
 introduction to, 169–72
 program for, 174–90
 summary of, 199
River Chart, 31, 133, 162
Road of Demons, *see* Gate of Demons

S

Sacrifice, 66, 284
 blood, 243, 249, 256–57, 261, 269
 Canon of, 262
 of dynastic legitimacy, 72, 152, 258, 272–73
 state, 254
 Taoist, x, 269, 287
Saints, *see* Four Saints
San-kuan ching, 56
San-t'ien nei-chieh ching, 24, 28, 171
San-yüan pao-ch'an, 177
Savior from Distress, *see* Heavenly Worthy Who Saves from Distress
Scarlet Palace, *see* Heart
Scripture of Salvation, the, *see Tu-jen ching*
Seal, 66–68, 145, 187, 279
 cloud-seals, 126
 five-thunder, 63, 80–81, 85–88, 102, 131, 174, 205, 215, 305, 318
 hand, 68
 phoenix-seals, 205, 208   seal-characters, 80, 112, 139, 155, 157–58, 203, 206, 210
 as True Form, 244, 266
Sealing the Altar, 32, 34, 56, 109–10, 227–28, 269, 303–305
 purification of altar in, 92–99
 sealing of borders in, 99–100
 sealing of Demon Gate in, 100–102
Shan-hai ching, 160
Shang-ch'ing ing-pao ta-fa, 158
Shen-hsiao, 205, 259
 see also Divine Empyrean
Sheng-hsüan pu-hsü chang, 29
Six Heavens, 28, 35, 46, 99, 246, 249
Six Masters, 37, 46, 56–57, 64–66, 77–79, 88, 105, 116, 147, 149
Smelting, *see* Sublimation
Somber Emperor, 244, 250–51, 257
Somber Warrior, 45–46, 96, 98, 299
Souls, celestial and terrestrial, 21, 43, 71–72, 79, 98, 104, 121, 123, 155–56, 183, 186, 191, 193
 clothing for, 183, 188–89, 192–93, 227, 234
 drowned, 158–59
 gathering of, 131, 164
 and god of soil, 172–73, 219, 227
 guilty, 229, 231, 234
 house for, 189–90
 lamps of, 176, 195–97, 199, 319

liberation from hell of, 182–83, 234–35, 321
mandate for, 177
and moon, 24
obstructed, 21, 29, 31, 35, 46, 99–100, 170–71, 208, 230
ordination of, 184–87
Removal of, 189
resentful, 21, 171, 218
solitary, 20, 28, 56, 58–59, 192
statuettes representing, 181, 184, 186–87, 189, 195–96, 198, 203, 227, 319
summons of, 56, 175–76, 183–85, 190, 192, 195, 319
visit to, 177–78, 188, 191, 201, 204, 212
Soul-banner, 172, 176, 179, 183, 185, 188–89, 196, 198–200, 205, 219, 227, 319–21
Spinal column, 43, 71–72, 234–35, 276
Ssu-ma Ch'eng-chen, 256
Starting the Drum, 54, 62
Sublimation (*lien*), 6–7, 9, 23, 29, 244, 249
ritual of, 73, 155, 192, 194, 231–35
Supreme Emperor, 54, 243, 245, 279
Sword, 76–77, 93–102, 130–32, 134, 166, 258, 291, 298, 303, 316
dance with, 47, 92–93, 128–29
gesture, 70, 75, 113, 119, 267
Symbol (*fu*), ix, 29, 34, 63–64, 66, 68–69, 79, 87–88, 102, 113–15, 123, 127, 140, 204, 228, 255, 260, 268–69, 271, 276–78, 281, 283–84
agents of the, 88, 100, 127, 131, 204, 226
to break open hell, 204–205, 208, 229, 231
contrasted with charts (*t'u*) and registers (*lu*), 161–62
entry, 34, 114–15
etymology of, 155
exit, 147
for healing, 170, 260, 262
and incantations, 229, 266–67
for ordination, 166

in Presentation of Memorial, 152 ff., 164, 214, 314–15
for purification of altar, 73–76, 95
rite for writing, 155 ff., 203
uniting of, 160, 181–82, 192
ways of writing, 267
of Wen Ch'iung, 244, 248
in the West, 10, 276–77
Symbol-candle, 221
Symbol-flag, 182, 193
Symbol-order, 62, 64, 76, 81–86, 113, 155, 177–78, 182–83, 203, 229, 298
Symbol-water, 58, 75–76, 79, 85–86, 88, 92–102 *passim*, 113, 127, 147, 174, 179, 183, 188, 190, 205, 219, 221, 227, 231, 303, 318
Symbolization, 8, 41, 152, 157–59, 166, 187, 215, 252, 269, 276

T

Ta-Ming hsüan-chiao li-ch'eng chai-chiao yi, 260
T'ai-p'ing kuang-chi, 31
T'ai-shan, 44, 71–72, 175, 200, 204, 230, 242, 291
T'ai-shang chi-tu chang-she, 213
T'ai-shang ming-chien chen-ching, 281
T'ai-sui, 28, 66, 99
Tao-fa hui-yüan, 45
T'ao Hung-ching, 271
Taoism, bureaucracy in, 209, 243–45, 247, 266, 286
compared with Biblical religion, 273, 276 ff.
defined, 6, 265–66, 285–87
epistemology of, 235, 246–52, 266, 275, 278–84
importance of in traditional society, x, xiii–xiv
as paganism, xv, 266–72
and popular religion, 201, 216, 228, 235, 241, 245–53, 256–58, 260–64, 267, 270–71

Taoism (*continued*)
and the state, xii, 253–60, 264,
270–75, 285
traditional views of, ix
Ten directions, 16, 35–37, 110, 113,
124, 142–43, 156–57, 178, 200
Teng Yu-kung, 83
Three Caverns, 29, 38–39, 126, 136
ff., 142
Three Days of Origin, 20–22, 24
altar for fast of, 30–35, 46, 65, 103,
130
Three Energies, 80, 104, 118, 142,
162–64
colors of, 43, 122, 156–57, 229
origin of cosmos, 103
and Three Heavens, 28–29
and Three Pure Ones, 38, 43, 54
Three Heavens, 64–66, 85, 122, 130,
162–64, 171, 204
in body, 122
in hand, 117, 119
opposed to Six Heavens, 28, 210,
246
source of pardon, 191, 193, 202,
206–207, 211, 213, 320
merit reported to, 245
Three luminaries, 75–76, 79, 81, 140,
156, 254
Three Officers, 44, 56, 91, 109,
114–15, 125, 129, 147, 167, 227
defined, 11–12
historical role of, 19–21, 107
place on altar, 46, 300
Taoists responsible to, 132, 144,
167
Three Pure Ones, 38, 46, 55, 81, 83,
121, 131, 140, 142, 150, 166,
183–84, 222, 287
addressees of Taoist ritual, 40–41,
51, 56–57, 107–110, 127, 147–48,
175, 177, 179, 181, 204, 247, 308,
319
Lao-tzu's dominance among, 43
in priest's body, 70, 119
secret names of, 54, 76
supremacy of, 67, 89, 111, 114–15,
124–25, 264

table of, 39
Three Realms, 63, 65, 69–70, 74, 83,
86, 88, 141, 155
generals of the, 83, 85, 94, 129, 215
"here-below", 39, 57, 139, 142, 162,
205
spiritual authorities of, 62, 66, 81,
87, 175, 206, 245
table of, 37, 45–46, 56, 76, 79, 128,
147, 173, 181, 184–85, 219, 226
Three Sovereigns, 26–30, 36–39,
92–93, 104
Three Terraces, 54, 73, 98, 113, 122,
156, 303
Step of the, 72, 92–94, 101–102
Three Treasures, defined, 43
synonym of Three Pure Ones, 39,
113, 115, 128, 131, 142, 186, 206
worship of, 136, 139, 141, 144–45,
175, 184–85, 192, 194, 196,
224–25, 261, 263
Three Virtualities, 11, 94
Thunder, 76, 165, 242
Duke of, 44, 81, 97, 313
five, 75, 80, 85, 215
and lightning, 44, 61, 71–72, 77, 86,
97, 118, 125, 170, 190, 244
and trigram *chen*, 15, 129, 230
and Yü, 154, 159
*Ti-ch'i shang-chiang Wen t'ai-pao
chuan*, 241
Ti-fu shih-wang pa-tu yi, 190
T'ien-p'eng, 76, 95, 96, 244, 250
Ting-character stance, 81, 94, 100,
318
Treasury, officers of, 175, 186, 188,
195
ritual for filling, 173, 186–89, 194
Triad, Taoist, 11, 23, 28, 46, 128, 140
Trigrams, 10, 32, 35, 46, 83, 133, 279
on altar, 30, 36–37, 111, 143
diagrams of, 14
in hand, 17, 118, 120
logic of, 14–17, 40
spirits of, 31, 165
on Taoist robe, 174, 291, 312
walk of, 84, 101, 128, 149
and Yü, 31

True Form, 98, 134
  of Feng-tu, 229, 232
  of generals, 80, 85, 87, 128
  of Wen Ch'iung, 244, 247, 250, 266
True Warrior, *see* Somber Warrior
True Writs, 32, 39, 44, 57, 62, 103,
    151, 267, 269, 286, 306, 315
Ts'an-t'ung ch'i, 16
Ts'ao Ts'ao, 255, 274
Tu Kuang-t'ing, 91 ff., 256, 259, 271
Tu-jen ching, 40, 127, 177–78, 180,
    212, 229, 234, 244
Tu-jen ching ssu-chu, 35
Tu-jen ta-fa, 73, 75, 86, 182, 205
T'u, 31, 160, 162, 267
Tung-chen huang-shu, 132–33
Turtle, 41–43, 72, 96, 166, 230, 256,
    273, 281, 299
  position of, 131–34, 245, 264, 269,
    287, 316
  see also Queen Mother
Tzu, 13–14, 17, 26–27, 29, 43, 70,
    101, 119–20, 132
Tz'u-pei pao-ch'an, 188

U

Underworld, Court of, 184, 186, 191,
    230, 243
  money, 185
  paths of the, 181
  road to, 197, 200
Universal Salvation, festival of, 52,
    56, 58, 61, 170–71, 189, 218, 237
  goal of Taoist ritual, xiii, 146, 192,
    198, 205, 208
Untying the Knots, 187, 291

V

Visualization, 87, 91, 94, 96, 122–24,
    131–32, 144, 153, 155 ff., 160,
    162–63, 209, 229, 230–31, 233–35,
    267
  of Lao-tzu, 281–82

  of messengers, 83
  to transform body, 71, 117, 122

W

Walking the Way, 90, 106, 110–11,
    121, 134, 142, 151–53
Wang Ch'i-chen, 43, 72, 200, 203,
    209–10
Wang Ch'in-jo, 257–58
Wang Yen, 256
Wei Ching-ssu, 256
Wen Ch'iung, biography of, 241–45,
    248
  Taoist angel, 44, 46, 248–52, 266,
    284, 286–87, 297, 313
Wishes, expression of, 111, 134, 136,
    138, 141, 146, 187–88, 192, 196,
    200–201
Wu Tao-hsien, 244–45, 249–50
Wu Tsung-ching, 244, 249, 266
Wu-lao ch'ih-shu ching, 39
Wu-liang tu-jen ching, 40
Wu-shang pi-yao, 26, 29–30, 33–35,
    44, 90, 167
Wu-tang shan, 45, 77, 96, 299
  Four Saints of, 56, 64, 88, 105, 142,
    152
Wu-Yüeh ch'un-ch'iu, 33, 42

Y

Yang Chieh, 95
Year Star, *see* T'ai-sui
Yeh Fa-shan, 248–49, 271
Yeh-pao yin-yüan ching, 190
Yellow Emperor, 34, 254, 258
Yen Tung, 35
Yin-yang, as cosmic entities, 8–9, 11,
    14, 20, 55, 82, 87, 96, 117, 125,
    147, 183, 208, 248, 272, 290–91,
    317
  directions, 27, 29, 38, 40, 192
  and magic squares, 133
  and musical instruments, 48, 55,
    62
  numbers, 16, 20

Yin-yang (continued)
  pure forms of, 41, 71
  rite, 190
  steps, 82, 128–29
  time, 22, 72, 74, 82, 118, 155, 191, 244
  and trigrams, 40
Yü, 22, 41, 96, 139, 159, ff., 246, 267–68, 270
  and altar, 33, 134, 201
  as god of soil, 23, 34–35, 201
    model for Taoist priest, 11, 29, 31–32, 46, 151–52, 154, 164, 166, 230
    Step of, xiv, 11, 23, 31, 40, 43, 72, 99–101, 118, 130, 134, 151 ff., 304
Yü-shu ching, 56
Yüan Miao-tsung, 71, 76, 92
Yüan-shih tung-chen tz'u-shan hsiao-tzu pao-en ch'eng-tao ching, 263
Yüeh-chüeh shu, 33